Modeling Economic Growth in Contemporary Poland

Entrepreneurship and Global Economic Growth

Series editor: Bruno S. Sergi, Harvard University, USA

Entrepreneurship and Global Economic Growth is Emerald's cutting-edge Global Economic Growth book series, presenting modern examinations of economic growth at national, regional and global levels. Each book in this series discusses different dimensions of the changing economic and industrial contexts, and examines in detail their impact on the nature of growth and development. For academics and senior practitioners, this series puts forward significant new research in the global economic growth field, opening discussions regarding new topics and updating existing literature

Published Titles in This Series

Modeling Economic Growth in Contemporary Russia, edited by Bruno S. Sergi
Modeling Economic Growth in Contemporary Belarus, edited by Bruno S. Sergi
Modeling Economic Growth in Contemporary Malaysia, edited by Bruno S. Sergi and Abdul Rahman Jaaffar
Modeling Economic Growth in Contemporary Greece, edited by Vasileiois Vlachos, Aristidis Bitzenis and Bruno S. Sergi
Modeling Economic Growth in Contemporary Hong Kong, edited by Michael K. Fung and Bruno S. Sergi
Modeling Economic Growth in Contemporary Indonesia, edited by Bruno S. Sergi and Dedhy Sulistiawian

Forthcoming Titles in This Series

Modeling Economic Growth in Contemporary India, edited by Bruno S. Sergi; Aviral Kumar Tiwari; Samia Nasreen
Modeling Economic Growth in Contemporary Czechia, edited by Daniel Stavárek and Michal Tvrdoň

Modeling Economic Growth in Contemporary Poland

EDITED BY

ELŻBIETA BUKALSKA
Maria Curie-Skłodowska University, Poland

TOMASZ KIJEK
Maria Curie-Skłodowska University, Poland

AND

BRUNO S. SERGI
Harvard University, USA & University of Messina, Italy

United Kingdom – North America – Japan – India – Malaysia – China

Emerald Publishing Limited
Emerald Publishing, Floor 5, Northspring, 21-23 Wellington Street, Leeds LS1 4DL

First edition 2024

British Library Cataloguing in Publication Data
A catalogue record for this book is available from the British Library

ISBN: 978-1-83753-655-9 (Print)
ISBN: 978-1-83753-654-2 (Online)
ISBN: 978-1-83753-656-6 (Epub)

Printed and bound by CPI Group (UK) Ltd, Croydon, CR0 4YY

INVESTOR IN PEOPLE

Table of Contents

Part 3 Prospects of Economic Growth in Poland: The Micro, Meso and Macro Perspective

List of Figures and Tables

About the Editors

Elżbieta Bukalska, PhD, D Sc, works as an Associate Professor at the Faculty of Economics at Maria Curie-Sklodowska University (Poland). She has teaching, research and practical experience in corporate finance. She gives lectures on corporate finance, financial analysis, business plan, capital structure and dividend policy and value-based management. She is the author or co-author of over 70 publications. Her research interests include capital structure, dividend and share repurchase policy, small and medium enterprises, IPO, and companies on the capital market.

Tomasz Kijek has been a Professor at the Department of Microeconomics and Applied Economics at University of Maria Curie-Skłodowska, Poland since 2017. He holds a doctoral degree in Economics. His current scientific interests include economics of innovation and knowledge, spatial aspects of innovation processes and productivity and efficiency analyses. He has had more than 100 articles published in refereed journals, and is a frequent speaker in international conferences. Recipient of two National Science Centre in Poland grants and Huygens scholarship.

Bruno S. Sergi, PhD, is an instructor at Harvard University, where his teaching portfolio includes courses on emerging markets and development economics. At Harvard, he is a Faculty Affiliate of the Institute for Quantitative Social Science and the Center for International Development. He is a Full Professor of Political Economy at the University of Messina, Italy. He is the Series Editor for *Cambridge Elements in the Economics of Emerging Markets* (Cambridge University Press) and *Entrepreneurship and Global Economic Growth* book series at Emerald Publishing. His areas of research and teaching are related to the broader subject of the political economy of emerging markets, with a focus on sustainable development and technology. To further research in these areas, he is the chairperson and co-director of the Lab for Entrepreneurship and Development (LEAD) based in Cambridge, USA.

About the Contributors

Marek Angowski, PhD works at the Department of Microeconomics and Applied Economics, Faculty of Economics, Maria Skłodowska-Curie University in Lublin. As far as research-didactic activity is concerned his interests encompass marketing and management problems in enterprises of agribusiness sector, research and analysis of food market consumer behaviours as well as entrepreneurship development on rural areas. He combines his didactic activity with practice through cooperation with territorial self-government (making expert opinions) as well as conducting trainings within entrepreneurship supporting. He is an author of many science publications, expert opinions as well as research and scientific studies; Participant of many conferences both domestic and international within competitiveness and management in agribusiness, marketing and consumers behaviours. He is the member of Polish Economic Society, Agriculture and Agribusiness Economists Association, Polish Scientific Society of Marketing and Eurasia Business and Economics Society.

Michał Bernardelli, Associate Professor in the Institute of Econometrics in the Collegium of Economic Analysis at the SGH Warsaw School of Economics (Poland). He is the Deputy Dean of Graduate Studies (2020–2024), Head of the Physical Education and Sports Centre since 2015. He has graduated from the Faculty of Mathematics, Informatics and Mechanics of the University of Warsaw in 2003 with two master's degrees: in mathematics and computer studies. At the same faculty, in 2008, he was awarded a doctoral degree in the mathematical sciences with a specialisation in applied mathematics. In 2020, he obtained his habilitation in the field of economic sciences. For more than 20 years he was a consultant and contractor of many scientific and commercial projects. The interdisciplinarity of his scientific works is based mainly on the use of the IT and mathematical apparatus to solve problems in areas related to data analysis and exploration, in particular in Big Data issues, predictive methods and optimisation.

Jakub Bis is an Economist with a PhD in Economics and currently he is an Assistant Professor at the Lublin University of Technology, Faculty of Management. In addition to his academic role, he holds the position of Vice President at the Lublin branch of the Scientific Society for Organization and Management. With over 16 years of experience as a lecturer and more than 11 years as a trainer, Dr Bis has authored or co-authored dozens of articles, monographs and scientific papers, and has participated in numerous training and research projects. He has completed various courses and training programs in management and personal development. Dr Bis is passionate about new trends and working with people. His scientific and research interests focus on the issues of foreign direct investments, special economic zones and startups.

Sebastian Bobowski, PhD in Economics and Finance, is an Associate Professor at the Wroclaw University of Economics and Business. He is the author and co-author of more than 100 research papers, 12 handbooks and monographs in the fields of trade regionalism, international business, innovativeness of regions and enterprises, GVCs. He is a member of the European Southeast Asian Studies Association (EuroSEAS), Eurasia Business and Economics Society (EBES), Polish Association for International Studies (PTSM) and Asia-Pacific Research Center in Wroclaw.

Piotr Bolibok is an Assistant Professor at the Department of Economic Policy and Banking at the John Paul II Catholic University of Lublin, Poland. His current research concentrates on financial macroeconomics and macroprudential policy with a special focus on the macroeconomic consequences of private sector leverage. He has authored or co-authored more than 50 peer-reviewed scientific publications, including monographs, journal articles and book chapters.

Anna Budzyńska, Institute of Economics and Finance, University of Maria Curie-Skłodowska (UMCS), pl. M. Curie-Skłodowskiej 5, 20-031 Lublin, Poland. Currently working as an Assistant Professor at the Department of Microeconomics and Applied Economics at UMCS. In 2019, she was awarded a PhD in Economic Sciences after defending her doctoral dissertation titled Competitiveness on the EU Sugar Market Against World Trends at the Collegium of Socio-Economics of the Warsaw School of Economics. She has also worked in the Controlling Department of a company listed on the Warsaw Stock Exchange. She is the author of two scientific monographs: European Sugar Market in the Conditions of Globalisation, UMCS Publishing House, Lublin 2020, and Sources of Competitiveness of the Polish Sugar Sector, written in collaboration with A. Matras-Bolibok, UMCS Publishing House, Lublin 2019. She has also published more than 20 articles in various scientific journals.

Wiesława Caputa is employed at the WSB University as a Professor. Her research interests focus on the process of creation and valuation of customer capital. She is the author or co-author of over 170 publications, including two monographs, funded by the National Science Centre.

Jakub Czerniak, PhD, D Sc, works as an Associate Professor at the Faculty of Economics at Maria Curie-Sklodowska University (Poland). He graduated from the Faculty of Economics in 2001 and from the Faculty of Law in 2002. Employed as an academic teacher at the Faculty of Economics since 2004, he has teaching and research experience mostly in macroeconomics and innovation policy. He is an author or co-author of almost 30 publications.

Arkadiusz Gola, D Sc, PhD Eng., works as an Associate Professor at the Department of Production and Computerisation at the Faculty of Mechanical Engineering of the Lublin University of Technology (Poland). In 2011, he received a PhD from Lublin University of Technology (Poland) and in 2019 he received a habilitation from Cracow University of Technology (Poland). He is an author or co-author of 7 scientific monographs, 102 research papers and 108 chapters. His actual H-index in Web of Science is 19 and 19 in the Scopus database. Arkadiusz Gola is an Editor-in-Chief of the Applied Computer Science journal, a President of the Polish Associate for Knowledge Promotion and a member of the Polish Society of Production Management. Since 2014, he has been an expert at the Polish National Centre of Research and Development. He specialises in manufacturing systems design, operation management and intralogistics.

Bartosz Jóźwik, PhD, is an Associate Professor and Head of the Department of International Economics at the Institute of Economics and Finance at The John Paul II Catholic University of Lublin in Poland. Prior to his current position, he held academic appointments at various institutions, including the Nanovic Institute for European Studies at the University of Notre Dame in the United States in 2017-2018. His research interests include European economic integration, economic growth in Central and Eastern Europe and environmental economics, with a focus on pollution, climate change and natural resource management. Recently, Jóźwik has published several articles and books related to these topics, such as the article 'Revisiting the environmental Kuznets curve hypothesis: A case of Central Europe' in Energies (2021) and the book 'Real economic convergence of the Central and Eastern European EU Member States. Transformation, integration and cohesion policy' (2017).

Armand Kasztelan is an Associate Professor in the Department of Economics and Agribusiness at the University of Life Sciences in Lublin (Poland). He was the Head of the Department from 2017 to 2021. He is employed as a Lecturer at the Zamość Academy. His research interests are in the economics of sustainable development with particular emphasis on the environmental determinants of regional and national competitiveness and the role of natural capital in economic growth and development processes. He is author or co-author of 75 scientific and popular science publications. The University of Life Sciences Rector repeatedly awarded him for scientific activity. In 2022, he received the Polish Association of Environmental and Resource Economists (PAERE) award for the best branch publication entitled: On the Road to a Green Economy: How Do European Union Countries 'Do Their Homework'? He has participated in more than 40 scientific conferences of national and international scope. He is a member of the European Regional Science Association Polish Section and the Polish Economic Society. He has participated in Erasmus+ programme and university coordinator for cooperation with the Association of Polish Banks.

Mariusz Kicia, Maria Curie-Skłodowska University (UMCS), Poland, is currently an Adjunct Professor at the Institute of Economics and Finance, Department of Banking and Financial Markets. Dean of the Faculty of Economics at UMCS since September 2020. Member of the Industrial Council for Competences in

Modern Business Services in Poland. His research interests are behavioural finance, fintech and agent-based modelling.

Arkadiusz Kijek, PhD, is an Associate Professor and Head of the Department of Statistics and Econometrics at the Institute of Economics and Finance at the Maria Curie-Skłodowska University, Poland. His primary research interests are econometrics, statistics, data analysis and business cycles. He has authored or co-authored over 50 articles published in refereed journals. Recently, he has published several articles and books in the field of convergence, such as the articles 'Club Convergence in R&D Expenditure across European Regions' in Sustainability (2022), 'The Patterns of Energy Innovation Convergence across European Countries' in Energies (2021), 'Club convergence of labour productivity in agriculture: Evidence from EU countries' in Agricultural Economics – Czech (2020) and the book 'Innovation and Regional Technological Convergence. Theory and Evidence' (2023).

Dominika Kordela, University of Szczecin, Poland, is currently an Assistant Professor at the Institute of Economics and Finance, where she has been a Scientific Council member since 2019. She received her PhD degree in economics based on a thesis on alternative markets. Her research interests focus on alternative markets, alternative finance and SME financing. She has experience teaching various courses in the finance field, also at foreign universities.

Aleksandra Kowalska is a Professor in the Institute of Economics and Finance at Maria Curie-Skłodowska University in Poland. Her research interests are in food integrity, the role of rapid alert systems and information technology in data exchange along the food supply chain, sustainable food systems, food security issues and consumer behaviour studies. She has published in numerous peer-review journals, authored book chapters and written two books in the area of food integrity and sustainable economy. Two-time project leader in projects funded by the National Science Centre in Poland and a team member in another research project funded by this institution.

Izabela Krawczyk-Sokołowska is a Professor employed at the Czestochowa University of Technology and is the author or co-author of over 150 publications. The main area of research interest is innovation, strategic management and sustainable development.

Sophia Lingham, PhD, is a Researcher at the Royal Agricultural University, UK. Her research is focused on sustainable food systems, food policy, food security and the socio-economic aspects of food networks and food SMEs; she concentrates on horizontal linkages between food and drink SMEs. She holds a Masters in Sustainable Agriculture and Food Security (with Distinction) from the RAU and a First Class Bachelors of Law Degree from the Open University.

Louise Manning is a Professor and works at the University of Lincoln, UK. She is an academic researcher, writer, communicator and educator. Her research is focused on the critical issues in society, food and farming including sustainability, resilience, values, integrity and trust. She has had over 100 papers published in peer-reviewed journals and has written and published many books for a range of audiences. She is Editor of British Food Journal.

Małgorzata Markowska is a Professor at the Department of Regional Economics at Wrocław University of Economics and Business, Poland, since 2013. Her research deals with econometric measurement, evaluation, variability and dynamics of development, competitiveness, knowledge-based economy, smart specialisations, convergence and innovativeness in European regional space. As an author or co-author she published more than 110 scientific papers and 25 chapters in books, and recently her own dissertation 'Dynamic Taxonomy of Regions' Innovativeness'. She took part in 12 scientific projects financed by National Science Centre in Poland and European Union, and in projects for governmental, local administration and business units.

Anna Matras-Bolibok is an Assistant Professor at the Department of Microeconomics and Applied Economics at Maria Curie-Skłodowska University in Lublin, Poland. Her research interests focus on the role of innovation in regional economic development. She has authored or co-authored over 50 peer-reviewed papers and scientific reports for local and regional government authorities.

Damian Maye is a Professor and works at the University of Gloucestershire, UK. His research covers agri-food studies, geographies of food and rural geography, with a particular focus on agri-food sustainability, governance and social innovation. He recently co-authored a major new book on Geographies of Food. He is an Associate Editor of Journal of Rural Studies and Chair of the RGS-IBG Food Geographies Research Group.

Anna Nowak, PhD, Associate Professor – Head of the Department of Economics and Agribusiness, University of Life Sciences in Lublin, Akademicka 13, 20-950 Lublin, Poland. Her research interests focus on agricultural competitiveness, convergence in agriculture, bioeconomy, development of agriculture and farms, productivity of production factors in agriculture, spatial differentiation of agriculture and international agri-food trade. She is the author or co-author of 139 publications and a reviewer of numerous scientific publications. Co-author of, for instance, 2-volume monograph titled Polskie rolnictwo wobec wyzwań współczesności. T. 1, Wymiar ekonomiczno-strukturalny (Contemporary Challenges for Polish Agriculture, V. 1, The Economic and Structural Dimension) and Polskie rolnictwo wobec wyzwań współczesności. T. 2, Wymiar społeczny i środowiskowy (Contemporary Challenges for Polish Agriculture, V. 2, The Social and Environmental Dimension). She is an observer in the Common Agricultural Policy Strategic Plan (2023–2027) Monitoring Committee at the Ministry of Agriculture and Rural Development.

Paweł Pasierbiak, PhD, is an Associate Professor of International Economics at Maria Curie-Skłodowska University, Poland. His scientific fields of interest are International Economics, Regional Economic Integration, European Integration, Asian Economic Integration, Economic Development and Labour Markets. Recently, he was a principal investigator and MCSU consortium coordinator of the EACEA project: Establishing a Europe-Asia Research Network on Strategies for Promoting Europe-Asia Connectivity (SPEAC) under Erasmus Plus, Jean Monnet Network. His current research concerns various aspects of global value chains (GVCs).

Artur Paździor is a Professor at the Lublin University of Technology, Head of the Department of Finance and Accounting at the Faculty of Management. He is the author or co-author of over 120 scientific publications and over 100 business projects on entities valuation, investment effectiveness, restructuring projects and strategic and financial analyses.

Dawid Piątek, Poznan University of Economics and Business, Poland. With Habilitation and PhD in economics, he is an Associate Professor at the Department of Macroeconomics and Development Studies of the Poznań University of Economics and Business. He is interested in macroeconomics, institutional economics and post-socialist transition. He studies institutional economic growth factors as well. He is the author and co-author of several dozens of scientific publications; Co-author of a course book and teaching materials for macroeconomics lectures and classes.

Michał Bernard Pietrzak, PhD, D Sc is an Associate Professor at the Gdansk University of Technology, Faculty of Management and Economics. He is an experienced econometrician specialising in the application of quantitative methods, with particular emphasis on the methods of multivariate comparative analysis, financial econometrics and spatial econometrics. His research results are confirmed by more than 90 articles published in the Web of Science Core Collection, where the Web of Science h-index is 18. The research problems he has undertaken have been related to the fields of Economics, Management and Finance.

Mariusz Próchniak, Professor in the Department of Economics II in the Collegium of World Economy at the SGH Warsaw School of Economics (Poland). He is the Dean of Collegium of World Economy (2020–2024). Since July 2022, he is a full Professor of social sciences in the discipline of economics and finance. In 2015, he received the habilitation degree in the field of economic sciences in the discipline of economics. He has worked at SGH Warsaw School of Economics since 2002 – at the beginning as an assistant, then Assistant Professor and Associate Professor, and currently – full Professor. He is the author of many articles published among others in the journals: Economic Modelling, Eastern European Economics, Post-Communist Economies, Gospodarka Narodowa, Ekonomista and Bank i Kredyt. He participated in many research projects funded, e.g. by the National Science Centre in Poland and the National Bank of Poland.

Mariusz Sagan, PhD is an expert and practitioner in stimulating strategic development, promoting entrepreneurship, devising development strategies for cities and attracting international investors. Since 2009, he is an Associate Professor in the Collegium of Business Administration at SGH Warsaw School of Economics. He is the author and co-author of over 100 publications on regional and urban development, international business and company management; this includes a considerable number of articles in prestigious magazines, e.g. Cross Cultural Management, Managing Service Quality, Marketing Education Review, Chinese Management Studies and Energies. He presented his research outcomes at conferences in several countries, e.g. China, the United States, Russia, Ukraine, Georgia, Portugal, etc. In the years 2014–2016, he is a member of the Global Advisory Board in the Center for Leadership and Management at Rutgers University in the United States.

Ilona Skibińska-Fabrowska, PhD, Department of Insurance and Investment (Faculty of Economics) at the Maria Curie Sklodowska University, Lublin, Poland. Her research focuses on finance and banking (particularly central banking, corporate capital structure and micro-enterprise finance). She is the author and co-author of numerous publications in this field.

Tomasz Sosnowski is an Assistant Professor at the Faculty of Economics and Sociology at the University of Lodz, Poland. He received his PhD in economics in 2013. His research interests focus on corporate governance, investment decisions, finance and accounting. He has conducted extensive research on topics such as private equity funds, IPO and corporate governance practices. In addition, he has also investigated issues related to financial reporting quality, earnings management and the influence of regulatory frameworks on corporate behaviour. He has published numerous papers in international and national journals and is a reviewer for several academic journals and conferences.

Adam Sulich is an Associate Professor at the Department of Advanced Research in Management, Wroclaw University of Economics and Business, Wroclaw (Poland) and Visiting Researcher at Schulich School of Business, York University, Toronto (Canada). His main scientific interests are the problems of ensuring sustainable development and the efficiency of enterprise operations in extraordinarily complex and dynamic environmental conditions. His research interests include green jobs, sustainable strategic management, green economy, network relationships, business ecosystems and sustainable development. He also gained scientific experience during the Erasmus+ exchange programs at Vrije Universiteit Brussels (Belgium) and Technical University in Ostrava (Czechia). In the business sphere, he specialises primarily in strategic analyses, including the valuation of intangible assets and the green jobs assessment. He developed or co-authored several business reports on strategic analysis and sustainable change management.

Andrzej Szablewski is a Professor of Economics. For the past 30 years, issues concerning various theoretical and practical aspects of liberalisation of the network industries, in particular the energy sector, have been his main field of interest. He is the author and co-author of over 100 publications on this area. He has participated in and led a number of research projects, including EU financed projects. Some of his recent and most important books include: Zarys teorii i praktyki reform regulacyjnych na przykładzie energetyki (2003), Liberalizacja a bezpieczeństwo dostaw energii elektrycznej (2012) and Regulacyjny wymiar liberalizacji. Wnioski dla sektora ciepłownictwa systemowego (2015). In addition to his academic and research activity, he advised numerous government bodies and committees on restructuring and regulation of energy sector as well as competition and energy policy. Currently, he is a Deputy Director of the Institute of Economics at the Polish Academy of Sciences in Warsaw.

Katarzyna Szarzec, Poznan University of Economics and Business, Poland. She is an Associate Professor at the Department of Macroeconomics and Development Studies at the Poznań University of Economics and Business in Poland (PUEB). She received her PhD and habilitation in economics from the PUEB. Her publications focus on political economy, macroeconomics, comparative economic systems and post-socialist countries. Her latest research is about state ownership and the role of state-owned enterprises in contemporary economies.

Anna Szelągowska, PhD, is a Full Professor of Social Sciences in the Department of Innovative City (Collegium of Business Administration) at the SGH Warsaw School of Economics. Her research focuses on finance and banking (particularly determinants of banking sector development), financial innovations, financial frauds, real estate finance, social housing policy and silver economy. She is an author of more than 200 publications, including 9 books and 16 edited books.

Bartosz Totleben, Poznan University of Economics and Business, Poland. An Assistant Professor at the Poznan University of Economics and Business, Institute of Economics, Poznań. In 2018 he received a PhD in economics from the Faculty of Economics, Poznan University of Economics and Business. His research interests include political analysis, determinants of state failure, rent-seeking activities and development in fragile states. He is the author and co-author for more than 15 scientific publications including articles, chapters and books.

Anna Wawryszuk-Misztal received her PhD in economics. She is an Assistant Professor at the Department of Corporate Finance and Accounting at the Maria Curie-Sklodowska University in Lublin, Poland. Her main area of research interest is financial management. She conducts research on corporate governance, board diversity, initial public offerings and financial disclosures. She is the author of the book entitled Financial factors and consequences of diversifying the composition of management and supervisory boards of Polish public companies, published by Wydawnictwo UMCS in Lublin in 2021.

Łukasz Wiechetek, PhD, is an Assistant Professor at the Faculty of Economics at Maria Curie-Sklodowska University (Poland). He has teaching, research and practical experience in deploying information systems and managing IT projects. Łukasz Wiechetek is the author or co-author of over 70 publications. His research interests include e-business, IT project management, digital society development, cybersecurity, automated data analysis and technology-enhanced teaching and learning.

Introduction

Over the past 15 years, Poland has been among the fastest-growing countries in the European Union. It was the only country in the EU that avoided economic recession during the global crisis in 2008–2009. Trying to explain the sources of Poland's economic success and decouple it from simple stylised facts on economic convergence anchored in the neoclassical growth models, this book shows how the Polish economy rapidly moved away from the communist economic system, which had ended up in an economic collapse, and took the road to unprecedented growth in income and the quality of life. The authors apply the three-way perspective on drivers and barriers to Poland's economic growth.

In the first part of the monograph, special attention is given to the transition and contemporary challenges of the Polish economy. Chapter 1 focuses on the main drivers of Polish economic growth from the perspective of the past, the present and the future. It emphasises the role of capital accumulation and labour force in explaining the growth of the Polish economy. The experience of Poland from the economic transition is then discussed in depth in Chapter 2. The authors deal with four aspects of the changes in the Polish economy, i.e. stabilisation, liberalisation, institutional reforms and privatisation. The following chapter outlines the topic of income convergence process among regions in Poland. The empirical analyses included in this chapter provide important insights into the effectiveness of regional policy in Poland. Chapter 4 shifts considerations towards the transformation of the Polish economy into the Green Economy (GE). The authors apply the Green Transformation Index to analyse the transformation towards GE in Poland. The current issues related to economic resilience of the Polish economy and food security are addressed in the next two chapters. The former studies the impact of the Covid-19 pandemic and the war in Ukraine on the situation of Polish consumers and the resulting behaviour in the context of business–consumer relations. The latter identifies and reviews food security challenges that governments and societies have faced during the Covid-19 crisis and beyond, with specific emphasis on Poland.

The second part of the monograph is dedicated to the issues related to the institutional and policy framework of the Polish economy growth. In Chapter 7, the authors investigate the impact of Polish monetary policy on investment outlays in contexts of high uncertainty. The fiscal and monetary policy are also subject to a broader discussion in the next chapter. It tackles dependencies between fiscal and monetary policy and the capital market in Poland. Chapter 9 is to deepen and widen the topics concerning mutual similarity among the characteristics of the financial sector (including the monetary policy by the central bank) and the characteristics of the real sector (e.g. economic growth), as well as cross-similarity between both sectors in Poland and selected Central and Eastern European countries. The further three chapters present non-macroeconomic policies that are key for reaping the sustainable growth in Poland. The first one portrays and evaluates the key developments in the innovation policy and national innovation system of Poland. Theoretical considerations in this chapter are supported by the empirical analyses of changes in Poland's innovation policy and innovation system frameworks. The second one shows new opportunities in Poland's decarbonisation energy policy. More specifically, it considers from an economic perspective the potential role of nuclear power in decarbonising the Polish power sector. The last part of the triptych tries to evaluate the significance of the common agricultural policy to the growth and development of agriculture and to structural transformations therein triggered primarily by the influx of additional CAP funds into Poland.

The final part of this book shows prospects of economic growth in Poland. These themes are discussed from the micro, mezo and macro perspectives. Chapter 13 tries to address the question whether imitation or innovation is the right key to the economic growth in Poland from both the conceptual and the empirical perspectives. The next chapter describes the present state and the trends in the ICT sector, which today is considered to be one of the most progressively developing part of the Polish economy. Changing the perspective, Chapter 15 presents the evolution of Poland's participation in global value chains since the mid-1990s, including its key determinants. Two further chapters bring attention to the challenges faced by the Polish companies. The first one provides a better understanding of the attitude of Polish companies towards diversity policies and reveals differences in actual and expected levels of gender diversity in corporate boards. The second one identifies the Polish companies' stability in the crisis situations especially during the Global Financial Crisis of 2007–2009 and COVID-19 crisis. This part of the monograph closes Chapter 16 relating to entrepreneurial ecosystems in Poland. It discusses and verifies the role of the entrepreneurship ecosystem in the development of enterprises in Poland.

This book is suitable for practitioners and academics interested in discovering the foundations for the Polish growth miracle and finding whether this growth will likely last in the future.

Preface

Leszek Balcerowicz

Warsaw School of Economics

Warsaw, 13th April, 2023

The post-communist transition in Europe is one of the most important trans-formations in modern history. Like other radical shifts in history, its timing and its crucial events were totally unexpected. Market-oriented reforms had been introduced under democratic political regimes in the post-communist transition. Therefore, the transition was both economic and political.

Poland was a pioneer in this transition respect entering the path towards a well-functioning market economy. The exceptional growth performance of the Polish economy after 1989 obviously poses questions about its causes. This book tries to give an answer to this question raised by tackling the most important issues from Poland's recent and past: the sources of economic success, the process of transition and structural achievements.

Poland's transition is analysed in the micro, mezo and macro perspectives and takes into account: the whole economy, financial market, fiscal policy, monetary policy, entrepreneurship behaviour and new technologies. The authors provide in-depth analyses and consider the changes in the Poland's external conditions: the 2007–2009 global financial crisis, the Covid-19 pandemic and the war in Ukraine. This book sheds light on actions providing food security, implementing a diversity policy and response to climate changes in the context of the Polish economy and firms. In my opinion, it deserves to be thoroughly read.

Part 1
Transition and Contemporary Challenges of the Polish Economy

Chapter 1

Factors of Polish Economic Growth – Past and the Future

Jakub Bis and Jakub Czerniak

Abstract

Research Background: Authors investigate the key factors contributing to Poland's economic growth since 1989, including capital accumulation, technological progress, labour force and productivity and European integration.

Purpose of the Article: Through the analysis of macroeconomic indicators, comparison with selected countries and review of relevant literature and policies, authors aim to offer a comprehensive understanding of Poland's growth story, providing valuable insights for informed policy recommendations and fostering sustainable economic development.

Methodology: This study utilises a mixed-methods approach, combining quantitative analysis of macroeconomic indicators with qualitative examination of literature, policy documents and expert opinions. This comprehensive analysis allows us to assess Poland's economic growth, compare its performance with selected countries and identify underlying factors driving growth and potential future challenges.

Findings: Understanding the drivers of Poland's growth is essential for effective policy formulation and promoting sustainable development, while acknowledging the potential threats to maintaining its high growth rate such as modest innovation performance, population ageing, growing public debt and reliance on coal-based energy. The findings provide valuable insights into Poland's economic trajectory and form the basis for informed policy recommendations.

Keywords: GDP growth rate; GDP per capita; capital accumulation; labour force; growth risks; population ageing

Modeling Economic Growth in Contemporary Poland, 3–13
Copyright © 2024 Jakub Bis and Jakub Czerniak
Published under exclusive licence by Emerald Publishing Limited
doi:10.1108/978-1-83753-654-220231001

Introduction

The Polish economy, located in Central Europe, has a dynamic history transitioning from a centrally planned system under communist rule to a thriving market-oriented economy. The fall of communism in 1989 marked a turning point, with Poland implementing economic reforms, including liberalisation, privatisation and stabilisation measures. EU membership in 2004 further accelerated growth, granting access to the Single Market and attracting investment. Over the past three decades, Poland has emerged as a leader in European economic growth. According to World Bank data, from 1990 ($1,731 in current prices) to 2021 ($17,999 in current prices), Poland's Gross Domestic Product (GDP) per capita increased over tenfold (World Bank, 2023d). Following the 1989 political transformation, the economy underwent numerous reforms, adopting policies of openness to global markets and integrating with the European Union. Despite rapid growth, Poland still lags behind the most advanced European economies. In 2021, its GDP per capita in purchasing power standard (PPS) was 77% of the EU average.

Understanding the factors driving Poland's economic growth after 1989 is crucial for formulating effective policies and fostering sustainable development. With a diverse economy, grasping the interplay of various factors can help navigate challenges and capitalise on opportunities. This chapter examines key factors contributing to Poland's economic growth, including capital accumulation, technological progress, labour force and productivity and European integration. By exploring these factors, we aim to provide insights into Poland's growth trajectory and potential future developments. The last section of this chapter also presents potential threats to maintaining the high growth rate of Polish GDP, such as modest innovation performance, population ageing, growing public debt and energy mix based on coal.

Polish GDP Growth in Comparison With Selected Countries.

Fig. 1 shows the rate of growth of Polish GDP, from 1993 to 2021, compared to the other Visegrad Group countries (Czechia, Hungary and Slovak Republic) and to its neighbouring country (and the biggest European economy as well) – Germany. During the last almost 30 years, the Polish economy usually experienced a higher rate of growth than the above-mentioned countries, both in times of expansion, and in times of slowdown or even recession. Poland demonstrated remarkable resilience during the 2009 global financial crisis. While most countries experienced economic contractions, Poland's economy continued to grow, albeit at a slower pace (2.83%). Like other countries in the region, Poland's economy contracted in 2020 due to the COVID-19 pandemic (−2.02%). However, the contraction was less severe than in Czechia (−5.50%) and the Slovak Republic (−3.37%).

Poland's economy rebounded in 2021 with a growth rate of 6.85%, showcasing its ability to recover from economic shocks. Although Germany has the largest economy in Europe, Poland's growth rates often exceeded Germany's during the

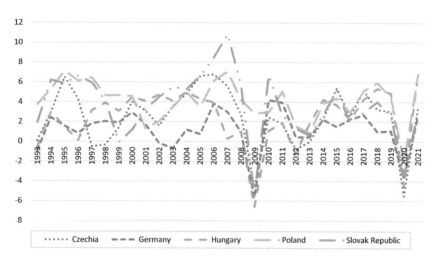

Fig. 1. GDP Growth (Annual %) 1993–2021 – Czechia, Germany, Hungary, Poland, Slovak Republic. *Source:* Own study based on https:// data.worldbank.org/ (World Bank, 2023c).

period of analysis. This suggests that Poland has made significant progress in catching up with more developed Western European economies. According to the latest OECD data, Poland's GDP rate of growth was 4.9% in 2022, but it is expected to shrink to 0.9% in 2023 and 2.4% in 2024 (OECD, 2023).

Capital Accumulation and Its Importance in Polish Economic Growth

Capital accumulation has played a significant role in driving Poland's economic growth. By increasing the stock of productive assets and enhancing the quality of these assets, capital accumulation supports higher output levels, improves productivity and fosters long-term growth. Gross fixed capital formation (GFCF) indicator represents the value of additions to fixed assets purchased by businesses, government and households within a country's economy. It is a measure of net investments in physical assets, such as infrastructure and machinery. According to the World Bank, Poland's GFCF as a percentage of GDP has remained relatively stable, hovering around 18%–20% since the early 1990s. The GFCF in Poland increased from $24.78 billion in 1995 to $115.8 billion in 2019, reflecting a strong trend in capital accumulation (World Bank, 2023b). Another indicator measure is gross domestic savings – the difference between a country's GDP and its total consumption. It provides an insight into the availability of domestic resources for investments in capital accumulation. World Bank data shows that Poland's gross domestic savings increased from $31.04 billion in 1995 to $168.97 billion in 2021 (World Bank, 2023e).

Investments are a crucial factor in socio-economic development, especially for underdeveloped countries. K. Rittenbruch emphasises the role of export-oriented investments, referred to as 'base activity' (Rittenbruch, 1968). In the 'big push' theory, P. N. Rosenstein-Rodan proposes autonomous investments, mainly in infrastructure, financed from public sources as a developmental impulse for underdeveloped areas (Rosenstein-Rodan, 1943). A. O. Hirschman suggests that the development of underdeveloped areas can be achieved through investments in 'bottlenecks' of development, and the surpluses obtained in this way can be reinvested to stimulate economic growth. These areas should implement appropriate incentives and investment incentives to stimulate the development of relevant sectors of the economy. A. O. Hirschman also warns of the social and psychological barriers present in underdeveloped countries, which can hinder development convergence (Hirschman, 1958). Like Rittenbruch and Hirschman, Kaldor highlights the crucial role of exports in accelerating the economic growth, arguing that export activity contributes to improving efficiency through internal and external savings. If wages do not rise as fast as productivity, the competitive position of the underdeveloped areas increases, leading to the inflow of further investments and economic growth (Kaldor, 1970).

N. G. Mankiw et al. present an empirical analysis that highlights the importance of investment in both physical and human capital for long-term economic growth. The authors extend Solow's growth model to include human capital, and their findings underscore the importance of investments in education and physical capital to increase productivity and drive economic growth (Mankiw et al., 1992). M. Mahmoodi and E. Mahmoodi studied the causality relationship between foreign direct investment (FDI), exports and economic growth in European and Asian developing countries, finding bidirectional causality between GDP and FDI in European countries, and between exports and economic growth in Asian countries. The study also reveals long-run causality between exports, FDI and economic growth for both panels. The results suggest that European countries can promote economic growth by attracting FDI, while Asian countries can achieve higher growth by increasing exports, with policy recommendations including expanding free trade zones, reducing export taxes and improving quality control and training programs (Mahmoodi and Mahmoodi, 2016). Interestingly, enough research shows that convergence in labour productivity levels among these nations appears to correspond to their convergence in schooling levels. However, econometric results mostly fail to show a significant impact of formal education, growth in educational attainment or interaction effects between schooling and R&D on country labour productivity growth (Wolff, 2000).

Investments in physical capital, such as infrastructure, have been crucial in modernising Poland's economy. Upgrades to transportation networks, energy systems and telecommunications have facilitated better connectivity, reduced logistics costs and increased the attractiveness of Poland as a destination for FDI. The development of industrial parks and special economic zones has further stimulated business activity and job creation. FDI represents an essential source of capital and knowledge transfer, which can contribute to economic growth. World Bank data indicates that Poland's FDI net inflows have increased over the past three decades, from $89 million in 1990 to $37.1 billion in 2021 (World Bank, 2023a).

Human capital investments have also contributed to Poland's growth. Prioritising education and skills development has led to a well-educated and skilled labour force, which in turn, has attracted multinational corporations seeking a competitive workforce. The enrollment rate in higher education in Poland has increased significantly over the past decades. In 1990, the gross enrollment ratio was 20%, while in 2019 it reached 70% (World Bank, 2023f). This trend demonstrates the growing emphasis on higher education in Poland. Another measure indicating the high quality of education in Poland is the Programme for International Student Assessment (PISA), which is an international study that evaluates 15-year-old students' performance in mathematics, science and reading. PISA scores serve as an indicator of the quality of education and the skills of the workforce. In 2018, Poland scored above the OECD average in all three subjects (OECD, 2018).

The European Union has had a significant impact on the growth of the Polish economy by providing financial support for various projects and initiatives aimed at modernising the country's infrastructure, enhancing human capital, fostering innovation and promoting regional development. Since the beginning of Poland's membership in the European Union (from May 2004 to August 2022), transfers amounted to over 224 billion euros, while during this time, Poland contributed to the EU budget just under 75 billion euros. The balance of settlements amounted to almost 150 billion euros (Ministry of Finance, 2023). These funds have accelerated economic growth, improved the business environment and attracted additional investments, contributing to Poland's impressive economic performance in recent years.

Polish Labour Force and Productivity

Poland's transition from a centrally planned economy to a market-oriented one in the early 1990s led to significant economic growth, mainly driven by the restructuring of the economy and the shift from heavy industries and agriculture to services and knowledge-based industries. This transformation required a change in the labour force, as people had to adapt to new industries and acquire new skills.

Education and skill development have been crucial factors in polish economic growth. Additionally, the Polish workforce is generally known for its strong work ethic, resilience and adaptability, which has contributed to increased productivity. Poland's accession to the European Union in 2004 facilitated the free movement of labour, leading to increased labour migration. Many young and skilled workers sought better job opportunities and higher wages abroad, resulting in a decline in the size of the labour force in Poland. This emigration led to a potential brain drain and labour shortage, which could negatively impact economic growth. Nowadays, in Poland we have a problem with the ageing population. As the population gets older, the labour force participation rate may decline, leading to a potential labour shortage in the future. This demographic shift may put additional pressure on social security and pension systems, potentially impacting economic growth (Fig. 2)

From 1992 to 2021, Poland experienced remarkable growth in GDP per capita, increasing from $26,605 to $74,890. This substantial increase suggests that labour productivity in Poland improved considerably during this period. The steady growth trajectory indicates that the Polish economy has been consistently enhancing its efficiency and output. From 1992 to 2021, Poland's GDP per capita increased significantly around 181%. During the same period, Germany's GDP per capita increased approximately 24%. Although Germany's GDP per capita remains higher than Poland's, Poland's growth rate has been considerably faster. Though Poland started with a lower GDP per capita than Czechia and Hungary and a similar GDP per capita to the Slovak Republic in 1992, it has experienced the fastest growth rate among the four countries from 1992 to 2021. This rapid growth reflects Poland's successful economic transformation and integration into the European and global economies. Czechia, Hungary and the Slovak Republic have also experienced substantial growth, but at a slower pace compared to Poland.

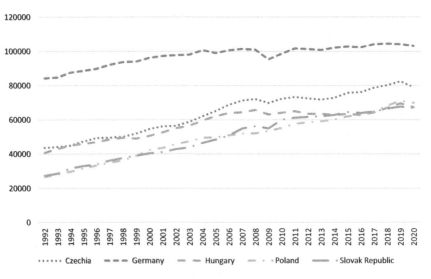

Fig. 2.   GDP per Person Employed (Constant 2017 PPP $) – Czechia, Germany, Hungary, Poland and Slovak Republic. *Source:* Own study based on https://data.worldbank.org/ (World Bank, 2023g).

Polish Future GDP Growth Risks

The Global Risks Report 2023 identified 35 risks that were included into the World Economic Forum's 2022 Executive Opinion Survey (EOS). The survey was administered between April and September 2022 and respondents were to choose five risks which are the most likely to pose the biggest threat to their country in the next 2 years. Risks were divided into five categories: economic, environmental, geopolitical, societal and technological. For each out of 121 economies surveyed, five main risks were presented. The results for Poland are as follows:

(1) Rapid and/or sustained inflation
(2) Breakdown of critical information infrastructure through cyber attacks
(3) Geoeconomic confrontation (including sanctions, trade wars, investment screening)
(4) Employment and livelihood crises
(5) Interstate conflict.

The main risk for the Polish economy in the near future is high inflation. Inflation rate (CPI) calculated by Polish central bank for February 2023 was 18.4% (change to the corresponding month of the previous year). This value was the fifth highest among OECD countries. In January 2023, Polish inflation rate (CPI) was 16.6%, significantly higher than the average for OECD which was 9.2% and for European Union which was 10.0%. Risks 3 and 4 are a direct consequence of Russian aggression in Ukraine (OECD Statistics). Fighting high inflation, forced to tighten the monetary policy, which has (and probably will have in the future) negative impact on consumption and investments, and thus on GDP growth. Furthermore, autumn 2023 general elections encourage the government to increase government spending. This expected expansionary fiscal policy can be considered as fuelling inflation.

In the more distant future the Polish economy can face some even more serious challenges for its GDP growth. Among them are modest innovation performance, population ageing, growth of public debt and an energy mix based mostly on coal.

In The Global Competitiveness Report 2017–2018, 137 economies were investigated. Based on the level of development, they were divided into three main categories: factor-driven (stage 1), efficiency-driven (stage 2) and innovation-driven (stage 3). There were also two transition stages indicated: transition from stage 1 to stage 2 and transition from stage 2 to stage 3. Poland, Slovak Republic and Hungary were at the transition from stage 2 to stage 3, while Germany and Czechia at stage 3 (Schwab and Sala-i-Martin, 2017). Being very close to the highest stage of development, means the Polish future growth depends strongly on the ability to create innovations. Unfortunately, this has been a weakness of the Polish economy for many years. According to the European Innovation Scoreboard 2022, Poland is in the place 24 (out of 27 EU member states), in the fourth (the last one) group of countries. The only three countries with poorer performance than Poland are Latvia, Bulgaria and Romania. What's even more disappointing is that Polish innovation performance doesn't seem to improve over time when compared to other countries and to the EU average (Fig. 3).

Polish innovation performance is not only the worst, but also quite stable over time while compared to the European Union, Germany and Hungary, and catching up a bit only when it comes to the Slovak Republic. However, Czechia started to perform significantly better. One of the main reasons explaining the low innovation potential of the Polish economy is very modest spending on research and development. Eurostat data for R&D spending (all sectors, euro per inhabitant, 2021) are as follows: Germany – 1357.1; EU – 734.5; Czechia – 444.4; Hungary – 260.1; Poland – 218.1; Slovak Republic – 168.2 (Eurostat, 2023a).

Another threat to Polish GDP growth is the ageing of the population. The old-age dependency (number of people at an age when they are economically inactive divided by the number of people of working age) in 2023 in Poland is 33.94. This is the 18th highest (so the 18th worst) result among 38 OECD member states. It means that nowadays Polish old-age dependency ratio is at average level while compared to other most developed economies, especially when compared to Germany (38.58), Czechia (35.99) and Hungary (35.43). However, the Slovak Republic has a better result (30.18) (OECD Statistics). Nevertheless, even with this current moderate old-age dependency ratio, the Polish pension system is facing difficulties in providing pensions at a reasonable level. Gross pension replacement rate for average earners at retirement age is 30.6% in Poland, which is fourth lowest (worst) among OECD countries. The value for Germany is 41.5; 49.0 for Czechia; 53.1 for Slovak Republic and 62.5 for Hungary. Average for OECD is 51.8 and the highest gross replacement rates show Portugal (74.9),

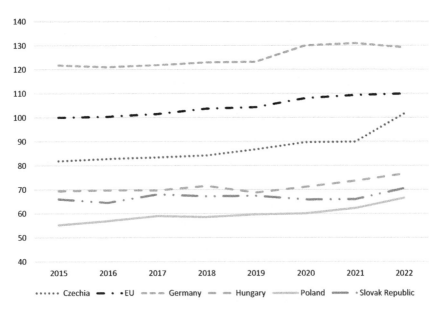

Fig. 3.   Summary Innovation Index Value (EU 2015 = 100) –
Czechia, Germany, Hungary, Poland, Slovak Republic, and the European
Union. *Source:* Own study based on Eurostat (Eurostat, 2023b).

Luxembourg (76.6) and Denmark (80.0). The situation is even more difficult when it comes to low earners in Poland. Gross pension replacement rate for low earners at retirement age is 31.8% (the second worst result in OECD). It is a slightly higher rate than for average earners, but it has to be kept in mind that this 31.8% is based on lower salary, so the amount of money is barely enough (or even not enough) for a living. Replacement rates for other comparison countries are higher: Germany (46.5%), Hungary (62.5%), Slovak Republic (62.6%), Czechia (81.2%) and 64.5% average for all OECD countries (OECD, 2021). Taking into consideration that these very low replacement rates (both, for average and low earners) appear in times of moderate old-age dependency ratio, situation in Poland will get extremely tough with the rising old-age dependency ratio and prospects in this matter are disturbing. It is expected for the Polish old-age dependency rate to reach 38.89 in 2030; 43.88 in 2040; 57.01 in 2050 and 68.20 in 2060. This 68.2 will be the sixth highest (worst) among OECD member states, higher than all comparison countries and much higher than OECD total (49.60). Combining current very low replacement rates in Poland with its population ageing, gives high risk of old-age poverty, especially for women who usually leave the labour market earlier but live longer. It also puts some extra pressure on fiscal sustainability. OECD calculations, based on the assumption of 'no policy change', stable replacement ratios and constant primary spending in other areas, show huge growth in Poland's public debt (Maastricht definition), from less than 60% of GDP today to almost 140% of GDP in 2050 (OECD, 2023).

There is another big challenge ahead of Poland's economy – electricity generation and electric power transmission. Growth of Poland's economy, despite using more energy-saving technology, still required more electricity. In 1990, Poland produced 136,311 GWh, while in 2021 it was 179,417 GWh. Not only the amount of produced electricity changed, but also the sources of Poland's electricity generation changed significantly. However, there is still a lot to be done. In 1990, coal was a source for 96.14% of electricity produced in Poland, 2.43% was produced by hydroelectric power plants and 1.15% from oil. In 2021, coal was still the main source for electricity production (72.28%), followed by wind (9.06%) and natural gas (8.79%) (International Energy Agency, 2023). Current Poland's energy mix, with more than 80% of electricity produced from fossil fuels, cannot be sustained in the time of fighting climate change and implementing the European Green Deal. By signing the declaration of resignation from the coal exploitation (during the World Climate Summit in 2021), Poland made a commitment to close all its hard coal mines by 2049. Fulfilling this commitment may be difficult, taking into account the huge share of coal in the Polish energy mix and at the same time growing demand for electricity. Another issue here is that coal plants in Poland are outdated and inefficient in many cases. It means that energy is more expensive and there is a high risk of power plant failure, which can lead to insufficient energy production and blackout. On the other hand, Polish grid infrastructure needs significant investments to be able to absorb electricity produced from renewable sources. It should be remembered that investments in power plants or in grid infrastructure are not only extremely costly, but also require more time than typical business investments.

Summary

The Polish economy has experienced robust GDP growth from 1993 to 2021, often surpassing the rates of other Visegrad Group countries (Czechia, Hungary, Slovak Republic) and Germany. Capital accumulation, investments in physical and human capital and EU support have played significant roles in driving this growth. Poland's GDP per capita has increased significantly from 1992 to 2021, showcasing a marked improvement in labour productivity. The Polish workforce's resilience, adaptability and strong work ethic have also contributed to increased productivity. However, Poland faces challenges such as an ageing population and potential labour shortages, which may impact future economic growth. Despite these challenges, Poland's rapid GDP growth indicates its successful economic transformation and integration into the European and global economies.

However, experts note many threats to Polish economic growth. Among the most important risks to Poland's future GDP growth are rapid and/or sustained inflation, breakdown of critical information infrastructure through cyber attacks, geoeconomic confrontation, employment and livelihood crises and interstate conflict. High inflation is currently the primary risk, with a consumer price index (CPI) of 18.4% in February 2023, the fifth highest among OECD countries. This, along with upcoming general elections, may lead to increased government spending, further fuelling inflation.

In the long term, Poland faces challenges such as modest innovation performance, population ageing, growth of public debt and an energy mix heavily reliant on coal. The country ranks poorly in the European Innovation Scoreboard and has low research and development spending. Additionally, Poland's old-age dependency ratio is expected to rise significantly in the coming decades, putting pressure on the pension system and increasing the risk of old-age poverty. Lastly, while Poland has made progress in diversifying its energy sources since 1990, further improvements are needed to ensure the sustainability of the energy sector.

References

European Commission, Directorate-General for Research and Innovation, Hollanders, H., Es-Sadki, N. and Khalilova, A. (2022), *European Innovation Scoreboard 2022*, Publications Office of the European Union, available at https://data.europa.eu/doi/10.2777/309907

Eurostat (2023a), available at https://ec.europa.eu/eurostat/databrowser/view/tec00114/default/table (accessed 11 March 2023).

Eurostat (2023b), available at https://ec.europa.eu/research-and-innovation/en/statistics/performance-indicators/european-innovation-scoreboard/eis (accessed 11 March 2023).

Hirschman, A. O. (1958), *The Strategy of Economic Development*, Yale University Press, New Haven.

International Energy Agency (2023), available at https://www.iea.org/countries/poland (accessed 22 March 2023).

Kaldor, N. (1970), The Case for Regional Policies, *Scottish Journal of Political Economy*, Vol. 17 No. 3, pp. 337–348.

Mahmoodi, M. and Mahmoodi, E. (2016), Foreign Direct Investment, Exports and Economic Growth: Evidence from Two Panels of Developing Countries, *Economic Research-Ekonomska Istraživanja*, Vol. 29 No. 1, pp. 938–949, https://doi.org/10.1080/1331677X.2016.1164922

Mankiw, N. G., Romer, D. and Weil, D. N. (1992), A Contribution to the Empirics of Economic Growth, *The Quarterly Journal of Economics*, Vol. 107 No. 2, pp. 407–437, https://doi.org/10.2307/2118477

Ministry of Finance (2023), available at https://www.gov.pl/web/finanse/transfery-polska-ue-unia-europejska (accessed 12 March 2023).

OECD (2021), *Pensions at a Glance 2021: OECD and G20 Indicators*, OECD Publishing, Paris, https://doi.org/10.1787/ca401ebd-en

OECD (2023), *Economic Surveys: Poland 2023*, OECD Publishing, Paris.

OECD (2018), available at https://www.oecd.org/pisa/publications/PISA2018_CN_POL.pdf (accessed 12 March 2023).

OECD Statistics, available at https://stats.oecd.org/ (accessed 27 March 2023).

Rittenbruch, K. (1968), *Zur Anwendbarkeit der Exportbasiskonzepte im Rahmen der Regionalstudien*, Duncker und Humblot, Berlin.

Ronsenstein-Rodan, P. N. (1943), Problems of Industrialization of Eastern and South-Eastern Europe, *The Economic Journal*, Vol. 53 No. 210/211. (June–September).

Schwab, K. and Sala-i-Martin, X. (2017), *The Global Competitiveness Report 2017–2018*, World Economic Forum, Geneva.

The Global Risks Report 2023 (18th Edition), Insight Report, World Economic Forum, Geneva.

Wolff, E. N. (2000), Human Capital Investment and Economic Growth: Exploring the Cross-Country Evidence, *Structural Change and Economic Dynamics*, Vol. 11 No. 4, pp. 433–472, https://doi.org/10.1016/S0954-349X(00)00030-8

World Bank (2023a), available at https://data.worldbank.org/indicator/BX.KLT.DINV.CD.WD?locations=PL (accessed 10 March 2023).

World Bank (2023b), available at https://data.worldbank.org/indicator/NE.GDI.FTOT.CD?locations=PL (accessed 10 March 2023).

World Bank (2023c), available at https://data.worldbank.org/indicator/NY.GDP.MKTP.KD.ZG?locations=PL-HU-SK-CZ-DE&most_recent_year_desc=false (accessed 10 March 2023).

World Bank (2023d), available at https://data.worldbank.org/indicator/NY.GDP.PCAP.CD?locations=PL& most_recent_year_desc=false (accessed 10 March 2023).

World Bank (2023e), available at https://data.worldbank.org/indicator/NY.GDS.TOTL.CD?locations=PL (accessed 10 March 2023).

World Bank (2023f), available at https://data.worldbank.org/indicator/SE.TER.ENRR?locations=PL (accessed 11 March 2023).

World Bank (2023g), available at https://data.worldbank.org/indicator/SL.GDP.PCAP.EM.KD?locations=PL-HU-SK-CZ-DE&most_recent_year_desc=false (accessed 11 March 2023).

Chapter 2

An Odyssey With a Happy End: The Polish Economic Transition – Outcome and Lessons

Katarzyna Szarzec, Dawid Piątek and Bartosz Totleben

Abstract

Research Background: At the beginning of the 1990s, the Polish economic situation was extremely difficult: high public debt, shortages, high inflation and more than 8,000 state-owned enterprises (SOEs) waiting to be restructured and/or privatised; along with a GDP per capita lower than in Ukraine.

Purpose of the Article: This chapter provides an overview of the Polish economic transition, and presents the results of this process, taking into account four aspects of the changes, i.e. stabilisation, liberalisation, institutional reforms and privatisation. Special attention is paid to intentionally unfinished privatisation and the still significant role of state-owned enterprises, which have remained important economic agents.

Methodology: Critical analyses were made of the literature dedicated to the economic transition and of the role and characteristics of state-owned enterprises. Empirical evidence is drawn from original datasets about the scale of SOEs in the contemporary economy and rotations in management and supervisory boards in Polish joint-stock companies.

Findings: Despite the unfavourable initial conditions, Poland soon emerged as a leader in economic growth, successfully stabilising, liberalising and privatising its economy. The institutional foundations of a democratic market economy were consistently built, and the applications for membership in the OECD, the EU and NATO were an important driver of institutional reforms. In terms of state institutions, political and economic freedom and quality of governance, Poland is more similar to the G7 countries than to the other post-socialist countries, though the need to

Modeling Economic Growth in Contemporary Poland, 15–31
Copyright © 2024 Katarzyna Szarzec, Dawid Piątek and Bartosz Totleben
Published under exclusive licence by Emerald Publishing Limited
doi:10.1108/978-1-83753-654-220231002

maintain high-quality state institutions is still a priority. The significant share of SOE is regarded as a challenge of the Polish economy because state-owned enterprises are an object of rent-seeking by politicians and political parties.

Keywords: Postsocialist economic transition; initial conditions; privatisation of enterprises; state-owned enterprises; liberalisation; state institutions

Introduction

The transition which took place in the countries of Central and Eastern Europe and in the territory of the USSR after 1989 was political, social and economic. All these countries at one point started the process of transition – from dictatorship to democracy, and from a centrally controlled economy based on state ownership to a market economy based on private property. Political changes involved introducing political freedom and the transition of the economy – increasing the scope of economic freedom and introducing the rule of law. Hence, such economic transitions required enormous institutional changes. On the one hand, the state had to withdraw from the functions it had performed in the previous system, on the other – it had to remain powerful and efficient enough to perform tasks while being part of the transition process, i.e. to stabilise the economy, liberalise the conditions for conducting business activity, privatise enterprises, and change the institutional environment (the so-called 'paradox of the adjusting state' (Ahrens, 2000).

Poland was one of the very first socialist countries to start its political and economic transition. It was Poland where social protests contributed to political changes thanks to which economic reforms were finally possible. The initial conditions of the Polish economy were regarded as so bad that 'near-universal pessimism (...) dominated discussions of Poland's economic prospects throughout the 1980s and early 1990s' (Slay, 2000). The Polish government decided to introduce rapid changes in the economic system and to restore economic freedom in all areas. Despite the pessimistic prospects, Poland succeeded in implementing both political and economic transitions.

This article aims to discuss and assess the results of Poland's economic transition – more than 30 years after it began. We address the following questions: (1) What are the results of the economic transition in Poland, in terms of stabilisation, liberalisation, privatisation and institutional reforms? and (2) What is the scale of state-owned enterprises which were not privatised and are regarded as a main challenge for the Polish economy? To answer these questions, critical analyses were made of the literature dedicated to the economic transition, and of the role and characteristics of state-owned enterprises. Empirical evidence is drawn from original datasets about the scale of SOEs in the contemporary economy and rotations in management and supervisory boards in Polish joint-stock companies.

This chapter presents the initial conditions of political and economic transition in Poland, with some comparison to other European countries that underwent transitions; briefly describes the process of political transition in Poland and the fundamental economic reforms introduced in 1990; presents the results of the economic transition in four main areas: stabilisation, liberalisation, institutional reforms, and privatisation; discusses the role of state-owned enterprises in contemporary Poland as a future economic challenge; and finally concludes.

The Initial Conditions of the Post-socialist Transition in Poland

The opinions of economists as to the importance of initial conditions for successful transition reforms are consistent (e.g. de Melo et al., 2001; Fischer and Sahay, 2000; Polanec, 2004; World Bank, 1996, 2002). These conditions were crucial at the beginning of the transition and had a decisive influence on the depth and duration of the transformational recession, although their impact definitely weakened over time. They were the effects of the common legacy of the central planning system, which can be characterised by four features: microbalance by direct control, coordination through plans, distorted relative prices, and low private ownership (de Melo, Denizer and Gelb, 1996). The initial conditions were weak in all post-socialist countries but there were significant differences among countries.

The initial conditions of the post-socialist transition can be considered using different categories. In this chapter, we used the categories proposed by de Melo, Denizer and Gelb (1996), i.e. structure, economic distortions and institutions.

The structure includes variables such as the initial income, the level of urbanisation, the level of industrialisation and natural resources. In 1989, Poland had a low initial income per capita (5150 PPP USD), similar to Bulgaria (5000 PPP USD), a little lower than Ukraine (5680 PPP USD) and much lower than the Czech Republic (8600 PPP USD) or Hungary (6810 PPP USD). Urbanisation could also be used as a proxy for the level of development. Poland had a fairly high level of urbanisation (measured by the percentage of the urban population). About 62% of Poles lived in towns and cities in 1990, which was a level of urbanisation similar to that of Croatia, Hungary, and Slovenia, and slightly lower than that in the Czech Republic (65%). Another indicator of development is industrialisation. However, overindustrialisation or industrial distortion was a common experience of socialist countries. The share of industry in GDP in Poland was 0.52%; this was rather high in the group of socialist countries and much higher than the predicted share of industry for a country at this level of development (de Melo et al., 2001). Poland also had a moderate endowment of natural resources compared to the entire group of socialist countries.

Economic distortions are related to factors such as suppressed inflation, black market exchange rates and trade shocks caused by the dissolution of the Soviet Union and the Council for Mutual Economic Assistance (CMEA). The Polish situation was characterised not only by chronic open inflation, and even hyper-inflation in the autumn of 1989, but also by high suppressed inflation. The increase in deflated wages minus the change in real GDP from 1987 through to 1990 in Poland was equal to 13.6, while in the Czech Republic and Hungary, it was −7.1 and −7.7, respectively. Furthermore, the black market exchange rate premium can be interpreted as a subsidy for imports, and the distortionary tax on exports was higher in Poland than in these aforementioned countries. The difference between the official and the free exchange rate was 277% in Poland, 185% in the Czech Republic and 47% in Hungary. Poland used to rely less on CMEA trade system than Bulgaria, Hungary and the Former Soviet Union (FSU) countries, so it experienced a little less disturbance from the trade shocks caused by the dissolution of the Soviet Union and the CMEA.

Institutions encompass such variables as years under central planning, location in relation to Western markets and experience with statehood. The number of years under central planning is used as a proxy for market memory, i.e. familiarity with market institutions. A shorter time for central planning could enhance the ability of societies to deal with the transition and to learn the rules of the market economy. Poland spent 41 years under central planning, and this was the shortest period of the entire group of transition countries. Moreover, the Poles had experience with several reforms of the central planning system. Although they were not successful, they resulted in institutional and social mentality changes, thanks to which Poland was better prepared than other countries (except Hungary) to build a market economy (Rosati, 1998). Locations that are defined as being in geographical proximity to prosperous market economies may be particularly important during the transition period because the latter have facilitated the introduction of market institutions and the adjustment of trading patterns. Poland benefited from better access to Western markets and stronger incentives for the adoption of the European Union's institutional framework due to its potential membership. The last feature is the experience of statehood, which was favourable in Poland. It had a long history of nationhood and, before the Second World War, had been an independent democratic state. Even after the Second World War, although dominated by the Soviet Union, Poland was formally independent, with its own parliament, justice system, army, etc. and with its own economic institutions, such as a central bank, customs bureau, fiscal policy, etc. Poland's historical political links with Western Europe gave it a clear sense of direction that the new FSU nation states did not have.

Taking into account the whole group of transforming countries, Poland belongs to the intermediate category. Its situation was not as good as that of the Czech Republic, which had a very favourable location, a stable macroeconomic situation, a relatively good economic structure and a low external debt. But it was not as bad as the situations of the smaller countries of the former Soviet Union, which inherited highly unstable economies and severe structural dependence on the Soviet market (Balcerowicz, 2002). At the same time, if one considers only the group of Central Eastern European countries, then Poland had had the most difficult initial conditions (Baszyński and Jarmołowicz, 2011), which were further complicated by hyperinflation, a large and inefficient coal mining sector, and a large foreign debt.

Programme of Economic Transformation in Poland

Political changes began in Poland earlier than in other socialist countries. The growing economic and social crisis made the authorities decide to start the Round Table talks with the opposition. They began on 6 February and ended on 5 April 1989. As a result, it was agreed that partially free parliamentary elections would be held. Elections to the Senate were to be entirely free, while in the Sejm, the opposition was given the opportunity to apply for 35% of seats, i.e. 161 mandates. Elections were held on 4 June. The opposition won, taking almost all the seats in the parliament it could compete for. In view of such a good electoral result, on 20 August 1989, President W. Jaruzelski appointed Tadeusz Mazowiecki as Prime Minister. On 12 September 1989, the government of T. Mazowiecki received a vote of confidence from the Sejm. The portfolio of the Minister of Finance and the position of Deputy Prime Minister were taken over by Leszek Balcerowicz (Slay, 2000). Work began on changing the economic system in Poland.

From the beginning, bringing down inflation was regarded as a necessary condition for the success of the economic transition. Therefore, disinflation became one of the priorities in the programme of changes adopted by the government in October 1989 (*Program gospodarczy rządu – główne założenia i kierunki*). 1 January 1990 was adopted as the date of implementation of most of the reforms. The programme assumed the introduction of a market economy based on private property, competition, strong and exchangeable money; open to foreign trade; and in which the state creates a stable framework for economic activity, but does not constrain it with bureaucratic regulations, and is not responsive to pressure from interest groups. On 17 December 1989, the government presented to the Sejm the drafts of 11 bills that constituted the programme of radical transformation, a complete overhaul of the country's economic system. Except for the act on limiting monopolistic practices, which was sent for further work, the Sejm adopted the presented drafts on 27 December, and on 31 December they were signed by President W. Jaruzelski (Balcerowicz, 1992).

Adopted and implemented on 1 January 1990, the programme of changes came to be called the 'Balcerowicz plan' after its main author. It consisted of five elements: restrictive monetary policy; fiscal policy aimed at reducing the budget deficit; price liberalisation; partial convertibility of the Polish zloty; and restrictive income policy (Dąbrowski, 1992). The restrictive nature of the monetary policy was evidenced by the reduction of the money supply and the policy of a positive interest rate in real terms, an increase of interest rates on previously granted loans, and a reduction in preferential loans. In addition, commercial banks were allowed to set the interest rate on deposits and loans. The restrictive approach also prevailed in fiscal policy. Subsidies were reduced, which was indispensable for controlling inflation and adjusting the budget to the conditions of a market economy (Owsiak, 1994). The reduction of subsidies was possible thanks to the liberalisation of prices. About 90% of all prices moved freely, while the prices of energy carriers, transport, medicines, and rents were administratively increased, often drastically. Partial (internal) convertibility of the zloty was also introduced. After the devaluation of the zloty, a fixed rate was established against the US dollar

(1 USD = 9500 PLZ), which was to act as an anti-inflationary anchor. These activities were accompanied by the liberalisation of foreign trade. All entities were allowed to trade with foreign countries, thus eliminating the state monopoly of foreign trade. In addition, domestic trade was liberalised. An important element of the programme was also a restrictive income policy. A fear of unleashing an inflationary spiral led to the decision to apply a 'wage brake', that is, a tax on excessive wage increases, called 'popiwek'. Exceeding a certain threshold of the wage increase rate entailed the need to pay the special tax. This was the second anti-inflationary anchor (Winiecki, 1992).

Using the commonly accepted division proposed by Islam (1993), four categories of changes are needed to transform a planned economy into a market economy, namely: stabilisation, liberalisation, institutional reforms and privatisation (SLIP). We can say that the 'Balcerowicz plan' was focused on macroeconomic stabilisation and microeconomic liberalisation. This radical therapy was aimed at introducing the marketisation of the economy and stopping hyperinflation simultaneously. However, building a market economy also required institutional changes and privatisation. After the introduction of stabilisation and liberalisation, the economy began to function according to market rules, but institutional changes and privatisation were necessary to maintain the stabilisation of the economy and to complete its transformation (Balcerowicz, 1997). Therefore, institutional changes were introduced. They included the liquidation of the institutional remnants of the central planning system, the introduction of local government and communal ownership, the introduction of social protection for the unemployed, and the creation of the Antimonopoly Office (Kaliński, 2004).

Privatisation also commenced. A 'small privatisation' was started in the first half of 1990s. Its essence boiled down to leasing property from cities and communes, most often by employees of a given shop or a small enterprise (Bałtowski and Miszewski, 2007). In August 1990, the Act on Privatisation came into force. The two main methods of privatisation provided for under this Act were capital (or indirect) privatisation and liquidation (or direct) privatisation. Capital privatisation was a two-stage process used for large state-owned enterprises: first, an enterprise was commercialised (transformed into a joint stock company wholly owned by the State Treasury), and second, shares of the newly established companies were made available to private investors through public offerings, tenders, or negotiations. Liquidation privatisation refers to the transfer of assets of an enterprise or a part thereof to private investors (Bałtowski and Kozarzewski, 2014).

Tremendous economic support for Poland came in the form of a write-off of its public debts. In April 1991, Poland signed a debt reduction agreement with the Paris Club of creditor governments, according to which the governments agreed to forgive half of this debt (some 15 billion USD), provided that Poland continued the economic transition programme begun in 1990. A similar agreement was reached in March 1994 with the London Club of Poland's commercial bank creditors, according to which 45% of Polish debts held by these institutions (some 13 billion USD) would be written-off (Slay, 2000).

The first 2 years of the Polish economic transition were characterised by the highest pace of change. After 1991, the changes continued, but not so dynamically. Although governments increasingly focused on current economic problems, all successive governments consistently continued the transition to a market economy. A clear confirmation of success on this path was Poland's accession to the OECD in November 1996 and to the EU in May 2004.

Main Effects of Transformation in Poland

In order to describe the results of the economic and political transition in Poland, four categories of changes proposed by Islam (1993), i.e. stabilisation, liberalisation, institutional reforms and privatisation, are used. The main goals of stabilisation were reducing inflation and restoring market balance. Poland's macroeconomic stabilisation efforts were largely successful in this regard. The positive effects of the stabilisation programme were spectacular and significantly changed the conditions for doing business. The main positive effects were (Bałtowski and Miszewski, 2007): markets – especially consumer goods – rebalanced quickly; the zloty became stable money, and a move away from the dollarisation of the economy began; a rationalisation of microeconomic decisions; the state budget was balanced; and hyperinflation was crushed. Although prices continued to rise quite rapidly in the first half of the 1990s, inflation in Poland finally began to decline. By 1996, the inflation rate had fallen below 20% and by 1999 it had dropped to single digits. The government continued to pursue sound economic policies and inflation stayed below 10% until 2022 (see Fig. 1). The

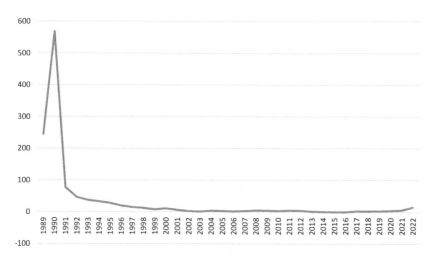

Fig. 1.   Inflation in Poland 1989–2022, Consumer Prices (Annual %).
Source: Authors' own elaboration based on publicly available data from
https://data.worldbank.org.

period of disinflation in Poland was an important step in Poland's economic development and laid the foundations for sustained growth and prosperity.

The actions taken at the beginning of the 1990s in Poland contributed to the rapid progress of liberalisation. We use the EBRD transition indicators to illustrate this (the value of the indicators ranges from 1 to 4.3; where 1 means a situation characteristic for a centrally planned economy and 4.3 represents the level characteristic of a developed market economy). As can be seen in Fig. 2, already in 1993, the Price liberalisation indicator and the Trade & Forex system indicator were already equal to 4. This means that prices in Poland were comprehensively liberalised and only a small number of administered prices remained. Furthermore, all significant export tariffs were removed, as were quantitative and administrative import and export restrictions; direct involvement in exports and imports by ministries and state-owned trading companies was insignificant and full current account convertibility was achieved. In 1998 these two transition indicators were equal to 4.3, which means that they were on a level characteristic of a developed market economy. This fast and comprehensive liberalisation in Poland made the development of new private enterprises possible. In fact, the development of new, private firms was faster in Poland than in the Czech and

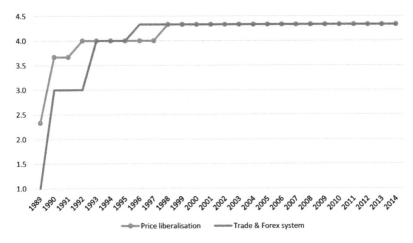

Fig. 2.   EBRD Price Liberalisation and Trade & Forex System Indicators in Poland 1989–2014. *Source:* Authors' own elaboration based on publicly available data from European Bank for Reconstruction and Development, https://www.ebrd.com/economic-research-and-data/transition-qualities-asses.html. The value of the indicators ranges from 1 to 4.3; where 1 means no change and 4.3 the level characteristic of a developed market economy. 2014 was the last year for which EBRD transition indicators were published.

Slovak Federal Republic and Hungary (Johnson, 1994). It was probably also the most important reason why Poland experienced a lower decline in production than any other post-communist country and explains why its economy had already begun to grow in 1992 (Winiecki, 2003).

Institutional reforms are inherently slower than stabilisation and liberalisation. At the beginning of the 1990s, the socialist countries of Central and Eastern Europe were quite a homogeneous group, at least with respect to their institutional environment. This homogeneity was the result of the lack of political and economic freedom and the low quality of governance. The economy was dominated by state ownership of the means of production and non-market, planned allocation of resources (Szarzec et al., 2014). In Poland, the pace of institutional reforms was relatively fast, and the scope of political and economic freedom increased rapidly (see Fig. 3). The institutional foundations of a democratic market economy were consistently built and the application for membership in international organisations (EU, NATO, WTO, OECD) was the important driver of institutional reforms (Piątek, Pilc and Szarzec, 2019). As a result, Poland joined these international organisations and is now – in terms of state institutions, that is,

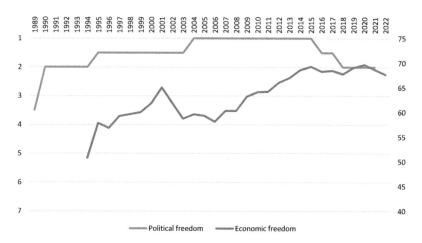

Fig. 3. Political Freedom Index and Economic Freedom Index in Poland 1989–2022. *Source:* Authors' own elaboration based on publicly available data from Freedom House, https://freedomhouse.org/report/ freedom-world; Heritage Foundation, https://www.heritage.org/index/. The political freedom index is the Freedom House Freedom Rating (ranges from 1 to 7; the lower the value, the greater the political freedom) and the economic freedom index is the Index of Economic Freedom of the Heritage Foundation (ranges from 0 to 100; the higher the value, the greater the economic freedom).

political and economic freedom and quality of governance – more similar to the G7 countries than to the other post-socialist countries (Piątek, 2016).

Privatisation in Poland was a big challenge. There were more than 8,400 state-owned enterprises (SOEs) at the beginning of the transition to a market economy. The Polish model of privatisation was eclectic and involved a combination of methods, including public share offerings, management/employee buyout, direct sales to strategic investors and voucher privatisation. As a result of the privatisation of SOEs and the growth of new private firms facilitated by liberalisation, the share of the private sector in GDP grew quickly, and in 1994 it was more than 50% (EBRD, 1996). Small scale privatisation also progressed rapidly, and by the end of 1992 was almost completed (Nellis, 2002). However, large-scale privatisation progress was a little slower (see Fig. 4). Overall, the Polish model of privatisation has been viewed as a success, with many experts considering it to be one of the most effective and well-managed privatisation programmes in the post-socialist countries (Kozarzewski, 2006). A factor contributing to the success of the Polish privatisation programme was highly efficient privatisation-related legislation (Mickiewicz and Bałtowski, 2000).

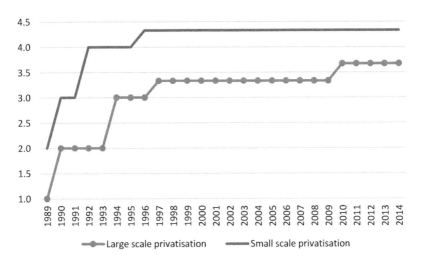

Fig. 4.   EBRD Large Scale Privatisation and Small Scale Privatisation Indicators in Poland 1989–2014. *Source:* Authors' own elaboration based on publicly available data from European Bank for Reconstruction and Development, https://www.ebrd.com/economic-research-and-data/transition-qualities-asses.html. The value of the indicators ranges from 1 to 4.3; where 1 means no change and 4.3 the level characteristic of a developed market economy. 2014 was the last year for which EBRD transition indicators were published.

However, there are still many SOEs in Poland that will not to be privatised, and in recent years we have even observed a privatisation reversal (Błaszczyk, 2016).

In the summary of the results of the transition in Poland, we pay attention to the changes in GDP as the most important macroeconomic result. The transformational recession was short (2 years), and the decline in GDP was lower in Poland than elsewhere (Piątek and Szarzec, 2011). After 5 years of transition, the Polish GDP was higher than at the beginning, which was the best result in the entire group of post-socialist countries. Since 1989, Poland has been the fastest converging economy in Europe, and the relative distance to the West in terms of income has never been shorter. Piątkowski (2018) called it 'the true Golden Age of Poland'. In 1990, Poland's level of income relative to the EU-15 was 35%, and it increased to 73% (compared to Euro-Area) in 2021. Poland was the fastest converging economy in Europe in that period.

Poland's transition to a market economy could generally be considered as very successful when one looks at the progress of stabilisation, liberalisation, institutional reforms and even privatisation or GDP growth. However, there were still some failures and problems during the transition, including the significant increase in the number of unemployed and the high level of unemployment in the first 15 years of transition, increasing poverty and increasing income inequality. But these problems were also largely common to other post-socialist states. Moreover, it is important to remember that Poland is still a young and unconsolidated democracy. In recent years, some problems have been observed with the quality of state institutions (Piątek, 2023), which could be detrimental to economic growth and could slow down the process of income convergence. It is even more important to maintain high-quality state institutions or 'good institutions' because SOEs continue to play an important role in the Polish economy and are objects that politicians seek to capture.

The Challenge of the Future: State-Owned Enterprises in Poland

Polish governments have declared that privatisation has been completed and that they do not intend to sell any more enterprises. One should rather expect and observe 'a reversal in the privatisation logic' and nationalisation through share buyouts in companies which have already been privatised (Szanyi, 2016). Governments claim that the reasons for maintaining state ownership are to limit market failures and ensure public security (in particular in network and strategic sectors).

The classification of enterprises as 'state-owned' and their operationalisation are not obvious (Bałtowski and Kozarzewski, 2016). We apply the following definition of a state-owned enterprise: an enterprise with at least 25.01% of a state ownership stake, and a dominant position of state shareholders or a dispersed ownership structure; or enterprise in which the state holds directly (or indirectly) an ownership stake of more than 50%. This is consistent with the results presented below of an estimation of the shares of SOEs, based on the dataset built by Szarzec, Dombi and Matuszak (2021) on the economic role of nonfinancial very large and large SOEs in 30 Western and post-socialist European countries. They showed that Russia and the Balkan countries that have not joined the European Union have the highest average share of SOEs in total assets in the countries' economy. Those countries are followed by EU Balkan countries as well as the Baltics and Central Europe countries. SOEs still play an important role in the Polish economy (with an average share of SOEs in total assets amounting to more than 30% in the years 2007–2016 and more than 22% in operating revenue), notwithstanding all privatisation processes (Fig. 5).[1] The remaining SOE portfolios in Poland tend to be strongly concentrated, mostly in the energy sectors, mining, oil industry and in finance (banking and insurance). They contribute significantly to exports, and among the top 25 exporters 6 SOEs were identified that have as much as a 55% share in the total average export in 2013–2015 (mainly due to one company – PKN Orlen, a conglomerate from the oil industry) (Szarzec, Nowara and Olejnik, 2020). All of the large Polish SOEs have their origins in the socialist period. Given their crucial role in the Polish economy, it is important to ask questions about the contribution of SOEs to economic growth, and the vulnerability of SOEs to being politically captured.

The impact of SOEs on the economic growth rate is non-linear. SOEs are potentially more effective in addressing market failures (Vickers and Yarrow, 1991) compared to privately owned enterprises (POEs). Moreover, SOEs are smoothing the business cycles by providing counter-cyclical investment expenditures (Telegdy, 2016). However, SOEs often have inadequate capabilities to innovate (Bognetti, 2020) and can strengthen the crowding out effect. Moreover, SOEs underperform financially when compared to private enterprises, which is due to agency problems, lack of well-defined groups of monitoring, soft budget

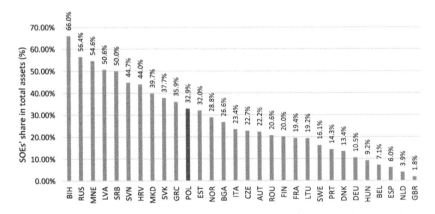

Fig. 5.   The Scale of State Ownership: Average Share of Non-financial Large SOEs in Total Assets of Enterprises (in 2016). *Source:* Authors' own elaboration based on publicly available data from Szarzec, Dombi and Matuszak (2021).

constraints, employing SOEs as 'political goods', and cronyism (Bałtowski and Kwiatkowski, 2022; La Porta et al., 2002; Megginson, 2017). Szarzec, Dombi and Matuszak (2021) claim that SOEs are neither negative nor positive for economic growth per se. Their impact is strongly and significantly correlated with the country's institutions. 'Good institutions' (measured by Worldwide Governance Indicators, WGI) contribute to the positive effect of SOEs on economic growth. 'Bad institutions' reduce the dynamics of economic growth. Poland – with an average WGI index equal[2] to 0.54 in 2021 – has a marginal effect of SOEs on economic growth: slightly above zero. This indicates that an improvement in the quality of the institutional environment in Poland would increase the rate of economic growth. SOEs could potentially boost economic growth also via the foreign direct investment channel. However this is not the case of Poland – the activities of Polish SOEs were concentrated in the domestic market and did not play an important role in the global scale (Szarzec, Nowara and Totleben, 2020).

All of the post-socialist countries are affected by political rent-seeking behaviour – to a greater or lesser extent (Hellman, Jones and Kaufman, 2000; Iwasaki and Suzuki, 2007). As a result, politicians and/or businessmen gain uncontrolled power to take decisions about access to economic resources, and their actions are not regulated by law. Additionally, SOEs are treated as the 'electoral booty' of 'political sinecures'. This means that politicians are able to collect different kinds of economic rents using SOEs, such as: offering jobs to people associated with the ruling political party (Kopecký and Spirova, 2011), financing political parties and electoral campaigns (Volintiru, 2015) and increasing lending from state-owned banks to companies in order to boost economic growth in election year (Dinc, 2005). To be more specific, this also includes replacing members of the supervisory or management boards of SOEs before (to receive relatively high severance payments) and also after winning parliamentary elections (Totleben, Szarzec, and Kardziejonek, 2019). To estimate the scale of these kinds of political rent-seeking, Szarzec, Totleben and Piątek (2022) used a full sample of all rotations in Polish joint-stock companies in the years 2001–2017. They found that the frequency of changes in supervisory and management boards is higher in SOEs than in POEs. The average number of changes in boards in SOEs was almost three times higher than in POEs. This phenomenon was a permanent feature. Moreover, the number of changes in the composition of boards of SOEs increases both before and after parliamentary elections. High up changes took place about 3–4 months before a new political election and approximately 9–10 months after an election. The frequency of changes was also higher after a new prime minister took office, peaking about 3 months after this. The scale of changes on boards was lower in the case of the replacement of a prime minister compared to political elections. The results of the analysis confirmed that changes in the boards of SOEs in Poland are driven more by political reasons than economic motives. These results were stable over time and were not dependent on any ruling political party. The capture of SOEs by rent-seeking politicians has become an informal institution and some kind of sanctioned tradition of taking the spoils after winning elections. Unfortunately, rotations in the boards of SOEs seem to be an endemic problem in Poland and

Polish SOEs are still vulnerable to political capture, which is a crucial threat to their efficiency and their positive impact on economic growth.

Conclusions

In this chapter, we investigated the process of economic transition in Poland, aiming to assess its results and completion. The main conclusions of our research are as follows. Despite unfavourable initial conditions, such as high public debt, shortages and high inflation, Poland soon emerged as a leader in economic growth, successfully stabilising, liberalising and privatising its economy. The Balcerowicz programme was aimed at simultaneously introducing the marketisation of the economy and stopping hyperinflation. By 1996, the inflation rate had fallen below 20%, by 1999 it had dropped to single digits, and stayed at that level until 2022. The successful process of disinflation in Poland laid the foundations for economic development. The transformational recession was short (2 years) and the decline in GDP was lower in Poland than in other post-socialist countries. The Polish economy was dominated by state ownership of the means of production and privatisation was a big challenge. In the second half of 1990s, one could already notice a reversal of the ownership structure of companies due to the privatisation of SOEs and the growth of new private firms facilitated by liberalisation. However, there are still many SOEs in Poland that, according to successive governments, are not to be privatised. State ownership seems to be persistent and SOEs play a crucial role in the Polish economy, in terms of their shares in total assets, turnover and export. Due to this, they are used by politicians for economic and personal rent-seeking and are treated as the well-deserved spoils of victory after elections.

Economic reforms were followed by fundamental institutional changes in the organisation of central and local governments, which had to perform new functions. The abovementioned reforms that aimed at the liquidation of the remnants of the central planning system and at the creation a sound democratic market economy appeared to be successful. In that sense, 'the transformational odyssey' of Poland had a happy ending. Poland joined international organisations such as the OECD, NATO and the EU, which confirmed the completion of political and economic transformation. However, the fundamental task for any future Polish governments remains to maintain high-quality institutions because that is never-ending work. They are essential for facilitating business and contribute positively to economic development. The experience of Poland may be an interesting lesson for other developing countries which are either already undergoing similar processes or will soon have to face important political and economic changes. Unfortunately, this still also concerns many of the non-EU post-socialist countries.

Notes

1. According to the OECD (Koske et al., 2015), among 56 countries surveyed in 2013, Poland, followed only by China, had the largest pervasiveness of state

ownership across 30 business sectors, measured as the share of sectors in which the state controls at least one company.
2. The WGI Index is calculated as the arithmetic average of the six sub-indexes: Political Stability and Absence of Violence/Terrorism, Government Effectiveness, Regulatory Quality, Rule of Law and Control of Corruption. Each sub-index is ranked from −2.5 (worse) to 2.5 (best).

References

Ahrens, J. (2000), "Toward a Post-Washington Consensus: The Importance of Governance Structures in Less Developed Countries and Economies in Transition", *Journal for Institutional Innovation, Development and Transition*, Vol. 4.

Balcerowicz, L. (1992), *800 dni. Szok kontrolowany*, Polska Oficyna Wydawnicza „BGW", Warszawa.

Balcerowicz, L. (1997), *Socjalizm, kapitalizm, transformacja. Szkice z przełomu epok*, Wydawnictwo Naukowe PWN, Warszawa.

Balcerowicz, L. (2002), *Post-communist Transition: Some Lessons*, IEA Occasional Paper No. 127.

Bałtowski, M. and Kozarzewski, P. (2014), *Zmiana własnościowa polskiej gospodarki (1989–2013)*, PWE, Warszawa.

Bałtowski, M. and Kozarzewski, P. (2016), "Formal and Real Ownership Structure of the Polish Economy: State-Owned versus State-Controlled Enterprises", *Post-Communist Economies*, Vol. 28 No. 3, pp. 405–419.

Bałtowski, M. and Kwiatkowski, G. (2022), *State-Owned Enterprises in the Global Economy*, Routledge, London and New York.

Bałtowski, M. and Miszewski, M. (2007), *Transformacja gospodarcza w Polsce*, Wydawnictwo Naukowe PWN, Warszawa.

Baszyński, A. and Jarmołowicz, W. (2011), „Warunki początkowe", in: *Liberalne przesłanki polskiej transformacji gospodarczej*, eds. Jarmołowicz, W. and Szarzec, K., PWE, Warszawa, pp. 216–233.

Błaszczyk, B. (2016), „Odwracanie prywatyzacji w Polsce i na Węgrzech", *Studia Ekonomiczne*, Vol. XCI No. 4, pp. 527–554.

Bognetti, G. (2020), "History of Western State-Owned Enterprises: From the Industrial Revolution to the Age of Globalization", in: *The Routledge Handbook of State-Owned Enterprises*, eds. Bernier, L., Florio, M. and Bance, P., Routledge, London and New York.

Dąbrowski, M. (1992), "Results and Prospects of the Polish Stabilization Program", *Eastern European Economics*, Vol. 30 No. 3, pp. 56–64.

de Melo, M., Denizer, C. and Gelb, A. (1996), *From Plan to Market: Patterns of Transition*, World Bank, Washington, DC.

de Melo, M., Denizer, C., Gelb, A. and Tenev, S. (2001), "Circumstance and Choice: The Role of Initial Conditions and Policies in Transition Economies", *The World Bank Economic Review*, Vol. 15 No. 1, pp. 1–31.

Dinc, I. S. (2005), "Politicians and Banks: Political Influences on Government-Owned Banks in Emerging Markets", *Journal of Financial Economics*, Vol. 77 No. 2, pp. 453–479.

EBRD (1996), *Transition Report 1996. Infrastructure and Savings*, European Bank for Reconstruction and Development, London.

Fischer, S. and Sahay, R. (2000), *The Transition Economies after Ten Years*, International Monetary Fund, Working Paper, No. 30.

Hellman, J. S., Jones, G. and Kaufmann, D. (2000), *Seize the State, Seize the Day: State Capture, Corruption, and Influence in Transition*, Policy Research Working Paper, No. 2444, World Bank, Washington, DC.

Islam, S. (1993), "Conclusion: Problems of Planning a Market Economy", in: *Making Markets: Economic Transformation in Eastern Europe and the Post-Soviet States*, eds. Islam, S. and Mandelbaum, M., Council on Foreign Relations Press, New York, pp. 182–214.

Iwasaki, I. and Suzuki, T. (2007), "Transition Strategy, Corporate Exploitation, and State Capture: An Empirical Analysis of the Former Soviet States", *Communist and Post-Communist Studies*, Vol. 40 No. 4, pp. 393–422.

Johnson, S. (1994), "Private Business in Eastern Europe", in: *Transition in Eastern Europe, Volume 2*, eds. Blanchard, O., Froot, K. and Sachs, J., University of Chicago Press, Chicago, pp. 245–292.

Kaliński, J. (2004), "Gospodarka Polski w procesie transformacji ustrojowej (1989–2002)", „Gospodarka polska na przełomie wieków. Od A do Z", supplement to Bank i Kredyt, No. 1.

Kopecký, P. and Spirova, M. (2011), "'Jobs for the Boys'? Patterns of Party Patronage in Post-Communist Europe", *West European Politics*, Vol. 34 No. 5, pp. 897–921.

Koske, I., Wanner, I., Bitetti, R. and Barbiero, O. (2015), *The 2013 Update of the OECD Product Market Regulation: Policy Insights for OECD and Non-OECD Countries*, OECD Economics Department Working Papers, No. 1200.

Kozarzewski, P. (2006), *Prywatyzacja w krajach postkomunistycznych*, ISP PAN, Warszawa.

La Porta, R., Lopez-De-Silanes, F. and Shleifer, A. (2002), "Government Ownership of Banks", *The Journal of Finance*, Vol. 57, pp. 265–301.

Megginson, W. L. (2017), "Privatization, State Capitalism, and State Ownership of Business in the 21st Century", *Foundations and Trends in Finance*, Vol. 11 No. 1–2, pp. 1–153.

Mickiewicz, T. and Bałtowski, M. (2000), "Privatisation in Poland: Ten Years After", *Post-Communist Economies*, Vol. 12 No. 4, pp. 425–443.

Nellis, J. (2002), *Privatization and Enterprise Reform in Transition Economies: A Retrospective Analysis*, The World Bank, Washington.

Owsiak, S. (1994), „Budżet państwa w okresie transformacji gospodarki polskiej", *Gospodarka Narodowa*, No. 7–8, pp. 6–11.

Piątek, D. (2016), *Instytucje państwa a wzrost gospodarczy w krajach post-socjalistycznych*, Wydawnictwo Uniwersytetu Ekonomicznego w Poznaniu, Poznań.

Piątek, D. (2023), "The Illiberal Model of State Capitalism in Poland", *Ekonomia i Prawo. Economics and Law*, forthcoming.

Piątek, D. and Szarzec, K. (2011), „Przebieg procesów transformacji", in: *Liberalne przesłanki polskiej transformacji gospodarczej*, eds. Jarmołowicz, W. and Szarzec, K., PWE, Warszawa, pp. 233–249.

Piątek, D., Pilc, M. and Szarzec, K. (2019), "What Determines the Institutional Change in Transition Economies?" *Argumenta Oeconomica*, Vol. 42 No. 1, pp. 235–269.

Piątkowski, M. (2018), *Europe's Growth Champion. Insights from the Economic Rise of Poland*, Oxford University Press, Oxford.

Polanec, S. (2004), *Convergence at Last? Evidence from Transition Countries*, LICOS Centre for Transition Economics, Katholieke Universiteit Leuven, Discussion Paper, No. 144.

Rosati, D. K. (1998), *Polska droga do rynku*, PWE, Warszawa.

Slay, B. (2000), "The Polish Economic Transition: Outcome and Lessons", *Communist and Post-Communist Studies*, Vol. 33 No. 1, pp. 49–70.

Szanyi, M. (2016), "The Reversal of the Privatisation Logic in Central European Transition Economies", *Acta Oeconomica*, Vol. 66 No. 1, pp. 33–55.

Szarzec, K., Baszyński, A., Piątek, D. and Pilc, M. (2014), *Institutions in Transition Countries*, Global Development Research Group, Poznań.

Szarzec, K., Dombi, A. and Matuszak, P. (2021), "State-owned Enterprises and Economic Growth: Evidence from the Post-Lehman Period", *Economic Modelling*, Vol. 99.

Szarzec, K., Nowara, W. and Totleben, B. (2020), "State-Owned Enterprises as Foreign Direct Investors: Insights from EU Countries", *Post-Communist Economies*, Vol. 33 No. 5, pp. 517–540.

Szarzec, K., Nowara, W. and Olejnik, I. (2020), "Exports and the Economic Performance of Large State-Owned Enterprises in Poland: Evidence from Firm-Level Data", *Ruch Prawniczy, Ekonomiczny i Socjologiczny*, Vol. 82 No. 1, pp. 265–282.

Szarzec, K., Totleben, B. and Piątek, D. (2022), "How Do Politicians Capture a State? Evidence from State-Owned Enterprises", *East European Politics and Societies*, Vol. 36 No. 1, pp. 141–172.

Telegdy, A. (2016), "Employment Adjustment in the Global Crisis. Differences between Domestic, Foreign and State-Owned Enterprises", *Economics of Transition*, Vol. 24 No. 4, pp. 683–703.

Totleben, B., Szarzec, K. and Kardziejonek, A. (2019), "Rent-Seeking by Politicians in State-Owned Enterprises", *Ekonomia i Prawo. Economics and Law*, Vol. 18, pp. 515–529.

Vickers, J. and Yarrow, G. (1991), "Economic Perspectives on Privatization", *Journal of Economic Perspectives*, Vol. 5 No 2, pp. 111–132.

Volintiru, C. (2015), "The Exploitative Function of Party Patronage: Does It Serve the Party's Interest?" *East European Politics*, Vol. 31 No. 1, pp. 39–55.

Winiecki, J. (1992), "The Polish Transition Programme: Underpinnings, Results, Interpretations", *Soviet Studies*, Vol. 44 No. 5, pp. 809–835.

Winiecki, J. (2003), "The Role of the New, Entrepreneurial Private Sector in Transition and Economic Performance in Light of the Successes in Poland, the Czech Republic, and Hungary", *Problems of Economic Transition*, Vol. 45 No. 11, pp. 6–38.

World Bank (1996), *From Plan to Market*, World Development Report.

World Bank (2002), *Building Institutions for Markets*, World Development Report.

Chapter 3

Income Convergence: Does the Catch-up Process Take Place in Polish Regions?

Arkadiusz Kijek and Bartosz Józwik

Abstract

Research Background: EU countries, including those in Central and Eastern Europe, seem to have increasingly similar economies, allowing for the study of real convergence as a process of equalising income levels (measured by GDP per capita). Studies of income convergence in the European Union also have a regional dimension and often focus on convergence at the NUTS2 or NUTS3 regional level. The level of development and income in Polish regions differ significantly. The regional policy implemented at the national and EU level focuses on reducing these differences.

Purpose of the Article: The main aim of the chapter is to analyse the income convergence process among regions in Poland and verify the effectiveness of regional policy implemented at the national and EU level.

Methodology: The study uses Barro type regression for panel data, log t convergence test, and club clustering algorithm introduced by Phillips and Sul to identify patterns of club convergence in Polish regions. The data used for the study is the Local Data Bank provided by Statistics Poland, which includes gross domestic product per capita at the NUTS-3 level for 73 Polish regions over the period of 2000–2020.

Findings: The results of the study indicate a very weak convergence process for all Polish NUTS-3 regions and suggest a club convergence. The club convergence is characterised by regions with similar income levels clustering together. The regional distribution of clubs is similar to the regional distribution of income. The study's findings provide important insights into the effectiveness of regional policy in Poland and suggest that policymakers need to focus on policies that promote catch-up growth in less developed regions. The study also highlights the importance of

Modeling Economic Growth in Contemporary Poland, 33–50

Published under exclusive licence by Emerald Publishing Limited
doi:10.1108/978-1-83753-654-220231003

supporting the most developed regions in the country as they can play a crucial role in driving the country's economic growth and prosperity.

Keywords: Income convergence; club convergence; catch-up process; regions of Poland; Poland; regional policy

Introduction

Income convergence is a term used to describe the phenomenon in which a region or country with a lower level of economic development eventually catches up with that of a more developed region or country. This process leads to a narrowing of the income gap between two regions and is typically the result of economic growth and development. The concept of income convergence has been a topic of economic analysis for over a century, with studies on the phenomenon beginning in the early 1900s.

In the mid-twentieth century, income convergence and inequality were recognised as important elements of economic growth theory. Solow (1956), Koopmans (1963) and Cass (1965) were among the economists who developed the foundations of convergence analysis. In the 1980s, research in the area of convergence and economic growth increased, with the use of empirical models to verify the neoclassical convergence hypothesis. Baumol (1986) and De Long (1988) conducted notable studies in this area.

When describing regional convergence, it is worth noting the studies conducted by Sala-i-Martin (1996) in the 1990s. According to his work, the estimated speeds of convergence across different countries have been relatively similar, with regions tending to converge at a rate of about 2% per year. Various factors, such as differences in population growth rates, labour force participation rates and savings rates between countries, as well as trade openness to international markets, may explain any differences in the speed of convergence. Technological diffusion also plays an important role since it can affect productivity levels, ultimately influencing economic development over time.

The study of income convergence of European countries has been ongoing for a while. Previously, evidence of this phenomenon was limited to Western European countries, but after 2004 it also covered member states of the European Union. This is an important distinction, as before 2004 the European Union was more economically homogenised and income convergence, due to economic cooperation and integration, could occur without radical reforms. Today, EU countries, including those in Central and Eastern Europe, seem to have increasingly similar economies, allowing for the study of real convergence as a process of equalising income levels (measured by GDP per capita). Additionally, studies of income convergence in the European Union also have a regional dimension and often focus on convergence at the NUTS2 or NUTS3 regional level. The results of these studies confirm the existence of income convergence in many countries.

In this paper we study the processes of income convergence at the NUTS3 regional level in Poland to verify the effectiveness of regional policy implemented at the national and EU level. We apply Barro and Sala-i-Martin (1992) type regression for panel data, log *t* convergence test and club clustering algorithm introduced by Phillips and Sul (2007, 2009). It allows us to verify the existence of absolute income convergence and identify the patterns of club convergence in Polish regions.

This chapter is constructed as follows: the theoretical part includes the identification of research problem, then data and methods are presented, the next section contains the results of econometric analyses and their comparison with previously published studies and the final section comprises conclusions and implications.

Literature Review

Regional Convergence and Its Drivers

Regional convergence is the process of different regions in a country or across countries becoming more similar over time (Barro et al., 1991). Usually they tend to grow at similar rates and converge towards similar levels of income and development. This phenomenon is often seen as a result of increased economic integration and globalisation, which allows for the spread of ideas, capital, and technology from more advanced regions to less advanced ones.

Regional convergence is a general term that encompasses the concept of club convergence, which is a more specific form of convergence. Club convergence refers to the phenomenon where a group of countries or regions with similar levels of income and development converge towards a common growth trajectory over time (Lyncker and Thoennessen, 2017). The club convergence hypothesis was developed by economists Robert Barro and Xavier Sala-i-Martin in the early 1990s. It states that countries with similar levels of economic development tend to converge towards each other over time, meaning they experience a narrowing gap between their incomes or GDP per capita. This is due to factors such as increased trade, technology transfer, capital flows and labour mobility which allow poorer nations to catch up economically with richer ones (Ben-David, 1998).

One of the key benefits of club convergence is that it allows countries and regions to learn from each other and to adopt the best practices and technologies that have been successful in other countries and regions. This can help them to overcome some of the constraints that might be preventing them from achieving more rapid and sustainable growth, such as a lack of infrastructure, a shortage of skilled labour, or a lack of access to financing. Another benefit of club convergence is that it allows countries and regions to pool their resources and to cooperate in areas where they have common interests and challenges. Despite the potential benefits of club convergence, there are also several challenges and limitations that must be taken into account. For example, club convergence may be hindered by differences in cultural, political and economic systems, as well as differences in the level of development and institutional capacity of the countries and regions involved.

The findings suggest that the drivers of regional convergence are a combination of economic, social, political and geographical factors. Economic factors include per capita output (GDP), competitiveness, structural funds assistance, investment levels, access to capital markets, labour mobility and productivity gains from technological advances (Corrado et al., 2005; Petrakos et al., 2011; Terrasi, 2002). Human capital, which refers to the skills, knowledge, experience, and abilities that people possess, is also considered an important driver of regional convergence. The presence of a well-educated workforce can lead to increased productivity, improved management practices and access to better technology (Lall and Yilmaz, 2001). Public capital, which includes infrastructure investments such as roads, bridges, and ports, can also play a role in regional convergence by reducing transportation costs and promoting trade (Lall and Yilmaz, 2001). Social factors such as education levels and policies, that promote equal access to education for all citizens regardless of their location or socio-economic background (Smętkowski, 2013), and health care quality can also play a role in determining how quickly one region catches up with another economically (Petrakos et al., 2011).

Political stability has a positive impact on regional development and, in turn, drives regional convergence. A stable political environment is attractive to foreign direct investment, which can bring in new technologies and increase competitiveness on the global market (Petrakos et al., 2011). Moreover, the political structure or form of government in a country can greatly influence its economic performance across regions (Quah, 1996). For instance, certain forms of government are better suited for promoting regional development and spurring economic growth. This highlights the important role of political stability in fostering regional convergence and promoting equitable economic growth and development. Another classic example of political influence on regional convergence is economic integration within the European Union (EU), which is crucial in reducing disparities between regions within member states. The integration process through trade, investment, and other economic activities helps lagging nations catch up with the more developed regions. In addition, the European Regional Policy, aimed at reducing inequalities among different parts of Europe, provides financial support for various development projects across sectors such as infrastructure, education and research & innovation (Boldrin and Canova, 2001; Geppert et al., 2008). These investments help bridge the gaps between richer and poorer areas, promoting regional convergence and improving income levels and living standards.

Geographical location can also influence regional convergence, as proximity to other countries and regions, and being located in core vs periphery areas within a region, can affect trade flows and spillovers (Quah, 1996). Technological diffusion, which refers to the spread of new technologies from one region to another, is another key driver of regional convergence. Spatial spillovers, which refer to positive externalities generated by activities taking place in one area that benefit other nearby locations, are also important drivers of regional convergence. Interregional specialisations and integration, where regions specialise in certain products or services and trade with other regions for complementary goods or services, can help reduce overall costs across multiple regions simultaneously (Cuadrado-Roura et al., 2002).

Examples of Regional Income Convergence

There are several examples of income convergence or divergence in different countries. For example, China has experienced rapid economic growth over the past few decades, and this growth has been characterised by significant income convergence across its regions. As the country has shifted from an agrarian-based economy to a more industrial and service-based one, its coastal regions, such as Guangdong and Shanghai, have experienced much faster rates of growth compared to its interior regions, such as Yunnan and Guizhou. There are many factors that could be influencing income convergence in China. These include economic policies such as trade liberalisation and deregulation; technological advances which can lead to increased productivity; investment in infrastructure projects like roads or railways; the development of human capital through education and training programs for workers; foreign direct investments and aid from international organisations or governments abroad. All these factors have been shown to contribute towards regional economic growth and thus influence income convergence between different regions within a country (Ma and Jia, 2015). However, in recent years, these interior regions have experienced faster rates of growth, closing the income gap with their coastal counterparts.

In the case of China, the study of X. Tian et al. (2016) found evidence for two distinct income clubs: seven east-coastal provinces (Shanghai, Tianjin, Jiangsu, Zhejiang Guangdong Shandong and Fujian), along with Inner Mongolia converging to form a high income club; while all other remaining provinces are forming a low income club. This suggests that there exists an unequal distribution in terms of economic resources between these two groups – i.e., those belonging to the higher-income group have access to more physical capital investments as well as better human capital development opportunities than their counterparts from lower-income regions do not enjoy such privileges or benefits. The strategies that can be used to promote regional convergence in China include: improving the infrastructure of industrialised buildings, such as roads and utilities; encouraging investment from both domestic and foreign sources into industrial projects; developing policies which incentivise businesses to invest in different regions across China; establishing a system for monitoring progress on development goals set by local governments or other organisations involved with promoting regional growth (Wang et al., 2021).

The European Union is another example of a region that has experienced income convergence. The EU has made substantial efforts to promote regional convergence through a number of initiatives and programs. This process was affected by policy changes in the mid-1980s, above all the implementation of an internal market programme. This meant reducing or eliminating barriers to trade between countries within Europe, such as tariffs and quotas on imports and exports. It also included harmonising regulations across different European nations so they could all compete fairly with each other for business opportunities (Neven and Gouymte, 1995). In recent years, these initiatives have included, among others, the European Regional Development Fund (ERDF) and the Cohesion Fund. The ERDF provides funding for a range of projects aimed at promoting economic development in EU regions, including infrastructure development, innovation, and support for small and medium-sized enterprises. The Cohesion Fund, on the other hand, is specifically targeted at EU regions that are lagging behind in terms of economic development and provides funding for projects aimed at reducing economic disparities within the EU (Jóźwik, 2017).

When discussing the convergence process in Europe, attention must be paid to the convergence of regions located in Central and Eastern Europe. Matkowski et al. (2016) investigated income convergence among 11 Central and Eastern European (CEE) countries that joined the EU in 2004, 2007, and 2013. The results confirm the existence of a clear-cut income-level convergence of the CEE countries towards the EU15 throughout the 1993–2015 period. The catching-up process took place between these two regions. The main factors driving income convergence among CEE countries are: economic policies such as trade liberalisation, privatisation of state owned enterprises and foreign direct investment; the accession to the European Union which has provided these countries with financial assistance for development projects in areas like infrastructure, education and health care; and improved macroeconomic stability due to better fiscal management by governments leading to increased investor confidence.

Slightly different research results are presented by Cieślik and Wciślik (2020). Authors found that there is convergence among the CEE (eight countries) countries and they seem to be converging towards two largest EU countries: Germany and France. But this study did not provide clear evidence for catching up behaviour of CEE economies towards old EU 15 member states but it confirms that integration process takes time and may take several years or even decades before complete catch up with western standards can happen. Kijek and Matras-Bolibok (2020) presented similar research results on the level of technological convergence across EU regions, offering a new perspective by applying spatial panel models. The study revealed a clear divide between Western European regions with high total factor productivity (TFP) values and Eastern European regions with lower TFP levels. Interestingly, the research also showed that the gap in productivity levels was reducing faster in Eastern Europe than in Western Europe. The analysis of spatial effects further emphasised the significance of spillover effects for regional development trajectories, indicating that the growth rate and level of TFP largely depend on the dynamics of neighbouring regions.

These examples demonstrate that income convergence is a common phenomenon across countries and regions, and it can occur as a result of various economic, technological, and structural factors. However, the pace and direction of income convergence can vary significantly from country to country, and it can be influenced by a range of factors, including economic policy, political stability, and infrastructure development.

Empirical Studies on Regional Convergence in Poland

In the case of Poland, income convergence has been a central policy goal since the country's transition to a market-oriented economy in the 1990s, and it has made significant progress in closing the gap with more developed economies in Europe and beyond. In recent years, various studies have been conducted to examine the convergence process in Poland, particularly in terms of labour productivity, real GDP per capita, economic growth, standard of living, and income levels. The results of these studies have provided a comprehensive understanding of the situation in Poland, highlighting the country's progress towards convergence with other developed economies in Europe and within a country.

Several studies have been conducted to analyse the convergence process among regions in Poland. The results of these studies are diverse, with some finding evidence of convergence while others indicating a lack of convergence or a diminished convergence process. For example, Misiak (2022) revealed that the idea of convergence of real GDP per capita in Poland and Western Poland was not supported by the data. However, 13 out of 17 regions displayed signs of convergence, which were grouped together in distinct clusters referred to as 'convergence clubs'. The study also found that there was no clear dividing line between the East and West regions. Adamowicz and Szepeluk (2022) indicate that the rural sectors of Poland experienced a partial convergence of labour productivity between 2003 and 2014. This was likely due to the European Funds offered to rural areas as part of the first two EU financial perspectives. However, after this period, the convergence process diminished for various reasons, including natural and socioeconomic factors. Krupowicz (2020) showed that there was evidence of absolute beta-convergence in the variables that characterise labour resources. Beta convergence refers to the equalisation of values across different regions over time, reducing differences between them. However, the study did not confirm sigma and gamma convergences, indicating that there was no significant decrease in diversification among regions or any shift in the positions of labour resources. Kowerski and Bielak (2019) suggested that there was a convergence in the standard of living among Polish voivodships (NUTS 2 regions) between 2006 and 2016, as verified by both beta-convergence and sigma-convergence. However, the estimated values were higher than anticipated, which the authors attributed to a clustering phenomenon.

On the other hand, multiple studies have explored Poland's economic convergence with other developed European economies. Próchniak (2019) found that Poland has experienced significant convergence in terms of income to the average EU level, with Polish incomes becoming more similar to those in other European Union countries over time. Additionally, the study found evidence of increasing economic integration between Poland and its neighbours within the EU, which suggests further potential gains from increased trade and investment flows. Kotlewski and Błażej (2020) suggested that there was a solid foundation for convergence between the Polish economy and other developed economies in Europe, as evidenced by KLEMS growth accounting. The study showed that Poland had the potential for economic growth by comparing the country with other European countries and analysing the distribution of growth among different industries and the contribution of various factors to this growth at the industry level. The results of these studies show that Poland has made considerable progress towards convergence with other developed economies in Europe.

However, there is still room for improvement, particularly in terms of ensuring a more equal distribution of economic growth and standard of living across the country.

The European Union (EU) funds have had a significant impact on regional income convergence in Poland, with the research showing both positive and negative effects. The studies indicate that structural funds have had a positive impact on regional economic growth in Poland, as measured by the amount of Cohesion Policy Funds allocated to each region (Piętak, 2021). Furthermore, EU funds have had a significant impact in reducing development gaps between regions, although they have also had a negative effect on the reduction of innovation gaps (Czudec et al., 2019). The accession to the EU in 2004 brought about a shift in Poland's regional development policy, adopting the polarisation and diffusion concept. This approach aimed to allocate public funds more efficiently and effectively, but it also resulted in disparities between regions in terms of economic growth over the short-term. However, despite the initial disparities, it was expected that the long-term outcome of the approach would be the elimination of disparities and the reduction of inequality between regions (Gaczek and Kisiała, 2017).

However, during the 2004–2015 period, the disparities between regions persisted, and this has contributed to the unequal distribution of wealth and development within Poland. Additionally, the accession to the EU gave an impulse for stronger development in western regions with good socio-economic situations, but it had much slower effects on eastern areas, which experienced only minimal growth. This could lead to the long-term preservation of low-level economic development in eastern areas and result in a draining of valuable resources from the east towards the west (Pietrzak and Balcerzak, 2017).

In conclusion, the EU funds have had a mixed impact on regional income convergence in Poland. While they have had a positive impact in reducing development gaps and promoting economic growth, they have also had a negative effect on the reduction of innovation gaps and have contributed to disparities between regions. The research highlights the need for a change in the structure of EU funds to provide stronger support towards entrepreneurship and job creation, and to stimulate the economic structures in peripheral regions. This is a prerequisite for reducing future discrepancies and intensifying convergence among regions, and for achieving a more equal distribution of wealth and development within Poland.

Data

Our main source of data is the Local Data Bank provided by Statistics Poland. We use gross domestic product per capita at the NUTS-3 level to study cross-unit income convergence. The sample consists of 73 NUTS-3 Polish regions over 2000–2020 ($T = 21$). Table 1 presents the descriptive statistics for GDP per capita in regions in the years 2000 and 2020. The average GDP in Polish regions increased almost three times from about 4500 EUR in 2000–12,400 EUR in 2020.

Table 1. Descriptive Statistics of GDP Per Capita (Thous. EUR) in Polish Regions in 2000 and 2020.

Year	Mean	Std. Dev.	Coef. of Var.	Min	Max
2000	4462	1717	38.48	2975	13,954
2020	12,398	5000	40.33	7190	39,164

Source: Own elaboration.

The increase of standard deviation was slightly higher. Variation of GDP in the regions was high, as evidenced by the coefficient of variation of around 40%. It confirms that Polish regions differ significantly in terms of income levels. This is the result of economic, social and historical conditions. Regional differences in GDP per capita are presented in Fig. 1. The first basic characteristic is the division into the poorer eastern regions and the richer western regions, as well the division in poorer northern regions and the richer southern regions. The second regularity in the distribution of income is its high level in metropolitan regions, where large corporations, industrial activities and university centres are concentrated.

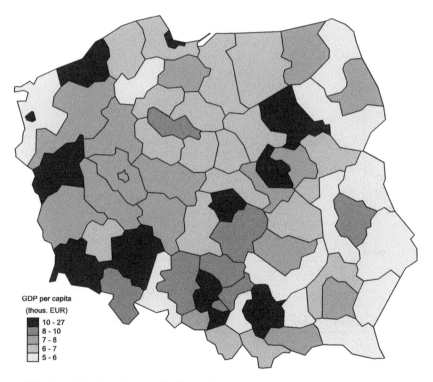

GDP per capita
(thous. EUR)

- 10 - 27
- 8 - 10
- 7 - 8
- 6 - 7
- 5 - 6

Fig. 1. Regional Distribution of GDP Per Capita in NUT-3 Polish Regions in 2000–2020. *Source:* Authors' own elaboration.

The initial level of GDP per capita in 2000 in Polish regions and growth rate of GDP in 2000–2020 are presented in Fig. 2. The scatterplot consists of five point types for each group of regions. The regions are grouped by income level, as shown in Fig. 1. The plot confirms heterogeneity of regional income. The regression line shows no relationship between the growth rate of GDP per capita and the initial level of GDP per capita in the entire sample. It indicates a lack of convergence for all regions. At the same time, dependencies within subgroups of regions are visible, which may suggest a club convergence. The outcomes of this study resemble the findings of Misiak (2022), who argued that the data did not support the notion of real GDP per capita convergence in Poland. Nonetheless, 13 out of 17 regions demonstrated signs of convergence, and they were classified into specific groups called 'convergence clubs'.

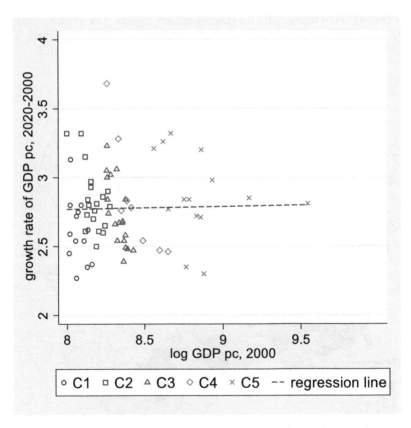

Fig. 2.   Scatter Plot of Initial Log GDP Per Capita and Growth Rate During 2020–2000. *Source:* Authors' own elaboration.

Methods

We study regional convergence processes in Poland using Barro and Sala-i-Martin (1992) type regression for panel data, log t convergence test and club clustering algorithm introduced by Phillips and Sul (2007, 2009).

Cross-section regression, called Barro regression, based on the neoclassical Solow-Swan model (Solow, 1956; Swan, 1956), is a commonly used tool to test the existence of convergence. β-convergence concept assumes that less developed countries or regions grow faster than more developed countries or regions. It means that the relationship between initial level of income and its growth rate is negative. Using cross-sectional data the average annual growth rate of GDP is regressed against the level of GDP in initial period. The classical regression used for testing β-convergence has the following form:

$$\frac{1}{T}\log\frac{y_{iT}}{y_{i0}} = \beta_0 + \beta_1\log y_{i0} + \varepsilon_i \tag{1}$$

where y_{i0} and y_{TT} are GDP in region i in initial period (0) and last period of time considered (T), β_0 is constant, β_1 is convergence parameter and ε_{ii} is error term.

The specification of Barro regression model for panel data is as follow (Barro, Sala-i-Martin et al., 1991):

$$\Delta\log y_{it} = \beta_0 + \beta_1\log y_{i,t-1} + \gamma_i + \varepsilon_{it} \tag{2}$$

where y_{ii} is GDP in region i at time t, β_0 is constant, β_1 is convergence parameter, γ_i is region-I specific effect and ε_i is error term. Eq. (2) is transformed to estimate its parameters to the following form:

$$\log y_{it} = \beta_0 + (\beta_1+1)\log y_{i,t-1} + \gamma_i + \varepsilon_{it} \tag{3}$$

The parameters of Eq. (3) are estimated using the generalised method of moments (GMM). The difference and system GMM estimators are designed for panel data analysis in such a case as ours, i.e. with current realisations of the dependent variable influenced by past one, and small a small number of time periods of available data T (many panels and few periods). For that reason we use the system generalised method of moment (GMM-SYS) estimator developed by Arellano and Bond (1991) and Blundell and Bond (1998).

Due to the possibility of club convergence in Polish regions, we employ the approach of Philipps and Sul (2007, 2009). They explain convergence variable as the product of a time-varying idiosyncratic factor loading δ_{it} and a common factor μ_t, which determines the common growth path:

$$\log y_{it} = \delta_{it}\mu_t \tag{4}$$

where δ_{it} is transition path of economy I to the common steady-state growth path determined by μ_t. An approach to modelling the transition elements is construction of the following relative transition coefficient:

$$h_{it} = \frac{\log y_{it}}{N^{-1}\sum_{i=1}^{N}\log y_{it}} = \frac{\delta_{it}}{N^{-1}\sum_{i=1}^{N}\delta_{it}} \tag{5}$$

which measures economy i's relative departure from the common steady-state growth path. The cross-sectional mean of h_{it} is unity, and hence its variance is given by:

$$H_t = N^{-1} \sum_{i=1}^{N} (h_{it} - 1)^2 \tag{6}$$

The convergence occurs if individual units approach the sample average over time. Then relative transition coefficient $h_{it} \to 1$ for all i as $t \to \infty$, and $H_t \to 0$ as $t \to \infty$.

To ensure overall convergence, Phillips and Sul propose the following semi-parametric form of δ_{it}:

$$\delta_{it} = \delta_i + \sigma_i \xi_{it} L(t)^{-1} t^{-\alpha} \tag{7}$$

where δ_i is time-invariant part of δ_{it}, σ_i is idiosyncratic scale parameter, ξ_{it} is iid(0, 1) across i and weakly dependent over t, and $L(t)$ is a slowly varying function (with $L(t) \to \infty$ as $t \to \infty$).

Phillips and Sul log t convergence test examines following hypotheses:
$H_0: \delta_i = \delta$ and $\alpha \geq 0$ against $H_1: \delta_i \neq \delta$ for all i or $\alpha < 0$.

The testing procedure consists of the following three steps:

(1) Calculation of cross-sectional variance ratios H_1/H_t ($t = 1, 2, \ldots, T$).
(2) Estimation of the following regression:

$$\log\left(\frac{H_1}{H_t}\right) - 2 \log L(t) = a + b \log t + u_t, \text{for } t = [rT], [rT] + 1, \ldots, T,$$

where $r \in (0, 1)$ is a truncation parameter. On the basis of Monte Carlo simulations, Phillips and Sul (2009) recommend the use of $r \in [0.2, 0.3]$.
(3) Application of autocorrelation and heteroskedasticity robust one-sided t test for $\alpha \geq 0$ using $\hat{b} = 2\hat{a}$ and a HAC standard error. The null hypothesis is rejected at a standard significance level (0.05) if $t_{\hat{b}} - 1.65$.

The rejection of null hypothesis means no overall convergence, but it does not rule out the existence of convergence in subgroups of units. Philips and Sul developed a club clustering algorithm to detect club convergence. It includes the four steps. First, the panel units are sorted in descending order with respect to the final period. Next, the core group including first k units ($2 \leq k < N$) is established by maximising $t_{\hat{b}}$ subject $t_{\hat{b}} > -1.65$ for each subgroup. Then one by one the units are added to the core primary group if the log t test statistic is greater than -1.65. The next groups are formed with the units for which the sieve condition fails in the previous step by performing the first three steps of procedure. The remaining units that do not satisfy convergence condition have divergent behaviour.

Results

At first, we estimate Barro type model for panel data to reveal the pattern of regional convergence processes in Poland. The estimation results are presented in Table 2. The

Table 2. Estimation Results of Absolute β-convergence Model.

Dependent Variable: *TFP*$_{i,t}$

TFP$_{i,\ t-1}$	0.9837***
	(0.0021)
Cons	0.2242***
	(0.0216)
β-convergence	0.9837
test	(0.0000)
N	219

Source: Authors' own elaboration.

Notes: *** indicate significance at the 1% level. Robust standard errors are displayed in parentheses. β-convergence test displays β-parameter and *p*-value in Wald test, i.e. H_0: $\beta = 1$, H_1: $\beta < 1$.

estimate of β parameter and *p*-value $= 0.000$ in β convergence test confirm β convergence hypothesis. Although the difference of β parameter from 1 is statistically significant, it is practically very small. It may mean that even if regional convergence processes for all Polish NUTS-3 regions take place, they are very weak.

According to the last conclusion, we employ the log *t* test proposed by Philips and Sul to verify the club convergence in Polish regions. Results of log *t* test performed for all regions (test statistic equal -13.853) gives strong evidence to rejects the null hypothesis of overall convergence. Then we apply the clustering algorithm to detect groups of converging regions. Table 3 presents the effects of this procedure.

Fig. 3 presents regional distribution of convergence clubs in Poland. The regional distribution of clubs is similar to the regional distribution of income which means that regional convergence takes place among regions with similar income. Thus, the clubs are divided into eastern and western and southern and northern regions. Club 4 consists of the regions with high GDP per capita, where industrial activities and university centres are concentrated. A specific group

Table 3. Log *t* Test Results.

Club	No. of Regions	$\hat{b}$	SE	*t*	meanGDP 2000	meanGDP 2020
1	2	1.6973	1.7514	0.9691	3093	7298
2	14	−0.1353	0.1323	−1.0226	3531.21	9270.5
3	31	0.1068	0.1051	1.0166	4451.39	12,598.26
4	21	−0.0946	0.0920	−1.0278	4926.76	13,694.48
5	4	0.2070	0.2284	0.9062	3665	10,843.75
No conv.	1				13,954	39,164

Source: Authors' own elaboration.

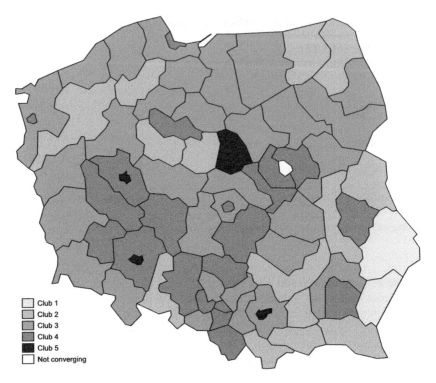

Fig. 3.   Regional Distribution of Convergence Clubs. *Source:*
Authors' own elaboration.

consists of regions in Club 5, three large cities (Krakow, Wroclaw, Poznan) and
płocki region. The only region that does not converge with the others is Warsaw,
which is distinguished by a much higher level of GDP than the others.

The club convergence phenomenon in Poland has several potential benefits. By
grouping regions with similar income levels, regional convergence can occur, which
could lead to more equitable economic growth and development across the country.
This could reduce regional inequalities and disparities in income and living standards. The identification of convergence clubs can also help policymakers and
investors focus on specific regions that have the potential for growth and development. For example, Club 4, which includes regions with high GDP per capita, could
be targeted for further investment in industrial activities and university centres,
potentially spurring economic growth in those regions. Additionally, the identification of regions that do not converge with others, such as Warsaw, could help
policymakers and investors understand why these regions may be lagging behind and
take steps to address those issues. Overall, the identification of convergence clubs can
provide insights into the economic development of regions in Poland and inform

policymaking and investment decisions aimed at promoting balanced and sustained economic growth.

The most developed regions, such as those ranked in Clubs 4 and 5, can play a significant role in the catch-up process that is crucial for Polish economic prosperity and living standards for its citizens. We should also focus on the catching up behaviour of all regions in Central and Eastern Europe towards the 15 old member states of the European Union. As mentioned earlier, a study by Cieślik and Wciślik (2020) did not provide clear evidence in this regard, but it confirms that the integration process takes time and may take several years or even decades before complete catch up with western standards can be achieved. When regions converge in terms of income levels, they tend to benefit from a more balanced and equitable distribution of wealth, which can result in reduced poverty and increased access to quality education, healthcare and other essential services. In addition, the catch-up process can also lead to increased economic growth and competitiveness at both the regional and national levels.

Summary

In this chapter, we studied the processes of income convergence in Polish regions to verify the effectiveness of regional policy implemented at the national and EU level. The results of the study indicate a very weak convergence process for all Polish NUTS-3 regions and suggest a club convergence. The club convergence is characterised by regions with similar income levels clustering together. The regional distribution of clubs is similar to the regional distribution of income. Therefore, the clubs are divided into eastern and western and southern and northern regions. The study found that the most developed regions, such as those ranked in Clubs 4 and 5, can play a significant role in the catch-up process that is crucial for Polish economic prosperity and living standards for its citizens.

The findings of the study offer significant insights into the effectiveness of regional policy in Poland, suggesting that policymakers should concentrate on policies that promote catch-up growth in less developed regions. Additionally, the study emphasises the significance of supporting the most developed regions in the country, as they can play a critical role in propelling the country's economic growth and prosperity. Therefore, policymakers can foster collaboration between regions within each convergence club to share knowledge and resources and work together towards shared economic objectives.

References

Adamowicz, M. and Szepeluk, A. (2022), "Regional Convergence of Labor Productivity in Rural Sectors of Poland during 2003–2019", *Agriculture*, Vol. 12 No. 11, p. 1774.

Arellano, M. and Bond, S. (1991), "Some Tests of Specification for Panel Data: Monte Carlo Evidence and an Application to Employment Equations", *The Review of Economic Studies*, Vol. 58 No. 2, p. 277.

Barro, R. J. and Sala-i-Martin, X. (1992), "Convergence", *Journal of Political Economy*, Vol. 100 No. 2, pp. 223–251.

Barro, R. J., Sala-i-Martin, X. X., Blanchard, O. J. and Hall, R. E. (1991), "Convergence across States and Regions", *Brookings Papers on Economic Activity*, Vol. 1991 No. 1, pp. 107–182.

Baumol, W. J. (1986), "Productivity Growth, Convergence, and Welfare: What the Long-Run Data Show", *The American Economic Review*, Vol. 76 No. 5, pp. 1072–1085.

Ben-David, D. (1998), "Convergence Clubs and Subsistence Economies", *Journal of Development Economics*, Vol. 55 No. 1, pp. 155–171.

Blundell, R. and Bond, S. (1998), "Initial Conditions and Moment Restrictions in Dynamic Panel Data Models", *Journal of Econometrics*, Vol. 87 No. 1, pp. 115–143.

Boldrin, M. and Canova, F. (2001), "Inequality and Convergence in Europe's Regions: Reconsidering European Regional Policies", *Economic Policy*, Vol. 16 No. 32, pp. 205–253.

Cass, D. (1965), *Studies in the Theory of Optimum Economic Growth*, Dissertations Publishing, Stanford University.

Cieślik, A. and Wciślik, D. R. (2020), "Convergence among the CEE-8 Economies and Their Catch-Up towards the EU-15", *Structural Change and Economic Dynamics*, Vol. 55, pp. 39–48.

Corrado, L., Martin, R. and Weeks, M. (2005), "Identifying and Interpreting Regional Convergence Clusters across Europe", *The Economic Journal*, Vol. 115 No. 502, pp. C133–C160.

Cuadrado-Roura, J. R., Mancha-Navarro, T. and Garrido-Yserte, R. (2002), "Regional Dynamics in the European Union: Winners and Losers", in: *Regional Convergence in the European Union, Facts, Prospects and Policies*, eds. Cuadrado-Roura, J. R. and Parellada M, Springer, pp. 23–52.

Czudec, A., Kata, R. and Wosiek, M. (2019), "Reducing the Development Gaps between Regions in Poland with the Use of European Union Funds", *Technological and Economic Development of Economy*, Vol. 25 No. 3, pp. 447–471.

Gaczek, W. M. and Kisiała, W. (2017), "Regional Convergence and Divergence in Poland", *Studia Regionalia*, Vol. 50, pp. 63–85.

Geppert, K., Happich, M. and Stephan, A. (2008), "Regional Disparities in the European Union: Convergence and Agglomeration", *Papers in Regional Science*, Vol. 87 No. 2, pp. 193–217.

Jóźwik, B. (2017), "Realna konwergencja gospodarcza państw członkowskich Unii Europejskiej z Europy Środkowej i Wschodniej: transformacja, integracja i polityka spójności", Wydawnictwo Naukowe PWN.

Kijek, A. and Matras-Bolibok, A. (2020), "Technological Convergence across European Regions", *Equilibrium*, Vol. 15 No. 2, pp. 295–313.

Koopmans, T. C. (1963), *On the Concept of Optimal Economic Growth*, Cowles Foundation Discussion Papers, 392.

Kotlewski, D. and Błażej, M. (2020), "Sustainability of the Convergence between Polish and EU Developed Economies in the Light of KLEMS Growth Accounting", *Bank i Kredyt*, Vol. 51 No. 2, pp. 121–142.

Kowerski, M. and Bielak, J. (2019), "Convergence of the Standard of Living in Polish NUTS2 Region", *Barometr Regionalny*, Vol. 17 No. 1, pp. 15–29.

Krupowicz, J. (2020), "The Convergence or Divergence of Labour Resources in Poland?" *Prace Naukowe Uniwersytetu Ekonomicznego We Wrocławiu*, Vol. 64 No. 4, pp. 75–100.

Lall, S. V. and Yilmaz, S. (2001), "Regional Economic Convergence: Do Policy Instruments Make a Difference?" *The Annals of Regional Science*, Vol. 35 No. 1, pp. 153–166.

Long, B. J. D. (1998), "Productivity Growth, Convergence, and Welfare: Comment", *The American Economic Review*, Vol. 78 No. 5, pp. 1138–1154.

Lyncker, K. von and Thoennessen, R. (2017), "Regional Club Convergence in the EU: Evidence from a Panel Data Analysis", *Empirical Economics*, Vol. 52 No. 2, pp. 525–553.

Ma, J. and Jia, H. (2015), "The Role of Foreign Direct Investment on Income Convergence in China after Early 1990s from a Spatial Econometric Perspective: Income Convergence in China after Early 1990s", *Review of Development Economics*, Vol. 19 No. 4, pp. 829–842.

Matkowski, Z., Próchniak, M. and Rapacki, R. (2016), "Income Convergence in Poland vis-à-vis the EU: Major Trends and Prospects", in: *Poland Competitiveness Report 2016. The Role of Economic Policy and Institutions*, SGH Warsaw School of Economics, Warsaw, pp. 37–55.

Misiak, T. (2022), "Is the Division of Western and Eastern Poland Still Valid? The Evolution of Regional Convergence in Poland", *Economics and Business Review*, Vol. 8 No. 2, pp. 145–169.

Neven, D. and Gouyette, C. (1995), "Regional Convergence in the European Community", *JCMS: Journal of Common Market Studies*, Vol. 33 No. 1, pp. 47–65.

Petrakos, G., Kallioras, D. and Anagnostou, A. (2011), "Regional Convergence and Growth in Europe: Understanding Patterns and Determinants", *European Urban and Regional Studies*, Vol. 18 No. 4, pp. 375–391.

Pietrzak, M. B. and Balcerzak, A. P. (2017), "A Regional Scale Analysis of Economic Convergence in Poland in the Years 2004–2012", in: *Regional Studies on Economic Growth, Financial Economics and Management: Proceedings of the 19th Eurasia Business and Economics Society Conference*, Springer International Publishing, pp. 257–268.

Piętak, Ł. (2021), "Structural Funds and Convergence in Poland", *Hacienda Publica Espanola/Review of Public Economics*, Vol. 236 No. 1, pp. 3–37.

Próchniak, M. (2019), "Income Convergence of Poland to the Average EU Level", in: *Poland. Competitiveness Report 2019*, World Economy Research Institute. SGH Warsaw School of Economics, pp. 85–98.

Phillips, P. C. B. and Sul, D. (2007), "Transition Modeling and Econometric Convergence Tests", *Econometrica*, Vol. 75 No. 6, pp. 1771–1855.

Phillips, P. C. B. and Sul, D. (2009), "Economic Transition and Growth", *Journal of Applied Econometrics*, Vol. 24 No. 7, pp. 1153–1185.

Quah, D. T. (1996), "Regional Convergence Clusters across Europe", *European Economic Review*, Vol. 40 No. 3–5, pp. 951–958.

Sala-i-Martin, X. X. (1996), "Regional Cohesion: Evidence and Theories of Regional Growth and Convergence", *European Economic Review*, Vol. 40 No. 6, pp. 1325–1352.

Smętkowski, M. (2013), "Regional Disparities in Central and Eastern European Countries: Trends, Drivers and Prospects", *Europe-Asia Studies*, Vol. 65 No. 8, pp. 1529–1554.

Solow, R. M. (1956), "A Contribution to the Theory of Economic Growth", *The Quarterly Journal of Economics*, Vol. 70 No. 1, pp. 65–94.

Swan, T. W. (1956), "Economic Growth and Capital Accumulation", *Economic Record*, Vol. 32 No. 2, pp. 334–361.

Terrasi, M. (2002), "National and Spatial Factors in EU Regional Convergence", in: *Regional Convergence in the European Union: Facts, Prospects and Policies*, pp. 185–209.

Tian, X., Zhang, X., Zhou, Y. and Yu, X. (2016), "Regional Income Inequality in China Revisited: A Perspective from Club Convergence", *Economic Modelling*, Vol. 56, pp. 50–58.

Wang, T., Wang, X., Wang, L., Au-Yong, C. P. and Ali, A. S. (2021), "Assessment of the Development Level of Regional Industrialized Building Based on Cloud Model: A Case Study in Guangzhou, China", *Journal of Building Engineering*, Vol. 44, p. 102547.

Chapter 4

Green Transformation of the Polish Economy

Armand Kasztelan and Adam Sulich

Abstract

Research Background: The transformation towards the Green Economy (GE) in Poland is a relatively new topic for researchers, policymakers and business practitioners. A comprehensive picture of the shift towards the GE can help mentioned groups translate theoretical assumptions into practice.

Purpose of the Article: This chapter presents the assessment of Poland's shift towards the GE, measured by the proposed Green Transformation Index (GTI).

Methodology: The set of GE indicators was elaborated in Structured Literature Review (SLR) variation method. Then, this set of indicators was compared with the Statistics Poland (GUS) secondary data and employed in the taxonometric calculation methods.

Findings: In the result, the GTI for the Polish economy was proposed and calculated between 2007 and 2020. The GTI allowed us to present a dynamic analysis of the transformation towards GE in Poland.

Keywords: Green Economy; taxonometric methods; Structured Literature Review; Green Transformation Index; Sustainable Development; Polish economy

Introduction

The transformation to the Green Economy (GE) is a multi-stage process covering many economic areas (Pearce, 1993). This green transformation is expected to contribute to the long-term goals of Sustainable Development (SD). On the other hand, reliable, properly selected and up-to-date data on the shift towards the GE are important for its measurement (Pretty, 2013). Selection of a unified and

Modeling Economic Growth in Contemporary Poland, 51–73
Copyright © 2024 Armand Kasztelan and Adam Sulich
Published under exclusive licence by Emerald Publishing Limited
doi:10.1108/978-1-83753-654-220231004

comprehensive set of indicators to assess progress towards a GE is a difficult task due to the complexity of the green transformation concept itself (Kasztelan, 2021).

This research aimed to assess Poland's transformation towards GE. First Structured Literature Review (SLR) variation method was used to define the most often co-occurring keywords describing the GE transformation. This method was developed with a bibliometric map in the VOSviewer software (version 1.6.18; Centre for Science and Technology Studies, Leiden University: Leiden, The Netherlands). The second taxonomic method was used based on the keywords describing the GE variables or indicators. Then a synthetic Green Transformation Index (GTI) measure was constructed and empirically verified on the public data from Statistics Poland (GUS). The analysis provided information about Poland's dynamic and overall level of green transformation. The results presented the dynamics of change for each year in the analysed period. The results presented in this chapter inform which areas require special attention and action in the coming years. The scientific contribution of this work is a set of indicators distinguished in SLR method variation and practical calculations of GTI in the Polish economy. The scope of the study covers the years 2007–2020, the broadest time horizon compared to the previous analyses in this area. In addition, an assessment of the green transformation processes in Poland in a dynamic approach was presented for the first time. The novelty of the research is based on the complementarity of the two used methods.

This chapter is organised as follows. The starting point is the SLR method on the GE measurement performed with the VOSviewer software. The results of this method were then compared with the GUS data areas and indicators. The next section presents the results of calculations for the synthetic GTI to assess the green transformation processes in Poland. The final section presents the conclusions and indicates potential directions for further research. In this chapter, the methodology description is presented alongside its results to increase the reproducibility and clarity of the research.

Literature Review

The Scopus scientific multidisciplinary database was the subject of the SLR variation research. The query used in SLR to explore Scopus was formulated as: (TITLE-ABS-KEY ('green economy') AND TITLE-ABS-KEY ('variables' OR 'indicators')). Neither limitations related to the discipline nor the period were applied; however, the syntax of the query limited the language of publications to English. Moreover, the query was interdisciplinary; hence, the subject area was not limited. There were 642 document results, which were downloaded as a CSV. file, for the bibliometric analysis in VOSviewer software to graphically explore the SLR method results. The exported data were used for analyses in a bibliometric programme, and the results are presented in a bibliometric map (van Eck and Waltman, 2010). The choice of the number of keywords co-occurrences determines the result obtained in its graphical presentation and influences bibliometric map clarity. Therefore, the full counting method was chosen for use in bibliometric software, and the default number of five keyword co-occurrences was primarily used to draw the bibliometric map (Fig. 1). Based on the query results in Scopus database research, the software drew this figure automatically in colours explained in Table 1. Additionally, there were keywords deselected from the list proposed by the VOSviewer software, including those related to the countries or cities' names, elements (water, air, etc.), research methods (integrated assessment, economic estimation, spatiotemporal analysis, etc.), calculation methods (structural equations) and too general keywords or subjects (decision making, trade, finance, economics, effectiveness, etc.). This influenced the number of analysed keywords and several clusters recognised in a bibliometric map (Fig. 1).

Each node in the bibliometric map represents a publication's keywords indexed in the explored Scopus database. The node size reflects the importance of the co-occurring keyword (van Eck and Waltman, 2010). The nodes are connected by edges, which represent the co-occurrences and can connect different keywords. Therefore, edges are the publications. Six different groups of scientific interests are visible, with keywords related to the GE variables or indicators mentioned directly in 642 scientific publications, as explored by the query in the Scopus database. The presented bibliometric map unveils pivotal areas and objectively illustrates linkages between articles focused on the GE indicators or variables.

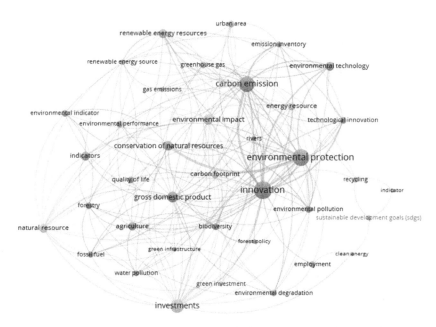

Fig. 1.   Bibliometric Map of Query Results for Scopus Exploration.
Source: Authors' own elaboration in VOSviewer software (version 1.6.18).

In Table 1, there are presented six clusters of keywords graphically represented by different colours as subnetworks of the bibliometric map in Fig. 1. These keywords proposed by the VOSviewer software are separated with commas and written in small letters despite their original writing form. The number of keywords caused the order of the clusters presented in Table 1. Despite that query syntax consisted of 'green economy' and 'variables', those are not present among the listed keywords.

The identified keywords are presented in alphabetical order. The red cluster is the most numerous and contains keywords related to the GE's different sectors. There is no surprise that 'forestry' and 'forest policy' are listed in this cluster together with 'agriculture' and 'biodiversity' because together with 'water pollution', 'gross domestic product' and existing 'green infrastructure' are elements of the 'quality of life' and are important in the GE (Sulich and Sołoducho-Pelc, 2022). The red cluster is related to economic activity using natural resources. There is a second green cluster related to the GE keywords representing the measurement of 'environmental performance' by 'environmental indicators'. The 'environmental protection' and 'conservation of natural resources', such as 'rivers', are also related to those GE indicators. Keywords automatically distinguished in the second cluster are related to the measurement of the pressure of human activity on the natural environment. The third cluster collects the keywords from scientific publications revolving around technological change to

Table 1. Clusters of Keywords Co-occurrences Visible in a Bibliometric Map for Scopus.

Cluster	Colour	Keywords
1	Red	agriculture, biodiversity, forest policy, forestry, fossil fuel, green infrastructure, gross domestic product, quality of life, water pollution
2	Green	conservation of natural resources, environmental indicators, environmental performance, environmental protection, indicators, rivers
3	Blue	carbon emission, emission inventory, environmental pollution, environmental technology, innovation, technological innovation
4	Yellow	carbon footprint, energy resource, environmental impact, green investment, investments, natural resource
5	Purple	clean energy, employment, environmental degradation, indicator, recycling, sustainable development
6	Teal	Gas emissions, greenhouse gas, renewable energy resources, renewable energy sources, urban area

Source: Authors' own elaboration based on Fig. 1.

reduce pollution and emissions. Therefore, in this blue cluster, the most important are 'innovation' and 'carbon emission'. In the fourth yellow cluster, 'investments' are the most often co-occurring keyword related to 'green investments', 'natural resource' and 'energy resource'. Interesting is the dispersion of all keywords belonging to this cluster. The keywords 'carbon footprint' and 'environmental impact' are close to the green economic activities' measurement, represented by the green cluster keywords intertwined with them. The fifth purple cluster consists of keywords related to the achieving of Sustainable Development Goals (SDGs) in the dimension of 'employment', 'clean energy' and 'recycling' to counteract 'environmental degradation' (Kozar and Sulich, 2023). In the last cluster, presented in Fig. 1 in teal or light blue, there are scientific publications revolving around renewable energy resources, 'urban area' and gas emissions. Keywords distinguished in this subcluster related to air pollution and climate changes ('gas emissions' and 'greenhouse gas') are located close to the similar subject area in the third cluster represented by keywords 'emission inventory' and 'carbon emission'. Among the indicated colour clusters, the most important keywords can be distinguished as carbon emission, investments, innovation, environmental protection, gross domestic product, conservation of natural resources and renewable energy resources. These terms can be considered the most popular and important GE indicators used in the scientific literature, proved by the SLR variation method. The results of the SLR were then analysed in Table 2 to construct the GTI.

Construction of the Green Transformation Index (GTI)

The evaluation of green transformation processes in Poland was carried out on the basis of a synthetic measure. In contrast to observing individual indicators, the synthetic index makes it possible to comprehensively assess the phenomenon under study from year to year, make comparisons and observe changes over time. The steps in constructing a synthetic measure have been widely discussed in the scientific literature (Mazziotta and Pareto, 2013; OECD, 2008).

The procedure used in the chapter is based on multivariate comparative analysis, which allows comparing objects (e.g. countries, individual years) described by multiple characteristics. One branch of multidimensional comparative analysis is the so-called taxonomic methods (Hellwig, 1995; Pluta, 1977). To construct the GTI, a taxonomic method of linear ordering was used, using the median and standard deviation formulas. This method is characterised by high robustness to the presence of extreme observations. Individual sites often show significant disparities in the asymmetry of indicator values. For this reason, the use of a synthetic metric with a median is most justified in this case (Grzebyk and Stec, 2015; Strahl, 2006).

The first step in creating the GTI was identifying the objects studied and the variables describing the object. The study's subject was the green transformation processes in Poland between 2007 and 2020. The choice of the time range is not accidental. First, in 2007, the global economic crisis in the financial markets

Table 2. Set of Variables Used in the Construction of the GTI Index.

SLR Method Results	Most Cited Sources	GUS Indicator (Statistical)	Symbol	Stimulant (S) or Destimulant (D)
Agriculture	(Pan et al., 2018; Pearce, 1993)	Gross value added in the agriculture, forestry, hunting and fishing section (% of total GVA in the economy)	x_1	S
		Agricultural and forest land excluded for non-agricultural and non-forest purposes (ha)	x_2	D
		Share of organic farmland in a total agricultural area (%)	x_3	S
Biodiversity	(Pan et al., 2018; Pearce, 1993; Pretty, 2013)	Farmland bird index	x_4	S
		Forest bird index	x_5	S
Forestry	(Ma et al., 2019; Shuai and Fan, 2020)	Forestry (%)	x_6	S
Forest policy	(Chen et al., 2017; Kardung et al., 2021; Rauf et al., 2018)	Timber harvesting (in cubic metres)	x_7	D
Fossil fuel	(Rodrigues et al., 2017; Sun et al., 2019)	Volume of PM_{10} emissions from fuel combustion and fugitive emissions from fuels (in kg)	x_8	D
Green infrastructure	(Pan et al., 2018; Rosasco and	Share of urban green areas in the	x_9	S

Table 2. *(Continued)*

SLR Method Results	Most Cited Sources	GUS Indicator (Statistical)	Symbol	Stimulant (S) or Destimulant (D)
	Perini, 2018; Sullivan, 2013)	total area of cities (%)		
Gross domestic product	(Pretty, 2013; Yi and Liu, 2015)	GDP per capita (current prices in PLN)	x_{10}	S
Quality of life	(Pretty, 2013; Zorpas et al., 2018)	Public expenditures on education in relation to GDP (in %)	x_{11}	S
		Poverty risk rate, including social transfers in income (in %)	x_{12}	D
		Households equipped with internet access (%)	x_{13}	S
		Percentage of population using the water supply system	x_{14}	S
		Percentage of population using sewerage network	x_{15}	S
Water pollution	(Pan et al., 2018; Rauf et al., 2018)	NA	NA	–
Conservation of natural resources	(Khan and Qianli, 2017; Yasmeen et al., 2019)	Legally protected areas (in hectares)	x_{16}	S
Environmental indicator	(Lutter et al., 2016; Merino-Saum et al., 2018)	Share of environmental taxes in total tax and contribution revenues (in %)	x_{17}	S

Table 2. *(Continued)*

SLR Method Results	Most Cited Sources	GUS Indicator (Statistical)	Symbol	Stimulant (S) or Destimulant (D)
Environmental performance	(Guo et al., 2018; Khan and Qianli, 2017)	Share of environmental technology patents in the total number of patents granted by the European Patent Office (in %)	x_{18}	S
		Share of inventions in the field of environmental protection technology in the total number of inventions filed with the Polish Patent Office (in %)	x_{19}	S
		Share of environmental technology patents in the total number of patents granted by the Patent Office of the Republic of Poland (in %)	x_{20}	S
		Final energy intensity of the economy (in kgoe/1000 PLN)	x_{21}	D
		Final energy intensity of households (in kgoe/1000 PLN)	x_{22}	D
		Primary energy productivity (in PLN/kgoe)	x_{23}	S

Table 2. *(Continued)*

SLR Method Results	Most Cited Sources	GUS Indicator (Statistical)	Symbol	Stimulant (S) or Destimulant (D)
		Resource productivity (in PLN/kg)	x_{24}	S
Environmental protection	(Guo et al., 2018; Shen et al., 2021)	Outlays on fixed assets for environmental protection in relation to GDP (%)	x_{25}	S
		Share of expenditures on environmental fixed assets in investment expenditures in the national economy (in %)	x_{26}	S
		Expenditure on environmental protection by households (at current prices in million PLN)	x_{27}	S
Indicator(s)	(Pan et al., 2018; Sun et al., 2019)	NA	NA	–
Rivers	(Shuai and Fan, 2020; Sun et al., 2019)	NA	NA	–
Carbon emission	(Shen et al., 2021; Sun et al., 2019)	Total carbon dioxide emissions (in thousands of tonnes of carbon dioxide equivalent)	x_{28}	D
Emission inventory	Guan et al. (2017)	NA	NA	–

Table 2. *(Continued)*

SLR Method Results	Most Cited Sources	GUS Indicator (Statistical)	Symbol	Stimulant (S) or Destimulant (D)
Environmental pollution	(Guo et al., 2018; Sun et al., 2019)	Volume of PM10 emissions (kg/per capita)	x_{29}	D
		Volume of PM2.5 emission (kg/per capita)	x_{30}	D
		Waste generated (excluding municipal waste) (in thousands of tonnes)	x_{31}	D
		Municipal waste collected in thousands of tonnes	x_{32}	S
Environmental technology	(Khan and Qianli, 2017; Maditati et al., 2018)	Environmental technology patents granted by the European Patent Office	x_{33}	S
		Environmental technology patents granted by the Polish Patent Office	x_{34}	S
Innovation	Shen et al. (2021)	NA	NA	–
Technological innovation	(Guo et al., 2018; Razzaq et al., 2021; Shen et al. 2021)	Environmental technology inventions filed with the Polish Patent Office	x_{35}	S
Carbon footprint	Pan et al. (2018)	NA	NA	-
Energy resource		Hard coal extraction (in	x_{36}	D

Table 2. *(Continued)*

SLR Method Results	Most Cited Sources	GUS Indicator (Statistical)	Symbol	Stimulant (S) or Destimulant (D)
	(Sun et al., 2019; Zhang et al., 2021)	thousands of tonnes)		
		Lignite extraction (in thousands of tonnes)	x_{37}	D
		Natural gas extraction (in million cubic metres)	x_{38}	D
Environmental impact	(Shen et al., 2021; Zhang et al., 2021)	Water intake for national economy and population (in hm^3)	x_{39}	D
		Nitrogen fertiliser consumption (in pure component) (in kg per hectare of agricultural land)	x_{40}	D
		Phosphorus fertiliser consumption (in pure component) (in kg per hectare of agricultural land)	x_{41}	D
Green investment	(Shen et al., 2021; Zhou, et al., 2020)	Expenditures on fixed assets for environmental protection (in thousands PLN)	x_{42}	S
Investments	(Sun et al., 2019; Zhang et al., 2021)	Investment expenditures (current prices in million PLN)	x_{43}	S

Table 2. *(Continued)*

SLR Method Results	Most Cited Sources	GUS Indicator (Statistical)	Symbol	Stimulant (S) or Destimulant (D)
		Internal R&D expenditures (per capita in PLN)	x_{44}	S
Natural resource	(Khan and Qianli, 2017; Shen et al., 2021)	Exploitable groundwater resources (in hm³)	x_{45}	S
		Hard coal resources (in million tonnes)	x_{46}	S
		Lignite resources (in million tonnes)	x_{47}	S
		Natural gas resources (in million cubic metres)	x_{48}	S
Clean energy	(Shen et al., 2021; Sun et al., 2019)	Share of energy from renewable sources in gross final energy consumption (%)	x_{49}	S
		Share of renewable energy in transport (%)	x_{50}	S
Employment	(Pan et al., 2018; Zhang et al., 2021)	Employed (in 1000)	x_{51}	S
		Registered unemployment rate (in %)	x_{52}	D
		Demographic dependency ratio (non-working age population per 100 people of working age)	x_{53}	D

Table 2. *(Continued)*

SLR Method Results	Most Cited Sources	GUS Indicator (Statistical)	Symbol	Stimulant (S) or Destimulant (D)
Environmental degradation	Shen et al. (2021)	Devastated and degraded land (in hectares)	x_{54}	D
Recycling	Maditati et al. (2018)	Selectively collected waste in relation to total municipal waste (in %)	x_{55}	S
Sustainable development	(Pearce, 1993; Sun et al., 2019)	NA		
Gas emissions	(Raza et al., 2019; Rodrigues et al., 2017)	Average number of days with exceedances of 120 $\mu g/m^3$ by total 8-hour ozone concentrations	x_{56}	D
Greenhouse gas	(Raza et al., 2019; Shuai and Fan, 2020)	Total greenhouse gas emissions (in thousands of tonnes of carbon dioxide equivalent)	x_{57}	D
Renewable energy (re) sources	(Chien et al., 2021; Zhang et al., 2021)	Renewable energy production (in thousands of tonnes of oil equivalent)	x_{58}	S
Urban area	(Ma et al., 2019; Zhang et al., 2020)	Population per 1 km^2 of total area	x_{59}	D
		Urbanisation index (%)	x_{60}	D

Source: Authors' own elaboration based on publicly available data from GUS data (Główny Urząd Statystyczny [Main Statistical Office in Poland], 2022). NA data not available.

began. Second, the study's introduction emphasises that the current process of defining and studying the GE began in 2008 with the establishment of the Green Economy Initiative.

The selection of variables used for the taxonomic method is presented in Table 2. In addition, it should be noted that the variables were selected to most fully reflect the various aspects of the green transition, expressed in most co-occurring keywords, the results of the SLR method. The source of information for the various indicators was the public data of Statistics Poland (GUS), primarily the database of GE indicators. An important selection criterion was the availability of data for individual indicators in the adopted time period. Thus, in the end, 60 indicators characterising individual areas of green transformation were extracted for the construction of the GTI index (Table 2). The presented disproportion between co-occurring keywords (36 results of the SLR method) indicating the variables used in the GE measurement and used by the GUS variables (60 indicators) proves the complexity of the green transformation.

The values of indicators (x_j, $j = 1, 2, \ldots, m$) in each year (y_i, $i = 1, 2, \ldots, n$) can be represented by a matrix of observations in the following form:

$$X = \begin{bmatrix} x_{11} & \cdots & x_{1m} \\ \vdots & \ddots & \vdots \\ x_{n1} & \cdots & x_{nm} \end{bmatrix} \tag{1}$$

Since the set of detailed indicators includes variables that cannot be directly aggregated (different units of measurement), they were normalised. Normalisation serves the purpose of ensuring that an increase in normalised indicators corresponds to an increase in the synthetic index. There are several ways to perform this operation. One of them is the min-max method (known in Poland as the zeroed unitisation method) used in this study (Fura et al., 2020; Kukuła, 2000; Petkovová et al., 2020):

for stimulants:

$$z_{ij} = \frac{x_{ij} - \min\left(x_{ij}\right)_i}{\max\left(x_{ij}\right)_i - \min\left(x_{ij}\right)_i} \tag{2}$$

for de-stimulants:

$$z_{ij} = \frac{\max\left(x_{ij}\right)_i - x_{ij}}{\max\left(x_{ij}\right)_i - \min\left(x_{ij}\right)_i} \tag{3}$$

where:

z_{ij} is the normalised value of the j-th variable in the i-th year.
x_{ij} is the initial value of the j-th variable in the i-th year.

After scaling, all z_{ij} values belong to the interval [0; 1], devoid of units, so that they can be added and compared. Values closer to 1 indicate a better situation in terms of the development of a given variable (indicator), and conversely, values closer to 0 indicate a worse situation in terms of a given indicator and, thus, a lower value of the GTI index in a given year. In the next step, the normalised values of specific indicators served as the basis for counting medians (Eqs. 4 and 5) and standard deviations (Eq. 6) (Grzebyk and Stec, 2015; Strahl, 2006):

$$Me_i = \frac{z_{\left(\frac{m}{2}\right)i} + z_{\left(\frac{m}{2}+1\right)i}}{2} \tag{4}$$

for an even number of observations, or:

$$Me_i = z_{\left(\frac{m}{2}+1\right)i} \tag{5}$$

for an odd number of observations, where:

$z_{i(j)}$ is the j-th statistical ordinal for the vector $(z_{i1}, z_{i2}, \ldots, z_{im})$, $i = 1, 2, \ldots, n; j = 1, 2, \ldots, m$.

$$Se_i = \sqrt{\frac{1}{m}\sum_{j=1}^{m}\left(z_{ij} - \bar{z}\right)} \tag{6}$$

In the last step, based on the following Eq. (7), the GTIs (GTI$_i$) were counted for each year:

$$GTI_i = Me_i(1 - Se_i); \ GTI_i < 1 \tag{7}$$

GTI index values closer to 1 indicate a relatively higher level of green transformation processes in a given year in Poland. Estimating synthetic measures made it possible to carry out a comparative analysis in individual years and assess the changes that have occurred throughout the period under study.

Results and Discussion

The results of the calculation of Poland's GTIs between 2007 and 2020 are shown in Fig. 2. The changes in the 'greening' of socio-economic processes in Poland were dynamic and should be evaluated very positively. Since 2017, one can even speak of an exponential increase in the value of the GTI index, which at the beginning of the period under study was only 0.0319, while in 2020, it was 0.6944, which means an almost 22-fold increase compared to the base year.

In the last year under review, 31 specific indicators (51.7%) had maximum levels of their normalised values (1.0000), while only 2 (x_{17} – share of environmental taxes in total tax and contribution revenues and x_{53} – demographic dependency ratio) had minimum levels of values (0.0000).

From 2007 to 2020, out of 60 indicators, unambiguously positive changes were observed for 43 of them (71.7%); on the negative side, we should evaluate the changes of 11 indicators (18.3%), while in the case of 6 (10.0%), it is not possible to make an unambiguous assessment, due to large fluctuations in values during

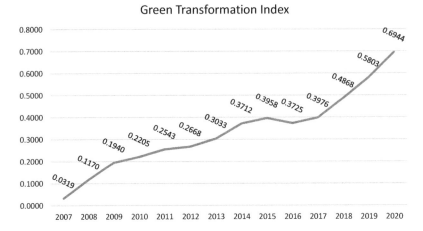

Fig. 2. The Value of the Green Transformation Index in Poland for 2007–2020. *Source:* Authors' own calculation based on publicly available data from GUS (Główny Urząd Statystyczny [Main Statistical Office in Poland], 2022).

the period under study (Table A1 – Appendix). What factors have negatively affected the overall assessment of green transformation processes in Poland? Considering the data for 2020, it is possible to distinguish those indicators for which satisfactory results have not been achieved so far. In addition to the demographic problems indicated early on and the underdeveloped system of green taxes (x_{17} and x_{53}), attention should be paid to the following:

- the reduction in the area of legally protected areas;
- the low level of innovation in environmental technology;
- successive deterioration of biodiversity, expressed, among other things, in the abundance index of common birds of the agricultural landscape;
- the growing area of agricultural and forest land excluded for non-agricultural and non-forest purposes;
- the still low share of outlays for environmental fixed assets in investment outlays in the national economy.

It seems, therefore, that within these areas, one should look for possible ways to continue the green transformation processes in Poland in the coming years. Given the war behind our eastern border, it should also be considered crucial to develop and implement an optimal energy mix for our country based on moving away from fossil fuels and combining renewable energy sources with nuclear power.

Using the synthetic index allowed a clear assessment of the green transformation processes in Poland from 2007 to 2020. On the other hand, the analysis of each of the specific indicators included in the GTI index allowed the identification of the weaknesses of these processes. In the course of the analysis, some limitations were encountered, which, as it were, set possible directions for further research. The construction of the GTI index was based on 60 indicators, even though nearly 80 indicators of green transformation were identified at the initial stage due to the existing information gap. Secondly, the latest available data on most of the specific indicators is from 2020; hence, it is not possible at this stage to say what changes occurred between 2021 and 2022. This was a time of exceptional challenges related to the need to combat the COVID-19 pandemic and Russia's aggression against Ukraine. This raises the question of how these conditions affected the overall process of balancing the Polish economy.

Summary

The green transformation of the Polish economy is related to the technological changes in the economy measured both quantitatively and quantitatively. Using the SLR method variation allowed us to build a collection of the GE indicators strongly harboured in the literature. The selected keywords were used in the second method of the taxonometric reference method.

The evaluation of green transformation processes in Poland is a complex issue requiring advanced analysis methods. Based on taxonomic methods, a synthetic evaluation index (GTI) was constructed, which made it possible to study this phenomenon in a multidimensional and dynamic manner. The added value of the research carried out is that, for the first time, a comprehensive assessment of the progress of the green transition from 2007 to 2020 was carried out. The informative value of the GTI index and the analysis of specific indicators should improve activities in monitoring, planning and implementing the goals of the GE in Poland.

In summarising the results of the study, it should be said that during the analysed period, there was a dynamic increase in the level of sustainability of socio-economic processes in Poland, which undoubtedly translated into the degree of achievement of the goals of the green transformation. A significant improvement in the value of the GTI index was noted, especially between 2017 and 2020. In turn, analysing changes in the values of specific indicators allowed us to identify those areas that still require corrective action.

Funding

The project is financed by the National Science Centre in Poland under the program 'Business Ecosystem of the Environmental Goods and Services Sector in Poland', implemented from 2020 to 2022; project number 2019/33/N/HS4/02957.

References

Chen, J., Wu, Y., Song, M. and Zhu, Z. (2017), "Stochastic Frontier Analysis of Productive Efficiency in China's Forestry Industry", *Journal of Forest Economics*, Vol. *28*, pp. 87–95, Elsevier GmbH.

Chien, F., Sadiq, M., Nawaz, M. A., Hussain, M. S., Tran, T. D. and Le Thanh, T. (2021), "A Step toward Reducing Air Pollution in Top Asian Economies: The Role of Green Energy, Eco-Innovation, and Environmental Taxes", *Journal of Environmental Management*, Vol. *297*, Academic Press.

van Eck, N. J. and Waltman, L. (2010), "Software Survey: VOSviewer, a Computer Program for Bibliometric Mapping", *Scientometrics*, Vol. *84* No. 2, pp. 523–538, Springer Netherlands, https://www.scopus.com/inward/record.uri?eid=2-s2.0-77953711904&doi=10.1007%2Fs11192-009-0146-3&partnerID=40&md5=77f9212dfdeda81adc0aafa9766aa55b

Fura, B., Stec, M. and Miś, T. (2020), "Statistical Evaluation of the Level of Development of Circular Economy in European Union Member Countries", *Energies*, Vol. *13* No. 23, p. 6401.

Główny Urząd Statystyczny [Statistics Poland] (2022), "Wskaźniki zielonej gospodarki w Polsce [Green Economy indicators in Poland], available at https://stat.gov.pl/obszary-tematyczne/srodowisko-energia/srodowisko/wskazniki-zielonej-gospodarki-w-polsce-2022,5,6.html (accessed 22 February 2023).

Grzebyk, M. and Stec, M. (2015), "Sustainable Development in EU Countries: Concept and Rating of Levels of Development", *Sustainable Development*, Vol. *23*, pp. 110–123.

Guan, R., Zheng, H., Hu, J., Fang, Q. and Ren, R. (2017), "The Higher Carbon Intensity of Loans, the Higher Non-Performing Loan Ratio: The Case of China", *Sustainability*, Vol. *9* No. 4, p. 667.

Guo, Y., Xia, X., Zhang, S. and Zhang, D. (2018), "Environmental Regulation, Government R & D Funding and Green Technology Innovation: Evidence from China Provincial Data", *Sustainability*, Vol. *10* No. 4, p. 940.

Hellwig, Z. (1995), *Taksonometryczne modele zmian struktury* [*Taxonomic Models of Structure Change*], Instytut Rozwoju i Studiów Strategicznych, Warsaw, Poland.

Kardung, M., Cingiz, K., Costenoble, O., Delahaye, R., Heijman, W., Lovrić, M., van Leeuwen, M., et al. (2021), "Development of the Circular Bioeconomy: Drivers and Indicators", *Sustainability*, Vol. *13* No. 1, pp. 1–24. MDPI AG.

Kasztelan, A. (2021), "On the Road to a Green Economy: How Do European Union Countries 'Do Their Homework'?", *Energies*, Vol. *14* No. 18, p. 5941.

Khan, S. A. R. and Qianli, D. (2017), "Impact of Green Supply Chain Management Practices on Firms' Performance: an Empirical Study from the Perspective of Pakistan", *Environmental Science and Pollution Research*, Vol. *24* No. 20, pp. 16829–16844. Springer Verlag.

Kozar, Ł. J. and Sulich, A. (2023), "Green Jobs: Bibliometric Review", *International Journal of Environmental Research and Public Health*, Vol. *20* No. 4, p. 2886.

Kukuła, K. (2000). *Metoda Unitaryzacji Zerowanej* [*The Zero Unitarization Method*], PWN, Warsaw, Poland.

Lutter, S., Giljum, S. and Bruckner, M. (2016), "A Review and Comparative Assessment of Existing Approaches to Calculate Material Footprints", *Ecological Economics*, Vol. *127*, pp. 1–10.

Ma, L., Long, H., Chen, K., Tu, S., Zhang, Y. and Liao, L. (2019), "Green Growth Efficiency of Chinese Cities and its Spatio-Temporal Pattern", *Resources, Conservation and Recycling*, Vol. *146*, pp. 441–451. Elsevier B.V.

Maditati, D. R., Munim, Z. H., Schramm, H.-J. and Kummer, S. (2018), "A Review of Green Supply Chain Management: From Bibliometric Analysis to a Conceptual Framework and Future Research Directions", *Resources, Conservation and Recycling*, Vol. *139*, pp. 150–162. Elsevier B.V.

Mazziotta, M. and Pareto, A. (2013), "Methods for Constructing Composite Indices: One for All or All for One?" *Rivista Italiana di Economia, Demografia e Statistica*, Vol. *67* No. 2, pp. 67–80.

Merino-Saum, A., Baldi, M. G., Gunderson, I. and Oberle, B. (2018), "Articulating Natural Resources and Sustainable Development Goals through Green Economy Indicators: A Systematic Analysis", *Resources, Conservation and Recycling*, Vol. *139*.

OECD (2008), *Handbook on Constructing Composite Indicators. Methodology and User Guide*, OECD Publishing, Paris, France, available at https://www.oecd.org/sdd/42495745.pdf

Pan, S.-Y., Gao, M., Kim, H., Shah, K. J., Pei, S.-L. and Chiang, P.-C. (2018), "Advances and Challenges in Sustainable Tourism toward a Green Economy", *Science of the Total Environment*, Vol. *635*, pp. 452–469. Elsevier B.V.

Pearce, D. (1993), *Blueprint 3: Measuring Sustainable Development*, Earthscan with Centre for Social & Economic Research on the Global Environment, London.

Petkovová, L., Hartman, D. and Pavelka, T. (2020), "Problems of Aggregation of Sustainable Development Indicators at the Regional Level", *Sustainability*, Vol. *12* No. 17, 7156.

Pluta, W. (1977), *Wielowymiarowa analiza porównawcza w badaniach ekonomicznych. Metody taksonomiczne i analizy czynnikowe* [*Multivariate Comparative Analysis in Economic Research. Taxonomic Methods and Factor Analysis*], PWE, Warsaw.

Pretty, J. (2013), "The Consumption of a Finite Planet: Well-Being, Convergence, Divergence and the Nascent Green Economy," *Environmental and Resource Economics*, Vol. *55* No. 4, pp. 475–499. Kluwer Academic Publishers.

Rauf, A., Liu, X., Amin, W., Ozturk, I., Rehman, O. and Sarwar, S. (2018), "Energy and Ecological Sustainability: Challenges and Panoramas in Belt and Road Initiative Countries", *Sustainability*, Vol. *10* No. 8, 2743. MDPI.

Raza, S. A., Shah, N. and Sharif, A. (2019), "Time Frequency Relationship between Energy Consumption, Economic Growth and Environmental Degradation in the United States: Evidence from Transportation Sector", *Energy*, Vol. *173*, pp. 706–720. Elsevier Ltd.

Razzaq, A., Wang, Y., Chupradit, S., Suksatan, W. and Shahzad, F. (2021), "Asymmetric Inter-linkages between Green Technology Innovation and Consumption-Based Carbon Emissions in BRICS Countries Using Quantile-On-Quantile Framework", *Technology in Society*, Vol. *66*, p. 101656. Elsevier Ltd.

Rodrigues, A., Bordado, J. C. and Dos Santos, R. G. (2017), Upgrading the Glycerol from Biodiesel Production as a Source of Energy Carriers and Chemicals – A Technological Review for Three Chemical Pathways, *Energies*, Vol. *10* No. 11. MDPI AG.

Rosasco, P. and Perini, K. (2018), "Evaluating the Economic Sustainability of a Vertical Greening System: A Cost-Benefit Analysis of a Pilot Project in Mediterranean Area", *Building and Environment*, Vol. *142*, pp. 524–533. Elsevier Ltd.

Shen, Y., Su, Z.-W., Malik, M. Y., Umar, M., Khan, Z. and Khan, M. (2021), "Does Green Investment, Financial Development and Natural Resources Rent Limit Carbon Emissions? A Provincial Panel Analysis of China," *Science of The Total Environment*, Vol. *755*, p. 142538. Elsevier B.V.

Shuai, S. and Fan, Z. (2020), "Modeling the Role of Environmental Regulations in Regional Green Economy Efficiency of China: Empirical Evidence from Super Efficiency DEA-Tobit Model", *Journal of Environmental Management*, Vol. *261*. Academic Press.

Strahl, D. (Ed.). (2006). *Methods for Evaluation of Regional Development [Metody Oceny Rozwoju Regionalnego]*, Academy of Economics Publishing House, Wrocław.

Sulich, A. and Sołoducho-Pelc, L. (2022), "Changes in Energy Sector Strategies: A Literature Review," *Energies*, Vol. *15*, No. 19, p. 7068.

Sullivan, S. (2013), "After the Green Rush? Biodiversity Offsets, Uranium Power and the 'Calculus of Casualties' in Greening Growth", *Human Geography*, Vol. *6* No. 1, pp. 80–101. SAGE Publications Inc.

Sun, H., Edziah, B. K., Sun, C. and Kporsu, A. K. (2019), "Institutional Quality, Green Innovation and Energy Efficiency", *Energy Policy*, Vol. *135*. Elsevier Ltd.

Yasmeen, R., Li, Y. and Hafeez, M. (2019), "Tracing the Trade–Pollution Nexus in Global Value Chains: Evidence from Air Pollution Indicators", *Environmental Science and Pollution Research*, Vol. *26*, No. 5, 5221–5233.

Yi, H. and Liu, Y. (2015), "Green Economy in China: Regional Variations and Policy Drivers," *Global Environmental Change*, Vol. *31*.

Zhang, D., Mohsin, M., Rasheed, A. K., Chang, Y. and Taghizadeh-Hesary, F. (2021), "Public Spending and Green Economic Growth in BRI Region: Mediating Role of Green Finance", *Energy Policy*, Vol. *153*. Elsevier Ltd.

Zhang, F., Deng, X., Phillips, F., Fang, C. and Wang, C. (2020), "Impacts of Industrial Structure and Technical Progress on Carbon Emission Intensity: Evidence from 281 Cities in China", *Technological Forecasting and Social Change*, Vol. *154*. Elsevier Inc.

Zhou, X., Tang, X. and Zhang, R. (2020), "Impact of Green Finance on Economic Development and Environmental Quality: a Study Based on Provincial Panel Data from China," *Environmental Science and Pollution Research*, Vol. *27* No. 16, pp. 19915–19932. Springer.

Zorpas, A. A., Voukkali, I. and Navarro Pedreño, J. (2018), "Tourist Area Metabolism and its Potential to Change through a Proposed Strategic Plan in the Framework of Sustainable Development", *Journal of Cleaner Production*, Vol. *172*, pp. 3609–3620. Elsevier Ltd.

Appendix

Table A1. Characteristics of the Diagnostic Variables Used in the Research.

Variable	Mean	Minimum	Maximum	Standard deviation	Coefficient of Variation [%]	Variable Change Between 2007 and 2020
x_1	3.2	2.7	3.7	0.3	10.1	Negative
x_2	4252.3	2441.0	6111.0	1075.3	25.3	Negative
x_3	3.5	1.8	4.6	0.8	24.2	Inconclusive
x_4	0.86	0.75	1.00	0.06	7.2	Negative
x_5	1.22	1.06	1.34	0.07	6.1	Positive
x_6	29.4	28.9	29.6	0.2	0.8	Positive
x_7	38947248.4	34273421.0	45589688.0	3383511.6	8.7	Negative
x_8	354116362.3	276571861.0	415137784.0	39155910.2	11.1	Positive
x_9	4.8	4.7	4.9	0.1	1.5	Positive
x_{10}	44949.4	31155.0	61231.0	9053.0	20.1	Positive
x_{11}	4.6	4.3	4.92	0.2	4.4	Positive
x_{12}	16.6	14.8	17.7	1.1	6.4	Positive
x_{13}	71.0	41.0	90.4	13.9	19.6	Positive
x_{14}	89.7	86.7	92.2	2.3	2.6	Positive
x_{15}	66.5	60.3	71.5	4.1	6.2	Positive
x_{16}	10141849.0	10101479.0	10182356.0	30255.0	0.3	Negative

Table A1. *(Continued)*

Variable	Mean	Minimum	Maximum	Standard deviation	Coefficient of Variation [%]	Variable Change Between 2007 and 2020
x_{17}	7.7	6.95	8.41	0.4	5.2	Negative
x_{18}	9.2	0.9	13.4	3.3	36.3	Positive
x_{19}	4.7	4.0	5.7	0.4	9.3	Negative
x_{20}	4.3	3.0	7.2	1.0	22.9	Positive
x_{21}	39.6	31.3	52.7	6.5	16.3	Positive
x_{22}	46.6	37.7	62.5	8.3	17.9	Positive
x_{23}	19.8	18.0	22.9	1.6	7.8	Positive
x_{24}	2.6	1.9	3.5	0.5	18.4	Positive
x_{25}	0.6	0.3	0.8	0.2	25.8	Negative
x_{26}	4.2	2.7	5.7	0.9	21.7	Negative
x_{27}	26808.4	17134.5	51 540.9	12222.1	45.6	Positive
x_{28}	402082.8	376038.5	420214.8	12542.6	3.1	Positive
x_{29}	10.8	8.9	12.3	1.0	9.2	Positive
x_{30}	8.3	6.7	9.6	0.8	9.9	Positive
x_{31}	120315.1	109466.0	131256.1	7665.2	6.4	Positive
x_{32}	10876.2	9473.8	13116.9	1215.5	11.2	Positive
x_{33}	18.3	0.3	48.8	15.5	84.6	Positive
x_{34}	126.8	74	161	20.4	16.1	Positive
x_{35}	186.4	113.0	264.0	39.0	20.9	Inconclusive
x_{36}	67020.1	48156.0	82779.0	7973.2	11.9	Positive
x_{37}	59705.4	47300.0	66139.0	4917.3	8.2	Positive

x_{38}	5268.5	4926.0	5839.2	286.8	5.4	Positive
x_{39}	10433.2	8666.3	11397.9	712.2	6.8	Positive
x_{40}	72.2	65.3	80.7	4.7	6.5	Negative
x_{41}	24.2	20.9	28.6	1.9	7.8	Inconclusive
x_{42}	10555906.5	6517035.4	15160046.4	2473265.7	23.4	Inconclusive
x_{43}	251068.9	191714.0	320937.0	36815.8	14.7	Positive
x_{44}	438.1	175.1	848.7	202.8	46.3	Positive
x_{45}	17592.1	16863.1	18439.5	482.8	2.7	Positive
x_{46}	71848.8	67878.0	78296.0	3623.7	5.0	Positive
x_{47}	24702.4	18162.3	27064.5	3324.8	13.5	Positive
x_{48}	137558.4	119187.2	149057.3	9430.1	6.9	Positive
x_{49}	11.3	6.9	16.1	2.6	23.4	Positive
x_{50}	5.5	1.7	6.9	1.4	26.0	Positive
x_{51}	14685.9	13771.1	16120.6	765.1	5.2	Inconclusive
x_{52}	9.9	5.2	13.4	2.8	28.2	Positive
x_{53}	59.6	55.0	68.0	4.5	7.5	Negative
x_{54}	62923.5	61161.0	64651.0	1092.9	1.7	Inconclusive
x_{55}	18.3	5.1	37.9	10.3	56.3	Positive
x_{56}	13.5	5.2	23.5	5.2	38.7	Positive
x_{57}	402082.8	376038.5	420214.8	12542.6	3.1	Positive
x_{58}	8589.5	4850.2	12518.2	2342.1	27.3	Positive
x_{59}	122.7	122.0	123.0	0.5	0.4	Positive
x_{60}	60.5	59.9	61.2	0.4	0.7	Positive

Source: Authors' won calculation based on publicly available data from GUS (Główny Urząd Statystyczny [Main Statistical Office in Poland], 2022).

Chapter 5

Economic Resilience in the Face of COVID and the War in Ukraine: Key Lessons From the Situation of the Polish Economy

Artur Paździor, Wiesława Caputa and Izabela Krawczyk-Sokołowska

Abstract

Research background: The Covid-19 pandemic and the war in Ukraine are a real example of how uncertainty can trigger radical changes in the socio-economic system on a macro and micro scale. The indicated events contributed to the increase in the level of uncertainty, and its effects appeared in the real conditions of the functioning of international communities.

Purpose of the Chapter: The purpose of the chapter is to determine the impact of the Covid-19 pandemic and the war in Ukraine on the situation of Polish consumers and the resulting behaviour in the context of business–consumer relations.

Methodology: This goal was achieved through literature studies, analysis of changes in selected indicators of the economic situation and analysis of basic variables determining the relationships between consumers and suppliers.

Findings: The presented research results allow us to conclude that both the pandemic and war had an impact not only on the economic indicators but also the financial standing of households. We are seeing an increase in the differences between the nominal and real value of these incomes. Inflation is on the rise, forcing households to change their spending structure and look for savings. Of course, there have been and will be companies that do not have to be significantly affected by the effects of these events. In this group, companies related to the provision of IT infrastructure and specialising in establishing multidimensional relationships in the digital space should be pointed out.

Modeling Economic Growth in Contemporary Poland, 75–87
Copyright © 2024 Artur Paździor, Wiesława Caputa and Izabela Krawczyk-Sokołowska
Published under exclusive licence by Emerald Publishing Limited
doi:10.1108/978-1-83753-654-220231005

Keywords: COVID pandemic; war in Ukraine; conditions of uncertainty; economic development; household situation; business relationship

Introduction

The Covid-19 pandemic and the war in Ukraine are a real example of how uncertainty can trigger radical changes in the socio-economic system on a macro and micro scale. The indicated events contributed to the increase in the level of uncertainty, and its effects appeared in the real conditions of the functioning of international communities. The identified areas of uncertainty include both the economy and the regulatory sphere. The changes caused by uncertainty and instability affect the behaviour of people (consumers, producers, stakeholders), the functioning of the existing supply chains of raw materials and goods and the forms of transfers and financial settlements.

This chapter reviews the literature on the identification and interpretation of changes caused by uncertainty and existing threats. Mainly in the context of the impact of economic uncertainty on all market participants in determining risk factors in decision-making processes, uncertainty typically influences many economic, financial and regulatory decisions at both individual and macro levels.

The purpose of this chapter is to determine the impact of the Covid-19 pandemic and the war in Ukraine on the situation of Polish consumers and the resulting behaviour in the context of business–consumer relations.

This goal was achieved through literature studies, analysis of changes in selected indicators of the economic situation and analysis of basic variables determining the relationships between consumers and suppliers. Based on the conducted research, an attempt was made to assess the impact of the Covid-19 pandemic and the armed conflict in Ukraine on the Polish economy in selected areas, mainly from the perspective of changes in consumer behaviour and business relations.

Theoretical Review

Conditions and Effects of Socio-Economic Uncertainty

The dynamic and uncertain environment of companies encourages them to take more risky strategies, e.g. hybrid organisation (Hitt et al., 2020), which can bring benefits by increasing legitimacy and access to resources, and by stimulating creativity and innovation (Wry et al., 2014). New organisational forms, i.e. hybrid ones, which could not function without the internet and complex spatial and temporal interactions (Wry et al., 2014).

According to Alpers, uncertainty is a subjective, multidimensional concept that changes depending on its source and the degree to which it is experienced – hence it is very difficult to measure (Wry et al., 2014). It should be assumed that this concept means the inability to accurately "predict something" and the simultaneous lack of confidence in one's knowledge to solve a specific problem. Two methods are most often used in uncertainty management: uncertainty reduction

(reduction of uncertainty into its specific forms without changing the company's strategy, e.g. gathering information and proactive cooperation) and dealing with uncertainty (affects the scope of uncertainty and often requires a change of strategy, e.g. flexibility, imitation and reactive cooperation) (Sniazhko, 2019).

The main difference between risk and uncertainty stems mainly from the fact that most risks can be predicted and measured with varying degrees of probability, while uncertainty is very difficult to measure and is also a subjective, multidimensional concept that varies depending on its source and degree, in how it is experienced (Alpers, 2019).

The economic disruptions caused by the pandemic and the war have significantly changed the approach and perception as well as the implementation of companies' obligations towards their stakeholders. According to Barney, non-owner stakeholders must receive value before shareholders, because the support of such stakeholders is essential to creating value in the first place (Barney, 2018), which confirms the need to change existing business models and the recognition that maintaining the company's reputation and integrity is its potential to create value in the long term, and shareholder profits may be less important. Value creators are more likely to manage threats when they work together than when they act alone.

Economic security is "undisturbed functioning of economies, i.e. maintaining basic development indicators and ensuring comparative balance with the economies of other countries" (Księżopolski, 2011). In other words, it means "conditions for harmonious development, which make it possible to create conditions for a relatively satisfactory standard of living for the citizens of the state. In macroeconomic terms, security means stable employment, low unemployment, and predictable prospects for economic development" (Żukrowska, 2013).

Despite the limited probability of predicting these events and the difficulties in estimating their effects at the initial stage of their occurrence, they had a significant impact on the socio-economic security and financial stability of citizens of many countries around the world (pandemic) and in particular the countries of Central and Eastern Europe (war). In addition, Poland has a complex and complicated situation in this respect, as a territorial neighbour and trade partner of both Russia and Ukraine (https://businessinsider.com.pl). It is enough to mention that before the outbreak of the war, i.e. in 2021, Russia was ranked 3rd among the largest partners in imports, and 7th in Poland's exports (https://pfr.pl). Poland's exports of goods to Ukraine in 2021 amounted to EUR 6.3 billion, and imports to EUR 4.25 billion (https://pfr.pl). The cited economic and geographical links of Poland, Ukraine and Russia, and the lack of clear forecasts regarding the pandemic, allow us to hypothesise that these events will significantly affect Poland's economic security.

On this basis, it could be argued that as a result of the introduction of the state of epidemic and the related lockdowns, many industries will be severely affected. It could be expected that this would apply in particular to companies from sectors sensitive to events, such as tourism and hospitality, sports and recreation, transport and logistics, etc. At the initial stage of the spread of the Covid-19 pandemic, hardly anyone assumed that apart[1] from companies from the sector of production and distribution of medicines and pharmaceutical products, in particular in the area of antiviral and anti-inflammatory drugs, vaccine manufacturers and manufacturers and distributors of personal protective equipment in the form of masks, gloves, as well as disinfectants, there will be other sectors of the economy that can be defined as victories in the pandemic economics.

In a situation when the world was still struggling with problems related to the Covid-19 pandemic, almost in the middle of Europe (https://www.britannica.com) war broke out. Disturbances in the global economy and numerous national and regional systems caused by epidemic restrictions, reflected, among others, in the broken logistic chains, abandoning or clearly limiting the mobility of employees, the collapse of the financial market and the banking system, disturbances in the functioning of public healthcare entities, uncontrolled changes in food prices caused by demand panic (Long Nguyen et al., 2021) and many others.

In a situation where the world has only just begun to cope with these problems with varying degrees of success, a war breaks out in Central and Eastern Europe, which, apart from human dramas, also brings economic consequences. Russia and Ukraine are the largest European countries in terms of territory. Due to the abundance of fertile soils in their areas, these countries provide a food base for a large part of the world, in particular for Africa, which is still struggling with food problems, and the economically powerful and densely populated countries of the Far East (https://www.osw.waw.pl). In addition to fertile soils, Ukraine's other natural wealth is scarce raw materials. In the light of numerous expert opinions, in Ukraine there are, among others, 10% of the world's iron resources, 6% of titanium and 20% of graphite, as well as numerous resources of hard coal and shale gas (https://www.renewablematter.eu). Russia, in turn, in 2021 was in second place among the largest producers of natural gas and 3rd on the list of the largest oil producers in the world (https://www.visualcapitalist.com). Taking into account the above-mentioned parameters, it seems reasonable to say that the armed conflict between these countries will contribute to destabilisation on the market of food products and energy resources. It could have been assumed that the scale of the conflict's impact would not be exclusively regional, and that the effects would be felt almost all over the globe. Therefore, it is necessary to anticipate that the Polish economy, due to geographical proximity and economic ties, will feel the consequences of armed aggression in a complex form and to a significant extent.

It should be assumed that the changes caused by the pandemic and the war in Ukraine will not last, permanently in business and its environment, but the current crisis will be a turning point. That is why it is important to try to indicate how the economy will function in the new normal?

Business Relations in Conditions of Uncertainty

The presented review of the literature gives grounds to conclude that the Covid-19 pandemic and the war in Ukraine radically change the conditions of farming. This consequently means that economics, being a science of management, is currently facing increasing pressure from threats and challenges, not only ecological but also civilisational. For many years, it has been commonly emphasised that farming conditions are characterised not only by huge qualitative changes but also these changes have less and less evolutionary features and are becoming more and more irregular (Dobiegała-Korona and Herman, 2006). Currently, this irregularity is associated with unpredictability. This does not mean, however, that all phenomena or processes exhibit such features.

There is no question that the farming conditions determine the process of creating business relationships. In the set of these relationships, the relationships between enterprises and their customers play a key role. The effects of establishing and developing these relationships at the macroeconomic level determine, among others, the situation on the labour market, the condition of households, the level of investment and also the acquisition of funds for the implementation of public tasks. On the other hand, at the microeconomic level, they determine customer satisfaction related to the level of satisfied needs and the ability to achieve business goals by the company, including mainly obtaining a sustainable capital supply.

At the basis of the relationship between the company and the customer is the dually defined value of the customer (Caputa and Krawczyk-Sokołowska, 2023). From the customer's perspective, this value is often referred to as customer value. Although (Grisaffe and Kumar, 1998; Ulaga and Eggert, 2005) this value is not uniformly defined, it is most often associated with the values perceived by the customer, resulting from customer preferences and priorities regarding: the attributes of the product itself, the process of its acquisition as well as experiences and expectations related to its use, but the basic element of the cost of acquisition is the price (Kotler and Bliemel, 2005). On the other hand, from the company's perspective, customer value is most often perceived as the economic value of business relationships and is referred to as customer *equity* (Blatberg and Deighton, 2001; Rudolf-Sipötz, 2001). This capital reflects the sum of benefits that the company connects with acquiring and retaining a customer throughout the entire period of maintaining the relationship with them (Dobiegała-Korona and Herman, 2006), which should result not only in a market transaction but also in the effect of such an information message from the client, which can be used in the value creation process. As a consequence, the customer's contribution to the value creation process can take direct (related to the purchase by the customer of a product offered on the market) or indirect power supply (resulting from the use of social and business relationships to launch an information transfer, the content of which is knowledge that can be used for creating value process for the client and the company) (Caputa, 2020).

The key determinant of the customer's market value is his income potential, which determines both the quantity and the value of purchases made. Therefore, when analysing the impact of the pandemic and war on business relations, attention should be paid to parameters such as changes in customer income, level and changes in prices, expenditure structure, product availability, on the one hand, and on the other hand, production costs, product and resource availability, as well as the security of establishing relationship, resources, applied business strategy and negotiated supply prices; it also indicates customer satisfaction (Peschke, 1997).

Research Methodology

The purpose of this study is to determine the impact of the Covid-19 pandemic and the war in Ukraine on the situation of Polish households (consumers). Taking into account the relatively short period of occurrence of the analysed phenomena, the formulated conclusions are only an attempt to make specific assessments. The analysis was carried out within changes in selected categories, which is mainly due to limited access or lack of data. In this study, we were interested in the changes caused by the Covid-19 pandemic and military operations in Ukraine. The key aspect was the behaviour of the Polish consumer and changes in business relations.

Business Relations Between the Company and the Client in the Light of Research

The result of the pandemic was not only restrictions on direct contacts between people but also a periodic lockdown. The increase in the number of infections prompted the Polish government to take radical measures to reduce the transmission of the coronavirus, including closing some industries (educational institutions, shopping malls, beauty salons, rehabilitation, hairdressing salons, hotels), limiting the number of people in commercial establishments and their actions, the introduction of a sanitary cordon on the borders of Poland and a ban on movement except in justified situations (https://www.gov.pl).

These activities were undertaken both on people's own initiative and as a result of decisions made at various levels of government administration. The intensity of these activities, as well as their effects, analysed in the context of business relations between customers and bidders, varied. The restrictions indicated in the table clearly indicate that the industry particularly vulnerable to the effects of the pandemic was, among others, hotel and gastronomy. This is confirmed by changes in indicators of the general economic climate (Table 1).

The ratios presented in the table are calculated as the arithmetic average of the balances of answers to questions from the monthly survey conducted among the management staff regarding the assessment of the current and expected economic situation of the enterprise. It is therefore clear that the aforementioned lockdowns had a significant impact on the perception of the condition of the surveyed entities. Most of the respondents evaluate it negatively. It should be noted, however, that with the easing of restrictions, we can observe a significant improvement. Although there is still a surplus of negative over positive assessments, compared to other sections assessing the economic situation negatively, this difference in 2022 is the smallest. As a result, the improvement of the economic situation is recorded in 14.3% of the surveyed companies, and its

Table 1. Indicators of the General Economic Climate in 2019–2022.

Specification of the Processing Industry	2019	2020	2021	2022	Long-Term Indicator
Industrial processing	4.3	−6.6	−0.9	−15.2	2.1
Construction	5.6	−15.4	−7	−15.3	−2.8
Wholesale trade	7.2	−4.6	6.2	−7	3.7
The retail trade	3.6	−9.8	−0.6	−8.1	−4.2
Transport and warehouse management	1.9	−12.7	5.3	−6.3	−0.5
Accommodation and gastronomy	**6.3**	**−19.3**	**−6.7**	**−4.9**	**−0.2**
Information and communication	16.9	5.4	13.4	11.8	18.5
Finance and insurance	26.9	2.7	12.2	9.2	26.3

Source: Authors' own elaboration based on publicly available data from Polish Main Statistical Office: Business tendency in manufacturing, construction, trade and services 2000–2022. https://stat.gov.pl/obszary-tematyczne/koniunktura/koniunktura/koniunktura-w-przetworstwo-przemysl owym-budownictwo-handlu- i-services-2000-2022-august-2022,4,64.html

deterioration in 19.2%. Other companies believe that their situation does not change (https://stat.gov.pl).

When analysing the presented research results, it is worth noting that only in two groups of entities representing the following departments: information and communication and finance and insurance, we observe an excess of positive assessments over negative ones. As a result, most of them declare an improvement in their situation and a positive attitude towards the future, regardless of the period of the research.

The pandemic, forcing the isolation of people, prompted all market entities to look for and use other ways of establishing relationships than before. This undoubtedly affects the positive assessment of those enterprises whose activities are related to enabling the establishment of relationships via the network, or the acquisition, processing and transfer of information.

Numerous studies show that the modern customer, among others: educated, impatient, sensitive to social needs, expects his needs to be met quickly, conveniently and cheaply (Caputa et al., 2021). The dynamically increasing access to the internet made the fulfillment of customers' expectations and their actual participation in the value creation process a reality. As a result, direct relationships with the customer, online relationships changed more and more often and the digital space itself was used by consumers in a multidimensional way even before the pandemic.

The legitimacy of this statement is confirmed by research on the use of the internet in Poland. These studies unquestionably show that although we have been observing an increase in the number of internet users for many years, in the last two years, which is the time of the coronavirus epidemic, the percentage of internet users has increased by almost 10%. The percentage of people using the network wirelessly via devices such as smartphones, tablets and laptops is also growing. As a result, despite isolation or restrictions on direct contacts, most Poles were able to quickly, comfortably and safely meet many needs that do not require establishing a direct relationship. In addition, in real time they could obtain and transfer information whose content is not indifferent to the business process, including the purchase or sale process (references, recommendations). For enterprises, this meant the need to change the existing business models, the foundation of which was the creation of customer value based on the use of digital space (https://www.cbos.pl). The latest internet research shows that almost 79% of all Poles use the internet, with almost 25.5 million doing it every day (https:// pbi.org.pl). Thus, we can talk about the widespread use of the internet. This does not change the fact that the intensity of its use is mainly related to age and, in the case of older people, also to education (https://www.cbos.pl).

The vast majority of internet users use the internet to make purchases. The increase in interest in this form of purchase is supported by a 7% increase in the total number of adult online shoppers before and after the pandemic. The increase in interest in conducting a business relationship (purchase/sale) in the online form is also supported by the increase in online sales, which in the same period increases by 8% among all internet users and as much as 10% among adult internet users. This confirms the growing interest in this form of purchasing process. It is worth noting, however, that this does not translate positively into the previously presented indicators of the general economic climate in retail trade. In 2022, when the Russian Federation invaded Ukraine, a significant deterioration of this indicator was recorded again. However, it should be noted that most retail products can be offered and purchased online. It is therefore worth paying attention to the development of e-commerce in Poland (Fig. 1).

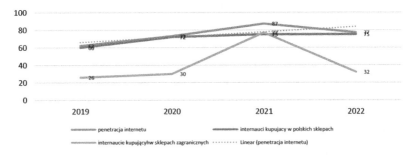

Fig. 1.   E-Commerce in Poland 2019–2022. *Source:* Authors' own elaboration based on publicly available data from e-Commerce Reports in Poland in 2019–2022.

The achieved dynamics of e-commerce growth in Poland is currently over 2.5 times higher than the European average, which puts us at the forefront of the continent in this respect (https://baselinker.com). As a result, according to the predictions of the above-mentioned report, the value of the e-commerce market in Poland in 2022 was to reach PLN 109 billion, which would be a 19% increase compared to 2021. Unfortunately, these were not accurate projections. In 2022, along with Russia's invasion of Ukraine, a sustained decline in the value of online sales was recorded, the share of which in June 2022 did not exceed 9% (stat.gov.pl).

Despite the Covid-19 pandemic, the financial situation of households in 2021 slightly improved. The level of the average monthly disposable income was 2.2% higher in real terms than the income from 2020. Over the same period, real spending was 3.5% higher than the previous year. It should be emphasised that in the analysed period, expenditure on consumer goods and services was higher by 3.6% (nominal 8.9%) in real terms than in the previous period. It should be emphasised, however, that although a slight increase in disposable income was maintained, the pandemic had a significant impact on both the level and structure of expenditure (Paździor and Majek, 2021). Starting from 2020, the share of expenses in disposable income is decreasing, and although we observe its increase in the following year it is small. These changes are undoubtedly related to the measures taken to limit the transmission of the coronavirus. Remote work and education, lack of travel opportunities, closure of hotels and catering outlets are just some of the reasons that affected the level of expenses. However, it is hard not to notice that along with the pandemic, pocket money decreases, the share of housing expenses, including energy, increases, but above all, inflation increases. This phenomenon is deepened by Russia's invasion of Ukraine. Its effect is a radical increase in energy prices, which affects the prices of all consumer goods and services.

All economies face this problem. Although in the initial period, inflation in Poland is one of the lowest in Europe, at the beginning of 2023, inflation in Poland was 17.2%. At this time, the rate of inflation in Poland was one of the highest in Europe – higher was only in Hungary 25.7%, Czech Republic 17.5%, Lithuania 21.5% or Latvia 20%. In the same period, in countries such as Germany (8.7%), France (6%) or Spain (5.9%), inflation does not exceed 10%. These countries were mostly dependent on supplies of raw materials (oil, gas) from Russia. However, it cannot be explained only by the increase in energy prices. Nevertheless, it can be concluded that this increase translates negatively into an increase in the prices of consumer goods and services, with a simultaneous decrease in the real income of the population, which could reduce the income and development potential of households, resulting in a slowdown in the economy and even recession.

Study Results

The presented research results allow us to conclude that both the pandemic and the outbreak of war had an impact on the relationship between the client and the company. The way of establishing relationships has changed as well as the implementation of the entire purchasing process, which, especially during the lockdown period, was carried out in the digital space. As a result, we are seeing a dynamic development of the e-commerce industry. However, it should be emphasised that the "loosening" of restrictions on the consumer goods market is accompanied by a decrease in the dynamics of online purchases/sales. It can therefore be concluded that in the coming years it should be expected that the discussed relations will be established and implemented in a hybrid form.

Although the pandemic has not disrupted the steady growth in household income since 2004, its dynamics have significantly slowed down. What's more, we are seeing an increase in the differences between the nominal and real value of these incomes. Inflation is on the rise, forcing households to change their spending structure and look for savings. It can therefore be assumed that in the next year the capital supply to many enterprises will not increase in real terms. Of course, there have been and will be companies that do not have to be significantly affected by the effects of these events. In this group, companies related to the provision of IT infrastructure and specialising in establishing multidimensional relationships in the digital space should be pointed out.

Discussion and Conclusions

After the pandemic subsides, long-term strategic changes may be needed to navigate the competitive landscape emerging in the "new normal" that is the result of technological, sociopolitical and institutional changes (Ahlstrom et al., 2020). The area of research may concern indications regarding the ability of companies that allow them to quickly and flexibly change their resources and capabilities in new conditions. It should be assumed that the post-pandemic and post-war reality will be very complex and dominated by various risk factors, which is a great challenge for companies, as they have to adapt to or shape their environment, while identifying, creating and using opportunities. It is essential to take into account the use of cognitive and emotional skills of stakeholders inside and outside the company (Hodgkinson and Healey, 2011).

A modern organisation should have a hybrid (Smith et al., 2019) character, as it must simultaneously face complex resource acquisition and organisational capacity development processes (i.e. orchestration of resources). Only such a flexible and ready to adapt company can meet the challenges of dynamically changing conditions (internal and external) of the company.

Note

1. The period during which it has not yet been officially diagnosed as a pandemic can be considered the initial stage of a pandemic, i.e. from the moment the first diagnosed case appeared (November 2019) to the official declaration of a pandemic by the WHO and the introduction of numerous lockdowns (March 2020) – cf. https://www.medicover.pl/o-zdrowiu/pandemia-koronawirusa-na-swie-cie-iw-polsce-kalendarium,7252,n,7,192 (accessed 2 March 2023).

References

Ahlstrom, D., Arregle, J.-L., Hitt, M. A., Qian, G., Ma, X. and Faems, D. (2020), "Managing Technological, Sociopolitical, and Institutional Change in the New Normal", *Journal of Management Studies*, Vol. 57, pp. 411–437.

Alpers, I. (2019), *Managing the "Unknowns": Exploring the Nature of Uncertainty and its Effects on Strategic Decisions* (Doctoral dissertation, University of St. Gallen). http://www1.unisg.ch/www/edis.nsf/SysLkpByIdentifier/4866/$FILE/dis4866.pdf

Barney, J. B. (2018), "Why Resource – Based Theory's Model of Profit Appropriation Must Incorporate a Stakeholder Perspective", *Strategic Management Journal*, Vol. 39, pp. 3305–3325.

Blatberg, R. C. and Deighton, J. (2001), "Manage Marketing by the Customer Equity Test", *Harvard Business Review*, Vol. 74, Juli-August, pp. 136–144.

Caputa, W. (2020), *Kapitał Klienta W Przestrzeni Wirtualnej*, Wyd. CeDeWu, Warszawa.

Caputa, W. and Krawczyk-Sokołowska, I. (2023, May), "Awareness of Network Security and Customer Value – The Company and Customer Perspective", *Technological Forecasting and Social Change*, Vol. 190, pp. 122430. https://doi.org/10.1016/j.techfore.2023.122430

Caputa, W., Krawczyk-Sokołowska, I. and Pierścieniak, A. (2021), "The Potential of Web Awareness as Determinant of Dually Defined Consumer Value", *Technological Forecasting and Social Change*, Vol. 163. https://doi.org/10.1016/j.techfore.2020.120443

Chadwick, A. (2007), Digital Network Repertoires and Organizational Hybridity, *Political Communication*, Vol. 24, No. 3, pp. 283–301, https://doi.org/10.1080/10584600701471666

Dalpiaz, E., Rindova, V. and Ravasi, D. (2016), "Combining Logics to Transform Organizational Agency: Blending Industry and Art at Alessi", *Administrative Science Quarterly*, Vol. 61, 347–392.

Dobiegała-Korona, B. and Herman, A. (2006), *Contemporary Sources of Enterprise Value*, Difin, Warsaw, p. 217 et seq.

Eggert, A. and Ulaga, W. (2002), "Customer Perceived Value: A Substitute for Satisfaction in Business Markets ?" *Journal of Business and Industrial Marketing*, Vol. 17, No. 2/3, pp. 107–118.

Grisaffe, D. and Kumar, D. B. (1998), *Antecedents and Consequences of Customer Value: Testing an Expanded Framework*, Working Paper 98-107, Marketing Science Institute, Cambidge.

Hitt, M. A., Sirmon, D. G., Li, Y., Ghobadian, A., Arregle, J.-F. and Xu, K. (2020), "Institutions, Industries and Entrepreneurial versus Advantage – Based Strategies: How Complex, Nested Environments Affect Strategic Choice", *Journal of Management & Governance*, https://doi.org/10.1007/s10997-020-09504-2

Hodgkinson, G. P. and Healey, M. (2011), "Psychological Foundations of Dynamic Capabilities: Reflexion and Reflection in Strategic Management", *Strategic Management Journal*, Vol. 32, pp. 15–16.

https://baselinker.com/pl-PL/blog/e-commerce-market-in-poland-trends-and-prospects-of-development/

https://businessinsider.com.pl/finanse/handel/oto-glowni-partnerzy-handlowi-polski-infografika/zvb80pr (accessed: 1 March 2023).

https://pbi.org.pl/badanie-mediapanel/wyniki-badania-mediapanel-za-grudzien-2022-informacja-prasowa/

https://stat.gov.pl/obszary-tematyczne/koniunktura/koniunktura/koniunktura-w-przetworstwo-przemyslowym-budownictwa-handlu- i-services-2000-2022-august-2022,4,64.html

https://www.bofit.fi/en/monitoring/weekly/2022/vw202227_v5/ (accessed: 1 March 2023).

https://www.britannica.com/event/2022-Russian-invasion-of-Ukraine (accessed: 3 March 2023).

https://www.cbos.pl/SPISKOM.POL/2022/K_077_22.PDF

https://www.gov.pl/web/koronawirus/

https://www.medicover.pl/o-zdrowiu/pandemia-koronawirusa-na-swiecie-iw-polsce-kalendarium,7252,n,192 (accessed: 2 March 2023).

https://www.osw.waw.pl/pl/publikacje/osw-comments/2022-05-06/production-and-export-food-from-ukraine-in-conditions-of-war

https://www.renewablematter.eu/articles/article/ukraine-all-lithium-reserves-and-mineral-resources-in-war-zones (accessed: 4 March 2023).

https://www.visualcapitalist.com/visualizing-the-worlds-largest-oil-producers/ (accessed 5 March 2023).

Kotler, Ph. and Bliemel, F. (2005), *Marketing-Management: Analyze, Planung und Verwirklichung*, 10. Foul., Stuttgart 2005, p. 58, R. Rust, KN Lemon, D. Narayandas, Customer Eguity Management, Pearson Prentice Hall, New Jersey.

Księżopolski, K. M. (2011), *Economic Security*, ELIPSA Publishing House, Warsaw, p. 32.

Long Nguyen, V. K., Hanh Le, T. M., Chau Tran, T. M., Hien Le, T. T., Mai Duong, T. N., Hien Le, T., Son Nguyen, T. and Hoa Vo, N. (2021), "Exploring the Impact of Pandemic on Global Economy: Perspective from Literatur Review", *Social Science and Humanities*, Vol. 29 No. 3, pp. 2074–2080.

Październik, A. and Majek, A. (2021), "Impact of COVID-19 on Household's Financial Situation in Poland", *European Research Studies Journal*, Vol. 24, No. 2, pp. 492–502.

Peschke, M. A. (1997), "Wertorientierte Strategiebewertung, Wiesbadden 1997, zugl. diss. Dortmund 1997, Peschke MA, Strategische Ziele im Value Management", in: *Praxis des Stretegische Managements: Konzepte-Erfahrungen-Perspektiven* eds. Welge, M. K., Al-Laham, A. and Kajüter, P. Wiesbaden 2000, pp. 95–112.

Polish Foreign Trade Compendium, Polish Development Fund (2022, April), pp. 14–16. https://pfr.pl/dam/jcr:a1156776-0c62-4599-a037-4504e100bc3/PFR_KompendiumHZ_202204.pdf (accessed: 1 March 2023).

Rudolf-Sipotz, E. (2001), *Kundenwert: Konzeption - Determinanten – Management*, Verlag Thexis, ISBN 3908545773, 9783908545774.

Smith, W. K. and Besharov, M. L. (2019), "Bowing before Dual Gods: How Structured Flexibility Sustains Organizational Hybridity", *Administrative Science Quarterly*, Vol. 64 No. 1, pp. 1–44.

Sniazhko, S. (2019), "Uncertainty in Decision-Making: A Review of the International Business Literature", *Cogent Business & Management*, Vol. 6, https://doi.org/10.1080/23311975.2019.1650692

Ulaga, W. and Eggert, A. (2005), "Relationship Value in Business Markts – The Construct and its Dimensions", *Journal of Business-To-Business Marketing*, Vol. 12, No. 1, pp. 73–99.

Wry, T., Lounsbury, M. and Jennings, P. D. (2014), "Hybrid Vigor: Securing Venture Capital by Spanning Categories in Nanotechnology", *Academy of Management Journal*, Vol. 57, 1309–1333.

Żukrowska, K. (2013), "Economics as the Sphere of State Security", in: *Interdisciplinarity of Security Sciences* Eds. K. Raczkowski, K. Żukrowska and M. Żuber, Difin, Warsaw.

Chapter 6

Food Security Through the COVID-19 Crisis and Beyond – Poland: A Case Study

Aleksandra Kowalska, Sophia Lingham, Damian Maye and Louise Manning

Abstract

Research Background: Applying mitigation measures during the COVID-19 pandemic resulted in 'locking down' of economies, and disrupted agri-food markets worldwide. Income losses and food price increases negatively affected food security. The 'stay-at-home' policy led some households towards a positive shift in eating habits and maintaining these changes could contribute to better nutrition. The Russia–Ukraine war and soaring energy and food prices contributes further to the pressure on the global food system and urgency to consider longer term resilience capacities of national food systems.

Purpose of the Chapter: The aim of the chapter is to identify and review food security challenges that governments and societies have faced during the COVID-19 crisis and beyond, with specific emphasis on Poland.

Methodology: The methodological approach was to undertake a narrative literature review and to analyse a number of indicators relating to food security at the national level. These were quantified using data from Economist Impact, the World Bank, the European Commission, FAOSTAT and Statistics Poland.

Findings: The 2019–2022 Global Food Security Index for Poland remained quite stable, but the number of food insecure people increased significantly. Hence, urgent government measures are needed to ensure food security for all. Since 2021, high food inflation has reduced food affordability and is expected to remain high due to the Russia-Ukraine war, market pressures on energy prices and climate-related weather conditions. Greater food self-sufficiency in Poland is a key strategy to build up the resilience of the national food system.

Modeling Economic Growth in Contemporary Poland, 89–108
doi:10.1108/978-1-83753-654-220231006

Keywords: Food security; COVID-19 pandemic; food supply; food prices; war; food consumption

Introduction

Security is a cornerstone of human and social development. Food security is ensured when 'all people, at all times, have physical, social and economic access to sufficient, safe and nutritious food that meets their dietary needs and food preferences for an active and healthy life' (CFS, 2014, p. 2). Everyone has a right to adequate food, as declared in the United Nations Universal Declaration of Human Rights of 10 December 1948 that applies to 193 countries which have obligations to provide food security for all (Kowalski and Kowalska, 2022). It represents, therefore, a basic human right. Food supply is adequate when it is sufficient with regards to quality, quantity, safety, variety and socio-cultural acceptability (Pangaribowo et al., 2013; Weingärtner, 2010). Only sustainable food systems can provide food security, being a public good that a purely market mechanism alone cannot supply (Kowalska et al., 2022; Zhang et al. 2022).

There is a particular challenge with ensuring food security in times of crisis, such as the financial crisis of 2007–2008, the COVID-19 pandemic or the ongoing climate-change crisis. It is impossible to provide public goods to all citizens at the appropriate level, including food security and sustainable development, without a strong public sector involvement. However, the responsibility for providing these goods is divided between different actors in a food system, including governments, non-governmental organisations, private companies and individuals (Kowalska et al., 2022; Oosterveer et al., 2014).

The World Health Organisation (WHO) determined COVID-19 as a pandemic on 11 March 2020 (WHO, 2020) and global priority was given to mitigating the threat of the pandemic. Globally, as of 28 February 2023, there have been over 758.3 million confirmed cases of COVID-19, including over 6.8 million deaths reported to WHO, and about 13.2 billion vaccine doses have been administered (WHO, 2023). Almost 1,19,000 people died due to COVID-19 in Poland (0.3% of the population). Over the period March 2020–December 2021, government COVID-19 related policies varied between countries and regions and have differed over consecutive waves of the pandemic and also between them. The containment and closure policy responses in Poland, and many other countries, included: schools and workplaces closing, cancelling public events, restrictions on gatherings, public transport networks closing, stay-at-home requirements, restrictions on internal movements and international travel controls (Hale et al., 2021). National health policy agendas comprised a mix of public information campaigns, testing policy, contact tracing after a positive diagnosis, emergency investment in healthcare, investment in vaccine development, facial coverings policy, vaccine delivery for different groups and protection for elderly and vulnerable people (Hale et al., 2021). The COVID-19 pandemic has contributed to a re-assessment of the role of 'government' and by inference, governance structures in most countries. The pandemic outbreak created extraordinary fiscal pressures for governments, requiring additional expenditure to mitigate the health and socio-economic consequences of the pandemic while at the same time the 'closing-down' of economies meant government tax revenues were falling (OECD, 2021a; Utz et al., 2020). General government expenditures increased in 2020 in all European countries, notably due to extensive spending on healthcare, higher non-repayable subsides granted to companies and income support for citizens suffering from the impact of the pandemic (OECD, 2021a).

As a consequence of 'locking down' economies agricultural and food markets faced major disruptions which affected the state of food and nutrition security. Operators in food supply chains have always faced disruptions arising from many types of events, including natural disasters, insect and rodent plagues, manmade events and industrial accidents, the latter leading to potential food safety and quality problems, e.g. adulterated food products (Ketchen and Craighead, 2020; Manning, 2021). Wieland (2021) reports that disruptions sparked by the pandemic resulted in the closure of numerous factories, and led to the loss of key suppliers, a problem which increased and impacted further as the pandemic elongated, disrupting existing supply chain relationships. The policy of closure showed the key role of food self-sufficiency in ensuring food security in times of crisis. The impact of the pandemic on all nations has been profound, potentially setting back the global delivery of the Sustainable Development Goals by 2030, specifically those related to food security and climate change (Fenner and Cerney, 2021). Furthermore, the Russia-Ukraine armed conflict and associated soaring food and input prices across the world continues to materially and financially stress the global food system, with food security consequently deteriorating in many countries globally for the last three years, starting in 2020 (EI, 2023a; Hellegers, 2022).

The aim of chapter is to identify and review food security challenges that governments and societies have faced during the COVID-19 crisis and beyond, with specific emphasis on Poland as a case study to help ground nexus relations in one particular political and social economy. The chapter is structured as follows: it firstly introduces the research context and food systems approach. In the second section, the influence of the COVID-19 pandemic on food security in both developed and developing countries is explored, leading to the third section where the methodological approach is described. The fourth section considers Poland's performance during the pandemic, particularly its response to food security. The fifth section concludes the chapter, including future lessons for food system resilience and capacity building.

Research Background

Food Systems: The Impact of COVID-19 on Food and Nutrition Security

The literature on the impacts of the COVID-19 pandemic on food systems and food security, including governments' policy responses on both the demand side and the supply side of the market, is extensive and expansive, ranging from system-level analysis to analysis and case studies of specific interventions and responses. The effects of demand and supply-side government policy interventions are synthesised in Table 1. The impacts of the pandemic on food supply arose in both developed and developing countries and varied across the world, being particularly severe for net food importing countries. The changes in consumer behaviour differed between lower income countries and higher income countries. Most of the effects of the pandemic that arose during the first lockdown periods lasted for a short time but had further consequences related to the food security situation across the world, related to, inter alia, food prices and consumer behaviour. These two aspects are considered further now.

Some analysts argue that COVID-19 demonstrated that food systems are effectively broken (Shanks et al., 2020), but this assertion is framed primarily through the lens of health inequalities and their relationship to the food system. Further studies suggest that due to government policy responses linked to the pandemic, a significant number of households have been exposed to reduced incomes in both developed and developing countries (Table 1), resulting in limited consumers' ability to buy adequate food. However, lockdowns or restrictions on movement have varied substantially by country and consequently the scale of the problem of income loss has been different across the world. In general, the world gross domestic product (GDP) per capita (constant 2017 international $) decreased by 3.01% between 2019 and 2020, but increased by 6% between 2020 and 2021 (WB, 2023b). This suggests on the one hand that the loss of income due to the COVID-19 crisis was a passing problem, and on the other that the average figure masks inequalities between those who did well during the crisis and those who were severely negatively affected.

Food access depends on the ability of people or households to obtain food, and this ability is determined by incomes and food prices. The FAO (2021, p. 1) stated that *while the global agri-food systems have remained resilient, income losses and food price spikes caused undernourishment to rise.* Indeed, the COVID-19 pandemic has contributed to the largest single-year increase in global hunger in decades. In 2020, there were 161 million more food-insecure people across the world than in 2019 (FAO, 2021). The FAO Food Price Index was up by 6.5% in December 2020 from its December 2019 value (FAO, 2020). The FAO Food Price Index has continued to rise through 2021 and into 2022. This index increased further by 20.7% over the period February 2021–February 2022 (FAO, 2022), undermining financial access to food for more vulnerable people. This was mainly a result of the pandemic and the pandemic-related restrictions (e.g. food export restrictions, restrictions on movement resulting in rising freight costs) (FREIGHTOS DATA, 2023; Kowalska et al., 2022). The key factor for the accelerated food prices was also a considerable increase in fossil fuel-based fertiliser prices (the price tripled over the period 2020–2022) (WB, 2023a). The FAO Food Price Index rose in February and March 2022 due to the outbreak of war in Ukraine but then fell markedly in the latter part of 2022, in particular Vegetable Oils Price Index (FAO, 2023). The overall FAO Food Price Index averaged 143.7 points in 2022, up by 14.3% from 2021, by 46.5% from 2020 and by 51.1% from 2019 (FAO, 2023), which supports the statement that food security situation has been deteriorating across the world for the last 3 years (EI, 2023a).

Table 1. Impacts of COVID-19 Pandemic on Food System in Developing and Developed Countries During the First Lockdown Periods.

Effect of the Pandemic	Country's Level of Development		Source
	Developed	Developing	
Impact on the supply side of food market			
Labour:	x	x	Laborde et al. (2020),
• Shortage on farms which caused crops to remain unharvested at the field level (farmers and farm workers were infected, potential farm workers were subject to travel restrictions, farmers and workers might have temporarily needed to self-isolate).			OECD (2021b), Prosser et al. (2022), Yaddanapudi and Mishra (2022), Zhu et al. (2022)
• Shortage in meat processing plants which forced them to operate at reduced capacity and left producers on farm with unsold mature animals that they had to feed.			
• Disruptions to container and truck transport of food due to limitations on crew changes, additional screening and mandatory quarantines.			
Logistics:	x	x	Laborde et al. (2020),
• Disrupted supply chains of specialised products that rely on air freight (high-value perishable horticultural products). Reduced number of tourism			OECD (2021b), Deconinck et al. (2020), Prosser et al. (2022), Rahimi et al. (2022), Kowalska et al. (2022)

Table 1. *(Continued)*

Effect of the Pandemic	Country's Level of Development		Source
	Developed	Developing	

related flights led to disruption of food supply as food was not transported.
- Introducing food export restrictions to protect domestic consumers; food importing countries were most affected.
- Border closures and delays in border inspections due to illness and social distancing requirements led to consignments being stuck in transit.
- Unsold commodities on farms that relied on supply routed to the hospitality sector, schools or restaurants which were temporarily closed and there were limited options to pivot commodities to alternative chains.
- Reduced quality, productivity and competitiveness of animal production systems caused by disruptions of animal feed supply chain, limited access to animal farming related services and animal health services,

Table 1. *(Continued)*

Effect of the Pandemic	Country's Level of Development		Source
	Developed	Developing	
decreased market opportunities for live-stock producers; export markets disrupted and little capacity in local markets.			
Finance: • Commodity and resource price insta-bility that affected cash flow, profitability and business viability.	x	x	Laborde et al. (2020)
Impact on the demand side of food market			
Financial: • Loss of consumers' income and assets that prejudiced the ability to buy food. • Increase in shopping online and buying in bulk where consumers' finances allowed. • Shifts in consumer demand towards cheaper and less nutri-tious foods in house-holds from lower socio-economic back-grounds. Eating less frequently and lesser amount during lock-downs in order to save food for later.	x	x	Béné et al. (2021), E.I.T Food (2020), Laborde et al. (2020), Hirvonen et al. (2021), Janssen et al. (2021), O'Meara et al. (2022)
Sustainable: • Enhanced consumer awareness of food waste. Increased	x	x	Burlea-Schiopoiu et al. (2021), E.I.T Food (2020), FSA (2021), O'Meara et al. (2022), Rodgers

Table 1. *(Continued)*

Effect of the Pandemic	Country's Level of Development		Source
	Developed	Developing	
awareness of the environmental consequences of food waste. Positive behavioural changes regarding food waste which differ by sociodemographic characteristics.			et al. (2021), Qian et al. (2020)
Sustainable: • Growing interest in healthy and sustainable diet. Shopping more locally to support local producers and not to travel further.	x		E.I.T Food (2020), Grunert et al. (2022), The Guardian (2020), FSA (2021), O'Meara et al. (2022)
Behaviour (general): • Increase in consumption of food products in almost every category (not in convenience foods). • Eating at home far more often that in the past. • Increase in spending time cooking. A sharp decline of sales of food away from home (consumed in restaurants, hotels, catering and cafés). • An increased level of consciousness among consumers regarding food safety issues and food prices.	x		E.I.T Food (2020), OECD (2021b), Acosta Market Research (2020), Grunert et al. (2022), Kitz et al. (2022)

Source: Authors' own elaboration based on publicly available data.

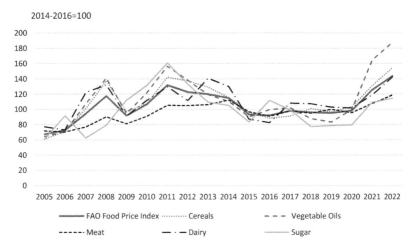

Fig. 1.   The FAO Food Price Index and FAO Food Commodity Price Indices from 2005 to 2022. *Source:* Authors' own elaboration based on publicly available data from (FAO, 2023).

Over the past 20 years or so, only three episodes of high food prices occurred, in 2007–2008, 2010–2011 and 2021–2022, which were periods of economic and social crisis (FAO, 2023) (Fig. 1). The likelihood of sudden price increases in the future is increasing due to the unpredictability linked to climate change which has increased volatility in food production and prices.

The first COVID-19-related lockdown caused a major shift in food-related consumer behaviour in several countries, including Poland (Acosta Market Research, 2020; Grunert et al., 2022; E.I.T. Food, 2020). The stay-at-home policy contributed to consumer behaviour changes forcing consumers to cook and eat most meals at home, a phenomenon called 'corona cooking' by Grunert et al. (2022). Social distancing led to working from home becoming the 'new norm' (Antonacopoulou and Georgiadou, 2021). The results of a survey conducted in Poland, Finland, Germany, France, Greece, Italy, Spain, Sweden and Romania in September 2020 indicated a number of trends (E.I.T Food, 2020): (1) enjoying food and diversified diet; (2) developing cooking skills; (3) giving priority to accessible food stores and access to food at affordable prices; (4) growing importance of healthy diet and healthy body weight; (5) being willing to buy more local food and reduce unsustainable packaging and food waste. Long-lasting remote working and remote learning have had an impact on sustaining these trends. Maintaining them could bring a higher level of nutrition security in households. Grunert et al. (2022) state that whilst being disruptive, the pandemic can be considered as an 'agent of change' and can form a foundation for emergent policy. Both health and environmental issues associated with food production and consumption were re-evaluated during the pandemic which has stimulated interest in organic food in several European countries including the United Kingdom and Poland (Wojciechowska-Solis et al., 2022). These new dietary patterns have created new scope for promoting a sustainable diet which contributes to ensuring food security of present and future generations.

Hence, there have been both positive and negative effects of the pandemic on societies. This crisis situation has created further threats to food and nutrition security, but it has also opened new opportunities regarding the nutritional dimension of food security due to changing consumer behaviour. This theory frames the study that we undertook here, with a particular focus on food security in the Polish context.

Methodology

To assess how Poland and other countries managed the consequences of government policy responses to the COVID-19 pandemic in respect of ensuring food security, and since that time have managed the outbreak of war between Russia and Ukraine, a narrative literature review was undertaken in 2021–2022. To supplement and triangulate the review findings, a number of food (in)security indicators were identified and analysed. These were quantified using the data of Economist Impact, the World Bank, the European Commission, FAOSTAT and Statistics Poland. The study focused on measuring food security at national level but there is also a need to measure individual and household food security, and this might be considered in future studies.

The first indicator considered was the Global Food Security Index (GFSI) which measures the efficiency of the food security system of a country and ranks 113 countries according to their food security performance. The GFSI comprises several dozen indexes grouped in four categories: (1) food affordability, (2) availability, (3) quality and safety and (4) sustainability and adaptation (Economist Impact (EI), 2023b). The *food affordability score* measures the ability of consumers to buy food and is mainly determined by changes in food prices, GDP per capita and the size of the population living under the global poverty line. The *food availability score* measures food supply sufficiency, agricultural output and on-farm capabilities and research efforts to increase agricultural production. The *food quality and safety score* measures the variety and nutritional quality of average diets, as well as the safety of food including water. The *sustainability and adaptation sub-index* assesses a country's exposure to the effects of climate change, its susceptibility and adaptive capacity to natural resource risks, and to demographic stresses (Economist Impact (EI), 2023a; Kowalska et al., 2022; Kowalski and Kowalska, 2022). These criteria fit within the four pillars of food security, i.e. availability related to food supply, access regarding ability to obtain that food, utilisation related to nutrition value and vulnerability (physical, environmental, economic, social and health risks affecting availability, access and use) (WFP, 2006).

GFSI is a synthetic index; thus, in order to gain a better insight into food security situation in Poland, we identified a number of specific indicators that determine the overall food security environment. The first specific indictor that can be used to measure the risk of food insecurity in a given country is *domestic food price inflation* which is measured as the year-on-year change in the food component of a country's Consumer Price Index (CPI) (WB, 2023a). CPI is calculated as a weighted average of the percentage price changes for a specific basket of consumer products of the following 12 categories: food and non-alcoholic beverages; alcoholic beverages; clothing and footwear; housing, water, electricity, gas and other fuels; furnishings, household equipment and routine household maintenance; health; transport; communication; recreation and culture; education; restaurants and hotels; miscellaneous goods and services (IMF, 2023).

The second specific indicator that can be used to determine the food security situation in an international food crisis situation is *food self-sufficiency*. This is defined by the ratio of food production to food consumption at the domestic level. The country is self-sufficient when domestic food production equals or exceeds 100% of the country's food consumption (Clapp, 2017). The self-sufficiency of a given country is usually assessed for individual products groups.

Results

Comparison of the country-specific GFSI values of 2019 with the figures of 2020 reveals that the food security situation in more than half of the 113 countries considered (55.8%) deteriorated during the pandemic (Kowalski and Kowalska, 2022). The number of countries whose overall GFSI scores have declined between 2020 and 2021 was the same, but the actual countries affected differed between the 2019–2020 and 2020–2021 list, suggesting that cultural differences, and the effects of the pandemic and the pandemic-related restrictions varied over time. Furthermore, some countries have proved to be resilient to the crisis because they were able to bounce back in terms of their food security situation (their GFSI score went down in 2020 and then up in 2021). These include Haiti, Nigeria, Ethiopia, Kenya, Myanmar, El Salvador, Malaysia, Turkey, China, Denmark and the Netherlands. However, the food security situation went down dramatically in Nigeria between 2021 and 2022 which was partly the result of the disruptions in the Black Sea region and a significant increase in food prices. The GFSI for Poland slightly dropped in 2020, but then increased to the 2019 level (EI, 2023a).

In 2022, Poland was ranked 21st in the GFSI ranking but the country was ranked 15th in terms of food quality and safety (which can be attributed to high nutritional standards and protein quality), although Poland's performance in the food safety score has deteriorated over the past 10 years and is below the global average (EI, 2023b). Poland ranked 17th in terms of sustainability and adaptation mainly due to the high level of political commitment to adaptation in the agricultural sector and good disaster risk management. When comparing the four scores for three chosen EU countries, Finland with the highest GFSI (first position in the world), Poland with the average overall score in the EU and Romania

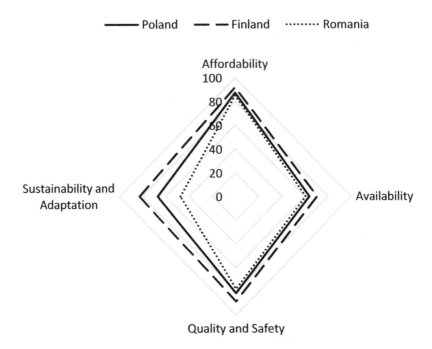

Fig. 2.   The Four GFSI's Sub-indicators for Poland, Finland and Romania in 2022. *Source:* Authors' own elaboration based on publicly available data from (EI, 2023a).

– the bottom country with the lowest GFSI in the EU (45th position in the world), it demonstrates that the main difference affecting the scoring of the food security outcomes lies in performing well in the sustainability and adaptation score (EI, 2023a) (Fig. 2). However, the performance of Poland in this score is pulled down by a very weak score in the indicator that measures the health of oceans, rivers and lakes. Availability is the weakest pillar for Poland due to moderate scores in agricultural R&D, farm infrastructure and volatility of agricultural production, and a very low score in food security and access policy commitments (EI, 2023b).

When considering the individual indexes that contribute to GFSI, it is evident that GDP per capita (constant 2017 international $) fell down by 2.4% in Poland in 2020 due to the COVID-19 crisis which could have endangered the access to food. This has been the first drop in GDP since 1991. GDP per capita in Poland went up again between 2020 and 2021 (by 7.3%) (WB, 2023c). Furthermore, the number of moderately and severely food insecure people in Poland increased considering the 3-year average values for the 2017–2019 period (1.6 million people; 4.2% of the population), the 2018–2020 period (2.2 million; 5.7%) and 2019–2021 period (2.8 million; 7.3%). It is worth noting that the number of moderately and severely food insecure people in Poland went down in each of the three previous 3-year periods, i.e. 2012–2014, 2013–2015, 2014–2016 (FAOSTAT. 2023). It can be suggested that food security situation of some Polish households was precarious due to the COVID-19 crisis.

We agree with Seiler (2020, 13) that *measuring and interpreting inflation is challenging during economic disruptions in general and the COVID-19 crisis in particular.* The fact is that food price inflation rates have continued to remain very high in Poland and the EU since 2021. The value for Poland was ca. 6 percentage points higher than the EU average in 2022 (Fig. 3). In Poland, the annual food inflation rate rose more rapidly in 2021, partially due to the greater share of food in consumer spending than the EU average. High food price inflation rates have been reducing food affordability in Poland and many other countries. The effects of high food inflation on child nutrition can be particularly severe. Surging domestic food and energy prices are key drivers of general inflation in Poland and other countries. Furthermore, high inflation and high interest rates, reduced investment and disruptions caused by the war between Russia and Ukraine have been the main reasons for slowing global growth. It is expected that food prices will remain high because of the Russia-Ukraine war, energy costs and extreme weather events as climate change progresses (WB, 2023a) and this level of disruption and the socio-economic vulnerability it creates should be taken into consideration by policy-makers and business people.

Considering production volumes and in-country demand of individual agricultural commodities in Poland over the period 2019–2020 shows that the level of self-sufficiency was high for many of the products concerned. These included eggs,

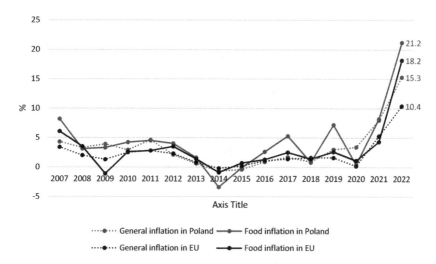

Fig. 3.   Annual Inflation Rates Comparing December Values in Poland and the EU Over the Period 2007–2022. *Source:* Authors' own elaboration based on publicly available data from (EC, 2023).

Table 2. Food Self-Sufficiency Ratios for Poland Over the Period 2019–2020.

	Production (in thousand tonnes)	In-Country demand (in thousand tonnes)	Self-Sufficiency (%)
Eggs	703	408	172.3
Sugar	2,075	1,522	136.3
Maize	3,734	2,816	132.6
Cereals	25,135	21,608	116.3
Vegetables	5,019	4,806	104.4
Dried pulses	380	374	101.6
Potatoes	6,600	6,566	100.5
Oleaginous seeds and fruit	2,432	2,787	97.3
Fruit	3,964	4,266	92.9
Vegetable fats and oils	1,162	1,983	58.6
	Production (in million litres)	In-country demand (in million litres)	Self-sufficiency (%)
Milk	14,456	11,054	130.8

Source: Authors' own elaboration based on publicly available data from (Statistics Poland, 2021).

sugar, maize, milk and cereals. Poland is also self-sufficient in vegetables, dried pulses and potatoes. However, Poland does not produce enough fruit, vegetable fats and oils and oleaginous seeds (e.g. rape, sunflower, soya bean, flax, groundnut, poppy seed, sesame) to meet consumption needs (Table 2). The self-sufficiency ratios for these commodities (below 100%) indicate that Poland relies on imports to meet demand. This might endanger the state of food security in terms of nutrients in the times of crisis. High self-sufficiency ratios for the majority of products provide for resiliency from volatility on international food markets, but also can create vulnerability in the event of a weather or disease incident within the geographic boundaries of Poland.

Summary

The COVID-19 pandemic, and mitigating measures introduced to control spread and impact of the virus, disrupted most facets of social and political economy globally and nationally. Impacts on food systems and the provision and access to food were to some extent no different, but for some economies and sectors of society the impacts were profound and deeply impactful, revealing wider weaknesses in food system resilience, social support frameworks and security. Impacts on agri-food markets have, thus, contributed to and instigated a re-assessment of the role of a state (government) in ensuring food and nutrition security for all, both globally and at the nation state level. Food security underpins growth and development within each country. 'Locking down' of economies resulted in labour shortages in the agri-food industry, disrupted supply chains, reduced quality, productivity and competitiveness of food production systems, and led to financial uncertainty. Income losses and food price increases that started in 2020 negatively affected food and nutrition security in many countries across the world. Remote working and remote learning led some consumers in European countries, including Poland, towards a positive shift in eating habits and maintaining them going forward could bring a higher level of nutrition security.

The GFSI for Poland remained quite stable over the period 2019–2022, although analysis of GFSI sub-indices shows several areas for improvement, i.e. food safety mechanisms, the health of rivers and lakes, agricultural R&D and farm infrastructure. When considering the number of moderately and severely food insecure people in Poland, a 75% growth in this figure is observed between 2017–2019 and 2019–2021 periods. This situation is alarming and warrants the application of well-thought-out government measures. Very high food price inflation rates have reduced food affordability in Poland and many other countries since 2021. Furthermore, the projections show that food prices will remain high because of the Russia-Ukraine war, energy costs and climate-related extreme weather events. Becoming isolated from eating out and developing cooking skills during the pandemic might contribute to maintaining a high level of nutrition security in a situation when inflation is high. High self-sufficiency ratios for the majority of food products allows Poland to buffer itself from volatility on international agri-food markets but this makes Poland more vulnerable in terms of capacities to adjust to difficult weather conditions and manage the events of animal or plant disease within the country.

The Polish government has focused on developing social policy in recent years. Given that there are three classes of food system policies, i.e. economy-wide policies, policies directed specifically at increasing food supply or improving the supply chain and safety nets for households (Savary et al., 2020), safety net policies dominate in Poland. These latter policies include minimum wage and welfare laws, social security system changes, food vouchers, etc. aiming at changing household access to food in the short term, but also causing food price increases and dissatisfaction of some groups in the society, e.g. people running small and medium-sized enterprises. Economy-wide policies, which include trade, price, tax and monetary policies, are thus equally important at times of crisis and influence the food and nutrition security situation in the longer term. Whilst policy aimed at providing a short-term safety net is essential to prevent hunger, in itself it does little to address the structural weaknesses in food systems. Policy-makers need to address the limitations of our current food systems to deliver food security in terms of access for all to affordable, nutritious and safe food. The examples used in the chapter demonstrate the complexity of this challenge and that an integrated stakeholder-led approach needs to be adopted at regional and national level to assure food security for all.

References

Acosta Market Research (2020), *New Acosta Report Details How COVID-19 Is Reinventing How America Eats*, available at https://www.acosta.com/news/new-acosta-report-details-how-covid-19-is-reinventing-how-america-eats (accessed 28 November 2021).

Antonacopoulou, E. P. and Georgiadou, A. (2021), "Leading through Social Distancing: The Future of Work, Corporations and Leadership from Home", *Gender, Work and Organization*, Vol. 28, pp. 749–767, https://doi.org/10.1111/gwao.12533

Béné, C., Bakker, D., Chavarro, M. J., Even, B., Melo, J. and Sonneveld, A. (2021), "Global Assessment of the Impacts of COVID-19 on Food Security", *Global Food Security*, Vol. 31, Article 100575, https://doi.org/10.1016/j.gfs.2021.100575

Burlea-Schiopoiu, A., Ogarca, R. F., Barbu, C. M., Craciun, L., Baloi, I. C. and Mihai, L. S. (2021), "The Impact of COVID-19 Pandemic on Food Waste Behaviour of Young People", *Journal of Cleaner Production*, Vol. 294, Article 126333. https://doi.org/10.1016/j.jclepro.2021.126333

Clapp, J. (2017), "Food Self-Sufficiency: Making Sense of it, and when it Makes Sense", *Food Policy*, Vol. 66, pp. 88–96, https://doi.org/10.1016/j.foodpol.2016.12.001

Committee on World Food Security (CFS) (2014), Global Strategic Framework for Food Security and Nutrition (GSF), available at http://www.fao.org/fileadmin/templates/cfs/Docs1314/GSF/GSF_Version_3_EN.pdf (accessed 1 January 2021).

Deconinck, K., Avery, E. and Jackson, L. A. (2020), "Food Supply Chains and Covid-19: Impacts and Policy Lessons", *EuroChoices*, Vol. 19 No. 3, pp. 34–39. https://doi.org/10.1111/1746-692X.12297

Economist Impact (EI) (2023a), Global Food Security Index 2022, available at https://impact.economist.com/sustainability/project/food-security-index/ (accessed:22 January 2023).

Economist Impact (EI) (2023b), *Country Report: Poland. Global Food Security Index 2022*, available at https://impact.economist.com/sustainability/project/food-security-index/reports/Economist_Impact_GFSI_2022_Poland_country_report_Sep_2022.pdf (accessed:30 January 2023).

E.I.T. Food (2020), *COVID-19 Impact on Consumer Food Behaviours in Europe*, available at https://www.eitfood.eu/media/news-pdf/COVID-19_Study_-_European_Food_Behaviours_-_Report.pdf (accessed 29 November 2021).

European Commission (EC) (2023), Consumer Food Inflation Snapshot, available at https://agridata.ec.europa.eu/extensions/FoodSecurity/FoodSecurity.html# (accessed 25 January 2023).

FAOSTAT (2023), Poland, available at https://www.fao.org/faostat/en/#country/173 (accessed 24 January 2023).

Fenner, R. and Cernev, T. (2021), "The Implications of the Covid-19 Pandemic for Delivering the Sustainable Development Goals", *Futures*, Vol. 128, Article 102726. https://doi.org/10.1016/j.futures.2021.102726

Food and Agricultural Organisation (FAO) (2023), FAO Food Price Index, available at https://www.fao.org/worldfoodsituation/foodpricesindex/en/ (accessed 30 January 2023).

Food and Agricultural Organisation (FAO) (2020, December 3), FAO - News Article: FAO Food Price Index Rises Sharply, available at http://www.fao.org/news/story/en/item/1334280/icode/ (accessed 29 September 2021).

Food and Agricultural Organisation (FAO) (2021), FAO's Response to COVID-19: Building to Transform, available at https://www.fao.org/3/ng635en/ng635en.pdf (accessed 30 November 2021).

Food and Agricultural Organisation (FAO) (2022), World Food Situation, available at https://www.fao.org/worldfoodsituation/foodpricesindex/en/ (accessed 18 March 2022).

Food Standards Agency (FSA) (2021), Food in a Pandemic, available at https://www.food.gov.uk/research/research-projects/food-in-a-pandemic (accessed 26 June 2021).

FREIGHTOS DATA (2023), Freightos Baltic Index (FBX): Global Container Freight Index, available at https://fbx.freightos.com/ (accessed 25 January 2023).

Grunert, K. G., Janssen, M., Christensen, R. N., Teunissen, L., Cuykx, I., Decorte, P., Lucia, A. and Reisch, L. A. (2022), ""Corona Cooking": The Interrelation between Emotional Response to the First Lockdown during the COVID-19 Pandemic and Cooking Attitudes and Behaviour in Denmark", *Food Quality and Preference*, Vol. 96, Article 104425. https://doi.org/10.1016/j.foodqual.2021.104425

Hale, T., Angrist, N., Goldszmidt, R., Kira, B., Petherick, A., Phillips, T., Webster, S., Cameron-Blake, E., Hallas, L., Majumdar, S. and Tatlow, H. (2021), "A Global Panel Database of Pandemic Policies (Oxford COVID-19 Government Response Tracker)", *Nature Human Behaviour*, Vol. 5, pp. 529–538. https://doi.org/10.1038/s41562-021-01079-8

Hellegers, P. (2022), "Food Security Vulnerability Due to Trade Dependencies on Russia and Ukraine", *Food Security*, Vol. 14, No. 6, pp. 1503–1510. https://doi.org/10.1007/s12571-022-01306-8

Hirvonen, K., De Brauw, A. and Abate, G. T. (2021), "Food Consumption and Food Security during the COVID-19 Pandemic in Addis Ababa", *American Journal of Agricultural Economics*, Vol. 103 No. 3, pp. 772–789. https://doi.org/10.1111/ajae.12206

International Monetary Fund (IMF) (2023), Consumer Price Index (CPI), available at https://data.imf.org/?sk=4FFB52B2-3653-409A-B471-D47B46D904B5 (accessed 26 January 2023).

Janssen, M., Chang, B. P. I., Hristov, H., Pravst, I., Profeta, A. and Millard, J. (2021), "Changes in Food Consumption During the COVID-19 Pandemic: Analysis of Consumer Survey Data From the First Lockdown Period in Denmark, Germany, and Slovenia", *Frontiers in Nutrition*, Vol. 8, Article 635859. https://doi.org/10.3389/fnut.2021.635859

Ketchen Jr, D. J. and Craighead, C. W. (2020), "Research at the Intersection of Entrepreneurship, Supply Chain Management, and Strategic Management: Opportunities Highlighted by COVID-19", *Journal of Management*, Vol. 46 No. 8, pp. 1330–1341. https://doi.org/10.1177/0149206320945028

Kitz, R., Walker, T., Charlebois, S. and Music, J. (2022). "Food Packaging during the COVID-19 Pandemic: Consumer Perceptions", *International Journal of Consumer Studies*, Vol. 46 No. 2, pp. 434–448. https://doi.org/10.1111/ijcs.12691

Kowalska, A., Budzyńska, A. and Białowąs, T. (2022), "Food Export Restrictions during the COVID-19 Pandemic: Real and Potential Effects on Food Security",

International Journal of Management and Economics, Vol. 58 No. 3, pp. 1–16. https://doi.org/10.2478/ijme-2022-0023

Kowalski, J. and Kowalska, A. (2022), "The Realization of the Human Right to Food: Preliminary Remarks on Assessing Food Security", *Przegląd Prawno-Ekonomiczny*, Vol. 1, pp. 9–31. https://doi.org/10.31743/ppe.13009

Laborde, D., Martin, W., Swinnen, J. and Vos, R. (2020), "COVID-19 Risks to Global Food Security", *Science*, Vol. 369 No. 6503, pp. 500–502. https://doi.org/10.1126/science.abc4765

Manning, L. (2021), "Safeguard Global Supply Chains during a Pandemic", *Nature Food*, Vol. 2, Article 10. https://doi.org/10.1038/s43016-020-00213-5

OECD (2021a), *Government at a Glance 2021*, OECD Publishing, Paris. https://doi.org/10.1787/1c258f55-en

OECD (2021b), *COVID-19 and Food Systems: Short- and Long-Term Impacts*. OECD Food, Agriculture and Fisheries Papers, No. 166, OECD Publishing, Paris. https://doi.org/10.1787/69ed37bd-en

O'Meara, L., Turner, C., Coitinho, D. C. and Oenema, S. (2022), "Consumer Experiences of Food Environments during the Covid-19 Pandemic: Global Insights from a Rapid Online Survey of Individuals from 119 Countries", *Global Food Security*, Vol. 32, Article 100594. https://doi.org/10.1016/j.gfs.2021.100594

Oosterveer, P., Adjei, B. E., Vellema, S. and Slingerland, M. (2014), "Global Sustainability Standards and Food Security: Exploring Unintended Effects of Voluntary Certification in Palm Oil", *Global Food Security*, Vol. 3 No. 3–4, pp. 220–226. https://doi.org/10.1016/j.gfs.2014.09.006

Pangaribowo, E. H., Gerber, N. and Torero, M. (2013), "*Food and Nutrition Security Indicators: A Review*", ZEF Working Paper, No. 108. https://doi.org/10.2139/ssrn.2237992.

Prosser, L., Lane, E. T. and Jones, R. (2022), "Collaboration for Innovative Routes to Market: COVID-19 and the Food System", *Agricultural Systems*, Vol. 188, Article 103038. https://doi.org/10.1016/j.agsy.2020.103038

Qian, K., Javadi, F. and Hiramatsu, M. (2020), "Influence of the COVID-19 Pandemic on Household Food Waste Behavior in Japan", *Sustainability*, Vol. 12, Article 9942. https://doi.org/10.3390/su12239942

Rahimi, P., Islam, M. S., Duarte, P. M., Tazerji, S. S., Sobur, M. A., El Zowalaty, M. E., Ashour, H. M. and Rahman, M. T. (2022), "Impact of the COVID-19 Pandemic on Food Production and Animal Health", *Trends in Food Science & Technology*, Vol. 121, pp. 105–113. https://doi.org/10.1016/j.tifs.2021.12.003

Rodgers, R. F., Lombardo, C., Cerolini, S., Franko, D. L., Omori, M., Linardon, J., Guillaume, S., Fischer, L. and Fuller-Tyszkiewicz, M. (2021), ""Waste Not and Stay at Home" Evidence of Decreased Food Waste during the COVID-19 Pandemic from the U.S. And Italy", *Appetite*, Vol. 160, Article 105110. https://doi.org/10.1016/j.appet.2021.105110

Savary, S., Akter, S., Almekinders, C., Harris, J., Korsten, L., Rötter, R., Waddington, S. and Watson, D. (2020), "Mapping Disruption and Resilience Mechanisms in Food Systems", *Food Security*, Vol. 12, pp. 695–717. https://doi.org/10.1007/s12571-020-01093-0

Seiler, P. (2020). "Weighting Bias and Inflation in the Time of COVID-19: Evidence from Swiss Transaction Data", *Swiss Journal of Economics and Statistics*, Vol. 156, Article 13. https://doi.org/10.1186/s41937-020-00057-7

Shanks, S., Van Schalkwyk, M. C. I. and McKee, M. (2020), "Covid-19 Exposes the UK's Broken Food System", *BMJ: British Medical Journal*, Vol. 370, Article m3085. https://doi.org/10.1136/bmj.m3085

Statistics Poland (2021), Statistical Yearbook of Agriculture, available at https://stat. gov.pl/en/topics/statistical-yearbooks/statistical-yearbooks/statistical-yearbook-of-agriculture-2021,6,16.html (accessed 24 January 2023).

The Guardian (2020), UK Organic Food and Drink Sales Boom during Lockdown, available at https://www.theguardian.com/environment/2020/sep/03/uk-organic-food-and-drink-sales-boom-during-lockdown (accessed 26 June 2021).

Utz, R., Mastruzzi, M., Ahued, F. V. and Tawfik, E. (2020), An Overview of the Potential Impact of the COVID-19 Crisis on the Accumulation of Government Expenditure Arrears, The World Bank Group, Washinton, DC, available at https://documents1.worldbank.org/curated/en/673331610536300640/pdf/An-Overview-of-the-Potential-Impact-of-the-COVID-19-Crisis-on-the-Accumulation-of-Government-Expenditure-Arrears.pdf (accessed 10 November 2021).

Weingärtner, L. (2010), The Concept of Food and Nutrition Security, in: K. Klennert (Ed.), *Achieving Food and Nutrition Security: Actions to Meet the Global Challenge – A Training Course Reader* (3rd ed.) (pp. 21–51), Inwent, Bonn.

Wieland, A. (2021), "Dancing the Supply Chain: Toward Transformative Supply Chain Management", *Journal of Supply Chain Management*, Vol. 57 No.1, pp. 58–73. https://doi.org/10.1111/jscm.12248

Wojciechowska-Solis, J., Kowalska, A., Bieniek, M., Ratajczyk, M. and Manning, L. (2022), "Comparison of the Purchasing Behaviour of Polish and United Kingdom Consumers in the Organic Food Market during the COVID-19 Pandemic", *International Journal of Environmental Research and Public Health*, Vol. 19 No. 3, Article 1137. https://doi.org/10.3390/ijerph19031137

World Bank (WB) (2023a), Food Security Update. https://www.worldbank.org/en/topic/agriculture/brief/food-security-update (accessed 26 January 2023)

World Bank (WB) (2023b), GDP, PPP (Constant 2017 International $), available at https://data.worldbank.org/indicator/NY.GDP.MKTP.PP.KD (accessed 24 January 2023).

World Bank (WB) (2023c), GDP, PPP (Constant 2017 International $) - Poland, available at https://data.worldbank.org/indicator/NY.GDP.MKTP.PP.KD?locations=PL (accessed 24 January 2023).

World Health Organization (WHO) (2023), WHO Coronavirus (COVID-19) Dashboard, available at https://covid19.who.int/?adgroupsurvey={adgroupsurvey}andgclid=EAIaIQobChMI9Mj0m_za_AIVTdOyCh193wsdEAAYASABEgKhPPD_BwE (accessed 22 January 2023).

World Health Organization (WHO) (2020), WHO Director-General's opening remarks at the media briefing on COVID-19-11 March 2020, available at https://www.who.int/director-general/speeches/detail/who-director-general-s-opening-remarks-at-the-media-briefing-on-COVID-19–11-march-2020 (accessed 10 November 2021).

World Food Programme (WFP) (2006), World Hunger Series – Hunger and Learning, available at https://docs.wfp.org/api/documents/WFP-0000118955/download/?_ga=2.204717527.691528589.1609848723-1064141307.160984872 (accessed 19 January 2023).

Yaddanapudi, R. and Mishra, A. K. (2022), "Compound Impact of Drought and COVID-19 on Agriculture Yield in the USA", *Science of The Total Environment*, Vol. 807, Article 150801. https://doi.org/10.1016/j.scitotenv.2021.150801

Zhang, L., Qin, K., Li, Y. and Wu, L. (2022), "Public-Public Collaboration for Food Safety Risk Management: Essence, Modes, and Identification of Key Influencing Factors Using DANP", *Frontiers in Public Health*, Vol. 10, Article 944090. https://doi.org/10.3389/fpubh.2022.944090

Zhu, X., Yuan, X., Zhang, Y., Liu, H., Wang, J. and Sun, B. (2022), "The Global Concern of Food Security during the COVID-19 Pandemic: Impacts and Perspectives on Food Security", *Food Chemistry*, Vol. 370, Article 130830. https://doi.org/10.1016/j.foodchem.2021.130830

Part 2
Institutional and Policy Framework for Polish Economy Growth

Chapter 7

Monetary Policy and Corporate Investment – Analysis of Different Monetary Policy Channels: Evidence from Poland

Anna Szelągowska and Ilona Skibińska-Fabrowska

Abstract

Research Background: The monetary policy implementation and corporate investment are closely intertwined. The aim of modern monetary policy is to mitigate economic fluctuations and stabilise economic growth. One of the ways of influencing the real economy is influencing the level of investment by enterprises.

Purpose of the Chapter: This chapter provides evidence on how monetary policy affected corporate investment in Poland between 1Q 2000 and 3Q 2022. We investigate the impact of Polish monetary policy on investment outlays in contexts of high uncertainty.

Methodology: Using the correlation analysis and the regression model, we show the relation between the monetary policy and the investment outlays of Polish enterprises. We used the least squares method as the most popular in linear model estimation. The evaluation includes model fit, independent variable significance and random component, i.e. constancy of variance, autocorrelation, alignment with normal distribution, along with Fisher–Snedecor test and Breusch–Pagan test.

Findings: We find that Polish enterprises are responsive to changes in monetary policy. Hence, the corporate investment level is correlated with the effects of monetary policy (especially with the decision on the central bank's basic interest rate changes). We found evidence that QE policy has a positive impact on Polish investment outlays. The corporate investment in Poland is positively affected by respective monetary policies through Narodowy Bank Polski (NBP) reference rate, inflation, corporate loans, weighted average interest rate on corporate loans.

Modeling Economic Growth in Contemporary Poland, 111–130
Copyright © 2024 Anna Szelągowska and Ilona Skibińska-Fabrowska
Published under exclusive licence by Emerald Publishing Limited
doi:10.1108/978-1-83753-654-220231007

Keywords: Central bank; Narodowy Bank Polski; monetary policy; corporate investment; transmission channel; monetary policy tools

Introduction

Investment is the engine of economic growth and one of the main transmission channels of monetary policy. The central bank interest rate is one of the most powerful levers to convince corporations to commit to an investment. Looking at the literature, it seems that determinants of investment outlays are closely tied to monetary policy. There is a wide literature on the determinants of corporate investment to monetary policy. According to Ottonello and Winberry (2020), monetary policy is less effective in recessions. In this context, although many economic variables have been discussed, central bank interest rates, inflation, loans and interest rates on loans have been often used variables in the literature. This study aims to investigate how Polish monetary policy influenced corporate investment outlays in Poland for the period 1Q 2000–3Q 2022. We examine the impact of Polish monetary policy on investment outlays at the enterprise level in the context of high uncertainty. We show the relationship between monetary policy (including the basic interest rates of the Narodowy Bank Polski (NBP), interest rates on corporate loans and inflation) and corporate investment of Polish enterprises. We argue that the level of corporate investment outlays is correlated with the effects of monetary policy. The empirical findings confirm the evidence that the QE policy positively impacts Polish investment outlays.

Literature Review

Impact of Monetary Policy on the Real Economy – Transmission Channels

Monetary policy is, apart from fiscal policy, the main instrument of the state's influence on stabilising the economic situation and mitigating fluctuations within business cycles. Current monetary policy in most countries is based on direct inflation targeting (Mishkin, 2006). This means that using monetary instruments (interest rates, open market operations, quantitative easing), the central bank indirectly affects the real economy (Mishkin and Schmidt-Hebbel 2001; Svensson, 2000; Égert and MacDonald, 2009). This interaction occurs through monetary transmission channels (Boivin et al., 2010; Loayza and Schmidt-Hebbel, 2002; Mishkin, 1996). Transmission channels have evolved over the last several years. Central banks' use of non-standard monetary policy instruments in response to crises (the Global Financial Crisis and the pandemic crisis) resulted in the diagnosis of the existence of new channels. It is also worth pointing out that the importance of individual channels is variable over time and different for different economies (Boivin et al., 2010; Chmielewski et al., 2020; Rey, 2015). In light of the latest research, the following transmission channels of monetary policy to the real economy are currently described (Boivin et al., 2010; Chmielewski et al., 2018; Chmielewski et al., 2020):

(1) Interest rate channel affects the level of investment (tightening the monetary policy results in an increase in the costs of financing investments and their decrease) and by way of intertemporal substitution on the level of consumption (tightening the monetary policy changes the slope of the consumption curve).

(2) Exchange rate channel – monetary policy tightening causes appreciation and then depreciation of the domestic currency.

(3) Asset price channel influenced by the Tobin q effect (a tightening of monetary policy results in a decrease in share prices, which would require more shares to be issued to obtain funds for investments. This, in turn, would decrease the share of existing shareholders in the capital. As a result, there is a decrease in investments) and the wealth effect (a decline in share prices in households' portfolios reduces the value of their wealth and consumption).

(4) Credit channel affecting the balance sheet effect (monetary policy tightening causes a decrease in share prices, and consequently a decrease in the value of corporate assets and their creditworthiness) and bank loans channel (monetary policy tightening affects the deterioration of the structure of banks' balance sheets and limits their ability to grant credits).

(5) When monetary policy is tightened, the redistribution channel affects the deterioration of borrowers (and net interest payers) and the improvement of lenders (and net interest recipients).

(6) The cost channel affects the price increase due to the tightening of monetary policy and higher costs of financing current assets.

(7) The risk-taking channel affects the tightening of financing conditions through risk perception and tolerance changes when monetary policy is tightened.

The described transmission channels affect the real economy through a direct impact on the level of investment by enterprises and through changes in household consumption.

Polish Monetary Policy

In the 1990s, the monetary policy was conducted by the NBP in the following regimes (Polański, 2004):

- Fixed exchange rate (in 1990–1991) – in this period, the main monetary policy instruments were the variety of refinancing credits and reserve requirements, and administrative ceilings on credit growth.
- Traditional monetary targeting strategy (1992–1995) – since 1993, NBP began to use open market operations as the primary instrument of monetary policy.
- Monetary base targeting (1996–1997) – in 1997, because of a significant increase in the supply of credit money, NBP introduced a non-standard instrument in the form of deposits directly from the public to reduce the economy's liquidity and domestic demand growth.

In 1997–1998, there were profound changes in the Polish legal system (Constitution, Act on the NBP) and the macroeconomic sphere. They allowed the central bank to move to implement the direct inflation targeting strategy. NBP has formally implemented this strategy since 1997 (Bednarczyk, 2019; Pietryka, 2008; Polański, 2004). It was implemented after nearly 10 years of disinflation. After the transitional period in the years 1999–2003, the current goal of the NBP is to stabilise the inflation rate at the level of 2.5% with the permissible fluctuation range of ±1 percentage point in the medium term (NBP, 2003). The short-term interest rate of the central bank (reference rate) became the primary monetary policy instrument. In addition, NBP uses traditional, conventional instruments, such as open market operations, deposit and lending operations and reserve requirements (of less and less importance) (NBP, 2022).

The global financial crisis, which did not significantly affect the Polish financial system (Kozinski, 2010), prompted the NBP to prepare a package of solutions, which included new monetary policy instruments in the form of bill discount credit and currency swaps. Only the latter instrument attracted interest from banks (this was the result of the crisis of confidence in the international money market and the limited access to financing in foreign currencies for Polish commercial banks with a portfolio of foreign currency loans). It should be emphasised that during the GFC period, the Polish central bank did not pursue an unconventional monetary policy in the form of quantitative easing. On the other hand, the asset purchase programme (quantitative easing) in the form of treasury debt securities and treasury-guaranteed debt instruments was launched by NBP after the outbreak of the SARS-CoV-2 pandemic in 2020. This was preceded by reducing the basic interest rate to a level close to zero (0.1%) (NBP, 2021).

Determinants of Tangible Investments of Enterprises

Physical investments of enterprises are one of the crucial elements creating gross domestic product (GDP). Therefore, the factors determining their level are the subject of theoretical analysis and empirical research. In addition, it is nowadays assumed, contrary to the assumptions of neoclassical theory, that investment decisions made in a company are very closely related to financial decisions regarding access to various sources of financing and the possibility of using financial instruments (Kokot-Stępień, 2016).

The literature describes two approaches to investment and their determinants (Regis, 2018). The first is the q-theory model (Chirinko and Schaller, 1995) and the second is the Euler equation (Chatelain and Teurlai, 2001; Delikouras and Dittmar, 2018). Both indicate the importance of access to external financing and the possibility of obtaining foreign capital, especially in the context of its costs. Enterprises with less access to this type of financing limit the level of investment and make it dependent on the generated profit (significance of cash flow) (Fazzari et al., 1987). Another trend of research indicates the impact of the company's debt level on the level of investment – the endogeneity of debt in relation to investment (Aivazian et al., 2005; Myers, 1977). Finally, the theory of the financial accelerator, which emphasises the existence of four indicators of the company's financial position with a significant impact on the level of investment, deserves to be pointed out (Riccetti et al., 2013; Vermeulen, 2000). These indicators are:

* financial leverage – debt in relation to total assets,
* liquidity – short-term debt in relation to current assets,
* availability – short-term debt in relation to total debt,
* creditworthiness – cash flow in relation to interest.

A common feature of all the approaches described above is the consideration of the cost of capital as an essential factor determining the level of investment. On the other hand, the cost of capital is a derivative of the monetary policy pursued by the central bank. This makes linking monetary policy with the real economy possible by influencing corporate investment. The second important factor is the availability of financing, which is the result of the lending policy of commercial banks and their propensity to take risks. These are also derivatives of the monetary policy conducted by the central bank.

Finally, attention should be paid to the results of research on Polish enterprises, which indicate a different channel of the impact of monetary policy on investment. Well, the restrictive approach of the monetary authorities and the tightening of the monetary policy led to a change in the structure of investments in enterprises, which ceased to conduct tangible investments, especially those of a replacement nature, and replaced them with investments in financial assets (Nehrebecka and Białek-Jaworska, 2016).

Methodology

The study attempts to determine which variables selected for analysis (assuming ceteris paribus) had the greatest impact on the change in the size of investment outlays of Polish enterprises. The research period covered data from 1Q 2000 to 3Q 2022, which resulted from the need to take into account the unified methodology of the studied variables. During this period, the Polish economy had experienced an intensive recovery from high inflation, and the central bank already had initial experience in using monetary policy instruments aimed at implementing the strategy of direct inflation targeting. The research problem adopted in the study concerned which factors had the greatest impact on the change in investment outlays of enterprises in Poland in the period under review. The dependent variable is investment outlays (in PLN mln). It was hypothesised that variation in investment outlays depends on the following independent variables:

* reference rate;
* inflation;
* value of corporate loans;
* weighted average interest rate on new corporate loans.

The empirical research is to build an econometric model for a relationship between investment outlays and reference rate, value of corporate loans and weighted average interest rate on corporate loans in Poland in 1Q 2000–3Q 2022. The scope of the research is to estimate and verify the model. In order to verify which of the selected independent variables had a statistically significant impact on the investment outlays of Polish enterprises, a correlation analysis and regression analysis using the backward elimination method was performed. We used the classical least squares method as the most popular in linear model estimation. The Gretl software package will be used to conduct the estimation. The evaluation includes model fit, independent variable significance and random component, i.e. constancy of variance, autocorrelation, alignment with normal distribution, along with Fisher–Snedecor test and Breusch–Pagan test.

The aim of the study is to assess the impact of the NBP monetary policy expressed by the level of the basic interest rate (reference rate) and inflation on the level of investment outlays of Polish enterprises. The research problem included in the study boils down to determining whether, and if so to what extent, the investment outlays of Polish enterprises are correlated with the effects of monetary policy.

The analysis draws on quarterly macroeconomics data for the period 1Q 2000–3Q 2022, with 91 observations. The statistical data were sourced from Statistics Poland (investment outlays and inflation), NBP (reference rate) and Polish Financial Supervision Authority (corporate loans, weighted average interest rate on corporate loans).

Findings

Correlation Analysis

The statistical significance of a correlation is tested by means of the t-Student test which includes calculation of its critical value:

$a = 0.05$ significance level
$t = 1.987$ t-Student statistic for $91 - 2 = 89$
                      degrees of freedom and significance level 0.05
$t^2 = 3.9481$

The critical value of the correlation coefficient presents Eq. (1):

$$r^* = \sqrt{\frac{(t^*)^2}{n - 2 + (t^*)^2}} = \sqrt{\frac{3.9481}{91 - 2 + 3.9481}} = 0.2061 \tag{1}$$

In the next step, the linear correlation coefficient is determined (Table 1).

The relationship between reference rate and investment outlays expressed by correlation coefficient $r = -0.4726$ is statistically significant. What is more, the relationship between corporate loans and investment outlays, expressed by correlation coefficient $r = 0.6937$, is also statistically significant. Similarly, the

Table 1. Linear Correlation Coefficients for Sample Observations 2000:1 to 2022:3.

Critical Value (for bilateral Critical region of 5%) = 0.2061 for $n = 91$

Investment outlays	Reference _rate	Corporate _loans	Inflation	Weighted_ average_interest_ rates_on_new- corporate_loans	
10.000	−0.4726	0.6937	0.0549	−0.4706	Investment_ outlays
	1.0000	−0.6635	0.2939	0.9931	Reference_rate
		10.000	0.1158	−0.6493	Corporate_ loans
			1.0000	0.2616	Inflation
				1.0000	Weighted_ average_ interest_ rates_on_new- corporate_loans

Source: Authors' own calculations using the Gretl package.

relationship between weighted average interest rates on new corporate loans and investment outlays, expressed by correlation coefficient $r = -0.4706$, is statistically significant. Additionally, the relationship between inflation and investment outlays, expressed by correlation coefficient $r = 0.0549$, is statistically insignificant. The strongest positive relationship between variables is noticeable in the case of corporate loans and investment outlays. The correlation between analysed variables is presented in Fig. 1.

The model after parameter estimation
Estimation of the linear parameter Model 1 performed by Gretl is presented below.

The significant variables are marked with asterisks. Lack of an asterisk means that the variable is insignificant and needs to be dismissed. Only one variable (corporate loans) is statistically significant, and the model fit is low at only 48.8%. Hence, the model fit and significance of independent variables was improved by introducing variables with a one-quarter lag (Model 2).

New significant variables appeared, and the model fit increased to 62.1%, which supports the model.

We will dismiss insignificant variables by means of step-by-step regression (Model 3).

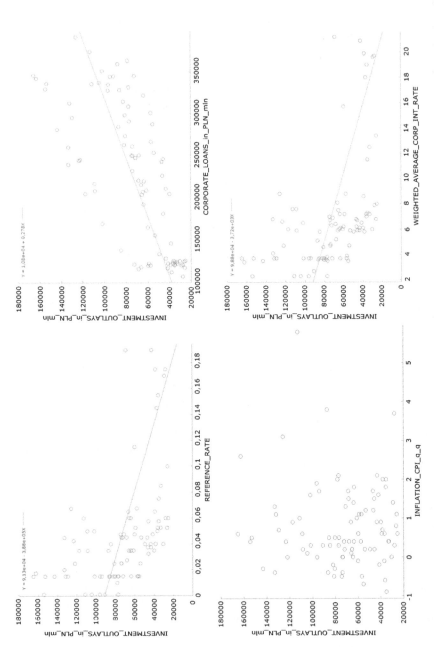

Fig. 1.   Correlation Charts for Sample Observations 1Q 2000–3Q 2022 (With Linear Regression). *Source:* Authors' own calculations using the Gretl package.

Model 1. Classical Least Squares Estimation, Observations Used: 2000:1 to 2022:3 ($T = 91$).

Dependent variable (Y): Investment outlays

Item	Coefficient	Standard error	t-Ratio	p-Value
Const.	20494.3	15729.7	1.303	0.1961
Reference rate	614453	608875	1.009	0.3157
Corporate loans	0.290643	0.0476036	6.105	<0.0001***
Inflation	−1923.87	3157.32	−0.6093	0.5439
Weighted average interest rate on corporate loans	−5756.92	5582.85	−1.031	0.3053
Arithmetic Mean	73386.53	Standard deviation Dependent variable	34935.25	
Residual sum of squares	5.62e + 10	Residual standard error	25565.37	
Coefficient of determination. R-squared	0.488280	Adjusted R-squared	0.464479	
$F(4, 86)$	20.51517	p-value for F-test	6.77e-12	
Log-likelihood	−1050.111	Akaike information criterion	2110.221	
Bayesian/Schwarz criterion	2122.775	Hannan–Quinn criterion	2115.286	
Residual autocorrelation-rho1	−0.367379	Durbin–Watson statistic	2.731682	

The model equation is given below:

$$\text{Investment}_{\text{outlays}} = 15192.5 + 1.218010 * \text{reference}_{\text{rate}} - 1.27$$
$$* \text{corporate}_{\text{loans}} + 1.63 * \text{corporate}_{\text{loans}_1} - 10193 * \text{Inflation}_1$$
$$- 9430.04 * \text{weighted}_{\text{average interest rate on corporate loans}_1}$$

An increase in reference rate by 1 p.p. increases investment outlays by PLN 1.218010 bln, mean estimation error is PLN 300.182 mln. An increase in value of corporate loans by PLN 1 mln decreases investment outlays by PLN 1.27 mln.

Model 2. Classical Least Squares Method Estimation, Observations Used 2000:2 to 2022:3 ($T = 90$).

Dependent Variable (Y): Investment Outlays in PLN mln

Item	Coefficient	Standard Error	t-Ratio	p-Value
Const.	14380.4	15789.9	0.9107	0.3651
NBP reference rate	773973	786096	0.9846	0.3278
NBP_1 reference rate	248013	852183	0.2910	0.7718
Corporate loans	−1.30018	0.427075	−3.044	0.0031***
Corporate loans_1	1.64993	0.430283	3.835	0.0002***
Inflation	747.744	3091.52	0.2419	0.8095
Inflation_1	−10612.8	3275.21	−3.240	0.0017***
Weighted average interest rate on new corporate loans	5395.64	9581.12	0.5632	0.5749
Weighted average interest rate on new corporate loans_1	−13064.1	7522.76	−1.737	0.0863*

Arithmetic Mean	73893.08	Standard deviation. Dependent variable	34793.28
Residual sum of squares	4.08e + 10	Residual standard error	22451.85
Coefficient of determination. R-squared	0.621027	Adjusted R-squared	0.583597
F(4, 86)	16.59192	p-value for F-test	2.75e–14
Log-likelihood	−1024.685	Akaike information criterion	2067.370
Bayesian/Schwarz criterion	2089.868	Hannan–Quinn criterion	2076.442
Residual autocorrelation-rho1	−0.094425	Durbin–Watson statistic	2.123421

Model 3. Classical Least Squares Method Estimation, Observations Used 2000:2 to 2022:3 ($T = 90$).

Dependent Variable (Y): Investment Outlays

Item	Coefficient	Standard Error	t-Ratio	p-Value
Const.	15192.5	13015.5	1.167	0.2464
NBP reference rate	1.21801e + 06	300.182	4.058	0.0001***
Corporate loans	−1.27043	0.415044	−3.061	0.0030***
Corporate loans_1	1.62999	0.417730	3.902	0.0002***
Inflation_1	−10193.0	3077.27	−3.312	0.0014***
Weighted average interest rates on new corporate loans_1	−9430.04	2549.31	−3.699	0.0004***

Arithmetic Mean	73893.08	Standard deviation. Dependent variable	34793.28
Residual sum of squares	4.10e + 10	Residual standard error	22102.00
Coefficient of determination. R-squared	0.619143	Adjusted R-squared	0.596473
$F(4, 86)$	27.31107	p-value for F-test	2.63e–16
Log-likelihood	−1024.908	Akaike information criterion	2061.816
Bayesian/Schwarz criterion	2076.815	Hannan–Quinn criterion	2067.864
Residual autocorrelation-rho1	−0.094328	Durbin–Watson statistic	2.124607

Mean estimation error is PLN 0.415 mln. An increase in value of corporate loans in the previous quarter by PLN 1 mln increases investment outlays in the current quarter by PLN 1.63 mln. Mean estimation error is PLN 0.418 mln. Increase in inflation quarter over quarter by 1 p.p. decreases investment outlays by PLN 10193 mln. Mean estimation error is PLN 3077.27 mln. Increase in weighted average interest rate on new corporate loans quarter over quarter by 1 p.p.

decreases investment outlays by PLN 9430.04 mln. Mean estimation error is PLN 2549.31 mln.

Evaluation of the model fit with the empirical data is performed to check if the model represents the dependent variable with sufficient accuracy. Various measures of alignment of the model with the empirical data can be used.

$$R^2 = 0.619 * 100\% = 61.9\%$$

The above value of the coefficient of determination indicates sufficient alignment of the model with the empirical data. The variability of the dependent variable is explained by independent variables in 62%.

Significance of Structural Parameters – Fischer–Snedecor Test

Due to testing the significance of the set of regression coefficients, we put forward the following hypothesis:

$$H_0 : \alpha_1 = \alpha_2 = 0 \text{ (no parameter irrelevant)}$$

$$H_1 : |\alpha_1| + |\alpha_2| \neq 0 \text{ (at least one relevant parameter)}$$

In order to test the set of hypothesis we use a statistical testing:

$$F = \frac{(n-k-1)}{k} \cdot \frac{R^2}{1-R^2}$$

Results provided by the software package are presented below:

$$F(5, 84) = 27.31107$$

Snedekor's F distribution $(k, n - k - 1)$

According to Fischer–Snedecor F test tables, the critical F^* value for significance level of 0.05, for $n1 = 1$ and $n2 = 18$ degrees of freedom is:

$F(5, 84)$
Right-sided probability = 0.05
Probability of complement = 0.95
Critical value $F^* = 6.41387$.

Since $F > F^*$ we reject H_0 and accept H_1, which means that at least one of its parameters is significant.

To investigate the significance of individual regression coefficients, we put forward hypotheses for each regression model coefficient:

$$H_0: \alpha_1 = 0 \; H_0: \alpha_2 = 0$$

$$H_1: \alpha_1 \neq 0 \; H_1: \alpha_2 \neq 0$$

We test the hypotheses with the t-student statistic.

Item	Coefficient	Standard error	t-Ratio	p-Value
Const.	15192.5	13015.5	1.167	0.2464
NBP reference rate	1.21801e + 06	300182	4.058	0.0001***
Corporate loans	−1.27043	0.415044	−3.061	0.0030***
Corporate loans_1	1.62999	0.417730	3.902	0.0002***
Inflation_1	−10193.0	3077.27	−3.312	0.0014***
Weighted average interest rates on new corporate loans_1	−9430.04	2549.31	−3.699	0.0004***

According to t-Student distribution tables, for the significance level of 0.05 and $90-5-1 = 84$ degrees of freedom, the critical value $t^* = 1.98$. From the inequalities below we conclude:

- $t(a_1) = 4.06 > t^*$, so for parameter a_1, we reject the null hypothesis and conclude that the parameter is significantly different from zero. Reference rate impacts investment outlays in a statistically significant way;
- $t(a_2) = 3.06 > t^*$, so for parameter a_2, we reject the null hypothesis and conclude that the parameter is significantly different from zero. Value of corporate loans impacts investment outlays in a statistically significant way;
- $t(a_3) = 3.9 > t^*$, so for parameter a_3, we reject the null hypothesis and conclude that the parameter is significantly different from zero. Value of corporate loans in the previous quarter impacts investment outlays in the current quarter in a statistically significant way;
- $t(a_4) = 3.3 > t^*$, so for parameter a_4, we reject the null hypothesis and conclude that the parameter is significantly different from zero. Quarter-over-quarter inflation impacts investment outlays in a statistically significant way;
- $t(a_5) = 3.3 > t^*$, so for parameter a_5, we reject the null hypothesis and conclude that the parameter is significantly different from zero. Weighted average interest rate on new corporate loans impacts investment outlays in a statistically significant way.

Having in mind the above calculations we carry out the random component analysis. In order to test for normal distribution of the random component, we put forward the hypothesis:

H_0: residuals have normal distribution
H_1: residuals have a distribution that is different from normal (Fig. 2).

Random component analysis using the Gretl package is presented below. Frequency distribution for residual, observations 2-91.

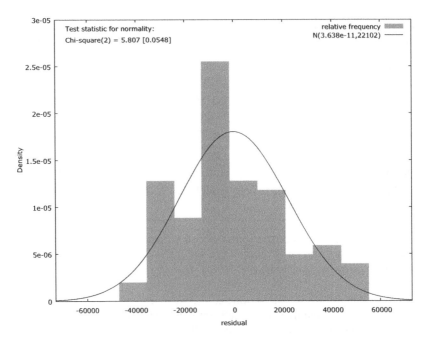

Fig. 2.   Test Statistic for Normality.
Source: Authors' own calculations using the Gretl package.

Number of intervals = 9; mean = 3.63798e-011; standard deviation = 22102.

Interval	Midpoint	Frequency	Relative	Cumulative
< −35541	−41203	2	2.22%	2.22%
−35541 – (−24215)	−29878	13	14.44%	16.67%*****
−24215 – (−12890)	−18553	9	10.00%	26.67%***
−12890 – (−1564.7)	−7227.4	26	28.89%	55.56%**********
−1564.7–9760.6	4097.9	13	14.44%	70.00%*****
9760.6–21086	15423	12	13.33%	83.89%****
21086–32411	26748	5	5.56%	88.89%*
32411–43736	38074	6	6.67%	95.56%**
>=43736	49399	4	4.44%	100.00%*

Source: Own calculations using the Gretl package.

Having in mind the null hypothesis: empirical function of distribution has normal distribution, we test for null hypothesis of normal distribution results in: chi-square(2) = 5.807 with *p*-value = 0.05483.

In the next step the Gretl conducts:

- a chi-square test;
- test for normal distribution of residuals.

The following null hypothesis is put forward: random component has normal distribution. According to tables, the chi-square critical statistic for 2 degrees of freedom = 5.991. Since chi-square test statistic = 5.807 < 5.991, there are no grounds for rejection of the null hypothesis, and we conclude that the distribution of the random component is normal. This supports the model.

Further, we conduct autocorrelation of the random component using the Breusch–Godfrey test, which indicates if autocorrelation of the random component takes place. Autocorrelation of random deviations is the relationship between random deviations from different time units. We put forward the following hypothesis:

H_0: $\rho(\varepsilon_t, \varepsilon_{t-1}) = 0$ lack of autocorrelation
H_1: there is positive autocorrelation.

where ρ – tier 1 coefficient of random component autocorrelation.
Results provided by Gretl software for Breusch–Godfrey test for first-order autocorrelation are presented below:

Estimation: classical least squares method. Observations used 2000:2 to 2022:3 ($T = 90$)
Dependent variable (Y): uhat

Item	Coefficient	Standard error	t-Ratio	p-Value
Const.	−127.822	13030.3	−0.009810	0.9922
Reference rate	−42150.0	304098	−0.1386	0.8901
Corporate loans	0.144971	0.445325	0.3255	0.7456
Corporate loans_1	−0.148402	0.449206	−0.3304	0.7420
Inflation_1	−155.294	3085.38	0.05033	0.9600
Weighted average interest rate on corporate loans_1	349.538	2581.15	0.1354	0.8926
uhat_1	−0.109398	0.120926	−0.9047	0.3683

Unadjusted R-squared = 0.009764

Test statistic: LMF = 0.818418
with p value = $P(F(1.83) > 0.818418) = 0.368$

(Continued)

Estimation: classical least squares method. Observations used 2000:2 to 2022:3 ($T = 90$)
Dependent variable (Y): uhat

Item	Coefficient	Standard error	t-Ratio	p-Value
Alternative statistic: $TR^2 = 0.878776$ with p value $= P(\text{chi-square }(1) > 0.878776) = 0.349$				
Ljung-Box Q' $= 0.741129$ with p value $= P(\text{chi-square }(1) > 0.741129) = 0.389$				

Source: Own calculations using the Gretl package.

According to tables, the critical chi-square value of the statistic for significance level of 0.05 and 1 degrees of freedom is:

Chi-square (1)
Right-sided probability = 0.05
Probability of complement = 0.95
Critical value = 3.84146

Since the statistic: $TR^2 = 0.88 < 3.841$ is smaller than critical value, there are no grounds for rejection of the H_0 hypothesis on lack of random component autocorrelation. There is no unfavourable autocorrelation in this model.

Next, we investigate the homoscedasticity of random components. One of the ways to test the constancy of variance of the random components is to verify the hypothesis that the variances of the random component are equal.

We verify the following hypotheses:

H_0: random component variance is constant in time (homoscedastic)
H_1: random component variance is not constant in time (heteroscedastic).

The results for Breusch–Pagan test for heteroscedasticity is presented below:

Estimation: classical least squares method. Observations used 2000:2 to 2022:3 ($T = 90$)
Dependent variable (Y): standardised uhat^2

Item	Coefficient	Standard error	t-ratio	p-value
Const.	−0.374251	0.708338	−0.5284	0.5986

(Continued)

Estimation: classical least squares method. Observations used 2000:2 to 2022:3 (T = 90)
Dependent variable (Y): standardised uhat^2

Item	Coefficient	Standard error	t-ratio	p-value
Reference rate	26.9323	16.3368	1.649	0.1030
Corporate loans	1.99327e-06	2.25879e-05	0.08825	0.9299
Corporate loans_1	5.30268e-06	2.27341e-05	0.2332	0.8161
Inflation_1	− 0.363570	0.167474	−2.171	0.0328**
Weighted average interest rate on corporate loans_1	− 0.174580	0.138741	−1.258	0.2118

Explained sum of squares = 22.1558
Test statistic: LM = 10.722206
with p-value = P(chi-square (5) > 10.722206) = 0.057175

According to tables, the critical chi-square value of the statistic for significance level of 0.05 and 5 degrees of freedom is:

Chi-square (5)
Right-sided probability = 0.05
Probability of complement = 0.95
Critical value = 11.0705

Due to the fact that the statistic TR^2 = 10.72 is lower than critical, there are no grounds for rejection of the H_0 on constant random component variance (homoscedasticity). This supports the model.

The level of corporate investment outlays is correlated with the effects of monetary policy. The empirical findings confirm the evidence that the QE policy positively impacts Polish investment outlays. We find, similarly to Fu and Liu (2015), that monetary policy has a significant effect on adjustment speed through monetary and credit channels. Our chapter is in line with the growing recent literature which considers the significance of the central bank in real economy.

Summary

The model has been successfully confirmed. In spite of the fact that the random component has a normal distribution, the model fits with empirical data is 62% and all other test results support the model. In addition, the model meets the condition of lack of residual autocorrelation. We know that model residuals are homoscedastic (their variance is constant in time), which means that the assumptions of applicability of the classical least squares method are met. The structural parameters, both grouped and individual, are statistically significant. So, the hypothesis on the relationship between investment outlays and the variables used in the model has been confirmed.

The study identifies that the investment outlays are directly correlated with the monetary policy effects. The greatest impact on the change in investment outlays of enterprises in Poland in the period under review had the reference rate. We find that investment outlays are positively affected by respective monetary policies through reference rate channels. The expected changes of reference rate have real consequences. Our findings suggest that decreasing the reference rate by NBP since 2000 contributed in a significant way to the investment outlays increase. Our results, as well, support Cohen et al. (2019) statement that both NBP and ECB's monetary policies have encouraged enterprises to raise their debt burden.

This study opens more questions than it provides answers. Among several possible avenues for further research, we are particularly interested in how monetary policy can accelerate investment outlays in other countries, especially in the era of post pandemic, war in Ukraine and considering the next global banking crises, which we plan to examine in further studies.

References

Aivazian, V. A., Ge, Y. and Qiu, J. (2005), "The Impact of Leverage on Firm Investment: Canadian Evidence", *Journal of Corporate Finance*, Vol. 11 No. 1–2, pp. 277–291.

Bednarczyk, J. L. (2019), "Polityka Pieniężna Narodowego Banku Polskiego a Wzrost Gospodarczy W Polsce Od Lat Dziewięćdziesiątych", in *Przemiany Spo- leczno-Gospodarcze w Polsce w latach 1989–2018. Wybrane Aspekty Makroeko- nomiczne*, ed. Kotowska-Jelonek M. (red.), Politechnika Świętokrzyska, Kielce, pp. 13–34.

Boivin, J., Kiley, M. T. and Mishkin, F. S. (2010), "How Has the Monetary Trans- mission Mechanism Evolved over Time?" in *Handbook of Monetary Economics*, Elsevier, (Vol. 3, pp. 369–422).

Chatelain, J. B. and Teurlai, J. C. (2001), "Pitfalls in Investment Euler Equations", *Economic Modelling*, Vol. 18 No. 2, pp. 159–179.

Chirinko, R. S. and Schaller, H. (1995), "Why Does Liquidity Matter in Investment Equations?" *Journal of Money, Credit, and Banking*, Vol. 27, No. 2, pp. 527–548.

Chmielewski, T., Kocięcki, A., Kapuściński, M., Kocięcki, A., Łyziak, T., Przystupa, J., Stanisławska, E. and Wróbel, E. (2018), *Monetary Transmission Mechanism in Poland what Do We Know in 2017?* NBP Working Paper No. 286.

Chmielewski, T., Kocięcki, A., Łyziak, T., Przystupa, J., Stanisławska, E., Walerych, M. and Wróbel, E. (2020), *Monetary Policy Transmission Mechanism in Poland What Do We Know in 2019?* NBP Working Paper No. 329.

Cohen, L., Gómez-Puig, M. and Sosvilla-Rivero, S. (2019), *Has the ECB's Monetary Policy Prompted Companies to Invest or Pay Dividends?* Research Institute of Applied Economics. Working Paper 2019/01, pp. 1–39.

Delikouras, S. and Dittmar, R. F. (2018), *Does the Simple Investment-Based Model Explain Equity Returns? Evidence from Euler Equations.* Working Paper, University of Miami.

Égert, B. and MacDonald, R. (2009), "Monetary Transmission Mechanism in Central and Eastern Europe: Surveying the Surveyable", *Journal of Economic Surveys*, Vol. 23 No. 2, 277–327.

Fazzari, S., Hubbard, R. G. and Petersen, B. C. (1987), *Financing Constraints and Corporate Investment*, NBER Working Paper 2387, https://doi.org/10.3386/w2387

Fu, Q. and Liu, X. (2015), "Monetary Policy and Dynamic Adjustment of Corporate Investment: A Policy Transmission Channel Perspective", *China Journal of Accounting Research*, Vol. 8, No. 2015, pp. 91–109. http://doi.org/10.1016/j.cjar.2015.03.001

Kliber, A., Kliber, P., Płucienik, P. and Piwnicka, M. (2016), "POLONIA Dynamics during the Years 2006–2012 and the Effectiveness of the Monetary Policy of the National Bank of Poland", *Empirica*, Vol. 43, pp. 37–59.

Kokot-Stępień, P. (2016), "Uwarunkowania Decyzji Inwestycyjnych w Przedsiębiorstwach Branży Hutniczej", *Finanse, RynkiFinansowe, Ubezpieczenia*, Vol. 82 No. 1, pp. 89–97.

Kozinski, W. (2010), "The International Banking Crisis and Domestic Financial Intermediation: the Experience of Poland", *BIS Papers*, Vol. 54, pp. 343–346.

Krušec, D. (2011), "Is Inflation Targeting Effective? Monetary Transmission in Poland, the Czech Republic, Slovakia, and Hungary", *Eastern European Economics*, Vol. 49, No. 1, pp. 52–71.

Loayza, N. and Schmidt-Hebbel, K. (2002), "Monetary Policy Functions and Transmission Mechanisms: An Overview", *Serieson Central Banking, Analysis, and Economic Policies*, No. 4.

Mishkin, F. S. (1996), *The Channels of Monetary Transmission: Lessons for Monetary Policy*, NBER Working Paper 5464.

Mishkin, F. S. (2006), *Monetary Policy Strategy: How Did We Get Here?* NBER-Working Paper 12515, https://doi.org/10.3386/w12515

Mishkin, F. S. and Schmidt-Hebbel, K. (2001), *One Decade of Inflation Targeting in the World: What Do We Know and what Do We Need to Know?* NBER Working Paper8397, https://doi.org/10.3386/w8397

Myers, S. C. (1977), "Determinants of Corporate Borrowing", *Journal of Financial Economics*, Vol. 5, No. 2, 147–175.

NBP (2003), *Monetary Policy Strategy beyond 2003*, available at https://www.nbp.pl/en/publikacje/o_polityce_pienieznej/strategy_beyond_2003.pdf (accessed February 21 2023).

NBP (2021), *Banking Sector Liquidity Monetary Policy Instruments of Narodowy Bank Polski*, available at https://www.nbp.pl/en/publikacje/instruments/instruments2020.pdf, (accessed February 20 2023).

NBP (2022), *Banking Sector Liquidity Monetary Policy Instruments of Narodowy Bank Polski*, available at https://www.nbp.pl/en/publikacje/instruments/instruments2021.pdf, (accessed February 20 2023).

Nehrebecka, N. and Białek-Jaworska, A. (2016), "Determinanty inwestycji przedsiębiorstw w środki trwałe. Zależność od cash flow i warunków kredytowych", *Econometrics. Ekonometria. Advances in Applied Data Analytics*, Vol. 3 No. 53, pp. 115–145.

Ottonello, P. and Winberry, T. (2020), "Financial Heterogeneity and the InvestmentChannel of Monetary Policy", *Econometrica*, November 2020, Vol. 88 No. 6, pp. 2473–2502.

Pietryka, I. (2008), "Monetary Policy of the National Bank of Poland in Period 1999-September 2008", *Equilibrium. Quarterly Journal of Economics and Economic Policy*, Vol. 1 No. 1–2, pp. 23–37.

Polański, Z. (2004), "Poland and the European Union: The Monetary Policy Dimension. Monetary Policy before Poland's Accession to the European Union", *Bank iKredyt*, Vol. 5, pp. 4–18.

Regis, P. J. (2018), "Access to Credit and Investment Decisions of Small and Medium sized Enterprises in China", *Review of Development Economics*, Vol. 22 No. 2, pp. 766–786.

Rey, H. (2015), *Dilemma Not Trilemma: The Global Financial Cycle and Monetary Policy Independence*. NBER Working Paper 21162, https://doi.org/10.3386/w21162

Riccetti, L., Russo, A. and Gallegati, M. (2013), "Leveraged Network-Based Financial Accelerator", *Journal of Economic Dynamics and Control*, Vol. 37 No. 8, pp. 1626–1640.

Svensson, L. E. (2000), "Open-economy Inflation Targeting", *Journal of International Economics*, Vol. 50 No. 1, pp. 155–183.

Vermeulen, P. (2000), *Business Fixed Investment: Evidence of a Financial Accelerator in Europe. SSRN 355985*.

Chapter 8

Effects of Fiscal Policy and Monetary Policy on the Capital Market in Poland

Mariusz Kicia and Dominika Kordela

Abstract

Research Background: Fiscal and monetary policies are essential to the development of a capital market. In this chapter, authors present how fiscal and monetary policy in Poland evolved and adjusted to economic challenges in 1998–2022. It is worth noticing that the Polish economy and financial market have been built from scratch after 45 years of socialism. Hence, it is scientifically interesting to study the relationship between fiscal and monetary policy, and capital market in a developing country, and in a relatively young economy.

Purpose of the Chapter: Both – the macroeconomic policy mix and development of the capital market – are the subject of analysis how fiscal and monetary policy impacted the capital market. As so the main aim of the chapter is the assessment of the nexus and dependencies between fiscal and monetary policy and the capital market.

Methodology: In the chapter, multiple linear regression was used for each dependent variable to discover which monetary and fiscal policy parameters significantly predicted selected variables describing the development of the capital market in Poland. Fiscal and monetary policy variables served as descriptors explaining capital market parameters in seven separate models.

Findings: Multiple regression models explain 77.3%–95.4% of the volatility of the capital market characteristics. The level of the central bank's reference rate is a variable that influences the capital market the most. In six out of seven models, the interest rate was a significant parameter. The development of the capital market was accompanied by a higher tax-to-GDP ratio. At the same time, a strong negative impact of the tax-to-GDP increase was noticed in domestic institutional investors' stock trading.

Modeling Economic Growth in Contemporary Poland, 131–144
Copyright © 2024 Mariusz Kicia and Dominika Kordela
Published under exclusive licence by Emerald Publishing Limited
doi:10.1108/978-1-83753-654-220231008

Keywords: Capital market; fiscal policy; treasury bonds; monetary policy; reference rate; Warsaw Stock Exchange

Introduction

Fiscal and monetary policies are essential to the development of a financial market. A well-functioning financial market is critical for an economy's development because it allows capital to be allocated to the most productive sectors, improves intermediation efficiency and lowers the cost of capital (Frank & Bernanke, 2007; Blanchard et al., 2010).

Fiscal policy refers to the decisions made by the government regarding spending and taxation. It has a direct impact on aggregate demand and has an impact on interest rates, inflation and economic growth. An increase in government spending, for example, stimulates demand and creates jobs, whereas a decrease in government spending causes a decrease in demand and job losses. Monetary policy, on the other hand, refers to the actions of a central bank to control the supply and demand for money. It is a critical tool for economic stabilisation, low inflation and long-term economic growth (Blanchard et al., 2010; Federal Reserve Bank of San Francisco, 2022; IMF, 2021).

A well-functioning financial market provides access to credit for individuals and businesses, and enables efficient allocation of resources. Furthermore, it also enhances financial literacy and provides financial education to individuals and businesses. This leads to the development of a more informed and responsible borrowing and investing culture, which is crucial for long-term financial stability (Bernanke and Gertler, 1995; Mishkin, 2007; Worldbank, 2020). The 2008 financial crisis is one of the most notable examples of the impact of fiscal and monetary policies on a financial market. It demonstrated the importance of having sound fiscal and monetary policies in place to avoid systemic risks and ensure financial system stability (Board of Governors of the Federal Reserve System, 2021; Goldstein, 1998).

In this chapter, authors present how fiscal and monetary policy in Poland evolved and adjusted to economic challenges in 1998–2022. Milestones in development of the Polish capital market were also presented. Finally, both – policy mix and development of the capital market – were subject of analysis to discover how fiscal and monetary policy impacted the capital market. The main aim of the chapter is the assessment of the nexus and dependencies between fiscal and monetary policy and capital market.

Literature Review

Fiscal Policy in Poland 1998–2022

From 1998 to 2022, Poland's fiscal policy was characterised by a series of reforms aimed at stabilising the country's economy, reducing the budget deficit and increasing the country's competitiveness in the global marketplace. Even at the end of the twentieth century, fiscal policy in Poland had to address issues left over from the first decade of the systemic transformation that began in 1989. The main factors in stabilising public finances in the 1990s were restrictive fiscal policy and tax reforms. It was also aided by a relatively high rate of economic growth during this time period (IMF, 2018).

The 1998 budget act aimed to reduce the budget deficit and increase fiscal stability in the country. The CIT rate was reduced from 40% to 36% and then reduced by 2 percentage points per year in subsequent years. The lowest PIT rate, at which 95% of taxpayers settled, was reduced from 21% to 19%. Simultaneously, the scope of reliefs was limited, but both changes resulted in a real-terms decrease in revenues, from 41.5% of gross domestic product (GDP) in 1994 to 38.6% in 1998. On the other hand, fiscal restraints in the 1990s and debt reduction negotiated after the start of the transformation reduced it from 83.3% of GDP in 1993 to 43% in 1999 (Dąbrowski et al., 2013; GUS).

In 1999, the pension reform was implemented, which had a significant impact on public finances. Pension reform was critical in the long run. The gradual transition from the pay-as-you-go to the funded pension system was extremely costly to the state budget. Maintaining the current level of pensions and transferring a portion of the contribution to the new system's capital accounts of pensions necessitated a greater coverage of transfers by the state budget. This resulted in persistent deficits and an increase in the national debt. Furthermore, the rate of economic growth slowed to around 1% per year in 2001–2002. In 2002, a 19% capital income tax was implemented. By 2004, the deficit had risen to around 7%, up from 3% in 1999. On the other hand, the pension reform resulted in the institutionalisation of the financial market, with the establishment of a dozen or so capital pension funds, which created a constant demand for financial instruments (primarily treasury bonds, but also shares, which accounted for 20%–30% of their portfolios) (Grabowski and Jarmulak, 2018; Rozkrut, 2003).

Accession to the European Union in 2004 increased access to funding and markets, resulting in an improvement in the country's fiscal position and the implementation of a comprehensive fiscal reform package in 2006 aimed at improving fiscal sustainability and increasing the country's competitiveness in the global marketplace. A further significant reduction in budget revenues was implemented in 2004. This was due not only to lower taxes, but also to changes in local government financing. These changes primarily took the form of increasing the proportion of local government revenues financed by centrally levied taxes (CIT and PIT), resulting in a reduction in state budget revenues.

In 2007–2011, continued efforts to improve country's fiscal position were made, including measures to reduce the budget deficit and increase tax revenues. The global financial crisis of 2008–2009 had direct negative consequences for the entire European Union's fiscal situation, as well as indirectly for Poland. In July 2010, the Polish government announced that the general VAT rate would be raised from 22% to 23%, and the reduced rate would be reduced to 8% (NBER). This was due to the European Union's Excessive Deficit Procedure (EDP).

Poland was subjected to two excessive deficit procedures during its first 10 years of EU membership, totalling nearly 8 years. The European Commission discovered an excessive deficit for the second time in 2009 with improvement expected until 2012. It has been extended twice until 2015. In 2012–2015, the country implemented a series of austerity measures aimed at reducing the budget deficit and improving fiscal sustainability. The government's pension reform in 2016, which included a drastic reduction in transfers to the capital part of the pension system and the transfer of more than 50% of pension fund assets to ZUS to keep the budget from exceeding the 55% threshold of public debt to GDP, as well as a ban on funds' investing in treasury bonds, only temporarily reduced the fiscal imbalance. The state's open debt to pensioners was written off and replaced with the Social Insurance Institution's undisclosed debt (ZUS). Nonetheless, despite the implementation of national expenditure rules and the existence of EU rules, Poland's lack of fiscal discipline is permanent. The rules themselves do not guarantee compliance. Despite this, fiscal policy became more expansive after 2015, owing primarily to increased social transfers and the implementation of protective measures aimed at mitigating the effects of the COVID-19 pandemic (2020–2021) and inflation (2022).

Monetary Policy in Poland 1998–2022

According to article 227 of the Polish Constitution, National Bank of Poland (NBP) is the central bank of Poland exclusively responsible for money issue and monetary policy. The fundamental objective of the NBP's activity is to maintain price stability. The Monetary Policy Council (MPC), one of the bodies of NBP, is responsible for setting interest rates. As the MPC was constituted on February 17, 1998, changes in monetary policy were announced. First of all the strategy has changed. The control of the money supply and the application of currency exchange rate fluctuation band were not the goals anymore. Inflation targeting strategy was introduced with focus on inflation rate (Sławiński, 2011). Inflation targeting in Poland was consistent with the world's trends and adjusted the monetary policy to the perspective of Poland's integration with the European Union (Przybylska-Kapuścińska, 2009).

The main tasks in the first years of the new strategy were to decrease the inflation rate below 4% by 2003 and to introduce a floating exchange rate; however, the possible interventions were maintained (Przybylska-Kapuścińska, 2009). The next steps in 2004 were to maintain Consumer Price Index (CPI) as an inflation target indicator and to set the fixed inflation target at 2.5% with 1 p.p. acceptable fluctuation band (Przybylska-Kapuścińska, 2009). From 2003 to 2009, the level of absolute deviation from the inflation target was not greater than 0.9 p.p. The level of the reference rate in whole period substantially decreased – from 19% in 2000 to as little as 3.5% in 2009. However, between 2000 and 2009, the short periods of increasing inflation rate were observed, followed by increase in reference rate. In the first 10 years of its activity, the main objective of the MPC was to prioritise inflation, hence the relatively high interest rates, and the secondary treatment of growth problems economic (Przybylska-Kapuścińska, 2009). Due to the 2008–2009 financial crisis, central banks had to deal with an additional goal which was to maintain the stability and liquidity of the financial market (Skibińska-Fabrowska, 2015). Although the financial system in Poland was not as affected by crises as the financial systems in Western Europe and the United States, the monetary policy still had to take into consideration the financial market situation. Decline in confidence in the interbank market consequently limited market activity. Hence, in response to the deteriorating liquidity situation in the interbank market in 2008, NBP also developed a set of measures to improve commercial banks' conditions. From 2010, the monetary policy NBP returned to the inflation target strategy, which was quite a challenge because of the increase of CPI above the target (Skibińska-Fabrowska, 2015). The raising interest rates in 2011 and 2012 were not consistent with the policy of other central banks that pursued an expansive monetary policy at those times (Skibińska-Fabrowska, 2015). As the inflation rate moved to the target at the end of 2012, MPC started to lower the interest rates, the minimum level 1.5% was reached in March 2015, and the interest rates were maintained until 2020 unchanged. In 2020, the COVID-19 pandemic hit the economy; it resulted in a suspension of the economic activity of many enterprises, disruption of supply chains and a general social and economic shock. Despite the fact that the CPI was above the inflation target from the beginning of 2020, MPC decided to lower interest rates three times, the reference rate reached the lowest level in the history of 0.1% in May 2020. The inflation target was maintained till the end of March 2021. From May 2021, CPI started to grow fast, reaching 6.8% in October. The period of rising interest rates began in monetary policy. The reference rate increased from 0.1% (September 2021) to 6.75% (September 2022) in just 1 year.

Capital Market in Poland 1998–2022

The capital market is a link between participants with a surplus of funds and units with a shortage of funds but with investment opportunities, and plays an important role in raising long-term funds for corporations, governments, banks and other entities. The Warsaw Stock Exchange (WSE) is in Poland, the main institution of the capital market. With the political and economic changes in Poland after the fall of socialism, the stock exchange was established by the State Treasury. The WSE was created from a scratch, and it was a challenge not only to set the legal framework and regulation but also to build credibility. Credibility was a core issue for both potential issuers and investors (Janicka, 2002). The development of the WSE has been dynamic. At the beginning, mainly thanks to the formerly state-owned companies; they used the stock exchange as a way to privatisation and restructuration.

The main market (the regular market for equity securities) operated since 1991. Attempts to establish an OTC market in the following years failed. The structural development of the exchange was successful in 2007 when the NewConnect market for a smaller and innovative enterprises was established. It operates as a multilateral trading facility (MTF), creates an alternative market for equity securities. In addition to the stock market, TGE (Towarowa Giełda Energii) commodity exchange in the WSE structure since 1999 and Catalyst debt market since 2009. TGE is a commodity exchange, where electricity, natural gas, property rights, CO2 emission allowances markets and agricultural and food commodities are traded.

According to the Federation of European Securities Exchanges (FESE) statistics, the WSE ranked fifth in terms of capitalisation among 15 European stock exchanges in 2021. Although the WSE is rated as a middle-sized stock market, it has a dominant position in the region. The WSE is the largest market in East Europe in terms of capitalisation (1.1 billion PLN or around 46% of GDP at the end of 2022).

The activity of investors on WSE has changed over time. In the first years, the share of foreign investors and individual investors in turnover amounted 38% each. In 2000, the share of individual investors was the highest – 50%; in the following years till 2008, it ranged from 29% to 37%. After the crisis, it fell under 20%. At the same time, the foreign investors in share trading reached 34%–47%. At the end of the 1990s, domestic institutional investors accounted for just over 20% of turnover, which increased to over 30% later on. During the last 10 years, in terms of turnover, the most active group on the main market of WSE were foreign investors (56%–65% share), followed by domestic institutional investors (19%–29%), and domestic individual investors remaining. While the NewConnect's trading was dominated by domestic individual investors (over 80%) (NBP, 2022).

The debt market in Poland was almost monopolised by banks for a long time. Banks on the primary market purchased debt securities and held them most often until the maturity date. As in 2009, the Catalyst, secondary market for debt instruments has been established, aimed at diversification of investors and increasing the involvement of individual investors. Market analysis after 13 years of its operation indicates that the banking sector still dominates in the debt market. The largest segment of the domestic market for long-term debt securities is the treasury bond market, which includes treasury bonds and bonds guaranteed by the State Treasury accounting over 85% of the domestic debt market in 2020–2022. The most important investors in this market were banks, followed by non-residents. Over 90% of transactions on the secondary market were traded on the OTC market, while the share of the Catalyst market in treasury securities turnover was quite low and did not exceed 1% (NBP, 2022).

Municipal bonds built 2.56% of the value of all debt instruments in 2021. In last 4 years, Catalyst markets traded from 15% to 21% of total value of municipal bonds. Most municipal bonds are non-marketable. According to data, in 2021, as much as 88% of municipal debt securities were traded on the OTC market, while on the Catalyst market, the turnover in these securities is negligible (NBP, 2022).

At the end of 2021, corporate bonds amounted to 7.35% of the total value of the market. Almost 30% of the value of corporate bonds were securities listed on the Catalyst market. Yet most of the issues were of a non-market nature. The main investors in the corporate bond market were investment funds and banks (NBP, 2022).

The data above prove the important role of the OTC market in debt trading and the dominance of the banking sector in it. The stock exchange at the same time is a key institution in equity trading.

Fiscal and Monetary Policy Mix and Capital Market – Empirical Review

Since there is a great number of publications regarding the interaction and influence of monetary policy on the stock market, only a few investigate the effects of fiscal policy on stock markets (Chatziantoniou et al., 2013; Foresti and Napolitano, 2016). The research on the relationship between monetary policy focuses on the effects of monetary policy on the performance of the capital market and stock prices (Ananwude et al., 2017; Babangida and Khan, 2021; Baykara, 2021; Bernanke and Kuttner, 2005; Bjørnland and Leitemo, 2005; Hojat and Sharifzadeh, 2017; Lütkepohl and Netšunajev, 2018), the impact of the reference rate of stock market volume (Bielicki, 2015) or stock market bubble (Gali and Gambetti, 2014). The studies analyse separately stock markets (Ananwude et al., 2017; Babangida and Khan, 2021; Baykara, 2021) as well as both stock and bond markets (Yang-Chaoet al., 2022). The subject of the research and discussion was also the reactions of monetary policy to events in the stock markets (Bernanke and Gertler, 2001; Bohl et al., 2007; Goczek and Partyka, 2016; Mishkin, 2011).

The research on the effects of fiscal policy on stock markets conducted on example of 11 countries of the Eurozone proved that stock markets react to both public expenditures and revenues. However, it has been also showed that the macroeconomic scenario is important and that fiscal policy is interpreted and conducted on the basis of the financial, debt and output cycles simultaneously (Foresti and Napolitano, 2016).

Investigating the impact of monetary policy on the stock market Bernanke and Kuttner (2005) in their vast research on US market found a relatively strong influence of unexpected monetary policy actions on the stock market. However, there is a differentiation in response across industry-based portfolios (Bernanke and Kuttner, 2005). Further studies on the US market Bjørnland and Leitemo (2005) focused on the interdependence between interest rate setting and stock prices. The main conclusion is that interest rate decisions are closely followed by the financial market and that monetary policy-making has an impact on the stock market (Bjørnland and Leitemo, 2005). In the European market, this relationship was examined by Lütkepohl and Netšunajev (2018). Their results partially in line with the results Bjørnland and Leitemo (2005) support the approach that the policy of the European Central Bank has a substantial impact on the stock market in Europe. To examine the impact of monetary policy on equity market not only the interest rate (in case of the USA federal funds rate FFR) has been used as variable but changes in money supply (M2), and federal funds futures on the expected rate of returns of publicly traded companies (Hojat and Sharifzadeh, 2017). Research conducted in Nigeria shows the monetary policy rate has a negative significant relationship with capital market performance while cash reserve ratio positively relates with the performance of the capital market (Ananwude et al., 2017).

Another study conducted in Australia (Brown and Karpavičius, 2017) focuses on the impact of unexpected decisions of the Reserve Bank of Australia (RBA) on the stock market's returns, and the impact from RBA announcements of the new target cash rate and the release of the explanatory meeting minutes. The research are generally consistent with the prior literature on the topic (Bernanke and Kuttner, 2005), but shows the response of the Australian stock market on monetary policy decisions by the RBA is limited. The stock market (equity prices) reacts negatively to the surprize change in the target cash rate.

Moreover, the scientific interest has been focused on the effects of both fiscal policy and monetary policy on the stock market (Chatziantoniou et al., 2013; Hsing, 2013). The research conducted on the United States, United Kingdom and German market studied not only the effects of monetary but also the fiscal policy shocks on stock market performance (Chatziantoniou et al., 2013). Authors presented different theories' approaches to the problem of the fiscal policy impact on stock market, showing the differentiation between Keynesian economics, classical economic theory and Ricardian perspective. The conclusions show there is *evidence suggesting that both fiscal and monetary policy affect the stock market, either directly or indirectly. More importantly, though, we find evidence that the interaction between the two policies is very important in explaining stock market developments* (Chatziantoniou et al., 2013).

Finally, the study of Hsing (2013) is limited to Poland. Applying GARCH model, and following variables: government deficit to GDP, interest rate, M3 money supply to GDP, industrial production, nominal effective exchange rate and CPI, the effects of the fiscal and monetary policy on the stock market have been investigated. The conclusions based on a sample from 1999. Q2 to 2012 indicate that fiscal policy does not have any significant impact on the stock index. Regarding monetary policy, the increase of interest rate has a negative impact on the stock index, whereas monetary easing has either a positive or negative impact on the stock index, depending on whether the ratio is less or greater than the critical value of 46.03% (Hsing, 2013).

Methodology

The analysis of the nexus between changes in fiscal and monetary policy and the parameters of the capital market in Poland was carried out based on annual data from 1998 to 2021. End-of-year data on parameters describing macroeconomic policies and parameters of the capital market were used. The data from the National Bank of Poland, the Ministry of Finance, the WSE and the Statistics Poland were collected (see Table 1).

The following parameters represented monetary policy:

$REFR_t$ – central bank's reference interest rate and a target for open market operations,

Table 1. Capital Market, Fiscal and Monetary Policy Data – Poland 1998–2021.

	Capital Market							Monetary Policy				Fiscal Policy			
Year	DEBTMV bln PLN	WSEMCAP bln PLN	NCMCAP bln PLN	PLINSWSE % Turnover	PLINDWSE % Turnover	FGNWSE % Turnover	WIG Points	REFR %	CPI %	M3 % GDP	DEFGDP % GDP	DBTGDP % GDP	GGSP % GDP	BGTSP % GDP	TXRV % GDP
1998	46.4	77.4	x	22.0	39.0	39.0	12795.60	15.5	11.8	36.9	-4.2	38.4	n/a	23.0	36.2
1999	73.6	123.4	x	22.0	44.0	34.0	18083.60	16.5	7.3	39.9	-2.3	38.9	n/a	20.5	35.9
2000	99.6	130.1	x	22.0	50.0	28.0	17847.60	19.0	10.1	40.2	-4.0	36.4	39.2	20.2	33.8
2001	140.8	103.4	x	29.0	37.0	34.0	13922.20	10.0	5.5	42.2	-4.7	37.3	42.2	22.1	33.9
2002	175.2	110.6	x	36.0	29.0	35.0	14366.70	6.8	1.9	40.2	-4.8	41.7	43.2	22.5	34.0
2003	203.9	167.7	x	39.0	29.0	32.0	20820.10	5.3	0.8	40.7	-6.0	46.6	43.1	22.3	33.5
2004	248.7	291.7	x	32.0	35.0	33.0	26636.20	6.5	3.5	40.5	-5.0	45.1	41.6	21.2	32.9
2005	303.2	424.9	x	33.0	26.0	41.0	35600.80	4.5	2.1	43.1	-3.9	46.6	41.6	21.0	33.9
2006	345.4	635.9	x	34.0	35.0	31.0	50411.80	4.0	1.0	46.3	-3.5	47.3	41.4	20.8	34.6
2007	389.3	1080.3	1.2[a]	37.0	30.0	33.0	55648.50	5.0	2.5	47.3	-1.9	44.5	40.7	21.2	35.5
2008	400.5	465.1	1.4	39.0	18.0	43.0	27228.60	5.0	4.2	51.8	-3.6	46.7	41.7	21.6	35.2
2009	446.0	715.8	2.5	37.0	27.0	36.0	39986.00	3.5	3.5	52.5	-7.3	49.8	43.0	21.7	32.3
2010	525.4	796.5	5.1	34.0	19.0	47.0	47489.91	3.5	2.6	54.6	-7.5	54.0	44.4	20.6	32.3
2011	574.3	642.9	8.5	35.0	18.0	47.0	37595.44	4.5	4.3	56.7	-5.0	55.1	42.7	19.5	32.8
2012	613.8	734.0	11.1	34.0	18.0	48.0	47460.59	4.3	3.7	57.1	-3.8	54.8	42.4	19.7	33.1
2013	670.8	840.8	11.0	39.0	16.0	45.0	51284.25	2.5	0.9	60.1	-4.3	57.1	42.9	19.7	33.1
2014	623.8	1253.0	9.1	38.0	13.0	49.0	51416.08	2.0	0.0	62.3	-3.7	51.4	42.1	18.4	33.1
2015	666.0	1082.9	8.7	36.0	12.0	52.0	46467.38	1.5	-0.9	64.2	-2.6	51.3	40.7	18.4	33.4
2016	740.7	1115.7	9.8	34.0	13.0	53.0	51754.03	1.5	-0.6	68.3	-2.4	54.5	40.4	19.5	34.3
2017	772.1	1379.9	9.6	31.0	14.0	55.0	63746.20	1.5	2.0	66.8	-1.5	50.8	39.9	19.0	35.0
2018	811.3	1128.5	7.4	27.0	12.0	61.0	57690.50	1.5	1.6	68.0	-0.2	48.7	40.5	18.4	36.0
2019	848.2	1103.8	9.7	23.0	11.0	66.0	57832.88	1.5	2.3	68.4	-0.7	45.7	40.4	18.1	36.0
2020	1097.3	1068.7	19.8	18.0	27.0	55.0	57025.84	0.1	3.4	78.0	-6.9	57.2	45.3	21.6	36.4
2021	1177.6	1312.7	19.2	21.0	21.0	58.0	69296.26	1.8	5.1	75.6	-1.8	53.8	n/a	19.9	n/a

Source: Authors' own elaboration based on publicly available data from National Bank of Poland (www.nbp.pl), Ministry of Finance (www.mf.gov.pl), Warsaw Stock Exchange[a] (www.gpw.pl), Statistics Poland (www.stat.gov.pl).
[a]Trading at WSE NewConnect initiated in 2007.

CPI_t – Consumer Price Index used by central banks to monitor inflation, which in turn plays a key role in determining monetary policy decisions,
$M3_t$ – M3 money supply measure to GDP.

Fiscal policy was observed with five independent variables:

$DEFGDP_t$ – general government deficit (surplus) to GPD,
$DBTGDP_t$ – general government debt to GPD,
$GGSP_t$ – general government spendings to GDP,
$BGTSP_t$ – government budget spendings to GDP,
$TXRV_t$ – all tax general government income to GPD.

Finally, seven measures of capital market were used as dependent variables and explained in model by monetary and fiscal policy parameters:

$WSEMCAP_t$ – market capitalisation of stocks listed at the main market of the WSE (Model 1),
$NCMCAP_t$ – market capitalisation of stocks listed at the NewConnect – alternative market of the WSE (Model 2),
WIG_t – value of WSE main index (Model 3),
$DEBTMV_t$ – market value of all issued debt instruments (Model 4),
$PLINSWSE_t$ – percent share of annual WSE stocks turnover by institutional domestic investors (Model 5),
$PLINDWSE_t$ – percent share of annual WSE stocks turnover by individual domestic investors (Model 6),
$FGNWSE_t$ – percent share of annual WSE stocks turnover by foreign WSE investors (Model 7).

Multiple linear regression was used for each dependent variable to discover which monetary and fiscal policy parameters significantly predicted selected variables describing development of capital market in Poland. Fiscal and monetary policy variables served as descriptors explaining capital market parameters in seven separate models as presented below:

$$Y_{i,t} = b_{0,i} + b_{REFR,i}\cdot REFR_t + b_{CPI}\cdot CPI_t + b_{M3,i}\cdot M3_t + b_{DEFGDP,i}\cdot DEFGDP_t$$
$$+ b_{DBTGDP,i}\cdot DBTGDP_t + b_{GGSP,i}\cdot GGSP_t + b_{BGTSP,i}\cdot BGTSP_t + b_{TXRV,i}\cdot TXRV_t + \xi_i$$

for $i = 1, 2, ..., 7$, where each $Y_{i,t}$ denotes one capital market parameter respectively.

Results and Discussion

The fitted regression models for each independent variable are presented in Table 2.

Multiple regression models explain from 77.3% to 95.4% of the volatility of the capital market characteristics. The level of the central bank's reference rate is a

Table 2. Results of Models' Estimation.

Independent Variable	WSEMCAP (Model 1)	NSMCAP (Model 2)	WIG (Model 3)	DEBTMV (Model 4)	PLINSWSE (Model 5)	PLINDWSE (Model 6)	FGNWSE (Model 7)
Regression statistics	$F = 31.164$ $p < 0.001$ Err = 27.2% Adj-R^2 = 0.804	$F = 20.944$ $p < 0.001$ Err = 22.6% Adj-R^2 = 0.822	$F = 22.646$ $p < 0.001$ Err = 18.6% Adj-R^2 = 0.797	$F = 65.564$ $p < 0.001$ Err = 12.3% Adj-R^2 = 0.954	$F = 15.979$ $p < 0.001$ Err = 9.7% Adj-R^2 = 0.773	$F = 22.855$ $p < 0.001$ Err = 18.7% Adj-R^2 = 0.832	$F = 22.414$ $p < 0.001$ Err = 9.1% Adj-R^2 = 0.854
Number of predictors (significant*)	3 (2)	3 (3)	4 (3)	7 (6)	5 (5)	5 (4)	6 (5)
Monetary Predictors (Standardised Beta Coefficients)							
β_{REFR} (p)	−0.605*** (<0.001)	−0.358* (0.035)	−0.416* (0.023)	−0.462* (0.011)		0.689*** (<0.001)	−0.856** (0.009)
β_{CPI} (p)				0.239 (0.051)	−0.373* (0.025)		0.447* (0.042)
β_{M3} (p)						−0.342* (0.032)	0.555* (0.012)
Fiscal Predictors (Standardised Beta Coefficients)							
β_{DEFGDP} (p)				−0.318* (0.012)	0.932** (0.001)	−0.311** (0.009)	
β_{DBTGDP} (p)		0.755*** (<0.001)	0.311 (0.095)	0.343** (0.008)	0.403* (0.046)		
β_{GGSP} (p)				0.188* (0.028)		0.241 (0.097)	−0.245* (0.047)
β_{BGTSP} (p)	−0.472*** (<0.001)		−0.374** (0.003)	−0.561*** (<0.001)	0.920*** (<0.001)		−0.326* (0.022)
β_{TXRV} (p)	0.198 (0.051)	0.413* (0.024)	0.263* (0.020)	0.522*** (<0.001)	−0.960*** (<0.001)	0.360** (0.009)	

Source: Authors' own elaboration.

*$p < 0.05$, **$p < 0.01$, ***$p < 0.001$.

variable that influences the capital market. In six models, the interest rate was a significant parameter. Lower central bank rate (monetary expansion) led to an increase in capitalisation of both stock markets, an increase of the stock market index, and market value of debt. These effects are in line with theoretical models of economy and capital market. The effect is similar to one observed by Hsing (2013) and Bjørnland and Leitemo (2005). An increase in interest rates is followed by a decrease in foreign investor activity on the Polish stock market. The latter seems to explain why, despite rising interest rates, individual investors have increased their activity in stock market turnover.

The parameters of the capital market and the activity of domestic institutional investors were positively affected by public debt in relation to GDP. At the same time, foreign investors reacted to its increase by lowering their activity, as in the case of other evidence of the expansiveness of fiscal policy: the increase in public sector expenditure to GDP and the general budget to GDP ratio.

In turn, the development of the capital market was accompanied by an increase in the share of tax revenues in relation to GDP. This effect can rather be explained by changes in the general activity of the economy, when a good economic situation (increase in income) is conducive to the accumulation of additional tax revenues, and is accompanied by an increase in risk appetite, interest in investing savings in the capital market and acquiring capital from the market as a source of financing accelerating investments. At the same time, a strong negative impact of tax-to-GDP increase was noticed in domestic institutional investors' stock trading.

Summary

The nexus between fiscal and monetary policy, and capital market, finds the interest among the researchers. Our studies contribute to this discussion. We employed three variables for the monetary policy description and five parameters describing the fiscal policy. As dependent variables, we selected seven characteristics of the capital market, which is not common in previous studies. Mostly the earlier research had focused on capital market size or capital market performance. In this chapter, we took into account stock markets capitalisation, market value of debt, performance and investors' activity, all of which allowed us to build seven models, which can be seen as a wider approach. Models explained 77.3%–95.4% of the volatility of the capital market characteristics with monetary and fiscal policy parameters. Our research is not free of limitation; however, we have made every effort to provide the most objective and comprehensive picture of the Polish capital market, and its link with policy mix.

References

Ananwude, A. C., Echekoba, F. N., Okaro, C. S. and Akuesodo, O. E. (2017), "Monetary Policy and Capital Market Performance: An Empirical Evidence from Nigerian Data", *Research Journal of Economics*, Vol. 1 No. 3, available at https://nbnresolving.org/urn:nbn:de:0168-ssoar-56320-3

Babangida, J. S. and Khan, A-U. I. (2021, June), "Effect of Monetary Policy on the Nigerian Stock Market: A Smooth Transition Autoregressive Approach", *CBN Journal of Applied Statistics*, Vol. 12 No. 1. https://doi.org/10.33429/Cjas.12121.1/6

Baykara, S. (2021), "The Impact of Monetary Policy Decisions on Stock Prices: An Event Study". *PressAcademia Procedia (PAP)*, Vol. 13, pp. 52–56, http://doi.org/10.17261/Pressacademia.2021.1422

Bernanke, B. S. and Gertler, M. (1995), "Inside the Black Box: The Credit Channel of Monetary Policy Transmission", *The Journal of Economic Perspectives*, Vol. 9 No. 4, pp. 27–48.

Bernanke, B. S. and Gertler, M. (2001), "Should Central Banks Respond to Movements in Asset Prices?" *The American Economic Review*, Vol. 91 No. 2, pp. 253–257.

Bernanke, B. S. and Kuttner, K. N. (2005), "What Explains the Stock Market's Reaction to Federal Reserve Policy?" *The Journal of Finance*, Vol. 60, https://doi.org/10.1080/23322039.2019.1598248

Bielicki, M. (2015), "Wpływ zmiany referencyjnej stopy procentowej na wolumen obrotów na Giełdzie Papierów Wartościowych w Warszawie", *Studia i Prace Wydziału Nauk Ekonomicznych i Zarządzania*, https://doi.org/10.18276/sip.2015.40/1-09

Bjørnland, H. C. and Leitemo, K. (2005), *Identifying the Interdependence between US Monetary Policy and the Stock Market*, Discussion Papers, No. 17/2005, Bank of Finland Research, Helsinki, ISBN 952-462-226-2.

Blanchard, O., Amighini, A. and Giavazzi, F. (2010). *Macroeconomics: A European Perspective*, Hoboken, Prentice Hall.

Board of Governors of the Federal Reserve System (2021), "The Federal Reserve's Role in the Financial Crisis", available at https://www.federalreserve.gov/econres/notes/feds-notes/the-federal-reserves-role-in-the-financial-crisis-20160323.htm (accessed 4 February 2023).

Bohl, M., Siklos, P. and Werner, T. (2007), "Do Central Banks React to the Stock Market? The Case of the Bundesbank", *Journal of Banking & Finance*, Vol. 31 No. 3, pp. 719–733.

Brown, A. and Karpavičius, S. (2017), "The Reaction of the Australian Stock Market to Monetary Policy Announcements from the Reserve Bank of Australia", *The Economic Record*, Vol. 93 No. 200, March 2017.

Cargill, T. F., Hutchison, M. M. and Ito, T. (2000), *The Asian Financial Crisis: Causes, Cures, and Systemic Implications*, Cambridge University Press.

Chatziantoniou, I., Duffy, D. and Filis, G. (2013), "Stock Market Response to Monetary and Fiscal Policy Shocks: Multi-Country Evidence", *Economic Modelling*, Elsevier, Vol. 30 No. C, pp. 754–769

Federal Reserve Bank of San Francisco (2022), "Monetary Policy", available at https://www.frbsf.org/education/publications/doctor-econ/2010/september/monetary-policy/ (accessed 4 February 2023).

Foresti, P. and Napolitano, O. (2016), *On the Stock Markets' Reaction to Taxation and Public Expenditure, LSE 'Europe in Question'*, Discussion Paper Series, No.115/2016.

Frank, R. H. and Bernanke, B. S. (2007). *Principles of Microeconomics*, New York, and Huntersville, McGraw-Hill/Irwin.

Gali, J. and Gambetti, L. (2014), *The Effects of Monetary Policy on Stock Market Bubbles: Some Evidence*, NBER Working Papers No. 19981, National Bureau of Economic Research.

Goczek, Ł. and Partyka, K. (2016), "Reakcja polityki pieniężnej na wydarzenia giełdowe", *Gospodarka Narodowa*, 5 (285), SGH. https://doi.org/10.33119/GN/10076

Goldstein, M. (1998), *The Asian Financial Crisis: Causes, Cures, and Systemic Implications*, Washington, Institute for International Economics.

Grabowski, M. and Jarmulak, M. (2018), *Fiscal Policy and Economic Performance in Poland, 1998–2017*, Warsaw: National Bank of Poland.

Hojat, S. and Sharifzadeh, M. (2017), "The Impact of Monetary Policy on the Equity Market", *International Journal of Applied Management and Technology*, Vol. 16 No. 1, https://doi.org/10.5590/IJAMT.2017.16.1.02

Hsing, Y. (2013), "Effects of Fiscal Policy and Monetary Policy on the Stock Market in Poland", *Economies*, Vol. 1, pp. 19–25. https://doi.org/10.3390/economies 1030019

International Monetary Fund (2018), "Poland: Selected Issues", available at http://www.imf.org (accessed 3 February, 2023).

International Monetary Fund (2021), "Fiscal Policies", available at https://www.imf.org/en/Topics/imf-and-covid19/Policy-Responses-to-COVID-19/Fiscal-Policies (accessed 2 February 2023).

Janicka, M. (2002), "Polski rynek kapitałowy w przededniu integracji z Unią Europejską", *Acta Universitatis Lodziensis, Folia Oeconomica*, Vol. 158 No. 2002, pp. 85–92.

Lütkepohl, H. and Netšunajev, A. (2018), "The Relation between Monetary Policy and the Stock Market in Europe", *Econometrics*, ISSN 2225-1146, Vol. 6 No. 3, pp. 1–14.

Mishkin, F. S. (2007), *The Economics of Money, Banking, and Financial Markets*, New Jersey: Pearson Addison Wesley.

Mishkin, F. S. (2011), "How Should Central Banks Respond to Asset-Price Bubbles? The "Lean" Versus "Clean" Debate after the GFC", *RBA Bulletin*, Reserve Bank of Australia, June quarter, pp. 59–70.

NBP (2022), *Narodowy Bank Polski, Report*, "Raport o rozwoju systemu finansowego w Polsce w 2021r", available at https://nbp.pl/system-finansowy/raporty-o-rozwoju-systemu-finansowego/ (accessed 20 February 2023).

Przybylska-Kapuścińska, W. (2009), "Dwudziestolecie Polityki Pieniężnej NBP. Wpływ Transformacji i integracji gospodarczej", *Ruch Prawniczy, Ekonomiczny i Socjologiczny*, Rok LXXI, zeszyt 2.

Rozkrut, M. (2003), "The Monetary and Fiscal Policy Mix in Poland", in: *Fiscal issues and Central Banking in Emerging Economies*, Papers, No 20, BIS.

Skibińska-Fabrowska, I. (2015), "Polityka pieniężna Narodowego Banku Polskiego w latach 2008–2014", *Zeszyty Naukowe Polskiego Towarzystwa Ekonomicznego w Zielonej Górze*, nr 2 - Współczesny kryzys finansowo-gospodarczy. Istota, przebieg i konsekwencje.

Sławiński, A. (ed.) (2011), *Polityka pieniężna*, C.H. Beck, Warszawa.

World Bank (2020), "Financial Market Development and Integration", available at https://data.worldbank.org/indicator/FM.AST.DOMS.GD.ZS (accessed 4 February 2023).

Yang-Chao, W., Jui-Jung, T. and Jingsi, X. (2022), "The Impact of Monetary Policy on China's Stock and Bond Markets", *China an International Journal*, Vol. 20 No. 2, May 2022.

Chapter 9

Innovation Policy and National Innovation System: Evidence From Poland

Anna Matras-Bolibok and Piotr Bolibok

Abstract

Research Background: Innovation policy and innovation systems undoubtedly play a crucial role in shaping the path of economic development of contemporary economies. A particularly interesting context for studying the evolution of this area is offered by post-transition economies which had to undergo fundamental structural changes and face the global competition where the advances in knowledge and technological progress ultimately decide between success or failure.

Purpose of the Chapter: The chapter aims to portray and evaluate the key developments in the innovation policy and national innovation system of Poland – one of the largest and most successful post-transition economies.

Methodology: The methodological framework of the study involves a descriptive analysis of the major changes in the regulatory and institutional settings as well as an analysis of statistical data on the crucial dimensions of Poland's innovation policy and innovation system over the period 2000–2021. Additionally, the overall effects of the policy have been assessed using the data from the European Innovation Scoreboard (over 2015–2022) and the Global Innovation Index (over 2008–2022).

Findings: The findings suggest that the significant changes in Poland's innovation policy and innovation system frameworks introduced since the mid-2000s have resulted in a dynamic increase in the intensity of R&D efforts, especially in the business enterprise sector, allowing to narrow the structural gaps dividing the country from more advanced economies and markedly improve its overall research and innovative performance. A key role in this process has been played by the direct and indirect government support for innovative activities.

Modeling Economic Growth in Contemporary Poland, 145–160

Copyright © 2024 Anna Matras-Bolibok and Piotr Bolibok

Published under exclusive licence by Emerald Publishing Limited

doi:10.1108/978-1-83753-654-220231010

Keywords: Innovation policy; national innovation system; Poland; research and development; innovativeness; public support for innovation

Introduction

In the light of the indisputable role of innovation in shaping the path of economic development, it is crucial to support innovation processes with a properly designed innovation policy. The importance of innovation policy is widely recognised and in both developed and developing economies governments are increasingly placing innovation at the centre of their growth strategies.

Innovation policy can be defined as a public intervention, designed and administered by government, including multiple agencies at various spatial levels, to support creation and diffusion of innovation (Edler et al., 2016).Within innovation policy framework, the state influences innovative activities by creating legal regulations, setting the long-term directions of scientific research and their priorities, deciding on allocation of financial resources for innovative activities, and supervising the functioning of public scientific institutions and the implementation of research programmes and projects (Jasiński, 2018).Theoretical as well as pragmatic approach to setting priorities for innovation policy is largely shaped by contextual factors to address relevant market failures, systemic component of technological progress or social and environmental challenges, and to be geared specifically to social, economic and environmental circumstances (Fagerberg, 2017).

The role of public support for innovative activity has been emphasised in the endogenous growth theory (Shaw, 1992). In contrast to neoclassical models of economic growth, where technological progress was considered as an exogenous and independent variable (Solow, 1957), endogenous growth results directly from technological progress, which is the effect of R&D activities. According to the assumptions of this theory, subsidising R&D activities may affect innovation performance and, in the long-term perspective, also the economic development (Jones, 1995; Romer, 1990).

Supporting the development of national innovation systems is also considered among key innovation policy goals aiming at enhancing the innovative performance and overall competitiveness of particular economies. The national innovation systems approach follows the assumption that the flows of knowledge among actors of innovation process, including enterprises, universities and government entities, are the key to successful innovative process. As demonstrated by Mazzucato (2011, p. 18), the governments of the contemporarily most advanced economies play important entrepreneurial role being actively engaged in innovation processes, creating the strategies for new high growth areas, funding the most uncertain and the least commercially attractive phases of R&D that the private sector is too risk-averse to undertake or managing and controlling further stages of innovation processes, including their final commercialisation. The role of modern governments goes, therefore, significantly beyond simply establishing the general infrastructural and regulatory conditions for creation of innovations.

The significance of innovation policy has also been acknowledged by countries trying to transform their economies to set them on dynamic growth trajectories. In the case of Poland, the beginnings of modern innovation policy can be traced back to the initial stages of the country's economic transition from a centrally planned to market economy in the early 1990s. Since that time, Poland's innovation policy has been constantly evolving, aiming to adopt the best practices of advanced economies on the one hand and trying to accommodate the specificity of local conditions on the other. The recent decades have brought significant changes in the country's innovation policy and national innovation system frameworks enabling it to markedly improve the overall innovation performance and to narrow the gaps in crucial structural dimensions of innovation policy dividing it from more advanced economies. Currently, Poland is assessed as an 'emerging innovator' among EU countries (taking 30th place in the European Innovation Scoreboard (2023)) and is ranked 38th among 132 countries according to the Global Innovation Index (2022).

The aim of the chapter is to characterise and evaluate the key developments in the Poland's innovation policy and national innovation system in the recent decades with a special focus on the extent and effects of direct and indirect government support for innovative activities in the business enterprise sector, as well as on the changes in the structure and the sources of funds for R&D expenditure in the major sectors of performance.

The remainder of the chapter is structured as follows. The next section considers the theoretical rationales for innovation policy and presents evolution and characteristics of innovation policy and national innovation system in Poland. The third section outlines the methodological framework of the study. The fourth section presents and discusses the results of empirical analyses. The chapter is closed with summary recapitulating its main findings.

Literature Review

Rationales for Innovation Policy

The relevant literature discusses three main rationales for innovation policy (Schot and Steinmueller, 2018). The first one is based on the assumption that government support for innovation contributes to economic growth and addresses market failure in private provision of new knowledge. The second approach emphasises the role of the national systems of innovation in knowledge creation and commercialisation. The third one is linked to contemporary social and environmental challenges supporting socio-technical transformations.

According to the first approach, the main premise for public support for innovation stems from the market failure perspective. Knowledge that is produced as a result of innovation policy, in particular during early stages of R&D, is considered as a public good (Hall et al., 2010). Difficulties in providing an effective protection against imitation of research results by competitors make companies reluctant to invest in R&D, given the threat of achieving an insufficient rate of return to compensate for the risk and cost incurred (Hall and Lerner,

2010). This, in turn, leads to a socially sub-optimal level of investment in creation of new knowledge, which justifies supporting this area with public funds. Numerous studies have shown a positive impact of government expenditure on R&D on the innovativeness of enterprises (Gonzàlez and Pazò, 2008; Kijek et al., 2016). Importantly, public funding has a positive impact on the growth of investment in R&D and is characterised by a higher social rate of return (Guellec and Van Pottelsberghe de la Potterie, 2004). It is worth emphasising that the empirical evidence on the impact of public financial support for innovative activities does not reveal any statistically significant crowding-out effect between public and private expenditures (Hall and Maffioli, 2008).

The other rationale for innovation policy is innovation system approach that is rooted in evolutionary economics which argues that neoclassical economics does not offer satisfactory explanations on economic growth and the key drivers of international competitiveness (Chaminade et al., 2018). The systems of innovation approach has emerged on the basis of seminal works by Freeman (1987), Lundvall (1992) and Nelson (1993) and initially put the main emphasis on the importance of development of such systems at a national level. In addition to the national approach, complementary variants: sectoral and regional approaches have emerged (Edquist, 1997). System of innovation is defined as the network of institutions, including enterprises, scientific institutions and government entities in the public and private sectors whose activities and cooperation contribute to creation and diffusion of innovation (Godin, 2009). The systemic approach to innovation, contrary to linear models of innovation process, is based on the assumption that innovation processes cannot be divided into several independent stages that take place in a strictly sequential order (Samara et al., 2012). Institutional change is not assessed through criteria based on static allocative efficiency but rather on how it promotes technological and structural change. In this approach, the quantity of R&D is not as important as its distribution throughout the economy, and often the crucial role in this process is played by the state.

The third approach, challenge-driven innovation policy, complements earlier rationales focused on boosting economic competitiveness by correcting market and system failures. The goals of innovation policy are focused on solving important societal challenges, as a consequence governments determine the directions of growth by supporting different sectors and fostering new industrial ecosystems, which the private sector can develop further, inducing cross-sectoral knowledge spillovers and increasing macroeconomic stability (Mazzucato et al., 2020).

It is worth to point out that the consecutive rationales for innovation policy do not replace the previous ones as they start to co-exist. As the result, the evolution of innovation policies may be shaped by competing framings (Schot and Steinmuller, 2018).

Evolution and Characteristics of Innovation Policy and National Innovation System in Poland

The first strategic documents setting out the directions of the national innovation policy in Poland were established in the mid-1990s as results of systemic transition process. The opening of the Polish economy to the outside world and the need to compete on a global scale forced fundamental regulatory changes, which resulted in the formulation of strategic goals aimed at building an innovative economy. The large dispersion of programmes, instruments and objectives resulted in an incoherent vision of the national innovation policy and a low effectiveness of actions aimed at creation of a national innovation system. Additionally, the first strategic documents defining the directions of innovation policy (Committee for Research Projects, 1999; Ministry of Economy, 2000) underlined the need to develop regional innovation systems by creating networks of innovation and technology transfer centres and supporting the creation of science, technology and industrial parks.

Poland's accession to the EU caused the country's innovation policy to be shaped by the EU's innovation policy. By becoming a member of the EU in 2004, Poland was automatically included in the implementation of the Lisbon Strategy objectives, and then in the implementation of the Europe 2020 Strategy (Ministry of Economy, 2011, 2012; Ministry of Economy, Labour and Social Policy, 2004). In accordance with both strategies, supporting innovation, entrepreneurship and knowledge-based economy has become the priority. It was assumed that the essential element of both strategies implementation should be the increase of the share of expenditures on R&D in gross domestic product (GDP) up to 3%, with 2/3 of these funds coming from private sources.

The turning point for innovation policy in Poland started with the inflow of funds under the EU programming period 2007–2013 when a coherent vision of innovation policy in Poland started to develop. It is worth emphasising that currently EU funds constitute the key external support for innovative activity in Poland. The main strategic documents devoted to improvement of innovativeness in Poland for the three sequential programming periods were: Innovative Economy Operational Programme 2007–2013 and Smart Growth Operational Programme 2014–2020, allocating €8.3 billion an €8.6 billion, respectively, and for the current programming period: European Funds for Smart Economy (EFSE) Programme 2021–2027, being the continuation of two previous programmes, with the allocation sum of €7.9 billion. The EFSE programme focuses its support on economic development, innovation and R&D, technology transfer, digitisation of enterprises and implementation of the European Green Deal in Poland with the goal to increase R&D expenditures to 2.5% of GDP by 2030.

The Polish government has developed and implemented several policy instruments to indirectly promote business R&D and innovation. In the Act of 29 July 2005 on selected forms of support for innovation activity, the government introduced the status of research and development centres to entrepreneurs, technology credit for the purchase of new technologies as well as tax incentives like tax relief giving the right to deduct from the tax base expenses incurred for the acquisition of new technologies (OECD, 2007). In 2016, new regulation introducing tax relief for R&D, available to entities that conduct R&D activities, regardless of their size, was introduced. The relief allows deduction of 200% of R&D costs in particular on staff remuneration and costs of raw materials and supplies. Other forms of indirect public support for innovation include: IP Box, introduced in 2019 for enterprises commercialising intellectual property (IP) rights created as the results of their own R&D activities or acquired as R&D services from other entities, but patented by the taxpayer. The prototype relief and tax relief for robotisation both introduced in 2022 were established under the Polish Deal Programme.

In the Polish national innovation system, the institution responsible for innovation policy is Ministry of Science and Education with its two executive agencies: National Science Centre and National Centre for Research and Development which are responsible for financing R&D projects and regulating a number of executive and legal acts related to the implementation of programmes financed with the EU funds (https://www.gov.pl/web/ncbr-en/ncbr). Besides government institutions which set policy directions and public sector intermediary agencies between governments and research organisations, the national innovation system in Poland encompasses research-performing organisations (universities and higher education institutions), research institutes of the Polish Academy of Sciences focused on basic research and branch R&D units which concentrate more on applied research (https://www.gov.pl/web/ncbr-en/polish-research–innovation-policy).

For the functioning of the innovation system in Poland, an important role is played by business environment institutions, including innovation and entrepreneurship centres and non-bank financial institutions. Over 1990–2021, their number increased from 27 to 382, including: 34 technology parks, 16 technology incubators, 16 academic entrepreneurship incubators, 52 technology transfer centres, 25 innovation centres, 103 training and consulting centres, and 41 entrepreneurship incubators, 64 loan funds and 31 credit guarantee funds (Mażewska et al., 2021).

Despite the intensified development of intermediary institutions, the collaboration on R&D activities between public and private research sectors is relatively weak. According to the European Innovation Scoreboard (2023), the number of public-private scientific co-publications per million population in Poland increased from 39 in 2014 to 75 in 2020 in comparison to 99 and 134, respectively, in EU. The share of cooperating enterprises is also relatively low. In 2014, only 3.5% of innovative small and medium-sized enterprises (SMEs) in Poland were collaborating in comparison to 9.5% in the EU, while in 2020, these shares grew to 6.7% and 11.7%, respectively. These results indicate that business-to-business and business-to-science linkages determining the knowledge spillovers within innovation system remain still underdeveloped in Poland.

Methodology

The research framework adopted in the present study encompasses two major stages. The first one aims to identify and evaluate the key developments in Poland's innovation policy over the period 2000–2021 using the data extracted from the databases and websites of Statistics Poland (2023), the Polish Ministry of Economic Development and Technology (2023), Eurostat (2023) and OECD.Stat (2023). First, we assess the changes in the composition, relative magnitude and general dynamics of funds used to finance the gross domestic expenditure on R&D, as compared to the EU averages. Next, we turn to the analysis of the scale and relative intensity of the direct and indirect government support for business R&D activities. Finally, we run an in-depth analysis of the allocation of R&D expenditure in the major sectors of performance, i.e. the business enterprise sector and the government and higher education sectors by type of research and field of R&D, as well the developments in the composition of the sources of funds for R&D activities within each sector. Due to breaks in data, the time frames of the in-depth analyses had to be adjusted accordingly with a general intention to cover the longest continuous time series possible.

The second stage of the research focuses on the assessment of the effects of Poland's innovation policy in the recent decades from the perspective of the country's overall research and innovative performance under two distinct evaluation frameworks, i.e. the European Innovation Scoreboard (2023) by the European Commission (over 2015–2022) and the Global Innovation Index (2023) by the World Intellectual Property Organization (over 2008–2022).

Findings

Key Developments in the Contemporary Innovation Policy of Poland

One of the most noticeable attainments of Poland's innovation policy in the recent decades is a fundamental change in the structure of the sources of funds for R&D activities (Fig. 1., Panel A.). In the years 2000–2010, the vast majority (56%–68%) of total gross domestic R&D expenditure (GERD) in Poland was financed by the government sector, whereas the share of the business sector remained relatively low (24%–34%). The year 2010, however, marks the beginning of the period of a dynamic increase in the magnitude of R&D activities in the Polish business enterprise sector which has led to a complete reversal of the above structure, bringing it much closer to the ones observed in more advanced European economies. In the result, over the recent years, the shares of both government and business sector financed GERD in Poland have been gradually nearing their respective average levels recorded across the entire EU. In 2021, the share of business enterprise R&D expenditure (BERD) in Poland reached 51% (as compared to the EU average of 58% in 2020). Simultaneously, the share of government financed GERD in 2021 arrived at 37% (with the EU average of 30% in 2020).

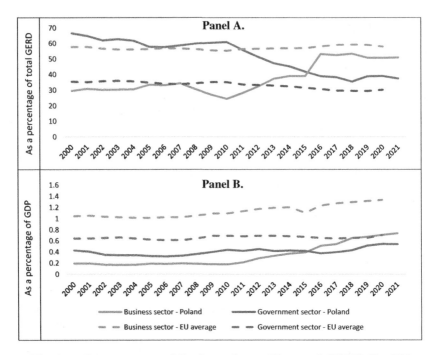

Fig. 1.   Government and Business Sector Financed GERD Vs. EU
Averages. *Source:* Authors' own elaboration.

Notwithstanding its dynamic growth since 2010, the BERD in Poland as a
percentage of GDP remains relatively low when compared not only to the most
advanced European economies but even to the EU average (Fig. 1., Panel B).
Although the gap dividing Poland from an average EU economy is progressively
closing, in 2020 the BERD as a percentage of GDP reached the level of 0.7, i.e.
roughly half of the EU average (1.3%). In contrast, the level of government
financed GERD as a percentage of GDP has been following the EU average more
closely, closing the gap up to 77% of the EU average in 2020 (i.e. 0.54% of GDP).
    The recent years have also brought a rapid increase in the direct and indirect
government support for BERD relative to GDP (Fig. 2.). Since 2002, the intensity
of this support increased nearly 12 times, reaching 0.17% of GDP in 2021.
    A noteworthy role in the above increase has been played by a system of new
income tax reliefs for innovative activities launched in 2016. In 2021, the estimated value of indirect government support for BERD reached nearly 0.05% of
GDP, i.e. about 28% of the total government support. Simultaneously, since 2002,
the intensity of direct government support (government financed BERD) has
increased more than eightfold, exceeding 0.12% of GDP in 2021.
    To make the analysis of the developments in Poland's innovation policy more
complete, we have investigated the structures of GERD by the type of research

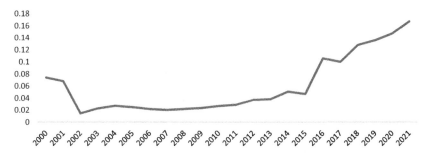

Fig. 2.   Government Financed BERD and Indirect Government Support Through Tax Incentives as a Percentage of GDP. *Source:* Authors' own elaboration.

and field of R&D and the composition of the sources of funds for R&D expenditure across the key sectors of performance, i.e. the business enterprise sector and the government and higher education sectors (Fig. 3.).

The results of the analysis clearly demonstrate that the dynamic increase in the business sector GERD since 2010 was attributable primarily to expenditure on experimental development (Fig. 3., Panel A.). In 2020, total expenditure of business sector on experimental development amounted to 0.65% of GDP and almost $^{3}/_{4}$ of total sector's GERD. The shares of expenditure on both basic and applied research in the business sector remained significantly lower, averaging 8% and 18% of GDP, respectively. In contrast, a majority of GERD in the government and higher education sectors (Fig. 3., Panel B.) was systematically allocated to basic research, which is largely consistent with the general principles of modern innovation policy. What is worth noticing, over the recent years the share of expenditure on basic research in the total GERD of government and higher education sectors in Poland significantly increased, averaging 75% in the years 2016–2020 as compared to 54% in the period 2005–2015. Not surprisingly, therefore, the shares of expenditure on applied research and experimental development in the government and higher education sectors remained significantly lower over the entire analysed period averaging about 20% of total GERD each.

As regards the structure of GERD by the field of R&D in both business as well as government and higher education sectors, the majority of expenditure was allocated to engineering and technology and natural sciences (Fig. 3., Panels C. and D.). If, however, in the government and higher education sectors, the shares of those two fields were largely similar in the entire analysed period, averaging about 29% and 33% of total GERD, respectively, in the case of the business enterprise sector the expenditures on engineering and technology were clearly dominating, averaging around 75% of the sector's GERD in 2004–2020 and being the main driver of its dynamic growth relative to GDP in the last decade. Interestingly however, since 2010 there has also been a noticeable increasing

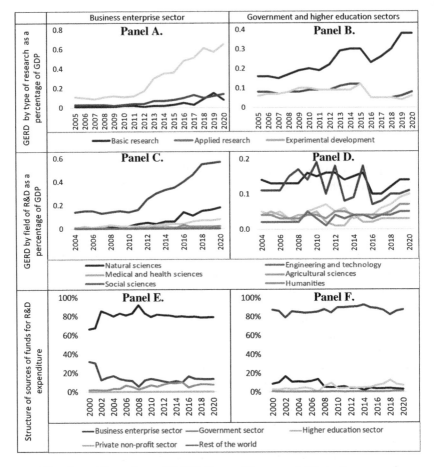

Fig. 3.   Allocation of R&D Expenditures and Their Sources of Financing in the Key Sectors of Performance. *Source:* Authors' own elaboration.

tendency in the share of BERD on natural sciences. Overall, the share of this field grew by 10 p.p., reaching 21% of the total sector's GERD in 2020. Simultaneously, the share of engineering and technology dropped by 12 p.p. to 66% of the sector's GERD in 2020. Other fields of R&D accounted for significantly lower shares of GERD in the investigated sectors of performance; however, it seems worth to underline a generally much more balanced composition of expenditure by field of R&D in the government and higher education sectors. The recent years have also brought a dynamic increase in the intensity of expenditure on medical and health sciences, which may be partially attributable to the impact of the COVID-19 pandemic. In the effect, in 2020, both in the business enterprise sector, as well as in the government and higher education sectors, the R&D expenditure in this field accounted for a similar percentage of GDP, i.e. 0.08% and 0.10%, respectively.

As demonstrated by the data, one of the most noteworthy achievements of Poland's innovation policy is strengthening the capacity of the business enterprise sector to self-finance its R&D expenditure (Fig. 3., Panel E.). In 2000, the funds of business enterprise sector financed slightly above 66% of total BERD, whereas in 2020, this share increased to about 79%. Simultaneously, the share of government financed BERD decreased from 32% in 2000 to barely 14% in 2020. These tendencies gain even more importance in the light of the dynamic growth in BERD observed since 2010. Thus, the business enterprise sector has not only been able to significantly increase its R&D expenditures in that period, but also has borne the highest burden of that increase. Moreover, a decreasing share of government financed BERD, occurring despite a dynamic increase in the value of direct government support for business R&D, suggests that in the last decade self-financed BERD has been increasing even more dynamically, which undoubtedly deserves a positive evaluation. It is also worth to point out the role of indirect government support for business R&D in the form of tax reliefs, as well as a gradually increasing share of BERD financed from foreign sources. In contrast, the R&D expenditures of the government and higher education sectors have been financed predominantly with the public funds which over the analysed period accounted on average for nearly 87% of total sources employed (Fig. 3., Panel F.). Such a strong reliance on public funds seems fully justified given the fact that government and higher education sectors focus primarily on basic research.

Evaluation of Poland's Innovation Policy

In order to assess the overall effects of the developments in Poland's innovation policy and innovation system in the recent years we first refer to the country's Summary Innovation Index (SII) within the European Innovation Scoreboard (2023) framework. The index offers a comprehensive assessment of the key dimensions of the research and innovative systems of the EU member states enabling a comparative analysis of their performance in that field. As demonstrated in Fig. 4., since 2015, Poland has exhibited a generally continuous progress in terms of SII. Despite still being considered an 'emerging innovator', between 2005 and 2022 the value of Poland's SII increased from 55 to 67 points. As of 2022, the country's overall innovative performance reached 60.5% of the EU average, compared to 56% in the whole block of 'emerging innovator' countries. What is worth to point out, Poland's innovative performance over the period 2015–2022 was increasing at a noticeably higher rate (11.3%) than the averages for the entire EU (9.9%) and the group of 'emerging innovator' countries (6.4%), allowing the country both to narrow the gap to the EU average and to increase the advantage over average 'emerging innovators'.

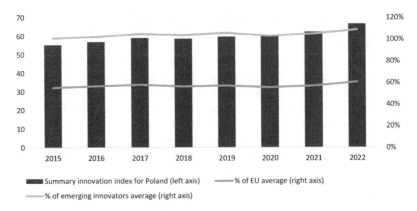

Fig. 4. European Innovation Scoreboard – Summary Innovation Index for Poland Vs. EU Averages. *Source:* Authors' own elaboration.

Another benchmark enabling a comprehensive assessment of the results of Poland's innovation policy in the recent years is offered by the *Global Innovation Index* (GII). Fig. 5 presents the changes in the Poland's position in the global rankings under the GII framework.

The data in Fig. 5 clearly confirm the overall progress made by Poland in each of the investigated dimensions of the GII framework. In the analysed period,

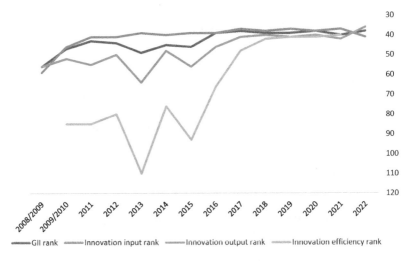

Fig. 5. Position of Poland in the Global Rankings Under the GII Framework. *Source:* Authors' own elaboration.

Poland has advanced from the 56th to 36th position in the world in terms of innovation output as well as from 59th to 41st position in terms of innovation input. As regards the overall position in the GII ranking the country has moved from 56th place in the period 2008/2009 to 40th in 2022. Even more noticeable advance was made in the global ranking based on the innovation efficiency ratio, designed to directly assess the efficiency of innovation systems and policies – after dropping to the 110th position in the world in 2013, Poland was able to reach 41st place in just 8 years, principally thanks to a significant improvement in the innovation output performance. The progress made by Poland in the analysed global innovation performance and efficiency rankings undoubtedly supports the validity of the principal assumptions and general directions of Poland's innovation policy.

Summary

The results of the study demonstrate that the successively introduced changes to Poland's innovation policy and innovation system framework since the mid-2000s have contributed to a significant increase in the overall intensity of R&D expenditure relative to country's GDP, especially in the business enterprise sector. This, in turn, has allowed to bring the general structure of GERD by sources of funds in the Polish economy much closer to the EU average. Moreover, both the direct government financing of BERD and the indirect support in the form of a systematically enhanced system of tax reliefs for innovative activities appear to have created strong incentives for business entities not only to continuously expand investments in R&D but also to finance them predominantly with their own funds. Although the value of direct government support for business R&D has been increasing very dynamically, its share in BERD has dropped more than two times over the last two decades as the rate of growth in self-financed BERD has turned out to be even higher. The business sector has, therefore, not only been able to significantly expand the magnitude of its R&D expenditures, but also has borne the highest burden of that increase. The empirical evidence also suggests that a pivotal role in that process has likely been played by the indirect government support for business R&D in the form of tax reliefs and in particular the tax relief for research and development launched in 2016. Strengthening the capacity of the business enterprise sector to self-finance its R&D expenditure is one of the most noteworthy achievements of Poland's innovation policy in the analysed period.

The dynamic increase in BERD since 2010 has been attributable primarily to expenditure on experimental development. The Polish business sector has, therefore, largely been focused on expenditure with the largest commercialisation potential. In contrast, consistent with the general principles of modern innovation policy, GERD in the government and higher education sectors has been increasingly dominated by basic research, which financial burden is commonly expected to be borne primarily by the public sector. Given the above, it comes as no surprise that the vast majority (nearly 90%) of R&D expenditures in the government and higher education sectors in the analysed period has been financed with public funds.

The majority of R&D expenditures in the key sector of performance was allocated to engineering and technology and natural sciences. Given the dominance of expenditure on experimental development in the business sector, not surprisingly the vast majority of BERD was spent in the former field, while in the case of government and higher education sectors the general composition of R&D expenditure was much more balanced, which seems largely justified by the fact that most of them were allocated for basic research.

As regards functioning of national innovation system, Poland still lags behind EU averages in collaboration on innovation activities. A dynamic progress in that field, however, allows to narrow the gap to more advanced European economies and creates favourable conditions for more intense collaboration and further exploiting the synergy potential of the system.

A significant progress made by Poland in terms of relative performance of its research and innovative systems as proxied by comprehensive measures employed under leading international benchmarks, such as the European Innovation Scoreboard or the Global Innovation Index, allows to assess positively the changes introduced to its innovation policy and innovation system frameworks over the recent years. Although Poland is still recognised as an 'emerging innovator', the successful development of strong incentives for sustainable increase in the business enterprise sector R&D combined with continuous support for basic research in the public one are likely to allow the country to speed up the process of narrowing the structural gaps to more advanced economies and build up competitive advantages necessary for strengthening the foundations of the long-term economic growth.

References

Chaminade, C., Lundvall, B. and Haneef, S. (2018), *Advanced Introduction to National Innovation Systems*, Edward Elgar Publishing Limited, Chentenham, Northampton.

Committee for Research Projects (1999), *Założenia polityki innowacyjnej państwa do 2002 r*, Warsaw.

Edler, J., Cunningham, P., Gök, A. and Shapira, P. (2016), *Handbook of Innovation Policy Impact*, Edward Elgar Publishing, Cheltenham/Northampton.

Edquist, C. (1997), "Systems of Innovation Approaches – Their Emergence and Characteristics", in: *Systems of Innovation: Technologies, Institutions and Organizations*, ed. Edquist, C., Pinter/Cassell, London.

European Innovation Scoreboard (2023), *EIS Interactive Tool*, available at https://ec.europa.eu/research-and-innovation/en/statistics/performance-indicators/european-innovation-scoreboard/eis (accessed 2 March 2023).

Eurostat (2023), "Eurostat Database", available at https://ec.europa.eu/eurostat/web/main/data/database (accessed 1 March 2023).

Fagerberg, J. (2017), "Innovation Policy: Rationales, Lessons and Challenges", *Journal of Economic Surveys*, Vol. 31, pp. 497–512.

Freeman, C. (1987), *Technology Policy and Economic Performance: Lessons from Japan*, Pinter, London.

Global Innovation Index (2023), "About the Global Innovation Index", available at https://www.globalinnovationindex.org/about-gii#reports (accessed 2 March 2023).

Godin, B. (2009), "National Innovation System: The System Approach in Historical Perspective" *Science, Technology & Human Values*, Vol. *34* No. 4, pp. 476–501.

González, X. and Pazó, C. (2008), "Do public subsidies stimulate private R&D spending?", *Research Policy*, Vol. *37* No. 3, pp. 371–389.

Guellec, D. and Van Pottelsberghe de la Potterie, B. (2004), "From R&D to Productivity Growth: Do the Institutional Settings and the Source of Funds of R&D Matter?" *Oxford Bulletin of Economics & Statistics*, Vol. *66* No. 3, pp. 353–378.

Hall, B. H. and Lerner, J. (2010), "Financing R&D and Innovation", in: *Handbook of the Economics of Innovation*, Vol. 1, eds. Hall, B. H. and Rosenberg, N., Elsevier, Oxford.

Hall, B. H., Mairesse, J. and Mohnen, P. (2010), "Measuring the Returns to R&D", in: *Handbook of the Economics of Innovation*, Vol. 2, eds. Hall, B. H., and Rosenberg, N., Elsevier, Oxford.

Hall, B. H. and Maffioli, A. (2008), "Evaluating the Impact of Technology Development Funds in Emerging Economies: Evidence from Latin America", *European Journal of Development Research*, Vol. *20* No. 2, pp. 172–198.

https://www.gov.pl/web/ncbr-en/ncbr (accessed 10 March 2023).

https://www.gov.pl/web/ncbr-en/polish-research–innovation-policy (accessed 10 March 2023).

Jasiński, A. (2018), "Polityka innowacyjna w procesie transformacji w Polsce: czy skuteczna?" *Optimum. Economic Studies*, Vol. *3* No. 93, pp. 221–239.

Jones, C. I. (1995), "R&D-Based Models of Economic Growth", *Journal of Political Economy*, Vol. *103* No. 4, p. 759.

Kijek, T., Matras-Bolibok, A. and Rycaj, E. (2016), "Do Public R&D Expenditures Foster Business R&D Investments?" *International Journal of Synergy and Research*, Vol. *5*, pp. 147–154.

Lundvall, B-Å. (1992), *National Systems of Innovation: Towards a Theory of Innovation and Interactive Learning*, Pinter, London.

Mazzucato, M., Kattel, R. and Ryan-Collins, J. (2020), "Challenge-Driven Innovation Policy: Towards a New Policy Toolkit", *Journal of Industry, Competition and Trade*, Vol. *20*, pp. 421–437.

Mazzucato, M. (2011), *The Entrepreneurial State*, Demos, London.

Mażewska, M., Bąkowski, A. and Rudawska, J. (eds.) (2021), *Business and Innovation Centers in Poland*, Study Report 2021, Polish Business and Innovation Centers Association in Poland, Warsaw.

Ministry of Economy (2000), *Zwiększanie innowacyjności gospodarki w Polsce do 2006 roku*, Warsaw.

Ministry of Economy, Labour and Social Policy (2004), *Strategia zwiększania nakładów na działalność B+R w celu osiągnięcia założeń Strategii Lizbońskiej*, Warsaw.

Ministry of Economy (2011), *Krajowy Program Reform na rzecz realizacji Strategii Europa 2020*, Warsaw.

Ministry of Economy (2012), *Strategia innowacyjności i efektywności gospodarki na lata 2012–2020*, Warsaw.

Ministry of Economic Development and Technology (2023), *Ulganabadania I rozwój* [*Tax Relief for Research and Development*], available at https://www.gov.pl/web/rozwoj-technologia/ulga-na-badania-i-rozwoj (accessed 1 March 2023).

Nelson, R. R. (ed.) (1993), *National Innovation Systems: A Comparative Study*, Oxford University Press, Oxford.

OECD (2007), *Policy Mix for Innovation in Poland Key Issues and Recommendations*, Warsaw.

OECD.Stat (2023), *OECD.Stat*, available at https://stats.oecd.org/ (accessed 1 March 2023).

Romer, P. (1990), "Endogenous Technological Change", *Journal of Political Economy*, Vol. *98* No. 5, pp. 71–102.

Samara, E., Georgiadis, P. and Bakouros, I. (2012), "The Impact of Innovation Policies on the Performance of National Innovation Systems: A System Dynamics Analysis", *Technovation*, Vol. *32* No. 11, pp. 624–638.

Schot, J. and Steinmueller, W. E. (2018), "Three Frames for Innovation Policy: R&D, Systems of Innovation and Transformative Change", *Research Policy*, Vol. *47* No. 9, pp. 1554–1567.

Shaw, G. K. (1992), "Policy Implications of Endogenous Growth Theory", *The Economic Journal*, Vol. *102* No. 412, pp. 611–621.

Solow, R. M. (1957), "Technical Change and Aggregate Production Function", *The Review of Economics and Statistics*, Vol. *39* No. 3, pp. 312–320.

Statistics Poland (2023), Science and Technology, available at https://stat.gov.pl/en/topics/science-and-technology/ (accessed 1 March 2023).

Chapter 10

New Opportunities in Poland's Decarbonisation Energy Policy – Prospects for the Development of Small-Sized Nuclear Power (SMRs)

Andrzej Szablewski

Abstract

Research Background: There are many indications that government policy-makers and supporters of large-scale nuclear expansion in Poland have not seriously grappled with arguments critical of this direction of the country's power development. Instead, there is a mood of euphoric elation in these circles without even an attempt to reflect on why this kind of nuclear power is in a state of perennial crisis and lack of development prospects in Western countries.

The Purpose of the Chapter: The purpose of this chapter is to consider from an economic perspective the potential role of nuclear power in decarbonising the Polish power sector. It needs to answer two questions: why not develop large-scale nuclear power and why small modular reactors (SMRs) can be a better alternative for decarbonisation of the Polish power sector.

Methodology: The primary research method used in the preparation of this chapter is a critical analysis and synthesis of the literature on the subject.

Findings: A technological revolution will offer electricity customers increasingly better alternatives. Among them there is also technology of SMRs which seems to be much less risky option in terms of its compatibility with the direction of the power sector's evolution as well as cost of sectors' decarbonisation.

Keywords: Large nuclear reactors; small nuclear reactors; economy of scale; reactor's flexibility; death spiral; modularisation and modularity

Modeling Economic Growth in Contemporary Poland, 161–174
Copyright © 2024 Andrzej Szablewski
Published under exclusive licence by Emerald Publishing Limited
doi:10.1108/978-1-83753-654-220231011

Introduction

Submitted several years ago, the proposal to build the potential of large-scale nuclear energy with a total capacity of 6 to 9 GW now seems to be entering the implementation phase. This is evidenced by the adoption of a government resolution to build the first nuclear power plant and the selection of Westinghouse as a contractor for this project. The contractor agreed that construction of the power plant consisting of three reactors with a total capacity of 3.7 GW would begin in 2026 and be completed in 2032. There are also declarations of government representatives about ongoing talks on the build of two further large nuclear power plants in Poland. These developments are very well received by the public. Support here reaches a record over 86%, and what more 70% of the the respondents declare approval for build a nuclear power plant near their place of residence ('Rekordowe poparcie 86% Polaków za budową elektrowni jądrowych w Polsce', 2022).[1] Therefore, it is not surprising that there is bipartisan support in the parliament, which is extremely rare case in recent years in the Polish political realities.

In the narrative prevailing in the media, development of nuclear power rises to the rank of the Polish raison d'état, and becomes a necessary condition of independence from fossil fuels (Stańczuk and Twardawa, 2022). However, the most appealing argument to the public in favour of nuclear power is related to the nature of the two main types of renewable energy sources (RES). As both depend on the fickle sun and wind, they cannot guarantee a stable supply of electricity. Recently, pro-nuclear narrative has also been reinforced by the war in Ukraine causing serious perturbations in fuel supplies. Therefore, it is postulated to change the approach to the energy transformation towards making nuclear energy its foundation. This is in line with the government's long undisguised reluctance to support the fastest possible development of renewable energy. Hence, nuclear power is even being treated as a better alternative than RES to decarbonise the domestic energy sector in both economic and environmental perspective (Kołodyńska-Magdziarz, 2020). The rhetoric of nuclear power supporters is also sharpening towards those who question the need for its development, which is even reflected in the comparison of opponents with anti-vaxxers (Wiech, 2022).

In this widespread and uncritical support for the development of large-scale nuclear energy, opposing views are usually ignored. This is worrisome given the huge financial dimension of this programme estimated in many tens of billions of dollars[2] and the risk that, if proceeded with, it would be the most expensive option for decarbonising the Polish power sector. The purpose of this chapter should be seen in this context. Referring to the title of this chapter, it is to consider from an economic perspective the potential role of nuclear power in decarbonising the power sector. The importance of this problem is indicated by the still very high, even by global standards, share of coal-fired power generation in Poland reaching around 70%, including 50% coal-fired and 25% lignite.

Two significant questions arise here and their discussion sets the structure of this chapter. First, why large-scale nuclear power should not be developed in Poland? Second, given growing hopes for the already advanced efforts to design and implement technology of SMRs (reactors sized up to 300MW – SMRs), another question concerns its potential advantages as a factor supporting the decarbonisation process.

Why Not Build Large-Scale Nuclear Energy?

Among the many arguments put forward against nuclear power, the most important one relates to its economics compared to other electricity generation technologies. According to the government, large-scale nuclear power plants '... are the cheapest generating units in the 2050 perspective.', and their inclusion in the energy mix is '...the cheapest way to carry out the energy transition in a sustainable manner'.[3] However, these statements depart grossly from what we know about the past and current state of competitiveness of such units in the United States and Western European countries and they do not take into account the implications of the growing share of increasingly cheaper RES for cost competitiveness of large-scale nuclear power in the future. Both issues need to be developed.

Main Lessons Learnt

To learn the most important lessons from the experience of Western countries, one must look at the development of nuclear power in these countries from a historical perspective. In the shortest terms, the history of nuclear power development in Western countries is clearly marked by three phases. *The first*, started in the late of 1950s, was the phase of its rapid development, driven by some factors (Wojtkowska et al., 2018). First of all, it was then strongly promoted by belief that the electricity thus generated would be 'too cheap to metre'. In addition to this hope, its development, especially in the United States as well as in France, was fostered by generous government support, including inter alia co-financing of research and even direct subsidies for investors. Nuclear power had also strong support of the public.

However, the main factor supporting its development was the then existing model of power sector regulation. It was based on administrative regulation of electricity prices which made it possible to transfer practically all the investment risk to consumers or taxpayers in cases where the investors were publicly owned companies. At the beginning of this phase, it was predicted that due to the rapid development of nuclear power, its share in the US electricity generation would increase to as much as 50% (Yergin, 2011). In Western European countries, the boom in power development energy moved forward by a decade and manifested itself in its most intense form in France, where a huge nuclear generation potential was built in a short time, supplying recently around 70% of the electricity domestic demand which is a world record level (The World Nuclear, 2022).

The second was the stagnation phase, whose slogan boiled down to the statement that it was 'too expensive to build'. An oft-cited symbol of the economic failure of nuclear power in the United States at the time was an assessment in Forbes Magazine in 1986 that it was '... the largest managerial disaster in business history, a disaster at the monumental scale'. (Warren, 2007). What proved the most destructive to the economics of nuclear power was the soaring costs of its expansion, increasingly exceeded the initial budgets. For some power plants commissioned in the 1970s, total construction costs were up to even seven times higher than budgets (Cooper, 2009). What more, the rapidly increasing construction time caused sharp growth of financing costs even up to 50% of total cost in case of high capital costs (Davies, 2012). Soaring total costs must have led to an unexpected escalation of costs of electricity production in new nuclear power plants. Estimates at the time of these costs dispelled illusions of extraordinarily cheap electricity, because they were more than twice the costs in coal fired power plants (Komanoff, 1992).

All of this radically boosted investment risk. It coincided with the start of the gradual economic liberalisation of the electric power industry and a shift away from regulated prices to prices set by market. This resulted in a radical change in the risk transfer mechanism from electricity consumers to investors. Given the high and difficult to predict initial costs, construction of new power plants as commercial ventures became practically impossible. Stopping the expansion of nuclear power was also aided by changing public attitudes towards it. The reason for this was widely publicised accident of one of the US nuclear plants (1979), and later the incomparably more dangerous Chernobyl disaster (1986). It is worth noting here that this rapid change of public opinion towards nuclear power indicates on high volatility of this factor and the risk of taking it too seriously in decisions on nuclear energy development made in democratic countries.

The scale of this turnaround in approach to nuclear energy in the United States can be illustrated by the following data. During the first two decades of its development, a total of 240 orders for nuclear reactors were placed. Fulfillment of all these orders would have resulted in the increase of nuclear power share in national energy mix up to the target level of 50%. However, since many of them were cancelled, finally its share increased to only 20%. The orders grew fastest during the 1971–1974 period, when 15, 20, 38 and 42 of them were placed annually, respectively. In 1975, the number dropped to 27, in 1978 to 5 and after 1979 no more orders were placed for the next 30 years (Davies, 2011). In the late 1980s, the previously uninterrupted growth in the number of net reactors came to a halt, and in 1990 the number of closures exceeded the number of new startups (The World..., 2022). In light of these data, it could not be surprising to see then a strengthening belief that nuclear energy no longer has a future (Nuttall and Taylor, 2008).

The third phase, which began in the late 1990s, basically continues to this day under the banner of waiting for the renaissance of nuclear power. The hope for its renaissance stemmed not only from the announcements made by nuclear industry promising significant reduction of construction costs but also from the growing importance of climate policy demands for emissions reduction. It seemed at the time that under conditions of high non-competitiveness of renewable energy, the only viable way to decarbonise was to focus again on the development of nuclear power. The message that '...the renaissance of nuclear power is inevitable' (Graaf, 2016) was highly publicised by representatives of various influential – especially in countries with extensive nuclear power plant construction industries – political and business circles, as well as organisations and individuals directly related to the nuclear power sector.

However, these announcements of the return of nuclear power development have not been confirmed by the facts. There were the negligible number of investments started – 2 out of 28 pledges announced in the United States at the beginning of renaissance phase – and only 3 builds in West Europe – in Finland, France and the United Kingdom. Much more embarrassing in economic terms was the manner in which these investments have been carried out. All of them – except for one in the United States which was discontinued due to excessive construction costs – fully confirmed the trend of rapid increases in construction costs – even more than four times the budgets – and significant extensions of construction time by up to 10 years (Szablewski, 2021).

Therefore, the construction of nuclear power plants still requires involvement of public finances or mechanisms that transfer construction costs to current or future electricity consumer as happened in the British case. The signing of the construction contract was preceded there by an estimate of the future price level, which can provide investors with a return on this investment. Ultimately, the price was determined at twice the level of the wholesale price in the UK electricity market in 2018 and will remain in effect after commissioning this power plant for the 35-year period of its amortisation. This makes the future nuclear plant the world's most expensive one (Watt, 2017). Given the past practice of repeatedly exceeding many times initial budgets, it can be assumed that its actual costs will be significantly higher.

Finally, it must be recognised that there is a large, but difficult to estimate, difference in the cost of building a nuclear power plant in a country that already has such facilities and a country that does not. In the first case, this kind of investment is often reduced to just replacing the old reactor with a new one. In the second case, the initial costs also include building the necessary infrastructure and human capital from scratch. In addition, these costs can be magnified by a lack of experience in managing such projects, as well as the costs associated with integrating new power plants into the national energy system (Popczyk, 2018). These aspects are rarely, if ever, taken into account by supporters of the nuclear power development in Poland.

Implications of Increasing Share of RES

Given that the constructions of large-scale nuclear power plants are a kind of investment with an extremely long-time horizon of up to 100 years, justification for their built cannot be based on today's challenges facing the energy sector. Instead, the starting point should be the recognition of the development trends in the power sector that are already emerging and an assessment made on this basis as to whether such large nuclear power plants will be compatible with the future architecture of the sector. Taking into account the enormous scale of capital expenditures, a key issue is whether it will be possible to at least recover them.

There is no doubt that the dominant direction of the architecture evolution is the rapid growth of RES in the energy mix. Due to the dispersed nature of these sources their expansion will lead to the gradual decentralisation of the generation subsector, as well as the entire energy system. In the latter case, this will be manifested through the creation of increasingly self-sustaining regional, local and micro-local energy systems with their own grid management and balancing systems. This raises a legitimate question about the ability of large-scale nuclear sources to operate efficiently in technical and economic terms within such an environment. There are at least two significant challenges facing large nuclear power plants that will be very difficult, if at all possible, to meet.

The first stems from limited capacity of large reactors to operate in a load-following mode (Khatib and Difiglio, 2016). It relies on the ability to adjust the volume of their production to changes in the volume of electricity demand. This requirement becomes much more important with the increase of the installed capacity of RES. Since their production fluctuates greatly, this will require nuclear sources to be flexible enough to adjust volume of their production or even to stop it. Therefore, to avoid such highly cyclical manner of their operation which results in faster equipment wear and costs, they are willing to offer negative prices (payment for the off-take of the electricity generated by them) as indicated by the many such cases in countries with a high share of RES (A World Turned Upside Down, 2017).

Even if it will be possible to solve this problem to some extent in new nuclear reactors designs, there is more important challenge concerning the economics of new large nuclear power plants operating in a load-following mode. As they will face a long depreciation period in which fixed costs will exceed up to 80% of total costs, their economics will depend a lot on the length of operating time and volume of electricity production. The shorter the time and smaller the volume of their production, the higher the unit costs and, consequently, the worse and worse profitability of these sources. Therefore, they are particularly highly exposed to the risk of becoming stranded assets, i.e. assets which are not able to earn an economic return.

It already happens in case of large coal and nuclear sources, which are beginning to be increasingly driven out of markets along with the increase in the share of RES implying a rapid deterioration of their economics. Striving to improve their profitability by raising the price of electricity triggers the so-called death spiral because higher price lead to another decline in sales – as customers shift to cheaper suppliers – and this necessitates further price increases. The ultimate result of this sequence of events is a gradual and permanent loss of revenue-generating capacity of high fixed cost generating units. Spiral death first appeared in the electricity industry with the start of its liberalisation and deregulation of electricity prices. It led many power plants to a permanent loss of profitability, as they could no longer sell energy at the price previously guaranteed by the regulator.

This threat is being treated as an increasingly serious problem for conventional large-scale power generation (Caldecott et al., 2017; Laws et al., 2017; The Economics of Grid Defection, 2014). In Europe, the hardest hit were Germany's largest electricity companies, which suffered huge losses and were forced to restructure and transfer their stranded assets to separate companies (Hopf, O'Brien Downs Pim, 2017; How to..., 2013). Three newly built coal-fired power plants in the Netherlands were also affected by the process (Wynn, 2016). To an even greater extent, the problem is of concern in the United States, where as many as 71% of electricity utilities saw the possibility of it happening (Strategic..., 2018). The threat of a death spiral has also begun to be recognised in Poland with regard to both the power (Chojnacki, 2019) and district heating sectors (Forum..., 2017).

Opportunities for a Nuclear Power Renaissance

Proposed Measures to Reduce Costs of Nuclear Power

The fundamental problem of high initial costs, long lead times and excessive construction delays that effectively constraints long-lasting expansion of large-scale nuclear power expansion has been recognised also by the nuclear industry and the pronuclear expert circles. So, in order to meet this challenge, two oriented efforts have been underway for quite some time (*The Future of...*, 2018). First, traditionally, promises are made to take action to reduce the cost and shorten time of large-scale nuclear builds through appropriate changes in reactor designs and improvement of investment processes in terms of their organisation and management. However, there are reasonable doubts about the effectiveness of such measures. They are of a more general nature and relate to the problems faced by the implementation of all over large-scale infrastructure investment projects.

Already numerous studies on the determinants of this type of investment, also called megaprojects, indicate that there are a number of reasons that make these projects usually over budget and late (Babaei et al., 2021; Locatelly, 2018). They are related to planning as well implementation stage of these projects. In the planning stage, there is a tendency to underestimate the costs of their implementation and overestimate the expected benefits. This is facilitated, among others, by extremely distant time horizon over which the mega-project efficiency calculus are carried out and large influence in the planning and decisions processes of non-commercial participants. This is because most of them are inclined to see primarily short-term benefits associated with the implementation phase of this kind of investment and underestimate the scale of the challenges involved in effectively managing such inherently complex investment processes. Therefore, failures of megaprojects are not incidental but rather the norm.

Given the above, much more promising is the second course of action which is expected to give the long-standing crisis a chance to be broken. The idea is to focus on the development of so-called SMRs, i.e. reactors, of varying power up to 300MW, mass-produced in a factory system, which could then be transported and installed at the deployment sites. There is already a large body of literature devoted to economic and technical issues of SMRs. During the period 2004–2019, 123 papers addressing these issues were identified, 65 of which were recognised as more in-depth analyses of various aspects of SMR technology (Mignacca and Locatelli, 2020). From the purpose of this study, two issues are particularly relevant, namely economics of SMRs and the time in which this technology will become commercially available.

Economics of SMR

Due to the fact that there are still no reactors of this type in operation, apart from Russia, the discussion around the economics of small reactors is largely hypothetical. Doubts about their economic viability (costs of generating electricity) of SMR relate to argument of economy of scale. At first glance, this argument looks very convincing in favour of large-scale reactors. According to some estimates, the so-called overnight capital costs, i.e. construction costs without financing costs (which, as mentioned earlier, increase significantly as construction time increases), fall by 20%–35% as the size of the reactor doubles (Mignaca and Locatelli, 2020). Therefore, the capital costs alone for SMRs can be as much as 70% higher per unit power than large-scale reactors being built today. This argument, however, ignores the fact that SMRs are not a simple miniaturisation of large reactors, but are characterised by important features, that large nuclear reactors do not possess but which can significantly or even completely cancel out the effect of losing economies of scale (Black et al., 2015, 2019; Ingerosoll, 2009; Mignaca and Locatelli, 2020). This is an important point that is overlooked by some Polish experts, who are critical of the sense of deploying them claiming that '...apart from the label small, there is little to distinguish them from large nuclear units' (Ciepiela, 2022).

The main feature refers to their modular construction. There are two important dimensions of modular construction expressed by words modularisation and modularity (Mignaca and Locatelli, 2020). The first indicates that plant is made up of modular factory-made modules which are transported–even by rail or trucks – to the destination and assembled there into a ready-to-operate reactors. The term modularisation, on the other hand, refers to the concept of building nuclear power plants as the sum of identical, assembled reactors, which will enable to enlarge them by adding successive reactors.

Both these dimensions imply the possibility of a number of important benefits which may determine their advantages over large reactors. These include firstly standardisation of the design and production process, facilitation of quality control of manufacturing and reduction of the cost of the whole process; secondly radical shortening time between the order of a reactor and its deployment; thirdly flexible adjustment of nuclear power plant capacity to electricity market size, which is particularly important in view of the increasing decentralisation of the power sector and the emergence of regional and local electricity markets; and fourthly simplification, shortening and reduction of decommissions costs of nuclear reactors. The varying size of reactors themselves and the possibility of combining them into larger generation sources make them much better suited, than large reactors, to the aforementioned power sector's architecture.

Another set of advantages is related to the multifunctionality of small reactors, as their use will not be limited to electricity generation alone. At least three of their additional potential applications are indicated. From the Polish perspective, the possibility of using SMRs in the district heating may be particularly promising option (Locatelli et al., 2016; Partanen, 2019). Poland, like other post-socialist countries, has in large and medium-sized cities combined heat and power coal plants and well-developed network systems which need to be decarbonised. Hence, nuclear reactors tailored to the size of individual district heating systems could be an attractive way to respond to this challenge. Another important application of SMRs could be the production of hydrogen, which in the not too-distant future is expected to serve not only as a fuel, but also as a means of storing electricity. In addition, in areas located by the sea, SMRs can perform the useful.

The variety of their potential uses can allow avoidance of triggering the death spiral mechanism, which, as mentioned above, is a huge threat to the viability of investment in large nuclear reactors. They can also be an attractive option for large energy consumers, as their own source of electricity supply, since it can create additional revenue streams from the sale of electricity and/or heat to regional or local customers. Crucial for commercial investors, advantage of SMRs is a much smaller size of initial costs and respectively a relatively lower risk of investment in nuclear power. This may make it easier for them to obtain necessary financing on favourable terms. Last but not least important advantage of SMRs lies in the chance of depoliticisation of the decision-making process when it comes to the choice of investment directions in the energy sector as well as investment implementation processes.

When Commercial Availability?

While it is true that this technology has not yet found practical application, it should be emphasised that variously advanced work on small reactor projects has long been underway in many countries. Just a few years ago, their number was estimated as 45 (Hidayatullach et al., 2015) , but now it reaches about 70 projects. There are various predictions of when this technology will be commercially available. According to some research teams, it is expected in the mid-2030s ('Advancing the Landscape...', 2019). However, some of these projects are already at a very advanced stage.

The leader here is a US corporation, which was the first to obtain design approval from the US Nuclear Regulatory Commission regulator in 2020 for its NuScale 77MW reactor design. In June 2022, the project has entered the pro-duction and delivery phase. NuScale reactors can be deployed in packages with a various number of reactors. Therefore, such packages are recommended as solution used to replace large power coal infrastructure ('NuScale SMR...', 2021). In addition, NuScale reactors are designed to operate also as suppliers of heat and desalinated water. There are also other projects that are considered advanced enough to be introduced in the near future. At the forefront of this race are projects being developed by GE Hitachi and Rolls Royce. A 100MW reactor project being prepared in China is also considered to be very advanced.

It may be surprising that despite the government's huge, not only by domestic standards, nuclear power development program, some large Polish companies are still interested in building their own small nuclear reactors. According to press reports (Ciepiela, 2022), four projects were reported to be under preparations for such investments in 2022. Two of them were for the purchase of 300MW reactors offered by GE Hitachi, and the other two for NuScale reactors. The most extensive program for the development of small-scale nuclear power was presented by a consortium involving Poland's largest state-controlled energy company Orlen and one of the largest private companies in the chemical industry.

They formed a company Orlen Synthos Green Energy which intends to deploy an entire fleet of GE Hitachi reactors. This concept is based on an assumption that it would be the best way to decarbonise not only power and heating but also industry. The company has undertaken intensive preparatory work and some first contracts have been signed. A construction permit application is also being prepared and is expected to be submitted in 2023. There is, however, no publicly available knowledge about the details of the activities carried out by other potential investors. It is only known that one of them has already decided to withdraw from its own nuclear project. The decision was justified by intention to join the government's program to build a large nuclear power plant.

Concluding Remarks

Given the above, starting a large-scale nuclear power construction programme exposes us to enormous economic risks because rapidly increasing investment costs may lead to a halt of investments already underway, and in the worst case, to a situation, that new power plants will not come on line due to unacceptable level of generation costs. The warning should be the history of large-scale nuclear power development which points to many such cases.

While SMR technology has a much better chance of breaking the multi-decade stagnation of nuclear power, the prospects for its development will depend on the rate at which two categories of technology – digitalisation of the power sector and short and long-term storage of electricity in large amounts – achieve commercial availability. Both categories are called enabling technologies because they may solve the intermittency problem of electricity supplied by RES. The faster they grow the less useful small nuclear power will be.

The last remark is of a more general nature. It concerns the gradually decreasing role of the state in the energy sector of which Polish politicians are unaware. A technological revolution will offer electricity customers increasingly cheaper alternatives. Therefore, the small nuclear power may turn out to be much less risky option in terms of its compatibility with the direction of the power sector's evolution as well as decarbonisation costs since its development will be done in a commercial mode.

Notes

1. Although this approval is eventually declining as demonstrated by the growing protests by residents of the villages where the first power plant is to be located.
2. There is still too little data to estimate the cost of entire program. According to some calculations, the costs of building just one power plant would amount PLN 110 billion (Bellon, 2022).
3. The cited quotes come from a press article written by the minister responsible for the nuclear energy development program in Poland (Naimski, 2020).

References

Advancing the Landscape of Clean Energy Innovation, (2019), Prepared for Breakthrough Energy by HIS Markit and Energy Futures Initiative, February, available at https://breakthroughenergy.org/wp-content/uploads/2022/10/ExecSummary_AdvancingtheLandscapeofCleanEnergyInnovation_2019.pdf (accessed 24 June 2022).

"A World Turned Upside Down", (2017), *The Economist*, 2017, 25 February.

Babaei, A., Loccately, G. and Sainati, T. (2021), "What Is Wrong with the Front-End of Infrastructure Megaprojects and How to Fix It. A Systematic Literature Review", *Project Leadership and Society*, Vol. 2. (accessed 12 October 2022).

Bellon, M. (2022), "Na duży atom w Polsce wydamy grube miliardy. Dlaczego koszty budowy elektrowni jądrowej są tak ogromne?", available at https://www.money.pl/gospodarka/na-duzy-atom-w-polsce-wydamy-grube-miliardy-dlaczego-koszty-budowy-elektrowni-jadrowej-sa-tak-ogromne-6738773876890528a.html (accessed 15 January 2023).

Black, G., Black, M. A. T., Solan, D. and Shropshire, D. (2015), "Carbon Free Energy Development and the Role of Small Modular Reactors: A Review and Decision Framework for Deployment in Developing Countries", Vol. 43, https://doi.org/10.1016/j.rser.2014.11.011

Black, G. A., Aydogan, F. and Koerner, C. L. (2019), "Economic of Light Water Modular Nuclear Reactors: General Methodology and Vendor Data", *Renewable and Sustainability Energy Reviews*, Vol. 103, 248–258.

Caldecott, B., Tulloch, D. J., Bouveret, G., Pfeiffer, A., Kriutwagen, L., McDaniels, J. and Derricks, G. (2017), *The Fate of European Coal-Fired Power Stations Planned in the Mid-2000s: Insights for Policymakers, Companies, and Investors Considering New Coal*, Working Paper, August, Smith School of Enterprise and the Environment, Oxford University Sustainable Finance Programme, available at https://www.google.com/search?client=safari&channel=mac_bm&q=4.%09Caldecott+B.+Tulloch+D.J.+Bouveret+G.+Pfeiffer+A.+Kruitwagen+L.+McDaniels+J+Derricks+G+(2017),+The+Fate+of+European+coal-fired+power+stations+planned+in+the+mid-2000s:+Insights+for+policymakers,+companies,+and+investors+c&spell=1&sa=X&ved=2ahUKEwin6euuo979AhUdCRAIHVpvCB0QBSgAegQIBxAB&biw=1324&bih=748&dpr=1 (accessed 16 January 2021).

Chojnacki, I. (2019), "Spirala śmierci wyzwaniem dla koncernów energetycznych", available at https://www.wnp.pl/energetyka/quot-spirala-smierci-quot-wyzwaniem-dla-koncernow-energetycznych,305493_1_0_0.html (accessed 10 November 2022).

Ciepiela, D. (2022), "Kolejny krok Synthosu do budowy małych reaktorów jądrowych w Polsce", wnp.energetyka, avaiable at https://www.wnp.pl/energetyka/kolejny-krok-synthosa-do-budowy-malych-reaktorow-jadrowych-w-polsce,633684.html (accessed 12 January 2023).

Cooper, M. (2009), "The Economics of Nuclear Reactors: Renaissance or Relapse", *Nuclear Monitor, WISE*, pp. 692–693, August 28, available at https://www.wiseinternational.org/sites/default/files/u93/2009%20The%20Economics%20of%20Nuclear%20Reactors%20%28Dr.%20M.%20Cooper%29.pdf (accessed 22 November 2020).

Davies, W. L. (2011), "Prospects for US Nuclear Power after Fukushima", *Energy Institute at Haas*, available at http://e.haas.berkeley.edu (accessed 21 May 2021).

Davies, W. L. (2012), "Prospects for Nuclear Power", *The Journal of Economic Perspectives*, Vol. 26 No. 1, Winter.

"Forum Energii: ciepłownictwu grozi ,spirala śmierci", (2017), Portal energetykacieplna.pl, available at https://www.energetykacieplna.pl/wiadomosci-i-komunikaty/forum-energii-cieplownictwu-w-polsce-grozi-spirala-smierci–134762-10# (accessed 10 November 2022).

Graaf, S. (2016), *Much Ado about Nothing? The Rethoric and Reality of Nuclear Renaissance*, University of Queensland, School of Political Sciences and International Studies, available at https://espace.library.uq.edu.au/data/UQ_396569/s4121846_final_thesis.pdf?Expires=1678985463&Key-Pair- (accessed 21 February 2022).

Hidayatullach, H., Susyadi, S. and Subki, M. H. (2015), "Design and Technology Development for Small Modular Reactors – Safety Expectations, Prospects and Impediments of Their Deployment", *Progress in Nuclear Energy*, Vol. 79, pp. 127–135.

How to Loose a Half Trillion Euros, (2013), *The Economist*, October 12.

Ingerosoll, D. T. (2009), *Progress in Nuclear Energy*, p. 51.

Khatib, H. and Difiglio, C. (2016), "Economics of Nuclear Power and Renewables", *Energy Policy*, Vol. 96, pp. 740–750

Kołodyńska-Magdziarz, N. (2020), Opcja atomowa byłaby najbardziej ekologiczna i ekonomiczna, Projekt Spięcie, Klub Jagieloński, available at https://krytykapolityczna.pl/gospodarka/opcja-atomowa-spiecie-nowa-konfederacja/ (accessed 11 November 2021).

Komanoff, C. H. (1992), "Fiscal Fission: The Economic Failure of Nuclear Power" – A Report in Historical Costs of Nuclear Power in he United States for Greenpeace by Komanoff Energy Associates, January, available at https://www.komanoff.net/nuclear_power/Fiscal_Fission_complete.pdf (accessed 16 September 2022).

Laws, D. D., Epps, B. P., Peterson, S. O., Laser, M. S. and Wanijru, G. K. (2017), "On the Utility Death and the Impact of Utility Rate Structure on the adoption of Residential Solar Photovoltaics and Energy Storage", *Applied Energy*, Vol. 185, pp. 627–641.

Locatelli, G. (2018), "Why Are Megaprojects, Incuding Nuclear Power Plants, Delivercd Overbudget and Late?" Center for Advanced Nuclear Energy Systems (CANES), Massachusetts Institute of Technology, available at https://arxiv.org/pdf/1802.07312.pdf (accessed 10 January 2023).

Locatelli, G., Firdaliso, A., Boarin, S. and Riccoti, M. E. (2016), "Cogeneration: An Option to Facilite Load Following in Small Modular Reactors", University of

Leeds, White Rose University Consortium, available at https://eprints.whiterose. ac.uk/110233/1/Load%20Following%20by%20Cogeneration%20V27%20to% 20deposit.pdf (accesseed 11 January 2022).

Mignacca, B. and Locatelli, G. (2020), "Economics and Finance of Small Modular Reactors: A Systematic Review and Research Agenda", *Renewable and Sustainability Energy Reviews*, Vol. 118, p. 109519.

Naimski, P. (2020), "Energia i niepodległość", *Rzeczpospolita*, 12 listopada.

Nuttal, W. J. and Taylor, S. (2008), *Financing the Nuclear Renaissance*, Working Papers in Economics, 0829, Faculty of Economics, University of Cambridge, Cambridge, available at https://www.google.com/search?client=safari&channel= mac_bm&q=21.%09Nuttal+W.J.+Taylor+S.+(2008),+%E2%80%9CFinancing +the+Nuclear+Renaissance,+Cambridge+Working+Papers+in+Economics,+ 0829,+Faculty+of+Econom&nfpr=1&sa=X&ved=2ahUKEwiW9KDetd79Ah WqAxAIHR7hC3gQvgUoAXoECAgQAg&biw=1324&bih=748&dpr=1 (accessed 10 January 2020).

Partanen, R. (2019), "Nuclear District Heating in Finland. The Demand Supply and Emissions Reduction Potential of Heating Finland with Small Nuclear Reactors", *Think Atom*, available at https://thinkatomnet.files.wordpress.com/2019/04/ nuclear-district-heating-in-finland_1-2_web.pdf (accessed 11 October 2022).

Pawlak, M. (2022), "Niezależność dzięki transformacji", *Rzeczpospolita*.

Popczyk, J. (2018), "Atom spowolni transformację", *Rzeczpospolita*, 31 grudnia 2020/ 1 stycznia 2021.

Rekordowe poparcie – 86% Polaków za budową elektrowni jądrowych w Polsce, (2020), Ministerstwo Klimatu i Środowiska, 15 grudnia, available at www.gov.pl

Stańczuk, M. and Twardawa, M, (2022), "Porozumienie w sprawie atomu racją stanu", *Rzeczpospolita*, 15–16 czerwca.

Strategic Directions Electricity Industry Report, (2018). Black@Veatch, available at https://www.bv.com/resources/2018-strategic-directions-electric-industry-report (accessed 2 December 2022).

Szablewski, A. (2021), *Transformacja energetyki i jej implikacje gospodarczo-spo-leczne*, Dom Wydawniczy ELIPSA, Warszawa.

Wojtkowska-Łodej, G., Motowidlak, T. and Szablewski, A. (2018), *Wybrane problemy zrównoważonego rozwoju elektroenergetyki*, Dom Wydawniczy ELIPSA, Warszawa.

The Economics of Grid Defection, (2014), Rocky Mountain Institute, available at https://rmi.org/wp-content/uploads/2017/05/RMI_Document_Repository_Public-Reprts_RMI_GridDefection-4pager_2014-06.pdf (accessed 12 January 2023).

The Future of Nuclear Energy in Carbon-Constrained World. An Interdisciplinary MIT Study, (2018), Massachusetts Institute of Technology, available at http://energy. mit.edu/research/future-nuclear-energy-carbon-constrained-world (accessed 15 September 2022).

The World Nuclear Industry Status Report 2022, (2022), A Mycle Schneider Consulting Project, Paris, October, available at https://www.worldnuclearreport.org/IMG/ pdf/wnisr2022-v3-hr.pdf (accessed 12 September 2022).

Warren, J. (2007), "Will We Pay, Again, for Nuclear Folly?" *NC WARN*, available at https://www.ncwarn.org/2007/07/nuclear-power-worst-managerial-disaster/ (accessed 12 September 2022).

Watt, H. (2017), "Hinkley Point: The 'Dreadful Deal' behind the World's Most Expensive Power Plant", *The Guardian*, December, available at https://www.theguardian.com/news/2017/dec/21/hinkley-point-c-dreadful-deal-behind-worlds-most-expensive-power-plant (accessed 16 January 2023).

Wojtkowska-Łodej, G., Szablewski, A. and Motowidlak, T. (2018), *Wybrane problemy zrównoważonego rozwoju elektroenergetyki*, ELIPSA, Warszawa.

Wynn, G. (2016), *The Dutch Coal Mistake: How Three Brand-New Power Plants in the Netherlands Are at Risk Already of Becoming Stranded Assets*, Institute for Energy Analysis, November, available at https://ieefa.org/wp-content/uploads/2016/11/The-Dutch-Coal-Mistake_November-2016.pdf (accessed 12 January 2023).

Wiech, J. (2022), "Antyatomowcy są jak antyszczepionkowcy: skąd niechęć wobec energetyki jądrowej?" *Gazeta Wyborcza*, 14 marca.

Yergin, D. (2011), *The Quest. Energy, Security, and the Remake of the Modern World*, The Penguin Press, New York.

Chapter 11

Impact of the Common Agricultural Policy on the Development of the Polish Agricultural Sector

Anna Nowak and Anna Budzyńska

Abstract

Research Background: Polish agriculture is one of the main sectors of the national economy that, under the influence of political transformations and European integration, is subject to measures stimulating its development. The instruments of the Common Agricultural Policy (CAP) have been an important supporting stimulus.

Purpose of the Chapter: This chapter aims to evaluate the significance of the common agricultural policy to the growth and development of agriculture and to structural transformations therein triggered primarily by the influx of additional CAP funds.

Methodology: The agricultural sector was examined together with its selected characteristics in the context of CAP instruments' impact after 2004. Data included the streams of funding for Polish agriculture and indicators illustrating changes in structural features, economic performance and productivity of production factors. The indicators included changes in the number, structure and potential of farmsteads, changes in the level of employment in agriculture, this sector's share in total gross value added, profitability of farmsteads, capital expenditure level and changes in labour and land profitability compared with changes in the level of employment and agricultural production intensity. They were calculated based on data from EURO-STAT, Statistics Poland and Farm Accountancy Data Network (FADN).

Findings: The outcomes confirm that common agricultural policy has contributed to create development processes in Polish agriculture. Changes in the sector affected structural characteristics, production factors productivity and the income of agricultural producers. Since Poland joined the

Modeling Economic Growth in Contemporary Poland, 175–188

Copyright © 2024 Anna Nowak and Anna Budzyńska

Published under exclusive licence by Emerald Publishing Limited

doi:10.1108/978-1-83753-654-220231013

European Union (EU), the percentage of agricultural workers declined by 8.4 p.p. and the number of farms decreased by nearly 30%. These changes were accompanied by a nearly twofold increase in agricultural labour productivity, 50% increase in land productivity and the profitability of land increased by 43%.

Keywords: Agriculture; common agricultural policy; agricultural development; Poland; structural transformation; direct payments

Introduction

Agriculture is a sector of the economy that is constantly changing under the influence of external and internal factors. These factors include primarily: the economic condition of the country, development of non-agricultural sectors, requirement for labour, national and foreign demand for foodstuffs, pricing in agriculture, innovations in agrarian structure, level of agricultural income, demand for foodstuffs and many other (Bański, 2018; Pawlak et al., 2021; Wicki, 2019). One of the most essential impulses to agricultural transformation in Poland was the political transformation, and recently the European integration, including the implementation of instruments available under the Common Agricultural Policy (CAP) in Polish agriculture. Numerous researchers have investigated the transformation of agriculture in the countries of Central Europe but their studies were usually limited to selected regions (Burger, 2001; Csaki and Jambor, 2015; Csaki and Lerman, 2000) or certain aspects of this process (Bański, 2014, 2020; Blacksell, 2010). However, the effect of the common agricultural policy on the development of the agricultural sector in new EU member states has been an interesting issue worth analysing in detail. Despite many reforms that have affected the European agricultural sector, CAP is one of the most stable European policies, which has preserved over time both its objectives and its construction philosophy (Vasile et al., 2015). Integration with the European Union gave rise to new conditions for the development of agriculture in Poland. Agricultural development programmes launched upon accession to the European Union are an example of measures stimulating transformations of the agricultural sector and rural development.

This chapter aims to evaluate the significance of the Common Agricultural Policy to the growth and development of agriculture and to structural transformations in agriculture. It is assumed that a significant actual increase in budget expenditure on agriculture since 2004, triggered by the influx of additional CAP funds to the sector, has become a strong fiscal stimulus which accelerated structural transformations and contributed to generating specified target income in agriculture. The analysis covers the period from Poland's accession to the European Union, that is, from 2004. This paper is an attempt to answer the following questions: Which CAP funds were allocated to the agriculture of Poland after its accession to the European Union? What kind of structural transformations took place in Polish agriculture at that time? How did it affect the position of this sector in the national economy? How was the profitability and productivity of agriculture affected?

Literature Review

The Common Agricultural Policy (CAP) is one of the oldest sector-specific policies in the European Union. It was programmed in 1957–1961 based on the Treaty of Rome of 1957 establishing the European Economic Community and was originally implemented from 1962 to 1970. In the 1970s and 1980s, it was supplemented and modified, and afterwards reformed in 1992. The establishment and subsequent expansion of the European Union entailed further modification of the CAP in terms of its objectives and instruments, and mostly of the cost of running such a policy (Adamowicz, 2018). In Poland, the first instance of support under CAP was SAPARD – a programme preparing the Polish agri-food sector for accession, in particular to the extent of alignment with the European Union's sanitary, hygienic and environmental protection requirements. The strategic objectives of agricultural policy after 2004 were: improved competitiveness of the agri-food sector, sustainable rural development, improved status of the natural environment, improved quality of life and diversification of the rural economy. Most measures undertaken from 2007 to 2013 were a continuation of those previously implemented (Wigier, 2013). The CAP until 2020 changed due to the emergence of new challenges, mainly due to increased focus on research and innovation, climate change and environmental protection (Czudec et al., 2017). Maier (2013) sees the policy's challenges for rural development and agriculture as a correlation of economic, spatial planning and environmental factors. The CAP rests on two 'pillars'; direct payments to farmers and other market-related mechanisms form the first one. The second pillar includes support to rural development (Grodzicki and Jankiewicz, 2022). In the perspective from 2021 to 2027, all CAP measures are programmed under the CAP's Strategic Plan for Poland from 2021 to 2027 (Wasilewski et al., 2021). The draft EC regulation on the new financial perspective from 2021 to 2027, adopted in 2018 under the Multiannual Financial Framework (MFF), gave rise to a completely new stage (model) of CAP's development. In fact, it follows up on two previous projections (CAP 2007–2013 and CAP 2014–2020) but provides for essential changes to priorities and measures (Pe'er et al., 2019).

Due to accession to the European Union, Polish farmers gained access to funds that made them able to improve the profitability of and conditions for production but also to implement structural changes expected to modernise the agricultural sector (Czyżewski et al., 2020). The funds were allocated, on the one hand, directly to increasing the farmers' income, for example, in the case of direct payments the value of which was significantly increasing and still remains high. By contrast, other first-pillar instruments such as market-based mechanisms and direct payments to agricultural producers, and from 2016 payments on account of climate- and environment-friendly agricultural practices, contributed to a general improvement in the market and environmental situation of agriculture in Poland.

The volume of disbursements and the stability of funding have also mitigated changes in the economic environment. In combination with high receipts from rural development programmes, Polish agriculture was offered a chance it should definitely utilise, which would be impossible to accomplish for the state budget alone (Czyżewski and Matuszczak, 2013).

Researchers often analyse the impact of CAP on the European Union's agriculture. However, authors often focus on certain aspects of agricultural change only, such as the level of employment (Mantino, 2017), or on selected CAP instruments (Žičkienė et al., 2022). Many studies also reviewed the significance of European Union's financial support to Polish agriculture. These, however, addressed a specific period of financing (Czyżewski et al., 2020; Sass and Tabaczyński, 2020), a specific instrument or group of instruments (Karwat-Woźniak, 2019), selected structural transformations or changes in the efficiency of agriculture (Poczta et al., 2012) or presented a regional approach to certain issues (Czudec et al., 2017). In contrast, a need arises for a comprehensive approach to this issue embracing multi-aspect changes in the agricultural sector throughout the duration of Poland's membership in the European Union.

Methodology

The subjective scope of research was Poland – a member state of the European Union. By contrast, the object of study was the agricultural sector and its selected characteristics in the context of CAP instruments' impact. The analysis covered the duration of Poland's membership in the European Union, that is, the period from 2004. The scope of the study was the streams of funding for Polish agriculture in that period and major changes in the sector. In order to fully illustrate support for Polish agriculture, EU funding was taken into account together with the state budget. In addition, the structure of funds was examined with reference to the two pillars of CAP. The effect of CAP funding on the growth and development of agriculture was evaluated based on changes in the sector. They were illustrated using several ratios referring to structural characteristics, economic performance and productivity of the production factors. The ratios were selected upon the assumption that labour productivity was a key parameter of economic development (Kijek et al., 2020). Furthermore, as the European Commission (2008) emphasises, productivity is the most reliable indicator of competitiveness in the long-term perspective. In addition, the increased level of funding for agriculture covered by CAP instruments was a booster to structural transformations and improvement in the economic performance of and income from agriculture (Czyżewski et al., 2020). The indicators addressed changes in the number, structure and potential of farmsteads, changes in the level of employment in agriculture, the sector's share in total gross value added, profitability of farmsteads, capital expenditure level and changes in labour and land profitability compared with changes in the level of employment and agricultural output intensity. Data needed for calculation derived from databases such as EUROSTAT, Statistics Poland and FADN. The FADN in Poland provides a sample of

12,100 commodity farms. The results are representative for about 730,000 farms accounting for 90% of the agricultural sector's commodity production.

Findings

The source of CAP funding for the entities concerned is the member state's budget and the community budget. The structure and volume of CAP expenditures varied throughout Poland's membership in the European Union. Polish agriculture from 2004 to 2021 received PLN 373.35 billion by way of various forms of support under the CAP, 78% of which were funds budgeted by the European Union. From its accession to the European Union's structures, Poland showed an upward trend characterising the volume of funds allocated to CAP. In 2015, agriculture in Poland received the biggest support in the entire period over which it was covered by CAP. The funds granted in 2015 were almost six times higher than those in the first year after Poland's accession to the European Union. Polish farmers were offered the greatest support in 2013, 2015–2016 and 2020 when the annual expenditure from CAP exceeded PLN 27 billion. In 2017, the aid decreased by 30% compared with the preceding year, but an upward trend was restored in subsequent years.

During the initial period of Poland's membership in the European Union, the CAP co-financing mechanisms required significant expenditure from the state budget. In 2004, as many as 71.6% of all funds were financed by Polish government. In the following four years, an average 48% of all grants under the CAP were derived from state funds. The structure of financing sources varied in terms of the volume of funding and its share in the overall financing of CAP mechanisms compared with that of the community funds. The largest expenditure from the Polish budget was made in 2007, corresponding to 62% of all the allocated funds. In contrast, the European Union spent the most on CAP funding for Polish agriculture in the record year 2015, which accounted for more than 90% of the total aid. From 2014, the share of EU funds ranged from 85% to 92% of all expenditure on CAP funding allocated to Polish agriculture.

The European Union granted more than PLN 290 billion to the Polish government for the co-financing of CAP mechanisms in support of Polish agriculture. On average, the value of EU funds increased year on year by more than 30% throughout the analysed period: from 2004 to 2021, but the highest increase was noted in 2005 (almost by five times) and 2008 (almost by two times). It should be mentioned that, during the first 4 years, the total EU grants equalled the amount of annual support from 2012 to 2016, which was the highest in the indicated years (Table 1).

The EU budget expenditure allocated to first pillar funding, exceeding PLN 191 billion, was nearly two times higher than that allocated to the second pillar, which from 2004 to 2021 amounted to almost PLN 99 billion. During the initial 5 years, expenditure on the second pillar, exceeding 60% of the EU's expenditure allocated to Poland, was predominant. Only after 2009 did the share of expenditure on funding tasks related to first-pillar direct aid increase. In 2016, due to

Table 1. CAP Expenditure in Poland From 2004 to 2021 [in mPLN].

Year	1st Pillar	2nd Pillar	Total Polish Budget	1st Pillar	2nd Pillar	Total EU Budget	Total	Polish Direct Payments	EU Direct Payments
2004	3,400	0	3,400	46	1,300	1,345	4,745	3,084	46
2005	5,029	0	5,029	3,505	2,638	6,134	11,163	3,638	3,505
2006	4,345	1,331	5,676	3,889	4,467	8,356	14 032	3,680	2,754
2007	5,762	3,727	9,489	2,543	3,291	5,834	15,323	5,529	2,310
2008	6,238	1,346	7,525	4,054	5,989	10,043	17,568	5,038	3,550
2009	4,554	1,011	5,565	8,135	4,612	12,747	18,312	4,554	6,450
2010	5,013	1,094	6,107	7,402	6,261	13,663	19,770	4,826	7,142
2011	4,653	1,500	6,153	10,113	7,259	17,253	23,406	4,613	9,524
2012	3,262	1,889	5,151	11,852	8,522	20,374	25,525	2,423	11,311
2013	3,258	1,883	5,165	13,556	8,776	22,332	27,497	2,469	11,134
2014	1,783	1,914	3,697	13,391	7,481	20,872	24,569	1,560	13,201
2015	552	3,597	2,746	15,283	9,905	25,188	27,934	413	12,660
2016	630	1,580	2,210	22,363	2,338	24,701	26,911	554	14,432
2017	242	1,539	1,781	14,543	2,615	17,158	18,939	172	14,109
2018	399	2,671	3,070	15,130	4,681	19,811	22,881	269	14,485
2019	217	2,696	2,913	15,005	5,061	20,066	22,979	78	14,874
2020	254	3,941	4,195	15,665	7,273	22,938	27,133	154	15,571
2021	163	3,354	3,517	14,957	6,195	21,152	24,669	109	14,823

Source: Authors' own elaboration based on publicly available data from The Ministry of Finance's state budget performance reports for 2004–2021 (https://mf-arch2.mf.gov.pl/web/bip/ministerstwo-finansow/dzialalnosc/finanse-publiczne/budzet-panstwa/wykonanie-budzetu-panstwa/sprawozdanie-z-wykonania-budzetu-panstwa-roczne), Supreme Audit Office's analyses of state budget performance from 2004 to 2021 (https://www.nik.gov.pl/kontrole/analiza-budzetu-panstwa/, Information on the outcome of the Supreme Audit Office's audit of performance of the Financial Plan of the Agency for Restructuring and Modernisation of Agriculture and performance of programmes co-financed from the European Union's budget from 2015 to 2021, Information on the outcome of the Supreme Audit Office's audit of performance of the Financial Plan of the Agricultural Market Agency in 2015 and performance of programmes co-financed from the European Union's budget.

changes in direct payments, expenditure on the first pillar exceeded 90% of all EU expenditure allocated to Polish farmers. In subsequent years, the first pillar accounted for more than 70% of CAP funds from the European Union.

The volume of expenditure from the Polish budget showed strong fluctuations. During the initial 4 years of Poland's membership in the European Union, expenditure on CAP co-financing increased: in 2007 almost three times (by 279%)

compared with the year of accession, that is, 2004. In the following years the expenditure from the state budget decreased until 2017 when it was the lowest.

Initially, most expenditures from the Polish budget (and over the first 2 years all of them) were allocated to financing the expenses eligible for the first pillar of CAP. From 2006 to 2014 funds financing operational programmes covered by the second pillar emerged. In the said years they constituted less than 30% of expenditures from the state budget. In the following years the situation was reversed and the second-pillar CAP financing aid for the operational programmes that since 2019 have accounted for more than 90% of the Polish state budget expenditure on CAP became the main item of Polish expenditure on rural development.

Among many CAP mechanisms direct payments play a special role. They facilitated partial alignment of the playing field for competitors on the common market by supporting the income of agricultural producers. Direct support offered to farmers during the initial 8 years after accession to the European Union showed an upward trend. The volume of direct payments in 2011 was above 4.5 times higher than in 2004. In the following years direct payments remained at an equal level. By contrast, the structure of disbursements according to funding sources changed significantly, as over the first 5 years it was the Polish government who covered most of the expenditure on direct payments – on average, nearly 70% of funds allocated to the financing of direct payments was disbursed at that time. In the following years the share of the Polish state budget declined; from 2012 to 2014 it was lower than 20%, and since 2017 it has been as low as about 1%.

A significant area of agricultural land in Poland sets the scene for developing agricultural production. However, increased fragmentation of land and a considerable number of small farmsteads (up to 5 ha) usually featuring low production efficiency is a limitation, in particular, to resource-based competitiveness (Karwat-Woźniak, 2019). Agricultural modernisation processes observed in the countries of Western Europe from the 1960s did not take place in Poland so its agrarian structure is not very modern. In 2004, more than 1.8 million farmsteads existed in Poland and their average surface area did not exceed 7.5 ha (Table 2). Accession of Poland to the European Union boosted structural transformations, which was also reflected in the changing number and structure of farms. The latest agricultural census showed that the number of farmsteads decreased to 1.3 million, and the farm's average surface area increased to 11 ha. Liquidation of farmsteads resulted in the flow of land to market-based entities, usually with a larger area.

It is worth emphasising that the changes were not uniform. Variations in the rate of transformation could be observed at three levels: temporal, referring to clusters of areas and spatial. The farm's area is a primary factor characterising its economic strength, since it determines the volume of agricultural output. Many researchers claim that farm size is a significant determinant of the farm's income from agriculture (Carletto et al., 2013; Noack and Larsen, 2019; Wicki, 2019). From 2004 to 2020, the structure of farming area and land use clearly changed. The share of the smallest farmsteads (up to 5 ha) decreased by 6.1% points, and in

Table 2. Selected Characteristics of Agriculture in Poland From 2004 to 2020.

Characteristic	2004	2020	Change
Average farm size (ha)	7.5	11.04	3.54
Number of farms larger than 1 ha UAA (in thousands)	1851.8	1284.6	−567.2
Percentage of 15 ha and larger farms (%)	10.5	15.4	4.9
Percentage of from 1 to 5 ha farms (%)	58.2	52.1	−6.1
Percentage of agricultural workers (%)	17.9	9.5	−8.4
Number of people employed in agriculture (thousand AWU[a])	2279.4	1,427.7	−851.7
Share of agriculture in total GVA (%)	3.7	2.8	−0.9
Agricultural production value according to fixed prices in 2010 (mEUR)	18124.41	24412.57	6,288.16
Gross value added of agriculture according to fixed prices in 2010 (mEUR)	6543.73	9567.68	3023.95
Capital expenditure in agriculture from 2004 to 2020 (mPLN)	2628.1	6000.0	3371.9
Gross fixed assets in agriculture from 2004 to 2020 (mPLN)	110935.4	154575.2	43639.8
Value of Food, beverage and tobacco exports (mEUR)	4959.6	35324.3	30364.7
Average farm net income (EUR)[b]	6110.0	10920.0	4810
Farm Net Income per 1 AWU (EUR per AWU)[b]	3471.6	7128.3	3656.7
Farm net value added per person employed on the farm (EUR per AWU)[b]	4080.0	8776.0	4696
Farm Net Income per 1 ha of UAA (EUR per 1 ha)[b]	388.4	555.4	167

Source: Authors' own elaboration based on publicly available data from EUROSTAT and FADN.
[a]AWU – Annual Work Unit
[b]FADN data for 2019

2020 they had 11.8% of agricultural land at their disposal, which was 6.9% points lower than in 2004. For farmsteads covering an area from 5 to 10 ha and from 10 to 15 ha, a slight increase in the farms' structure was recorded, while their share in agricultural land declined. The significance of farms with an area bigger than 15 ha increased both in terms of their number and share in the total number of farmsteads and the surface area of agricultural land at their disposal (Table 2).

Karwat-Woźniak (2019) underlines that the concentration of land went smoothly. However, its scope is insufficient from the point of view of the agricultural sector's competitiveness. The European Union has no policy which would directly influence the way respective member states manage their agricultural land or affect national land development policies. Still, certain conditions were set by the directions of support provided under the CAP. In consequence, transformations in the agrarian structure largely resulted from the CAP (Karwat-Woźniak, 2019). Structural pensions granted to farmers at pre-retirement age who would give up their farming activity and hand their agricultural land over to other farmers in order to increase the area of another farm, or to successors who have not run farming activity before, had a direct impact on the structure of land. The Agency for Restructuring and Modernisation of Agriculture (ARiMR) reported that ca. 73,800 farmsteads were handed over in exchange for structural pensions.

Changes in Polish agriculture during EU membership also included employment in the sector. Structural transformations in the economy along with progress in agriculture have reduced the number of workers in the sector and simultaneously enhanced socio-economic development (Baum et al., 2006). Wicki (2012) underlines that, on the one hand, high labour resources are an indication of the agriculture's potential for development, while, on the other hand, they reduce the dynamics of modernisation processes in that sector. In 2004, Polish agriculture employed 2.28 million workers on a full-time basis. By 2020, this figure declined to 1.43 million, which is equivalent to a decrease by 37.4% (Table 2). The average reduction in the number of agricultural workers in Poland was 75,200 workers per annum in the analysed years.

Capital expenditure is a source of renewing agricultural fixed assets resources. Investing in the means of mechanisation in agriculture is closely linked with the economic conditions in agriculture, level of agricultural producers' income and the structure of CAP instruments (Pawlak, 2016). When Poland became the member of the European Union, mechanisms of financial support for agriculture were launched. This process leaded to increase in capital expenditure and grew gross value of fixed assets (Fig. 1). On average, from 2004 to 2020, capital expenditure in Poland increased by PLN 259.6 million per annum and was accompanied by an increase in the gross value of this sector's fixed assets. In the opinion of Urban and Kowalska (2015), a shift in the farmers' approach to investing was triggered by grants oriented at the common agricultural policy of the European Union and the increasing demand for Polish agricultural products and foodstuffs on the single European market.

The growing demand for Polish agricultural products was accompanied by a real increase in their prices and income of agricultural producers. According to FADN, an average farm's income from 2004 to 2020 increased by 78.7% and reached EUR 10920. Income per full-time agricultural worker (annual work unit – AWU) was two times higher in the said period and income per 1 ha of utilised agricultural area (UAA) increased by 43% (Table 2).

Agricultural output intensity affects the level of farmers' income as well as the productivity and competitiveness of agriculture (Zakrzewska and Nowak 2022). The basic measure of output intensity is the cost of agricultural production per 1 ha

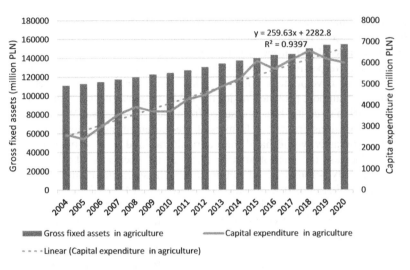

Fig. 1.   Capital Expenditure and Gross Fixed Assets in Polish Agriculture From 2004 to 2020 (mPLN). *Source:* Authors' own elaboration based on publicly available data from Statistics Poland.

of UAA. Fig. 2 illustrates the costs of intermediate consumption per 1 ha UAA. Following the methodology of FADN, they include direct costs (products made and used in the process of production on a farm) and general economic costs accompanying the operations in the accounting year. In Poland, they were growing in the analysed period, reaching EUR 1001.2 per 1 ha in 2021. However, output intensity is still lower than in the member states forming the so-called 'old' EU-15 where in the same year the ratio was 2059.6 EUR/ha. An upward trend is also observed for land productivity, expressed as the value of agricultural output per 1 ha UAA. The growth rate in Poland was similar to that seen in the EU-15, but the modulus of productivity in Poland is considerably lower. The ratio of land productivity in Poland to its value in the 'old EU' was 0.48 in 2021, and improved in comparison to the year 2004 when it reached 0.39.

Fig. 3 illustrates changes in labour productivity in Poland and EU-15 using the example of changes in the level of employment. Labour productivity was calculated as gross value added to number of agricultural workers. In 2021, in Polish agriculture it was EUR 5592.3 per capita, which was much lower than in the old member states. However, from 2004 to 2021, its growth dynamics was higher (194.8) than in EU-15 (158.6), which was accompanied by a decline in the percentage of agricultural workers from 17.9% in 2004 to 8.3% in 2021.

Accession of Poland to the European Union also had a positive effect on changes in the foreign agri-food trade. From 2004 to 2021, exports of Polish agri-food products increased seven times and trade surplus increased ten times. In 2021, exports of food, drinks and tobacco according to Standard International

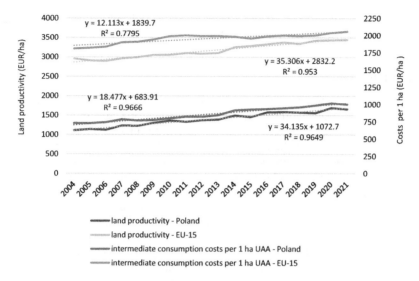

Fig. 2. Intermediate Consumption per 1 ha UAA and Land Productivity in Polish Agriculture Compared With EU-15 From 2004 to 2021. *Source:* Authors' own elaboration based on publicly available data from EUROSTAT.

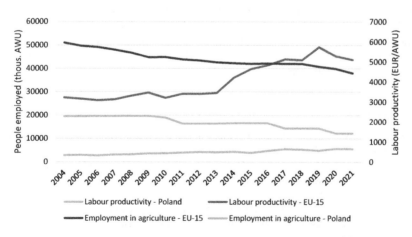

Fig. 3. Changes in Labour Productivity Illustrated by Changes in the Number of Agricultural Workers in Poland and in w EU-15 From 2004 to 2021. *Source:* Authors' own elaboration based on publicly available data from EUROSTAT.

Trade Classification (SITC) 0 and 1 were EUR 35324.3 million, and the balance of trade amounted to EUR 14032.8 (Eurostat, 2022).

Summary

The CAP is an underlying premise for the operation of agriculture in Poland, simultaneously contributing to creating development processes in this sector and in rural areas. The introduction of CAP opened up funding for the Polish agricultural sector on a scale that had not been recorded before. The funds provided development-oriented commodity farms with an opportunity to significantly increase their output and, above all, modernise their equipment. In addition, for Polish agriculture, the accession of Poland to the European Union signified a substantial change in the economic conditions of production – the method of supporting this sector changed along with the scope and terms of intervention on main agricultural markets, barriers to foreign trade in agri-food products with EU member states were lifted and new forms of support to agriculture, including direct payments and structural funds, were implemented. The stream of funding and options due to unrestrained access to the EU market have become the key elements of the agricultural sector in Poland. Changes in agriculture affected structural characteristics, production factors productivity and the income of agricultural producers. Since Poland joined the European Union, the percentage of agricultural workers has declined by 8.4 p.p. and the number of farms has declined by nearly 30%. These changes were accompanied by a nearly twofold increase in agricultural labour productivity, a 50% increase in land productivity, while the profitability of land increased by 43%. The subsequent financial perspective of CAP for 2023–2027 puts more emphasis on environmental issues and climate than in the previous periods and assumes increased support to small and medium-sized enterprises. This can signify a slower transformation in the structure of farms in Polish agriculture and, as a consequence, inhibit development processes in the entire agricultural sector.

References

Adamowicz, M. (2018), "Present Changes in the Common Agricultural Policy of the European Union", *Problems of World Agriculture*, Vol. 18 No. 1, pp. 7–22.

Bański, J. (2014), "Structure and Ownership of Agricultural Land in Poland in the First Years of New Millennium", *Journal of Agricultural Science and Technology B*, Vol. 4, pp. 85–93.

Bański, J. (2018), "Phases to the Transformation of Agriculture in Central Europe – Selected Processes and Their Results", *Agricultural Economics – Czech*, Vol. 64, pp. 546–553.

Bański, J. (2020), "Selected Aspects of the Transformation of Agriculture in the CEECs Following the Fall of the Eastern Bloc", *Studia Obszarów Wiejskich*, Vol. 56, pp. 5–31.

Baum, S., Cook, P. A., Stange, H. and Weingarten, P. (2006), "Agricultural Employment Trends in an Enlarged European Union: Does the CAP Reform/

Introduction Matter?" in *Annual Meeting, August 12–18, 2006, Queensland, Australia 25395, International Association of Agricultural Economists.*

Blacksell, M. (2010), "Agriculture and Landscape in 21st Century Europe: The Post-communist Transition", *European Countryside*, Vol. 1, pp. 13–24.

Burger, A. (2001), "Agricultural Development and Concentration of Land in a Central European Country: A Case Study of Hungary", *Land Use Policy*, Vol. 18, pp. 259–268.

Carletto, C., Savastano, S. and Zezza, A. (2013), "Fact or Artifact: the Impact of Measurement Errors on the Farm Size–Productivity Relationship", *Journal of Development Economics*, Vol. 103, pp. 254–61.

Csaki, C. and Jambor, A. (2015), "After the Transition: The Impacts of EU Membership upon the Agriculture of the New Member States", in: *Agricultural Transition in Post-Soviet Europe and Central Asia after 25 Years. Studies on the Agricultural and Food Sector in Transition Economies*, Vol. 79, eds. Kimhi, A. and Lerman, Z., Leibniz Institute of Agricultural Development in Transition Economies IAMO, Halle.

Csaki, C. and Lerman, Z. (eds.) (2000), *Structural Change in the Farming Sector in Central and Eastern Europe.* World Bank Technical Paper No. 465, World Bank, Washington DC.

Czudec, A., Kata, R. and Miś, T. (2017), *Effects of European Union Agricultural Policy at Regional Level*, Bogucki Wydawnictwo Naukowe, Poznań (in Polish).

Czyżewski, A., Kata, R. and Matuszczak, A. (2020), "Impact of Budget Expenditures on Structural Changes and Income in Agriculture under the Conditions of CAP Instruments Operated in Poland", *Ekonomista*, Vol. 6, pp. 781–811.

Czyżewski, A. and Matuszczak, A. (2013), "Income and Expenditure in the Polish Agricultural Budgets in Past Financial Perspective 2007–2013", *Journal of Agribusiness and Rural Development*, Vol. 28 No. 2, pp. 33–43.

European Commission (2009), *European Competitiveness Report 2008.* European Commission, Brussels, Belgium.

Eurostat (2022), available at https://appsso.eurostat.ec.europa.eu/nui/show.do?dataset=ext_lt_intratrd&lang=en (accessed 4 November 2022).

FADN (2022), available at https://agridata.ec.europa.eu/extensions/FADNPublic Database/FADNPublicDatabase.html (accessed 4 November 2022).

Grodzicki, T. and Jankiewicz, M. (2022), "The Role of the Common Agricultural Policy in Contributing to Jobs and Growth in EU's Rural Areas and the Impact of Employment on Shaping Rural Development: Evidence from the Baltic States", *PLoS ONE*, Vol. 17, No. 2, pp. e0262673.

Karwat-Woźniak, B. (2019), "Impact of Selected Instruments of the Common Agricultural Policy on Strengthening and Slowing Down Development Processes in Polish Agriculture", *Nierówności Społeczne a Wzrost Gospodarczy*, Vol. 57 No. 1, pp. 304–315.

Kijek, A., Kijek, T. and Nowak, A. (2020), "Club Convergence of Labour Productivity in Agriculture: Evidence from EU Countries", *Agricultural Economics – Czech*, Vol. 66, pp. 391–401.

Maier, L. (2013), "Rural Development in the 2014–2020 Period: Elements for a Result-Oriented Policy", in *EC DG AGRI, 2nd Development Conference: the CAP in the 2014–2020 Period and the Shaping of National Strategy*, Athens.

Mantino, F. (2017), "Employment Effects of the CAP in Italian Agriculture: Territorial Diversity and Policy Effectiveness", *EuroChoices*, Vol. 16 No. 3, pp. 12-17.

Noack, F. and Larsen, A. (2019), "The Contrasting Effects of Farm Size on Farm Incomes and Food Production", *Environmental Research Letters*, Vol. 14, pp. 084024.

Pawlak, J. (2016), "Investment Outlays in Polish Agriculture", *Problems of Agricultural Economics*, Vol. 348 No. 3, pp. 143–158.

Pawlak, K., Smutka, L. and Kotyza, P. (2021), "Agricultural Potential of the EU Countries: How Far Are They from the USA?" *Agriculture*, Vol. 11, pp. 282.

Pe'er, G., Zinngrebe, Y., Moreira, F., Sirami, C., Schindler, S., Müller, R., Bontzorlos, V., Clough, D., Bezák, P., Bonn, A., Hansjürgens, B., Lomba, A., Möckel, S., Passoni, G., Schleyer, C., Schmid, J. and Lakner, S. (2019), "A Greener Path for the EU Common Agricultural Policy", *Science*, Vol. 365, pp. 449–451.

Poczta, W., Pawlak, K. and Czubak, W. (2012), "Production and Income Situation in Polish Agriculture after Accession to the European Union", *Berichte über Landwirtschaft*, Vol. 90 No 1, pp. 133–158.

Sass, R. and Tabaczyński, L. (2020), "Effect of Direct Payments on Farm Income", *Zagadnienia Doradztwa Rolniczego*, Vol. 3, pp. 21–35 (in Polish).

Statistics Poland (2022), available at https://stat.gov.pl/en/ (accessed 10 November 2022).

Urban, S. and Kowalska, A. (2015), "Investments and Basic Fixed Assets in Agriculture", *Wiadomości Statystyczne*, Vol. 9, pp. 66–76 (in Polish).

Vasile, J., Panait, A. and Alecu, A. (2015), *Transformations of European Agricultural Sector, Market and Model under the Influence of Common Agricultural Policy (CAP)*, MPRA Paper No 69556, 12 September 2015, Romania.

Wasilewski, A., Krzyżanowski, J. and Chmieliński, P. (2021), "Complementarity of the Measures of the Common Agricultural Policy and the Cohesion Policy for Rural Development between 2021 and 2027 in the Light of Programing Documents", *Problems of Agricultural Economics*, Vol. 367 No 2, pp. 31–47.

Wicki, L. (2012), "Convergence of Labour Productivity in Agriculture in the European Union", *Economic Science for Rural Development*, Vol. 27, pp. 279–284.

Wicki, L. (2019), "Size vs Effectiveness of Agricultural Farms", *Annals PAAAE*, Vol. 21 No 2, pp. 285–296.

Wigier, M. (2013), "The Model of Development of Polish Agriculture in the Light of the CAP Implementation", *Problems of Agricultural Economics*, Vol. 1, pp. 22–41.

Zakrzewska, A. and Nowak, A. (2022), "Diversification of Agricultural Output Intensity across the European Union in Light of the Assumptions of Sustainable Development", *Agriculture*, Vol. 12, pp. 1370.

Žičkienė, A., Melnikienė, R., Morkūnas, M. and Volkov, A. (2022), "CAP Direct Payments and Economic Resilience of Agriculture: Impact Assessment", *Sustainability*, Vol. 14, pp. 10546.

Chapter 12

The Analysis of Economic Growth and Monetary Policy for Poland and Selected Central and Eastern European Countries With the Use of Dynamic Time Warping[1]

Michał Bernardelli and Mariusz Próchniak

Abstract

Research Background: The comparison between economic growth and the character of monetary policy is one of the most frequently studied issues in policymaking. However, the number of studies incorporating a dynamic time warping approach to analyse the similarity of macroeconomic variables is relatively small.

The Purpose of the Chapter: The study aims at assessing the mutual similarity among various variables representing the financial sector (including the monetary policy by the central bank) and the real sector (e.g. economic growth, industrial production, household consumption expenditure), as well as cross-similarity between both sectors.

Methodology: The analysis is based on the dynamic time warping (DTW) method, which allows for capturing various dimensions of changes of considered variables. This method is almost non-existent in the literature to compare financial and economic time series. The application of this method constitutes the main area of value added of the research. The analysis includes five variables representing the financial sector and five from the real sector. The study covers four countries: Czechia, Hungary, Poland and Romania and the 2010–2022 period (quarterly data).

Findings: The results show that variables representing the financial sector, including those reflecting monetary policy, are weakly correlated with each other, whereas the variables representing the real economy have a solid mutual similarity. As regards individual variables, for example, GDP fluctuations show relatively substantial similarity to ROE fluctuations –

Modeling Economic Growth in Contemporary Poland, 189–205
Copyright © 2024 Michał Bernardelli and Mariusz Próchniak
Published under exclusive licence by Emerald Publishing Limited
doi:10.1108/978-1-83753-654-220231014

especially in Czechia and Hungary. In the case of Hungary and Romania, CAR fluctuations are consistent with GDP fluctuations. In the case of Poland and Hungary, there is a relatively strong similarity between the economy's monetisation and economic growth. Comparing the individual countries, two clusters of countries can be identified. One cluster includes Poland and Czechia, while another covers Hungary and Romania.

Keywords: Economic growth; monetary policy; time series similarity; dynamic time warping; financial sector; central banking

Introduction

The question of comparing various time series has been considered among economists for many years. There is no single measure to compare phenomena. Different indicators to assess the level of similarity between various objects can be found in the literature (e.g. Walesiak, 2016). One of the newest and less explored economics tools used, among others, to analyse the similarity between time series is Dynamic Time Warping (DTW). It is an advantageous method that allows you to capture various aspects of the time series behaviour. It was initially introduced independently by Vintsyuk (1968) and Sakoe and Chiba (1978) in speech application. However, it turns out to be a valuable tool for analysing variables of an economic nature. The examined variables are compared to each other in terms of the direction and amplitude of fluctuations, the time extension of cycles, the frequency of occurrence of turning points (peaks and troughs), non-linearities, and time shifts (leads and lags). DTW is a method of measuring similarity in a transparent and interpretable way, whereas ordinary methods fall behind by focusing only on one or more selected aspects. For example, the cross-correlation coefficient only represents the correlation extended to account for leads and lags.

Looking at the economy, many macroeconomic variables are undoubtedly mutually correlated due to, among others, their direct relationships, dependence on the same external factors, or similarly defined. The economy is a very complex organism where all the individual items interact following some patterns. An especially interesting area is to assess the similarity between economic growth and the other macroeconomic variables. Economic growth affects society's standard of living and is a crucial measure of interest among many economists.

This chapter examines the similarity between economic growth and selected other macroeconomic variables. We include variables representing the real and financial sectors, primarily influenced by monetary policy. The comparison between economic growth and the character of monetary policy is one of the most frequently studied issues in policymaking.

The goal of the study is an analysis of the mutual similarity among various variables representing the financial sector (including the monetary policy by the central bank) and the mutual similarity of various variables representing the real economy (e.g. economic growth, industrial production, household consumption expenditure), as well as cross-similarity between the financial and the real sector.

In the literature, one can find many studies on, for example, the synchronisation of business cycles or turning points, trend and cyclical component identification of various time series. Most are based on the most popular research methods applied in the literature for many years. However, the number of studies incorporating a DTW approach to analyse the similarity of macroeconomic variables is relatively small (the selected research papers are described in the literature review in the next section of this chapter).[2] This measure carries a value that allows data-based inference to be made without violating the assumptions of applicability of classical similarity measures.

The added value of the research is to show the authentic patterns of the links between the financial and real sectors as well as within these sectors. The analysis considers all the elements the DTW method allows to capture (e.g. different time length and magnitude of variables' fluctuations, different distribution of peaks and troughs).

The review of the literature shows that there is no single variable that fully accounts for all the aspects of the financial sector's stability and development. The financial sector is described by many different variables representing a variety of financial and monetary policy issues which may be directly independent. Therefore, to fully assess the behaviour of the financial sector, we include a few financial variables, measuring banks' financial outcomes, the volume and structure of loans, as well as the monetary policy.

This chapter consists of five points. After the introduction, there is a literature review. Then, the data and the applied research method are described, followed by the presentation and interpretation of the findings. The last section concludes.

Literature Review

The DTW method is almost non-existent in economics. It is widely used in engineering, computer science, medicine, physics and mathematics. However, the application to economics is very rare. However, some studies incorporating the DTW approach to macroeconomic research can be found. The most important papers from the point of view of this study are presented here with a short indication of their contents.

Focardi (2001), in a theoretical paper, indicates that concepts of similarity, such as dynamic time-warping, used in a wide range of application domains (e.g. speech recognition, medicine, biomathematics, seismology) might be useful in the context of finance and economics which is done in the current study.

Raihan (2017) applies the DTW algorithm to predicting recessions in the United States. It turns out that DTW successfully predicted the 1999 and 2007 recessions. The predictions are more robust when an asymmetric step-pattern is adopted. Also, compared to other non-parametric methods, DTW raises significantly fewer false signals of recessions.

Franses and Wiemann (2020) use DTW to examine similarities of business cycles in US states based on quarterly data for the 2006–2017 period. The cited study shows that the DTW method is superior to the parametric models. As such,

DTW allows for the possibility that lead and lag relations can change during the sample period. With a few examples, the analysis showed that this switching behaviour is more common than rare and parametric models to allow for this behaviour will quickly become parameter-heavy.

D'Urso et al. (2021) proposed a robust clustering method capable of neutralising the negative effects of possible outliers in the clustering process. They apply the DTW algorithm to 40 of the most traded stocks in the Italian Stock Exchange that make up the FTSE MIB (Financial Times Stock Exchange Milano Indice di Borsa) index. The clustering method achieves its robustness by adopting a suitable trimming procedure to identify multivariate financial time series more distant from the bulk of data. The proposed clustering method is applied to the stocks composing the FTSE MIB index to identify common time patterns and possible outliers.

Gassouma et al. (2023) analyse the similarities between Islamic and conventional banks in the Gulf countries in the 2006–2015 period using the clustering method based on DTW distance. The study includes 44 Islamic and 46 conventional banks from Saudi Arabia, Kuwait, United Arab Emirates, Bahrain, Qatar and Oman.

As we can see based on the literature review, there are some studies (although not many) that apply the DTW approach to the financial sector. However, we have not found the analysis to answer the research questions formulated in this study.

The financial sector can be analysed based on a variety of variables. There are studies in which the authors use individual variables and composite indicators covering a wide range of aspects. Gadanecz and Jayaram (2009) provided a good review of available measures.

Pawlowska (2016) used non-performing loans to check the relationship between the competition in the banking sector and the financial stability in the EU27 countries during 2004–2012. The studies on the relationship between financial development, bank stability and non-performing loans were also conducted by, among others, Guy and Lowe (2011), Ozili (2019), and Kozarić and Dželihodžić (2020). Diallo and Al-Mansour (2017) use the Z-Score measure in the financial sector in their analysis (Z-Score equals ROA + EA/s.d.(ROA), where ROA is the rate of return on assets, EA - the ratio of equity to assets, and s.d.(ROA) - the standard deviation of ROA). Hallak (2013), as a measure of financial stability, incorporates interest rate spread.

Since the financial sector can be characterised in many uncorrelated aspects, many authors examine a broad range of variables. Cernohorska (2015) – in her study of the stability of the banking sector in Czechia and the UK during 2006–2013 – employs net interest margin, interest rate spread, loans-to-deposits ratio, after-tax profits, bank capital-to-assets ratio, capital adequacy ratio, rate of return on equity, and rate of return on assets. Yiadom et al. (2022) – in the analysis of 45 Sub-Saharan African countries during the 1982–2018 period – use, apart from the composite financial development (FD) index compiled by the IMF, the following variables: M2-to-GDP ratio, credit-to-GDP ratio, and the volume of stocks traded (% of GDP). Xue (2020) employs the following proxies of the size and quality of financial sector development: credit-to-GDP ratio, credit-to-deposits ratio, bank return on equity, capital adequacy ratio, non-performing loans, and Z-score. In the cited study, the author estimates regression models to assess the relationship between the financial sector development and the GDP fluctuations in a wide sample of 50 countries during the 1997–2014 period.

Some researchers construct custom indices of financial stability. Elsayed et al. (2023) build a new composite financial stability index which includes the banking sector, the equity market, the bond market and the foreign exchange market. Svirydzenka (2016) elaborated on an aggregate financial development index, measuring the depth, access and efficiency of financial institutions and financial markets. Index proposed by her includes a huge number of individual variables, including credit-to-GDP ratio, interest rate spread, rate of return on assets, rate of return on equity and market capitalisation of listed companies (% of GDP).

Methodology

The dynamic time warping technique compares time series data by warping the time axis to minimise the distance between them. It helps identify patterns, predict and detect anomalies in time series data. It is commonly applied in speech recognition, audio alignment, music analysis, gesture recognition, robotics and other fields that require temporal alignment. DTW algorithm uses chosen dissimilarity measures between two points in the time series (e.g. Euclidean distance or the Manhattan distance) and finds the optimal alignment between the time series to minimise the overall distance (Kate, 2016; Müller, 2007). DTW is invariant to time shifts between series and therefore helps compare time series with different lengths and dynamics of change.

Comparison of variables of different magnitudes requires normalisation. In this research, we followed the formula:

$$\tilde{x}_t = \frac{x_t}{\max\limits_{s}|x_s|}$$

It is not a typical normalisation technique as it sets the target value range between -1 and 1 rather than [0, 1]. Adopting this approach makes it possible to balance the high and low points of cycles, even if they have been measured with markedly different amplitudes.

In addition to determining the distance between time series, the DTW can be used as a measure of grouping time series (Paparrizos and Gravano, 2016) according to their patterns or shapes, even if these patterns are not synchronised. K-means clusterisation method based on the DTW similarity provides an exceptional opportunity for in-depth exploration.

Data Characteristics

DTW similarity measure, together with the clusterisation method, was used in the empirical analysis. Based on the literature review, the study includes 10 time series: five variables representing the financial sector and five from the real sector. The financial sector is described by the following time series:

(1) broad money M3 (% of GDP) [MONEY],
(2) domestic credit (% of GDP) [CRED],
(3) non-performing loans (% of total loans) [NPL],
(4) return on equity of the deposit takers (%) [ROE],
(5) capital adequacy ratio of the banking sector (%) [CAR].

The first two variables best represent monetary policy. The monetisation ratio measures the size of the broad money supply. In contrast, the share of credit in GDP indirectly reflects the monetary policy as the central bank is responsible for setting interest rates, which show the cost of credit and influence the credit expansion. The remaining three variables are also partially related to monetary policy. Non-performing loans depend on the level of interest rates (high rates increase the probability of insolvency). Still, they also highly reflect the current state of the economy: many people and firms may become bankrupt during recessions when income decreases. The last two variables measure the financial outcomes of banks which depend on many factors, including the character of monetary policy, macroeconomic performance, and the level of competitiveness in the banking sector in a given country.

The following variables describe the real sector:

(1) real GDP growth rate (against a corresponding quarter of the previous year) (%) [GDPGR],
(2) industrial production growth rate (against a corresponding quarter of the previous year) (%) [IP],
(3) investment (% of GDP) [INV],
(4) private consumption (% of GDP) [CONS],
(5) government consumption (% of GDP) [GOV].

The first variable is the fundamental variable in business cycle analysis for which turning points and cycles are identified. Industrial production (the second one) is an alternative measure, as fluctuations in industrial production are very similar to those in the whole economy. The last three variables represent the output structure from the demand-side perspective (investment and consumption are GDP components). The fifth variable (government spending on consumption) represents fiscal policy.

The study covers four countries: Czechia, Hungary, Poland and Romania, which are homogenous economies from the point of view of the goal of this analysis. The sample selection results from three reasons. Firstly, all these countries are advanced inflation targeters. Czechia adopted the inflation targeting monetary policy regime in 1998, Hungary – in 2001, Poland – in 1999, and Romania – in 2005. Secondly, the chosen countries have individual currencies (the euro has not been introduced yet), meaning that their monetary policy depends only on domestic central bank actions. Thirdly, they all are EU members implying that their institutional environment is similar and they share a similar model of capitalism (the so-called patchwork capitalism) (Rapacki, 2019, Rapacki et al., 2019).

The calculations are based on quarterly data starting from *Q1* 2010 and ending – in the case of most time series – in *Q3* 2022.

Findings

The analysis results are presented in Tables 1–4 and Fig. 1. The tables present the values of similarity coefficients obtained by the DTW algorithm for each of the four examined countries of Central and Eastern Europe. To facilitate the interpretation of the results, different background colours were used in the tables: the closer the values are to zero (i.e. the more similar the two variables are), the brighter the background (in the case of total similarity, i.e. comparing a variable with itself, the similarity coefficient is 0 and the corresponding cell has a white filling).

Several conclusions can be drawn from the results presented in Tables 1–4. Firstly, variables representing the financial sector, including those reflecting monetary policy, are weakly correlated with each other. The dark grey colour of the cells is dominant in the upper left corner. It means that the similarity between the individual financial variables is slight. This result can be justified by the fact that there is no single universally accepted measure of the development and stability of the financial sector. The financial sector can be described by many variables that represent various aspects of this sector and are influenced by multiple, often independent factors. For example, monetary policy primarily affects the monetisation ratio and the volume of loans (including non-performing loans). Still, it plays a lesser role in shaping banks' financial results where the other factors, including microeconomic ones, also matter. As a result, variables such as capital adequacy ratio or rate of return on assets may follow a completely different path than, for example, the size of the money supply.

Secondly, in the case of real variables, the mutual dependence is more significant from the theoretical point of view. For example, according to Okun's law, fluctuations in the unemployment rate, employment and GDP are synchronised, except that the unemployment rate behaves countercyclically, whereas the amplitude of fluctuations and possible leads or lags may also differ. Unlike the real sector, our results evidently imply that there is no single commonly used measure of the development and stability of the financial sector. To fully describe fluctuations in the financial sector, a broad set of variables covering various aspects of the financial sector should be considered. The single financial variables behave differently and cover multiple areas of the country's financial system and monetary policy.

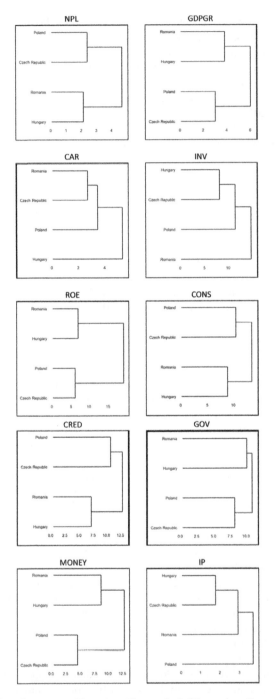

Fig. 1.   Dendrograms Showing Countries' Clustering Based on DTW
Similarity Coefficients. *Source:* Authors' own calculations.

Table 1. The DTW Similarity Coefficients Between Financial and Real Variables for Czechia.

Variable	NPL	CAR	ROE	CRED	MONEY	GDPGR	INV	CONS	GOV	IP
NPL	0	29.79	7.76	15.19	32.77	14.61	17.46	7.86	15.94	15.00
CAR	29.79	0	22.84	12.28	5.04	14.73	8.75	22.42	9.90	12.00
ROE	7.76	22.84	0	12.32	21.02	5.59	11.16	5.45	13.06	8.04
CRED	15.19	12.28	12.32	0	10.55	10.88	10.49	11.08	10.37	8.91
MONEY	32.77	5.04	21.02	10.55	0	15.41	8.37	22.19	9.54	13.17
GDPGR	14.61	14.73	5.59	10.88	15.41	0	9.66	6.25	13.88	7.29
INV	17.46	8.75	11.16	10.49	8.37	9.66	0	11.01	10.99	9.94
CONS	7.86	22.42	5.45	11.08	22.19	6.25	11.01	0	13.33	6.99
GOV	15.94	9.90	13.06	10.37	9.54	13.88	10.99	13.33	0	10.99
IP	15.00	12.00	8.04	8.91	13.17	7.29	9.94	6.99	10.99	0

Source: Authors' own calculations.

Note: The lower value, the more similar time series and the brighter filling of cells.

Michał Bernardelli and Mariusz Próchniak

Table 2. The DTW Similarity Coefficients Between Financial and Real Variables for Hungary.

Variable	NPL	CAR	ROE	CRED	MONEY	GDPGR	INV	CONS	GOV	IP
NPL	0	18.20	18.93	8.47	16.80	13.93	18.80	11.28	12.83	14.09
CAR	18.20	0	12.34	19.58	12.24	8.42	9.13	17.29	13.68	12.00
ROE	18.93	12.34	0	17.85	10.93	7.25	12.03	16.20	12.88	7.89
CRED	8.47	19.58	17.85	0	8.12	10.87	12.82	9.08	8.78	9.54
MONEY	16.80	12.24	10.93	8.12	0	9.52	10.06	10.29	8.77	9.33
GDPGR	13.93	8.42	7.25	10.87	9.52	0	9.02	12.61	10.17	3.77
INV	18.80	9.13	12.03	12.82	10.06	9.02	0	14.91	11.66	9.40
CONS	11.28	17.29	16.20	9.08	10.29	12.61	14.91	0	10.70	11.64
GOV	12.83	13.68	12.88	8.78	8.77	10.17	11.66	10.70	0	9.98
IP	14.09	12.00	7.89	9.54	9.33	3.77	9.40	11.64	9.98	0

Source: Authors' own calculations.

Note: The lower value, the more similar time series and the brighter filling of cells.

Table 3. The DTW Similarity Coefficients Between Financial and Real Variables for Poland.

Variable	NPL	CAR	ROE	CRED	MONEY	GDPGR	INV	CONS	GOV	IP
NPL	0	25.25	4.05	14.87	22.15	12.37	14.75	12.71	12.26	12.36
CAR	25.25	0	23.40	10.33	5.46	11.95	12.69	18.52	14.14	12.08
ROE	4.05	23.40	0	15.12	20.40	10.11	14.30	11.36	10.91	9.86
CRED	14.87	10.33	15.12	0	7.23	10.73	12.46	15.53	11.55	9.99
MONEY	22.15	5.46	20.40	7.23	0	8.90	12.40	15.97	13.15	9.25
GDPGR	12.37	11.95	10.11	10.73	8.90	0	13.12	13.34	12.36	6.57
INV	14.75	12.69	14.30	12.46	12.40	13.12	0	15.06	13.58	11.54
CONS	12.71	18.52	11.36	15.53	15.97	13.34	15.06	0	13.40	12.40
GOV	12.26	14.14	10.91	11.55	13.15	12.36	13.58	13.40	0	11.57
IP	12.36	12.08	9.86	9.99	9.25	6.57	11.54	12.40	11.57	0

Source: Authors' own calculations.

Note: The lower value, the more similar time series and the brighter filling of cells.

Table 4. The DTW Similarity Coefficients Between Financial and Real Variables for Romania.

Variable	NPL	CAR	ROE	CRED	MONEY	GDPGR	INV	CONS	GOV	IP
NPL	0	20.66	26.17	10.12	16.86	11.24	20.63	14.10	12.56	11.13
CAR	20.66	0	9.41	21.03	14.41	7.96	14.27	16.66	9.55	14.39
ROE	26.17	9.41	0	23.73	12.56	11.60	13.85	20.07	11.73	11.80
CRED	10.12	21.03	23.73	0	11.53	12.46	16.88	8.93	11.57	10.28
MONEY	16.86	14.41	12.56	11.53	0	13.37	14.43	10.11	10.34	13.57
GDPGR	11.24	7.96	11.60	12.46	13.37	0	13.26	12.60	9.59	5.29
INV	20.63	14.27	13.85	16.88	14.43	13.26	0	15.12	14.83	14.06
CONS	14.10	16.66	20.07	8.93	10.11	12.60	15.12	0	9.65	10.63
GOV	12.56	9.55	11.73	11.57	10.34	9.59	14.83	9.65	0	10.15
IP	11.13	14.39	11.8	10.28	13.57	5.29	14.06	10.63	10.15	0

Source: Authors' own calculations.

Note: The lower value, the more similar time series and the brighter filling of cells.

Thirdly, when analysing financial variables individually, certain relationships can be found. The capital adequacy ratio follows an entirely different path compared to the volume of non-performing loans. The respective DTW similarity coefficients are equal to 29.79 for Czechia, 18.20 for Hungary, 25.25 for Poland, and 20.66 for Romania. Such a discrepancy is due to the fact that the volume of non-performing loans depends on factors like the level of household income in the case of individual loans and the profitability of business activity in the case of corporate loans, which is not the case of capital adequacy ratio that depends primarily on the other determinants. A relatively substantial similarity can be observed between the variables representing the total volume of loans and the value of non-performing loans (similarity coefficients range between 8 and 15 for the analysed countries). Such a result is economically justified, as these variables represent similar aspects of the financial sector and are influenced by similar factors.

Fourthly, the variables representing the real economy have a solid mutual similarity. Looking at Tables 1–4 as a whole, the cells at the bottom right corner of the table (representing the mutual similarity of the real sector variables) have a relatively bright filling. A strong resemblance is especially visible when comparing the GDP growth rates with the growth rates of industrial production. The most substantial similarity between these variables occurs for Hungary (the similarity coefficient stands at 3.77) and Romania (5.29). A strong relationship was also evidenced for Czechia and Poland, with coefficients of 7.29 and 6.57, respectively. This outcome is consistent with the economic theory, stating that industrial production shows similar dynamics to changes in general economic activity. As a result, the industrial production index is often used as an alternative measure to analyse business cycles and identify turning points, mainly because the data are available on a monthly basis.

Fifthly, an interesting result refers to the relatively high similarity between the investment rate and economic growth rate. The corresponding similarity coefficients range from 9–10 in Hungary and Czechia to 13–14 in Poland and Romania. This outcome confirms the theoretical view that investments are an important source of economic growth and strongly react to changes in economic activity. Slower economic growth decreases business confidence about the future and discourages investment.

Sixthly, some worth mentioning interactions can be found between monetary policy (and, more broadly, the financial sector) and economic growth. GDP fluctuations show relatively substantial similarity to ROE fluctuations – especially in Czechia and Hungary, where the similarity coefficients equal 5.59 and 7.25, respectively (in Poland and Romania they are also relatively low, standing at 10.11 and 11.60, respectively). Additionally, in the case of Hungary and Romania, CAR fluctuations are consistent with GDP fluctuations (similarity coefficients at the level of 8.42 and 7.96, respectively). These results show that economic activity changes affect the banking sector's profitability, which theoretical foundations support.

Seventhly, in the case of Poland and Hungary, there is a relatively strong similarity between the economy's monetisation and the economic growth rate.

The corresponding similarity coefficients are 8.90 for Poland and 9.52 for Hungary. This result may lead to the conclusion that monetary policy in Poland and Hungary was partly coordinated with fluctuations in general economic activity (although it should also be borne in mind that the monetisation ratio, i.e. the ratio of money supply to GDP, depends by definition on the size of GDP).

Eighthly, two more interesting relationships exist between the real and financial sectors. In three CEE countries (all except Poland), there is some similarity between household consumption and the volume of loans (the corresponding similarity coefficients are 11.08 for Czechia, 9.08 for Hungary and 8.93 for Romania). This relationship has a strong theoretical basis, as a large part of household consumption expenditure is financed by credit. Therefore, these variables follow a similar path. In the same three countries, fluctuations in public consumption (as % of GDP) are akin to fluctuations in money supply (also in % of GDP), with similarity coefficients at the level not exceeding 10.5. This can be interpreted as coordination (at least partial) of fiscal and monetary policy – similar factors shaped the central bank's activities in the area of the money supply to the actions taken by the government in the area of public spending on consumption.

The DTW method can also be used to cluster countries. Fig. 1 presents dendrograms showing the grouping of countries into clusters. The individual graphs in Fig. 1 include a dendrogram for a single variable and show what groups of countries can be distinguished for one particular time series.

Based on Fig. 1, two clusters of countries can be identified. One cluster includes Poland and Czechia, while another covers Hungary and Romania. These two clusters of countries can be distinguished based on as many as 7 out of 10 analysed variables: non-performing loans, the volume of credit, ROE, the monetisation ratio, GDP growth rate, household consumption and government expenditure on consumption.

A relatively high similarity between Poland and Czechia results from a few factors. Both countries play a prominent role in the European Union, achieve comparable results in terms of per capita income, share analogous institutional environments and – finally – are neighbours of each other. They are exposed to analogous demand and supply shocks, both internal and external, which makes the cyclical fluctuations of the financial and real sectors very akin. The sources of similarity between Romania and Hungary can be traced to historical and geographical factors, including that they are neighbouring countries and a sizeable Hungarian minority lives in Romania. For the above-mentioned seven variables, countries are divided into clusters, which can be explained by economic, institutional, political and historical factors.

Regarding two variables (investment rate and industrial production), Czechia can be clustered with Hungary due to the closer DTW measure than with the other two countries (Poland and Romania). In the case of CAR, there is only one compact cluster with Czechia and Romania, while Poland and Hungary are far away from each other and do not form a separate cluster (in terms of the DTW distance).

Summary

The study aims at assessing the mutual similarity among various variables representing the financial sector (including the monetary policy by the central bank) and the mutual similarity of various variables representing the real economy (e.g. economic growth, industrial production, household consumption expenditure), as well as cross-similarity between the financial and the real sector. The analysis is based on the dynamic time warping method which allows to capture various dimensions of changes of considered variables, including different time length and magnitude of variables' fluctuations, different distribution of peaks and troughs, non-linearities and time shifts (leads and lags). The DTW method is almost non-existent in economics, so the study contributes much to the economic literature.

The analysis includes five variables representing the financial sector and five from the real sector. The study covers four countries: Czechia, Hungary, Poland and Romania, which are advanced inflation targeters. The calculations are based on quarterly data starting from *Q1* 2010 and ending – in the case of most time series – in *Q3* 2022.

The results show that, on the one hand, variables representing the financial sector, including those reflecting monetary policy, are weakly correlated with each other. On the other hand, the variables representing the real economy have a solid mutual similarity.

Looking at the individual variables, the analysis indicates that capital adequacy ratio follows an entirely different path compared to the volume of non-performing loans. A relatively substantial similarity can be observed between the variables representing the total volume of loans and the value of non-performing loans. In terms of real variables, a strong resemblance is also especially visible when comparing the GDP growth rates with the growth rates of industrial production. There is also a relatively high similarity between the investment rate and economic growth rate.

Some worth mentioning interactions can be found between monetary policy (and, more broadly, the financial sector) and economic growth. GDP fluctuations show relatively substantial similarity to ROE fluctuations – especially in Czechia and Hungary. In the case of Hungary and Romania, CAR fluctuations are consistent with GDP fluctuations. These results show that economic activity changes affect the banking sector's profitability. In the case of Poland and Hungary, there is a relatively strong similarity between the economy's monetisation and the economic growth rate.

Comparing the individual countries, two clusters of countries can be identified. One cluster includes Poland and Czechia, while another covers Hungary and Romania. These two clusters of countries can be distinguished based on 7 out of 10 analysed variables.

The DTW algorithm turned out to be a useful tool to compare macroeconomic time series. Its further use in economics and finance is widely recommended and opens the area for further studies on the subject.

Notes

1. The contribution by Mariusz Próchniak has been financed by the National Science Centre in Poland (project no. 2018/31/B/HS4/00164).
2. For example, when exploring the ScienceDirect database with the term 'dynamic time warping' for the 2000–2023 period, there appear 5,078 articles among which there are exactly zero articles in the subject area related to economics.

References

Cernohorska, L. (2015), "Impact of Financial Crisis on the Stability Banking Sectors in the Czech Republic and Great Britain", *Procedia Economics and Finance*, Vol. *26*, pp. 234–241.

Diallo, B. and Al-Mansour, A. (2017), "Shadow Banking, Insurance and Financial Sector Stability", *Research in International Business and Finance*, Vol. *42*, pp. 224–232.

D'Urso, P., De Giovanni, L. and Massari, R. (2021), "Trimmed Fuzzy Clustering of Financial Time Series Based on Dynamic Time Warping", *Annals of Operations Research*, Vol. *299*, pp. 1379–1395.

Elsayed, A.H., Naifar, N. and Nasreen, S. (2023), "Financial Stability and Monetary Policy Reaction: Evidence from the GCC Countries", *The Quarterly Review of Economics and Finance*, Vol. *87*, pp. 396–405.

Focardi, S.M. (2001), *Clustering Economic and Financial Time Series: Exploring the Existence of Stable Correlation Conditions*, Discussion Paper, No. 2001–04, The Intertek Group.

Franses, P. H. and Wiemann, T. (2020), "Intertemporal Similarity of Economic Time Series: An Application of Dynamic Time Warping", *Computational Economics*, Vol. *56*, pp. 59–75.

Gadanecz, B. and Jayaram, K. (2009), "Measures of Financial Stability – A Review", *Irving Fisher Committee on Central Bank Statistics (IFC) Bulletin*, No. *31*, pp. 365–380.

Gassouma, M. S., Benhamed, A. and El Montasser, G. (2023), "Investigating Similarities between Islamic and Conventional Banks in GCC Countries: A Dynamic Time Warping Approach", *International Journal of Islamic and Middle Eastern Finance and Management*, Vol. *16* No. 1, pp. 103–129.

Guy, K. and Lowe, S. (2011), "Non-performing Loans and Bank Stability in Barbados", *Economic Review*, Vol. *37* No. 3, pp. 77–99.

Hallak, I. (2013), "Private Sector Share of External Debt and Financial Stability: Evidence from Bank Loans", *Journal of International Money and Finance*, Vol. *32*, pp. 17–41.

Kate, R. J. (2016), "Using Dynamic Time Warping Distances as Features for Improved Time Series Classification", *Data Mining and Knowledge Discovery*, Vol. *30*, pp. 283–312.

Kozarić, K. and Dželihodžić, E. Ž. (2020), "Effects of Macroeconomic Environment on Non-performing Loans and Financial Stability: Case of Bosnia and Herzegovina", *Journal of Central Banking Theory and Practice*, Vol. *9* No. 2, pp. 5–17.

Müller, M. (2007), "Dynamic Time Warping". in: *Information Retrieval for Music and Motion*, Springer, Berlin, Heidelberg.

Ozili, P. K. (2019), "Non-performing Loans and Financial Development: New Evidence", *The Journal of Risk Finance*, Vol. *20* No. 1, pp. 59–81.

Paparrizos, J. and Gravano, L. (2016), "K-shape: Efficient and Accurate Clustering of Time Series", *SIGMOD Record*, Vol. *45* No. 1, pp. 69–76.

Pawlowska, M. (2016), "Does the Size and Market Structure of the Banking Sector Have an Effect on the Financial Stability of the European Union?", *The Journal of Economic Asymmetries*, Vol. *14* No. A, pp. 112–127.

Raihan, T. (2017), *Predicting US Recessions: A Dynamic Time Warping Exercise in Economics*, SSRN Working Paper, No. 3047649.

Rapacki, R. (ed.) (2019), *Diversity of Patchwork Capitalism in Central and Eastern Europe*, Routledge, London.

Rapacki, R. (ed.), Próchniak, M., Czerniak, A., Gardawski, J., Horbaczewska, B., Karbowski, A., Maszczyk, P. and Towalski, R. (2019), *Kapitalizm patchworkowy w Polsce i krajach Europy Środkowo-Wschodniej* (*Patchwork Capitalism in Poland and the Countries of Central and Eastern Europe*), Polskie Wydawnictwo Ekonomiczne, Warszawa.

Sakoe, H. and Chiba, S. (1978), "Dynamic Programming Algorithm Optimisation for Spoken Word Recognition", *IEEE Transactions on Acoustics, Speech, and Signal Processing*, Vol. *26* No. 1, pp. 43–49.

Svirydzenka, K. (2016), *Introducing a New Broad-Based Index of Financial Development*, IMF Working Paper, No. WP/16/5.

Vintsyuk, T. (1968), "Speech Discrimination by Dynamic Programming", *Cybernetics*, Vol. *4* No. 1, pp. 81–88.

Walesiak, M. (2016), "The Choice of Groups of Variable Normalisation Methods in Multidimensional Scaling", *Przegląd Statystyczny*, Vol. *63* No. 1, pp. 7–18.

Xue, W.-J. (2020), "Financial Sector Development and Growth Volatility: An International Study", *International Review of Economics & Finance*, Vol. *70*, pp. 67–88.

Yiadom, E. B., Mensah, L. and Bokpin, G. A. (2022), "Environmental Risk and Foreign Direct Investment: The Role of Financial Sector Development", *Environmental Challenges*, Vol. *9*, 100611.

**Part 3
Prospects of Economic Growth in Poland:
The Micro, Meso and Macro Perspective**

Chapter 13

Innovation or Imitation: The Right Key to Growth in Poland

Tomasz Kijek and Małgorzata Markowska

Abstract

Research Background: This chapter deals with the issue of the role of imitation and innovation in explaining economic growth in the context of the Polish economy, taking the endogenous growth theory and the technology catch-up theory as guidelines. This issue is extremely important as Poland faces the urgent need to reduce productivity gap through investments in R&D and/or the absorption of foreign technologies.

Purpose: The aim of this chapter is to find the effects of innovation and imitation on economic performance of Poland and shed light on possible outcome differences between these two kinds of activities.

Methodology: The empirical analysis uses data on innovation, imitation and Gross Domestic Product (GDP) of the Polish economy between 2005 and 2021, collected from a few statistical sources. We apply the autoregressive distributed lag (ARDL) model to find the impact of innovation and imitation on economic growth.

Findings: The results suggest that R&D investments positively affect economic performance of the Polish economy, whereas the impact of imitation activities on GDP appears to be insignificant.

Keywords: Innovation; imitation; economic growth; ARDL model; Poland; catch-up effect

Introduction

As part of the theoretical discussion on sources of economic growth, innovation is identified as the key driver of productivity increase. In line with the first and second generation of endogenous growth models any R&D policy change affects

Modeling Economic Growth in Contemporary Poland, 209–219
Copyright © 2024 Tomasz Kijek and Małgorzata Markowska
Published under exclusive licence by Emerald Publishing Limited
doi:10.1108/978-1-83753-654-220231016

permanently the growth rate of productivity or has an impact on the steady-state growth rate (Minniti and Venturini, 2017). On the other hand, the literature on technology diffusion and technology transfer points out the importance of imitation for productivity growth of economies at the earlier stages of economic development (Veeramani, 2014). The question about choosing between innovation and imitation is extremely important for the Polish economy, which, despite its high economic growth, remains a laggard in terms of overall spending on R&D.

In line with the European Innovation Scoreboard (EIS) Poland is classified as an Emerging Innovator with performance at 60.5% of the EU average (Hollanders, Es-Sadki and Khalilova, 2022). A relative strength of Polish economy within the investment-related framework of EIS is its high propensity to absorb new technology through, inter alia, investments in equipment and machinery and the acquisition of patents and licences. These activities are classified as non-R&D innovation expenditures and can be grouped into three main categories: (1) minor improvements in terms of existing products and processes by applying engineering knowledge, (2) imitations of user-driven innovations and (3) new combinations of existing knowledge (Lopez-Rodriguez and Martinez-Lopez, 2017). It should be noted that there is a decreasing trend in non-R&D expenditures in Polish economy compared to the EU average over recent years. As for R&D innovation expenditures, Poland took 16th place among all 27 EU Member States in 2021, spending 1.44% of GDP on innovation. Importantly, R&D intensity in Poland was constantly growing in 2006–2021 period (apart from the exceptional years of 2013 and 2016). The trends observed for innovation activities in the Polish economy may imply a shift from passive transfer of technology to innovation or at least creative imitation. Unfortunately, little empirical research exists on the impact of innovation and imitation on economic growth in Poland. The few studies that deal at the same time with economic effects of innovation and imitation activities have mainly a regional dimension. For example, Świadek and Szajt (2018) find that R&D expenditures affect productivity of Polish regions in the short run and long run, while investments in machinery and equipment only in the short run.

Therefore, the aim of this study is to find the effects of innovation and imitation on economic performance of Poland and shed light on possible outcome differences between these two kinds of activities. This chapter provides the literature review on the relationships between innovation, imitation and economic growth. It also describes the data, variables and econometric model we use; followed by results and discussion; and finally concludes.

Literature Review

Innovation and Economic Growth

The link between innovation and economic growth is at the centre of ongoing interest in both academic and policy-oriented research. In the neoclassical approach, exogenous and completely unexplained technical progress is a source of long-run productivity growth, since capital exhibits diminishing returns (Solow, 1957). In contrast, the new growth theory goes beyond the neoclassical model by explaining technical progress as the result of R&D activities. In the models developed by Aghion and Howitt (1992), Grossman and Helpman (1991) and Romer (1990) the productivity growth rate should be rising when the growth rate of R&D is positive. These models are referred to as the first-generation fully endogenous models. On the other hand, the semi-endogenous growth models pioneered by Jones (1995) postulate that R&D has at most transitory effect on productivity growth. Finally, the second-generation fully endogenous models (Howitt, 1999; Young, 1998) show that the deleterious effect of product proliferation offsets the growth spurring effect of increasing R&D investments.

In the literature on economic growth, many empirical studies tried to verify the impact of R&D on economic growth at the country level. The results of a meta-analysis of econometric studies based on economy-wide data and published over 2000–2010 suggest that the mean and median rate of return to R&D amount to 0.41 and 0.53 and range from a lower quartile of 0.12 to an upper quartile of 0.64. Moreover, the mean and median social rate of return to R&D amount to 1.7 and 2.2 and the variation in estimated social rates of return to R&D spans from a minimum of 0.2 to a maximum of 3 (Appelt, 2015). It is worth noting that the R&D rates of return in developed economies are likely to be in the 20%–30% range, but they may be also as high as 75% (Hall, Mairesse and Mohnen, 2010). In case of developing countries the situation is mixed (Table 1). For example, Samimi and Alerasoul (2009) find no significantly positive impact of R&D on the level of GDP in the sample of 30 developing countries, including Poland. The similar conclusion is drawn by Inekwe (2015) for lower income economies. In turn, Tuna, Kayacan and Bektaş (2015) show that there is no causality relationship between R&D and economic growth at the national level in Turkey.

Interpreting the results presented in Table 1, it should be noted that various types of R&D investments may have different economic impacts. The most commonly used distinction of R&D is privately vs. publicly financed R&D. In Poland, there was the successive increase in the share of the business sector in internal R&D investments (from 31.1% to 63.1%, between 2005 and 2021) and a gradual decline in the share of the government sector. For the higher education sector, its share continues to be around 30% (Karpińska, 2021). It is a welcome situation, since, as suggested by Scotchmer (2004), economic effect of public R&D is expected to be smaller than that of private R&D spending.

Imitation and Economic Growth

Gerschenkron (1962) introduced the term 'backwardness advantage' according to which developing countries have an advantage over developed countries, since they can faster and less riskily imitate technologies and products that were invented in advanced countries. Moreover, the higher the distance of a country from the world's technology leaders is, the greater the possible gains it can get from this advantage. In the same vein, Howitt (2000) argues that a country that is

Table 1. Selected Studies on the Impact of R&D on Economic Growth.

Author(s)	Sample	Time Period	Main Findings
Lichtenberg (1992)	74 countries	1964–1989	There is the positive impact of R&D investment on the level and growth of productivity growth
Sylwester (2001)	20 OECD countries	1989–2006	There is not found to be a strong association between R&D and output growth, but in the sub-sample of G-7 countries a positive association between industry R&D expenditures and economic growth is reported
Samimi and Alerasoul (2009)	30 developing countries	2000–2006	There is no significantly positive impact of R&D on the level of GDP
Petrariu, Bumbac and Ciobanu (2013)	15 CEE countries	1996–2010	R&D spending level has a negative impact on economic growth
Inekwe (2015)	66 countries	2000–2009	The effect of R&D expenditure on growth is positive for upper middle-income economies while insignificant in lower income economies
Gumus and Celikay (2015)	52 countries	1996–2010	The research shows that R&D expenditure has a positive and significant effect on economic growth in the long run
Tuna, Kayacan and Bektaş (2015)	Turkey	1990–2013	There is no long-term relationship between real R&D expenditures and economic growth series

Source: Authors' own elaboration.

far beyond the world technology frontier may experience faster growth than a country that is situated close to the technology frontier, since the less developed country is supposed to make more technological progress when one of its sectors moves to the world frontier. On the other hand, Abramovitz (1986) advocates that social capability is needed to effectively adopt external technology. His arguments are in line with a theory of absorptive capacity developed by Cohen and Levinthal (1989). This theory assumes that the ease with which countries absorb technology spillovers depends on their R&D intensity.

Coe, Helpman and Hoffmaister (1997) identify four channels through which knowledge produced in one country affects economic growth in other countries. All channels are related to international contacts and trade, which allow a country to purchase advanced equipment and machinery from abroad. These imports may facilitate learning process about production methods and product design. Moreover, they enable a country to copy foreign technology and enhance productivity of its own innovation and imitation processes. Although technology spillovers may take place between developed countries, the process of technology diffusion seems to be a relatively more important driver of productivity growth for developing than for developed countries. In general, developing countries have a comparative disadvantage in producing knowledge-advanced capital goods, since they are endowed with a lower stock of knowledge capital.

The effects of international trade on domestic productivity are analysed in a vast empirical literature. In their pioneering paper Brada and Hoffman (1985) find that the accumulation of imported capital contributes significantly to technological progress in developing countries. In turn, Coe and Helpman (1995) and Coe, Helpman and Hoffmaister (1997) prove that a country can gain benefits from importing goods produced by other countries with large cumulative experiences in R&D. Going beyond the simple relationship between trade openness and growth, Veeramani (2014) shows that the types of imported capital goods and the sources of their origin matter for growth. As regards the specifics, capital goods exert a stronger impact on growth than intermediates, and, as expected, the group of developing countries gains more from imported capital goods than the group of developed countries. These results contrast with findings of Keller and Yeaple (2009), who find that productivity spillovers from imports are not straightforward.

Apart from international trade (i.e. import and export) there are also other channels that are likely to be the source of technology spillovers. One of them is foreign direct investment (FDI). When multinational corporations (MNCs) join a domestic market, the novel technology is transferred from the firms' R&D centres to the foreign subsidiaries located in the host country. It is also possible that knowledge generation can take place in an R&D centre established within organisational structures of subsidiaries. Blyde (2003) also analyses other mechanisms of knowledge spillovers induced by FDI. These include, inter alia, migration and turnover of MNCs workers, sharing knowledge with MNCs suppliers and buyers, which could therefore lead to the increase in productivity in upstream and downstream sectors, and MNCs competitive pressure on domestic firms to update their technologies.

As for empirical studies on FDI and productivity growth, Meyer and Sinani (2009) provide a meta-analysis of 66 empirical studies on FDI productivity spillovers in developing countries, transition economies and developed countries. They show that many of the early studies in developed and developing economies find significant positive effects. In contrast, some recent panel data studies in developing and developed countries identify negative effects. In the case of transition economies, the evidence is equally inconclusive. For Poland, Zukowska-Gagelmann (2000) reveals that the effect of FDI on the scope of productivity growth of locally owned firms is negative. Interestingly, Golejewska (2009) indicates the lack of spillovers in Polish manufacturing as a whole. On the other hand, Wojciechowski (2016) concludes that there exists a long-term relationship between FDI and Gross Value Added (GVA) of the Polish economy.

Data and Methods

The databases from the Statistics Poland and the Polish Patent Office are the sources of the data used in the research. Four variables are taken into account as potential explanatory variables in our model for economic performance of the Polish economy. The first two of them describe innovations and the next two proxy imitations. The variables in currency units are expressed in fixed prices from 2005. Imputation of missing data has been carried out by regression analysis with complete variables as independent ones. Original values have been deflated by index of investment goods prices and consumer prices index, respectively – making prices constant at 2005 level.

The following variables are the proxies for innovation: applications for patent in Polish Patent Office – PAT (pcs), internal expenditures for R&D – RD (1000 PLN).The proxies of imitation are as follows: total foreign direct investment expenditures in enterprises – FDI (1000 PLN), investment expenditures for imported machinery and equipment (related to innovation activities) – IMP (1000 PLN).

After considering different approaches to measuring economic performance, i.e. GDP level and growth – total volume (million PLN) and per capita (PLN), and yearly dynamics of them (%), we use GDP total, since it seems to be the best proxy for the development level of the Polish economy. We use the variables in natural logarithms to control for potential heteroscedasticity. The natural logarithm of the PAT, RD, FDI, IMP and GDP series is displayed in Fig. 1.

To find the impact of innovation and imitation on economic performance of the Polish economy, we apply the ARDL model. This model is often used to model the dynamic relationship between variables in a single-equation time-series framework (Kripfganz and Schneider, 2022). The ARDL approach can deal with both I(0) and I(1) variables, so we refrain from unit root pretesting. A general ARDL model, in which the regression error term u_t is free of serial correlation, is given by:

$$y_t = \alpha_0 + \sum_{i=1}^{p} \beta_i \Delta y_{t-i} + \sum_{i=1}^{q} \delta_i \Delta x_{t-i} + u_t$$

where: α_0 – intercept, p, q – lag orders and $p \in (1, p^*)$, $q \in (1, q^*)$.

Results and Discussion

Applying the optimal lag selected on the basis of likelihood ratio (LR) test and three information criteria (AIC, the HQIC and SBIC), we have tested for

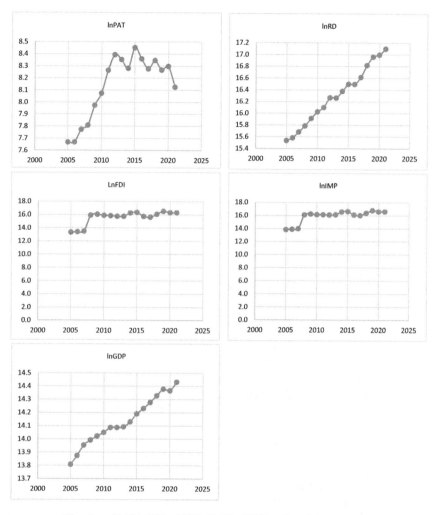

Fig. 1.   PAT, RD, FDI, IMP, GDPseries (2005–2021).
Source: Authors' own elaboration.

cointegration using Pesaran, Shin, and Smith (PSS) bounds test (Pesaran, Shin and Smith, 2001) with Kripfganz and Schneider (KS) critical values and approximate p-values. As a result, we have failed to reject the null hypothesis of no long-run relationship. Thus, we estimate ARDL model with optimal lag orders determined on the basis of the Schwarz/Bayesian information criterion, but apart from an equilibrium correction term. The results of ARLD model estimation are presented in Table 2. As a part of diagnostics of ARDL estimation, we have

Table 2. Results of ARDL Model Estimation ($R^2 = 0,98$).

Dependent Variable: lnGDP	Coef.	Std. Err.	*p* Value
lnGDP$_{t-1}$	0.479	0.251	0.080
lnPAT	−0.024	0.063	0.716
lnRD	0.213	0.094	0.047
lnFDI	0.166	0.245	0.513
lnIMP	−0.195	0.281	0.504
Cons.	4.620	2.135	0.056

Source: Authors' own elaboration.

examined the residuals of the estimated model for autocorrelation using Breusch-Godfrey LM test. The resulting estimates of Breusch-Godfrey LM test with four lags confirm that the residuals of the estimated ARDL model are free from autocorrelation. We also have tested for heteroscedasticity in the residuals using Cameron and Trivedi's decomposition of IM-test. The test results confirm that the residuals are homoscedastic.

The results in Table 2 indicate that only R&D within the set of innovation and imitation variables has significantly ($p < 0,05$) positive performance effect on the Polish economy. This finding is partially consistent with the results reported by Świadek and Szajt (2018) for Polish regions. It is worth noting that they show the positive impact of R&D on productivity not only in the short run, but also in the long run. There are also other studies that reveal a beneficiary effect of R&D for Polish regions. For example, Brodny and Turak (2022) use a synthetic measure of regional capacity based, inter alia, on R&D expenditures and reveal its positive impact on a synthetic measure of economic development. Importantly, patent applications have an insignificant impact on GDP. The plausible explanation of this situation is the fact that institution from public sector in Poland (i.e. universities, research institutes and scientific entities of the Polish Academy of Sciences) are more eager to apply for patent protection than firms from private sector. In addition, considering the private sector is typically favoured for commercialisation of inventions due to markets ensuring that firms are more efficient than public agents no relationship between patent applications and economic growth is quite understandable.

As regards the effect of FDI on GDP in Poland, it appears to be insignificant. The reason for this may be threefold. Firstly, as suggested by Konings (2001), foreign firms decrease the productivity of domestic firms through competition effect. Secondly, learning process from MNCs may require domestic firms to spend more time, which short run analyses do not take into account. Finally, foreign firms may efficiently protect their know-how. Our results also provide no evidence for imports-related technology spillovers, which may be associated with a relatively low scale of innovation activities involved with importing machinery and equipment in the Polish economy.

Summary

Our chapter fits with the ongoing discussions on the role of innovation and imitation in the growth of the Polish economy. The theoretical background of our research has been grounded in the endogenous growth theory and the convergence theory. We analyse a relatively broad spectrum of empirical studies on the impact of imitation and innovation on economic performance of developed and developing countries, including Poland. Unfortunately, few studies deal with economic effects of both innovation and imitation in the comparative context. We try to fill this gap by studying the relationship between a set of proxies for innovation and imitation and performance of the Polish economy. The results show the positive effect of R&D investments and no significant effects of imitation activities. However, this does not mean that innovation is the only appropriate mean for economic growth in Poland. In our opinion innovation and imitation should be regarded as the complementary sources of growth. To fully exploit the benefits of foreign technology, the economy needs the absorptive capacity.

Our study is not without limitations. As regards the methodology of research, we have faced with the problem of modelling short time-series, which undoubtedly affects the robustness of the results. Moreover, the proxies for innovation and imitation used in our study have their disadvantages widely identified in the literature. To overcome these limitation, future studies in this field should be based on longer time-series and apply the direct measures of innovation and imitation, e.g. sales of products that are 'new to the market' and sales of products that are 'new to the firm'.

References

Abramovitz, M. (1986), "Catching Up, Forging Ahead, and Falling behind", *The Journal of Economic History*, Vol. 46 No. 2, pp. 385–406.

Aghion, P. and Howitt, P. (1992), "A Model of Growth through Creative Destruction", *Econometrica*,Vol. 60 No. 2, pp. 323–351.

Appelt, S. (2015), "The Impact of R&D Investment on Economic Performance: A Review of the Econometric Evidence", OECD, DSTI/EAS/STP/NESTI(2015)8, pp. 1–59.

Brada, J. and Hoffman, D. (1985), "The Productivity Differential between Soviet and Western Capital and the Benefits of Technology Imports to the Soviet Economy", *Quarterly Journal of Business and Economics*, Vol. 25 No. 1, pp. 6–18.

Blyde, J. S. (2003), "The Role of Foreign Direct Investment and Imports of Capital Goods in the North-South Diffusion of Technology", *Journal of Economic Integration*, Vol. 18, pp. 545–562.

Brodny, J. and Tutak, M. (2022), "Assessing the Level of Innovation of Poland from the Perspective of Regions between 2010 and 2020", *Journal of Open Innovation, Technology, Market and Complexity*, Vol. 8, 190.

Coe, D. T., Helpman, E. and Hoffmaister, A. W. (1997), "North-South R&D Spillovers", *The Economic Journal*, Vol. 107 No. 440, pp. 134–149.

Coe, D. T. and Helpman, E. (1995), "International R&D Spillovers", *European Economic Review*, Vol. 39 No. 5, pp. 859–887.

Cohen, W. M. and Levinthal, D. A. (1989), "Innovation and Learning: The Two Faces of R&D", *The Economic Journal*, Vol. 99 No. 397, pp. 569–596.

Gerschenkron, A. (1962), *Economic Backwardness in Historical Perspective: A Book of Essays*, Belknap Press of Harvard University Press, Cambridge.

Golejewska, A. (2009), *Are There Labour Productivity Spillovers from Foreign Direct Investment? Evidence from the Polish Manufacturing Sector 1993-2006*, Working Papers of Economics of European Integration Division, No. 902, pp. 2–16.

Grossman, G. and Helpman, E. (1991), "Quality Ladders in the Theory of Growth", *Review of Economic Studies*, Vol. 58 No.1, pp. 43–61.

Gumus, E. and Celikay, F. (2015), "R&D Expenditure and Economic Growth: New Empirical Evidence", *Margin: The Journal of Applied Economic Research*, Vol. 9 No. 3, pp. 205–217.

Hall, B. H., Mairesse, J. and Mohnen, P. (2010), "Measuring the Returns to R&D", in: *Handbook of the Economics of Innovation*, eds. Hall, B. and Rosenberg, N., North-Holland, Amsterdam, pp. 1033–1082.

Howitt, P. (1999), "Steady Endogenous Growth with Population and R&D Inputs Growing", *Journal of Political Economy*, Vol. 107 No. 4, pp. 715–730.

Howitt, P. (2000), "Endogenous Growth and Cross-country Income Differences", *American Economic Review*, Vol. 90 No. 4, pp. 829–846.

Inekwe, J. N. (2015), "The Contribution of R&D Expenditure to Economic Growth in Developing Economies", *Social Indicators Research*, Vol. 124, pp. 727–745.

Jones, C. (1995), "R&D-Based Models of Economic Growth", *Journal of Political Economy*, Vol. 103 No. 4, pp. 759–784.

Hollanders, E., Es-Sadki, H. and Khalilova, N. (2022), "*European Innovation Scoreboard 2022*", Publications Office of the European Union, available at: https://data.europa.eu/doi/10.2777/309907 (accessed 11 March 2023).

Keller, W. and Yeaple, S. R. (2009), "Multinational Enterprises, International Trade, and Productivity Growth: Firm Level Evidence from the United States", *The Review of Economics and Statistics*, Vol. 91 No. 4, pp. 821–831.

Karpińska, K. (2021), "Situation of the R&D Sector in Poland in the Face of the Current Crisis", *Studies in Logic, Grammar and Rhetoric*, Vol. 66 No. 79, pp. 409–424.

Konings, J. (2001), "The Effects of Foreign Direct Investment on Domestic Firms: Evidence from Firm Level Panel Data in Emerging Economies", *Economics of Transition*, Vol. 9, pp. 619–633.

Kripfganz, S. and Schneider, D. C. (2022), *Ardl: Estimating Autoregressive Distributed Lag and Equilibrium Correction Models*. Research Center for Policy Design Discussion Paper TUPD-2022-006, available at: https://www.nber.org/papers/w4161 (accessed 3 March 2023).

Lopez-Rodriguez, J. and Martinez-Lopez, D. (2017), "Looking beyond the R&D Effects on Innovation: The Contribution of Non-R&D Activities to Total Factor Productivity Growth in the EU", *Structural Change and Economic Dynamics*, Vol. 40, pp. 37–45.

Meyer, E. and Sinani, E. (2009), "When and Where Does Foreign Direct Investment Generate Positive Spillovers? A Meta Analysis", *Journal of International Business Studies*, Vol. 40 No. 7, pp. 1075–1094.

Minniti, A. and Venturini, F. (2017), "The Long-Run Growth Effects of R&D Policy", *Research Policy*, Vol. 46 No. 1, pp. 316–326.

Romer, P. (1990), "Endogenous Technological Change", *Journal of Political Economy*, Vol. 98 No. 5, pp. 71–102.

Samimi, A. J. and Alerasoul, S. M. (2009), "R&D and Economic Growth: New Evidence from Some Developing Countries", *Australian Journal of Basic and Applied Sciences*, Vol. 3 No. 4, pp. 3464–3469.

Solow, R. (1957), "Technical Change and the Aggregate Production Function", *Review of Economics and Statistics*, Vol. 39 No. 3, pp. 313–330.

Lichtenberg, F. R. (1992), "*R&D Investment and International Productivity Differences*", NBER Working Paper, No. 4161, available at: https://www.nber.org/papers/w4161 (accessed 3 March 2023).

Pesaran, M. H., Shin, Y. and Smith, R. (2001), "Bounds Testing Approaches to the Analysis of Level Relationships", *Journal of Applied Econometrics*, Vol. 16 No. 3, pp. 289–326.

Petrariu, I. R., Bumbac, R. and Ciobanu, R. (2013), "Innovation: A Path to Competitiveness and Economic Growth. The Case of CEE Countries", *Theoretical and Applied Economics*, Vol. XX No. 5, pp. 15–26.

Scotchmer, S. (2004), *Innovation and Incentives*, MIT Press, Cambridge, MA.

Sylwester, K. (2001), "R&D and Economic Growth", *Knowledge, Technology & Policy*, Vol. 13 No. 4, pp. 71–84.

Świadek, A. and Szajt, M. (2018), "Impact of Innovation Expenditures on Manufacturing in Poland in 2006–2015 – Regional Diversification", *Studies of the Industrial Geography Commission of the Polish Geographical Society*, Vol. 32 No. 3, pp. 54–68.

Tuna, K., Kayacan, E. and Bektaş, H. (2015), "The Relationship between Research & Development Expenditures and Economic Growth: The Case of Turkey", *Procedia – Social and Behavioral Sciences*, Vol. 195, pp. 501–507.

Wojciechowski, L. (2016), "The Impact of FDI on Gross Value Added in Host Country with Particular Emphasis on Manufacturing Sector", *Studies of the Industrial Geography Commission of the Polish Geographical Society*, Vol. 30 No. 1, pp. 143–158.

Veeramani, C. (2014), "World's Knowledge Spillovers: Beyond Openness and Growth", *Journal of Economic Integration*, Vol. 29 No. 2, pp. 298–328.

Young, A. (1998), "Growth without Scale Effects", *Journal of Political Economy*, Vol. 106 No. 1, pp. 41–63.

Zukowska-Gagelmann, K. (2000), "Productivity Spillovers from Foreign Direct Investment in Poland", *Economic Systems*, Vol. 24 No. 3, pp. 223–256.

Chapter 14

Development of Polish ICT Sector: Education, Governmental Policy, Employment and Future Trends

Łukasz Wiechetek and Arkadiusz Gola

Abstract

Background: This chapter describes the present state and the trends in the Polish information and communications technology (ICT) sector, which today is considered to be one of the most progressively developing part of the national economy. Special attention is given to economic background, ICT employment and governmental policy. Some forecasts for future development were also proposed.

Purpose of the Chapter: The purpose of this chapter is to present the background, dynamics and future trends in the Polish ICT sector.

Methodology: The statistical data (Statistics Poland, Eurostat), market reports and scientific articles were analysed. Microsoft Excel and QGIS software was used to analyse the data and visualise the results.

Findings: Polish ICT market has stable fundaments, good infrastructure, qualified workers and a good location. Despite the developed infrastructure, e-commerce and e-administration usage is relatively low compared to the average level of EU27. The Polish ICT market specialises in software implementation, IT outsourcing and computer game development. The Polish ICT market development is associated with cloud computing, outsourcing, e-commerce, cybersecurity, big data, artificial intelligence (AI) and Industry 4.0. Poland is also in the top 10 countries for IT outsourcing worldwide, with the leading ICT centers in Warsaw, Cracow and Wrocław.

The growth of the ICT sector was (is) supported also by central programmes and government strategies: Operational Programme Digital Poland, Digital Competence Development Program and Cybersecurity Strategy. In the last 2 years, the development of ICT was also boosted by the

Modeling Economic Growth in Contemporary Poland, 221–233

Copyright © 2024 Łukasz Wiechetek and Arkadiusz Gola

Published under exclusive licence by Emerald Publishing Limited

doi:10.1108/978-1-83753-654-220231017

COVID-19 pandemic. Market reports and forecasts show that the sector's future development will be related to artificial intelligence, Industry 4.0 and data analytics and financed by private business and central government contracts. The increase in remote work will also be significant.

Keywords: ICT sector; IT; Polish market; IT education; ICT development; ICT policy

Introduction

Poland is located in Central Europe and has about 38 million citizens. It is the sixth-largest and one of the fastest-growing economies in the European Union. The Polish economy has many advantages such as huge internal demand, low costs, a stable financial sector and high staff potential (PARP, 2017). Unfortunately, the disadvantages can be a low investment in R&D and innovation, also a complicated regulation system.

The digital economy and society in Poland are at a moderately developed level. 92% of households have access to the internet and 54% (in 2019) used the internet for ordering goods and services. In 2021, about 47% of Poles used internet to interact with public administration, while the average for 27 EU countries was 58%. Also, the e-business sector in Poland is growing rapidly and still has great potential.

Over 95% of enterprises in Poland have broadband access to the internet, and 70% give their employees portable devices for a mobile connection to the Internet. In 2021 about 15% of enterprises received orders online (at least 1%). Finally, the

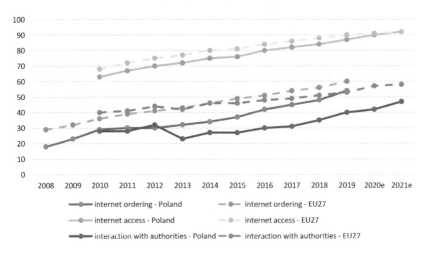

Fig. 1.   Dynamics of Digital Society Development in Poland. *Source:* Authors' own elaboration based on publicly available data from Eurostat.

share of enterprises' turnover on e-commerce was about 18% (the average for EU 27 in 2021 was 20%). Fig. 1 and Fig. 2 show the dynamics of digital society and e-business development in Poland.

From a technical point of view, Poland is ready for fast digital development. The communication infrastructure is good, and the level of internet access is similar to the EU average. However, we can observe a lower level of internet ordering 7 p.p. less in Poland compared to the EU27 average, especially in e-administration. In this case, Poland loses 11 p.p. The comparisons show that there is still great potential for digital society development in Poland.

For the last decade in Poland, we could notice the stable development of e-business. We have strong positive dynamics in this area. In 2010, only 8% of enterprises received more than 1% of orders online, while in 2021, almost 20% of companies accepted online orders. Also, the share of e-commerce turnover nearly doubled between 2010 and 2021 from 8% to 15%.

The Eurostat data confirms the stable economic foundation for the growth of the Polish digital economy and society. However, there is still great potential and much to be done in this area to compare with European leaders: Denmark, Finland, Norway, Ireland, and the Netherlands. According to the PARP (2017), in the following years, the Polish economy and the information and communications technology (ICT) sector will have to overcome the problems related to decreasing EU funds and increasing labour costs. Therefore, Polish companies

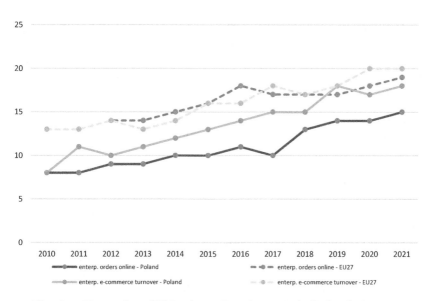

Fig. 2.   Dynamics of E-business Development in Poland. *Source:* Authors' own elaboration based on publicly available data from Eurostat.

must look for new, innovative products and services and market niches. The market will also have excellent potential for establishing ICT-related start-ups.

ICT Sector in Poland

ICT solutions are the foundation of modern industry end economy. The economy can be prosperous only if ideas and efficiency are combined with innovation. IT solutions can improve and optimise the existing business processes and might also be the source of new business paths. Poland's demand for ICT hardware, software and services is still growing. The COVID-19 pandemic has strongly sustained the growth. During the pandemic, it turned out that many activities, education, entertainment, and even everyday work could be or even must be performed online.

According to the Polish Investment & Trade Agency (PITA, 2022), there are about 60,000 ICT companies in Poland, which is growing rapidly. The sector employs above 400,000 specialists. Eurostat (Eurostat, 2022) data shows that in 2019, Polish ICT sector generated 3.6% of the GDP and used about 2.7% of working-age employees. The IT/ICT companies are the most innovative and responsible for about 90% of expenditures on R&D in Poland. The development of the Polish ICT sector is also seen outside the country. The value of exported services was about *5.6 billion EUR in 2017.*

The ICT market comprises three sectors (hardware, software and services). The hardware sector is the biggest (over 50% of the market). However, its share has declined recently, proving that the ICT market is maturing. The software and services sectors increase their share. The development of the ICT market is based mainly on three components: providing infrastructure for big public contracts, developing and selling software and services outsourcing. The local market development is driven by digitalisation in the entertainment sector (computer games), education (online learning and teaching) and business sector (remote work). The Polish ICT market specialises in software implementation, IT outsourcing and computer game development (PARP, 2017; Computerworld, 2020). Although the Polish labour market offers a lot of well-qualified workers, ICT companies still have problems recruiting highly skilled specialists, and the gap between labour supply and demand is still significant.

The main drivers for ICT sector development in Poland are qualified workers (e.g. talented programmers) (PITA, 2021), well-prepared educational programmes in mathematics, algorithms and data analytics and good background for investment. Therefore, Poland became a good place for locating big tech companies' R&D centres and service hubs.

The development of the domestic ICT market is associated with cloud computing, outsourcing, e-commerce, cybersecurity, big data, Artificial Intelligence (AI) and Industry 4.0 (PARP, 2019). Cloud services are one of the fastest-growing segments of the Polish IT market. Enterprises use cloud solutions because of scalability, flexible payments, no need to buy hardware and licences and the possibility of reducing operational costs. Polish IT companies provide data centre and cloud computing services and locate their centres in Poland, Western Europe, the United States and Asia (Comarch, 2022). Heavy amounts of data provided by individuals and companies must proceed with specialised analytical tools. Therefore, new analytical needs created the demand for big data services. The growing demand for big data causes universities and technical colleges to open new fields of study and develop curricula integrating IT, management and economics. New study fields are created, such as business analytics or data science. Estimates show that the big data sector can grow about 10% year-to-year. According to Gartner (Gartner, 2021), cloud and AI are very much sought-after services. These technologies are used in many areas like healthcare, automotive, finance, e-commerce, logistics, entertainment and industrial production.

According to Google Trends (Fig. 3), Polish internet users in the last two decades were mainly interested in cloud computing, outsourcing and e-commerce. Less often, the searches addressed big data and Industry 4.0. We can observe that interest in outsourcing has declined in recent years while cloud computing and e-commerce have become exciting topics.

Poland is in the top 10 countries for IT outsourcing worldwide because of its low costs, good infrastructure, low prices and negligible risk. Essential facts are also the high rate of human development index and knowledge of the English language, especially among young people. The main centres for outsourcing in Poland are Cracow, Warsaw, Katowice, Wrocław and Rzeszów.

The e-commerce sector is developing very fast, about 20% each year. These services are widely used because most Polish e-commerce users are motivated by lower delivery costs and more attractive prices than traditional stores.

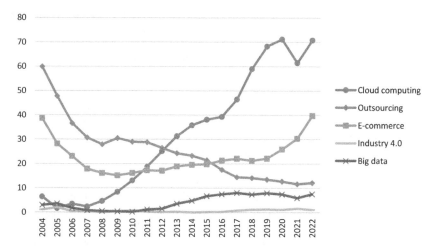

Fig. 3.   Interest in ICT Areas From 2004 to 2022. *Source:* Authors' own elaboration based on publicly available data from Google Trends.

E-commerce development and generated incomes were boosted recently also by the COVID-19 pandemic. During the pandemic, we could observe both increased internet sales volume of existing shops and a growing number of new online shops and services. The lockdown also contributed to a vast increase in the popularity of online shops offering food products. According to Statista (2022a), the e-commerce revenue in 2025 will grow in Poland to nearly 26.3 billion US dollars.

Development in the cybersecurity segment is caused mainly by changes in legal regulations, increased online activities due to the COVID-19 pandemic and new cyberterrorism threats related to the geopolitical background. Poland's cybersecurity industry revenue is estimated to increase to 1.4 billion US dollars by 2027 (Statista, 2022b). The gains in this segment are generated mainly by cybersecurity systems and services.

New technologies and services like AI significantly impact the national economy. Therefore, the Polish government prepared a policy for AI development. The document indicates activities and aims in the following areas: society, innovative companies, education, international cooperation and AI for the public sector. These activities should increase AI development dynamics and generate new well-paid jobs (GovTechPolska, 2020).

Industry 4.0 is recognised by more than half of the companies in Poland. About 70% of companies familiar with the Industry 4.0 term are willing to implement it in an organisation. This solution is primarily attractive to cars and device producers. The main drivers for implementing Industry 4.0 solutions were increasing efficiency and lowering operational costs. The main barriers identified in this area were: user resistance and insufficient funds (PSI Polska, 2019).

The source of ICT development in Poland are also the start-ups. Due to the availability of specialists and investors, most of the ICT start-ups are located in big Polish cities, Warsaw, Cracow, Gdansk, Poznan, Łodz and Wroclaw. They are based on different technologies like AI and 3D Printing. Frequently, start-ups are also innovative platforms supporting educational, sports and commerce activities. Compared to the EU27 average, Poland has a higher concentration of start-ups in enterprise software, marketing solutions, fintech and gaming (PFR, 2020).

One of Poland's most critical drivers of ICT sector development are government-financed projects. Almost 25% of demand generated in the ICT market is related to e-administration. Despite many efforts and programmes that financed the development of e-government, Poland is still below the EU average regarding the percentage of individuals using the internet to interact with public authorities (Fig. 4).

According to Eurostat, in 2021, 47% of Polish citizens interacted online with public authorities, while the average for EU27 was 58%. The leaders in e-government, like Iceland, Denmark, Norway and Ireland, exceeded 90%. Poland has fewer achievements in this area than neighbouring countries, Germany, Czechia, Slovakia and Lithuania. Like other countries, we can observe significant differences in ICT solutions in Poland between big, medium and small enterprises. Small organisations have fewer possibilities to use sophisticated technology and employ highly qualified specialists.

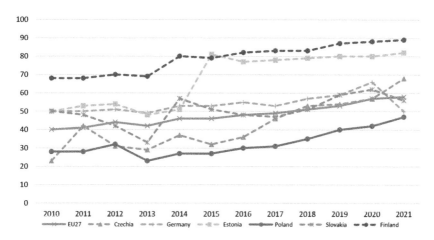

Fig. 4.   Individuals Using the Internet for Interaction With Public Authorities. *Source:* Authors' own elaboration based on publicly available data from Eurostat.

The ICT market in Poland has strong fundaments but is still a young and fast-developing part of the national economy. The development of the market is supported by the educational system, domestic companies and international ICT companies looking for well-educated young IT specialists, and government policy indicating the directions of development.

ICT Education and Employment

Poland has the most significant number of IT professionals in Central and Eastern Europe (CEE). The country has about 86,000 students in ICT, with about 11,000 graduates each year (PITA, 2022). Polish ICT specialists are recognised as top-class programmers. Therefore, international companies and start-ups and companies from Europe and around the world are opening their offices in Poland. According to the CEE tech ecosystem outlook report (PFR, 2020), in 2019, Poland had the largest pool of IT developers, with about 400,000 specialists. About 25% of software developers from CEE are Polish.

Every major city in Poland has a technical university. The main centres of ICT and Business and Administration education in Poland are shown in Fig. 5.

Each voivodship has its own centres of ICT and Business and Administration Education (Fig. 6). The important role is played by both higher education institutions and international schools. Most ICT education centres are located in mazowieckie, małopolskie and dolnośląskie voivodship.

In 2021, due to the COVID-19 pandemic, digital transformation in Poland boosted. We could observe an increasing volume of job offers in IT. According to the NoFluffJobs portal (https://nofluffjobs.com), the increase between 2020 and

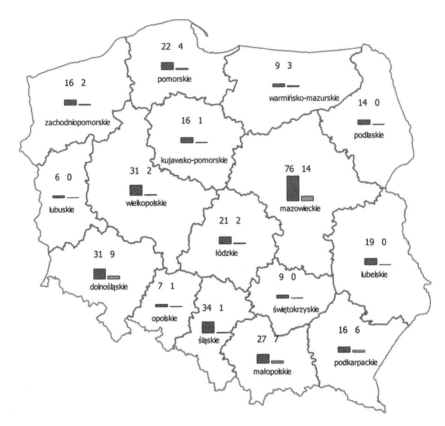

Fig. 5. The Main ICT and Business & Administrationeducation
Centres in Poland (Blue – Higher Education Institutions, Grey –
International Schools). *Source:* Authors' own elaboration based on publicly
available data from https://publikacje.paih.gov.pl/Poland_ICT_-
_Succeed_With_Poland (accessed 12 October 2022).

2021 was about 240%. Also, the average salary has grown year-to-year by 8%.
Analysis of job offers indicates that the most popular were backend offers.
However, non-technical jobs like project manager, UX designer and business
analyst gained popularity. The number of offers addressing cybersecurity and AI
almost quadrupled. The highest salaries (B2B contracts) were offered in the
cybersecurity, DevOps and big data categories (from EUR 3,000 up to EUR
5,000 per month). Considering the technology, the most paid offers for developers
included Java, Python and iOS. We can also notice a vast increase in telework.
Most of the offers presented on nofluffjobs.com (33%) were remote. Most of the
stationary job offers were in the biggest Polish cities: Warsaw, Cracow, Wroclaw,
Poznan, Gdansk and Katowice (NoFluffJobs, 2021).

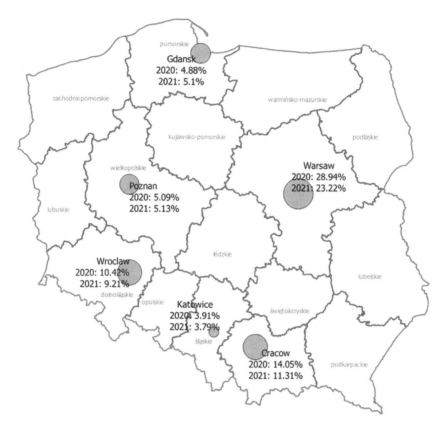

Fig. 6.   The Most Popular Location of Job Offers in IT. *Source:*
Authors' own elaboration with QGIS based on publicly available data from
https://nofluffjobs.com/insights/raport-rynek-pracy-it-2021/ (accessed 12
October 2022).

Comparing the two pandemic years, 2020 and 2021, we notice an increase in
remote work by 260%. The remote offers in 2021 accounted for almost one-third
of all published offers. Poland's top three ICT markets were still Warsaw, Cracow
and Wroclaw.

ICT Development Policy

The educational sector, business organisations and government policy support the
development of the Polish ICT sector. The regulations and programmes established by the government are aimed at both developing e-business and
e-administration, increasing digital society development and building internal and

external awareness. Many of the programmes were (are) supported also with European funds.

To ensure the stable development of the ICT sector, the Polish central government established the Digitization Council (Ministry of Digitalization, 2011).The Council supports the Ministry of Digitalization with knowledge and experience and gives opinions on strategic documents related to digitisation, connectivity and the development of the information society. It cooperates in digital integration, online privacy protection and eliminating barriers to developing the electronic economy. Members of the Council can also provide and generate new ideas related to the country's digital development.

In the years 2014–2020, the Operational Programme Digital Poland was conducted (Digital Poland, 2014). The Programme's main aim was to strengthen the digital foundations for the country's development. The main directions of support were the development of broadband networks and the improvement of the quality and efficiency of public services through their digitisation. The key supported areas in e-administration were the labour market, social security, healthcare, justice and judiciary, education, public contracts, safety and emergency. The Programme contained five priority axis common access to high-speed internet, e-administration and open government, digital competencies of the society, technical support and digital development of local government. EUR 2,172 million was allocated under the Digital Poland Programme in 2014–2020. EUR 1,223 million was spent on eliminating territorial differences in the possibility of accessing high-speed broadband internet, greater access to local and central government via the internet costed EUR 728 million and EUR 163 million was spent on developing digital skills. The primary beneficiaries of the activities under the Digital Poland Programme were not only telecommunication companies, municipalities, state research institutes, government administration, but also courts and prosecutor's office units, cultural institutions, state archives, nationwide radio and television broadcasters, scientific departments, non-governmental organisations, entrepreneurs and higher education institutions (Digital Poland, 2020).

The central government also established Digital Competence Development Program 2023–2030. The Program contains five priorities development of digital education; providing the opportunity to develop digital competencies; supporting digital competencies of employees from various sectors; development of advanced digital competencies; and strengthening the management of the development of digital competencies. The main aims of the Program planned for 2030 are 80% of the population with at least basic digital competencies, 40% of the population with above-basic digital competencies, 6% of the employed will be ICT specialists, 29% of women in ICT professionals, and finally a well-established and proven mechanism for coordinating and monitoring activities supporting the development of digital competences (Digital Competences, 2022).

Cybersecurity issues are significant for a solid digital ecosystem and stable ICT market development. Therefore, Polish government developed the Cybersecurity Strategy of the Republic of Poland for 2019–2024 (Cybersecurity Strategy, 2019).The document defines strategic goals, appropriate policy and regulatory measures that need to be implemented to make information systems, operators of crucial services, operators of critical infrastructure and public administration resistant to cyber threats. The strategy's main goal is to increase the level of resistance to cyber threats and the level of information protection in both public, military and private sectors. The sub-objectives are the development of the national cybersecurity system, increasing the resilience of public administration and private sector information systems and achieving the capacity to effectively prevent and respond to incidents, increasing the national potential in the field of cybersecurity technologies, building awareness and social competences in the field of cybersecurity and, finally, building a strong international position of the Republic of Poland in cybersecurity.

We can state that mentioned programmes and strategies established by the central government are also the catalysts for the development of the IT market. In some cases, they guarantee the stable development of the ICT sector. Implementation of the goals set in these documents provides and will provide massive demand for hardware, software and ICT services. Their performance will also involve many IT specialists. Therefore, the government strategy and central programmes will increase the speed of the Polish ICT market development and can generate many new jobs for IT specialists.

Summary

The Polish ICT market is still a young and fast-developing sector of the economy. The digital skills of Polish society are at a moderate development level. The gap between Poland and developed EU27 countries can still be observed mainly in e-commerce and e-administration. The main strengths of the market are still human capital, geographical location, low costs and good infrastructure. However, the barriers to stable development include geopolitical situation, lack of external financing sources and increasing wage requirements.

The future development of the ICT sector will be closely related to AI, Industry 4.0 and data analytics and financed by private capital and big central government contracts, which implement strategic government plans. In the following years, ICT services outsourcing should still be one of the leading development drivers. The ICT market growth in Poland can also be enhanced by start-ups providing innovative products and services and addressing new market niches that generate new demand for hardware, software and ICT services.

At present main centres of ICT in Poland are Warsaw, Cracow and Wroclaw. However, due to massive competition in these locations and increasing wage requirements of current and new employees, many IT companies are looking for specialists and opening branches in other sites like Łódz, Poznań, Gdansk, also Lublin, Rzeszów and Szczecin. The ICT market in Poland has strong fundaments. It is still a young and fast-developing part of the national economy with good prospects for further development. The market's growth is supported by educational system, domestic companies and international ICT companies looking for well-educated young IT specialists. Finally, its stable development is protected and supported by central government policy.

References

Comarch (2022), "Zaczynając na Data Center, kończąc na Chmurze", available at https://www.comarch.pl/handel-i-uslugi/ict/data-center/?gclid=Cj0KCQjwy5maBh DdARIsAMxrkw2iCpf4YzXfXOZjYdZZYID2NeJRfnxBIWZlR5er1nINHgaa_ vRTDMwaAoIoEALw_wcB (accessed 7 October 2022).

Computerworld (2020), "Raport 7N: Polska wśród najlepszych krajów do out-sourcingu IT", available at https://www.computerworld.pl/news/Raport-7N-Polska-wsrod-najlepszych-krajow-do-outsourcingu-IT,424143.html (accessed 7 October 2022).

CybersecurityStrategy (2019), "Strategia Cyberbezpieczeństwa Rzeczypospolitej Pol-skiej na lata 2019–2024", available at https://www.gov.pl/web/cyfryzacja/strategia-cyberbezpieczenstwa-rzeczypospolitej-polskiej-na-lata-2019-2024 (accessed 11 October 2022).

Digital Competences (2022), "Program RozwojuKompetencjiCyfrowych", available at https://www.gov.pl (accessed 11 October 2022).

Digital Poland (2014), "Program Operacyjny Polska Cyfrowa na lata 2014–2020", available at https://www.polskacyfrowa.gov.pl/media/107357/POPC_2_2022_ REACTEU_15032022.pdf (accessed 11 October 2022).

Digital Poland (2020), *Report on the Implementation of the Operational Programme Digital Poland for 2020*, available at https://www.polskacyfrowa.gov.pl/strony/o-programie/raporty/sprawozdania/#/domyslne=1 (accessed 11 October 2022).

Eurostat Database (2022), available at https://ec.europa.eu/eurostat/data/database (accessed 5 October 2022).

Gartner (2021), "Gartner Launches Emerging Technologies Radar 2021", available at https://blogs.gartner.com/tuong-nguyen/2020/12/07/gartner-launches-emerging-technologies-radar-2021/(accessed 5 October 2022).

GovTech Polska (2020), "Polityka rozwoju AI w Polsce przyjęta przez Radę Minis-trów – co dalej?" available at https://www.gov.pl/web/govtech/polityka-rozwoju-ai-w-polsce-przyjeta-przez-rade-ministrow–co-dalej (accessed 7 October 2022).

Ministry of Digitalization (2011), "Ministry of Digitalization Public Information Bulletin", available at https://mc.bip.gov.pl/rada-do-spraw-cyfryzacji-2021/ dzialalnosc-rady-do-spraw-cyfryzacji-2021-2023.html (accessed 5 October 2022).

NoFluffJobs (2021), *Rynek pracy IT w 2021 roku – Zarobki w Polsce, najpopu-larniejsze specjalizacje i wymagania w ofertach pracy*, available at https:// nofluffjobs.com/pl/praca-zdalna?page=1 (accessed 12 October 2022).

PARP (2017), "ICT Industry Development Prospects Until 2025", available at https:// www.parp.gov.pl/component/publications/publication/perspektywy-rozwojubranz y-ict-do-roku-2025 (accessed 6 October 2022).

PARP (2019), "IT/ITC Sector in Poland", *Polish Agency for Enterprise Development*, available at https://www.trade-old.gov.pl/pl/f/v/570995/PPE_PL_IT%20ICT% 20SECTOR%20IN%20POLAND.pdf (accessed 5 October 2022).

PFR (2020), *Polish and CEE Tech Ecosystem Outlook*, available at https://pfr.pl/dam/jcr:0d64a858-2b4e-4dbd-b933-50591f82c638/Polish-and-CEE-tech-ecosystem-outlook-Final-2.pdf (accessed 12 October 2022).

PITA (2021), "Succceed with Poland. The Information and Communications Technology Sector, Polish Investment and Trade Agency", available at https://publikacje.paih.gov.pl/Poland_ICT_-_Succeed_With_Poland/(accessed 12 October 2022).

PITA – Polish Investment & Trade Agency (2022), available at https://www.paih.gov.pl/sectors/ict (accessed 5 October 2022).

PSI Polska (2019), "Polska produkcja gotowa na Przemysł 4.0?" available at https://przemysl-40.pl/index.php/2019/11/04/cztery-raporty-o-przemysle-4-0-w-polsce/ (accessed 7 October 2022).

Statista (2022a), "E-commerce Revenue Forecast in Poland 2017–2025", available at https://www.statista.com/statistics/960912/poland-e-commerce-revenue/ (accessed 5 October 2022).

Statista (2022b), "Forecast of the Cybersecurity Market Revenue in Poland 2016–2027", available at https://www.statista.com/forecasts/1325264/cybersecurity-market-revenue-poland (accessed 5 October 2022).

Chapter 15

Evolution of Poland's Participation in Global Value Chains Since the Mid-1990s

Paweł Pasierbiak and Sebastian Bobowski

Abstract

Research Background: The last three decades have witnessed strong development of global value chains (GVCs). Also, the Polish economy developed international production links along with the systemic transformation from the beginning of the 1990s. This led to changes in Poland's participation in GVCs.

The Purpose of the Chapter: The study's primary purpose is to characterise the evolution of Poland's participation in GVCs since the mid-1990s, including its key determinants.

Methodology: Several research methods were used to achieve the study's goal, including critical literature analysis, statistical data analysis and descriptive methods. To determine Poland's share in the GVCs, the method of estimating domestic and foreign added value was used, which allowed for measuring the scale of production fragmentation and related trade in value-added.

Findings: The analysis allowed us to conclude that Poland has increased its share in GVCs, mainly inside the EU. Also, the industrial structure underwent positive changes. The increasing Poland's participation in the GVCs was primarily due to the inflow of FDI-related technology, the transformation of the economic structure, institutional and geographical factors. The improvement in the conditions for the functioning of the Polish economy has been reflected in international competitiveness rankings, where such attributes as geographical location, macroeconomic performance, human capital, market size, technical infrastructure and innovativeness are indicated. On the other hand, however, the tightness of the law, the efficiency of the government and public administration remains a challenge.

Modeling Economic Growth in Contemporary Poland, 235–248
Copyright © 2024 Paweł Pasierbiak and Sebastian Bobowski
Published under exclusive licence by Emerald Publishing Limited
doi:10.1108/978-1-83753-654-220231019

Keywords: Global value chains (GVCs); Poland; foreign trade; production networks; international competitiveness; value-added trade

Introduction

The last three decades have been a period of strong growth in the global internationalisation of production. Technological progress and favourable institutional and political changes made it easier for enterprises to organise the production process in such a way that the value of the final product is the result of the value added by entities from different countries. Consequently, there has been a significant increase in international trade in parts and components and the provision of services. Therefore, since the mid-1990s, the development of global value chains (GVCs) has largely driven the process of economic globalisation. The possibility of deepening the fragmentation of production processes and transferring production abroad led to a finer international division of labour, bringing the benefits of specialisation to the involved entities.

At the beginning of the 1990s, along with the progress of political and socio-economic transformation, the post-socialist countries of Central and Eastern Europe, including Poland, began to engage in production internationalisation. The development of cooperation between Polish companies and their foreign partners resulted in changes in Poland's participation in GVCs.

These issues are the subject of interest in this study. The main research objective of the study is to characterise the evolution of Poland's participation in GVCs since the mid-1990s, including its key determinants. The structure of the study was subordinated to this goal. In the first part, a literature review is presented. The second section describes the methodological issues. The following section analyzes changes in Poland's GVC participation. The fourth section offers the most critical factors for the growth of Poland's participation in GVCs. The chapter ends with conclusions.

Several research methods were used to achieve the study's goal, including critical analysis of the literature, statistical data analysis and inference and descriptive methods. The time range of the study covers the years 1995–2018, mainly determined by the availability of statistical data.

Literature Review

GVCs have become an inherent attribute and the new structural feature of the global economy since the advent of hyperglobalisation era (Ambos et al., 2021), its 'backbone and central nervous system' (Cattaneo et al., 2010, p. 7). Enhanced by liberalisation and deregulation of international macroeconomic policies, as well as development of information and communication technologies (ICTs), multinational enterprises (MNEs) shifted away from internalisation of overseas investments in favour of outsourcing and offshoring (Kano et al., 2020). Disaggregation and dispersion in geographical space relate both to pimary and support activities within the value chain, including more and more sophisticated knowledge-intensive processes (Coe and Yeung, 2015). Due to pandemic experiences, and its trade-distorting effects, GVCs may become more regional or local to secure supplies at the expense of productivity and cost efficiency (Shih, 2020; Zhan, 2021).

A critical aspect of GVC activities is the location decision, aimed at the most effective geographical configuration of the business activities, and maximisation of the value created and captured. In most cases, MNEs originating in technologically advanced countries account for upstream stages of the GVCs (Buckley and Tian, 2017). As argued by Ancarani et al. (2019), progressive industrial automation and robotics may lead to backshoring in case of MNEs oriented on quality rather than costs. On the other hand, according to Antràs (2020), digital innovations such as high speed Internet and e-commerce have increased the inclusiveness of GVCs by reducing entry barriers for enterprises originated in the lower cost countries.

Methodology

Measuring international trade in value-added terms is based on the assumption that the value of the final product is equal to the sum of the value added in successive countries participating in international production processes.[1] The primary methodological assumption in the case of international fragmentation of production is the possibility of estimating the national contribution to the product's final value. Koopman et al. (2014) developed a comprehensive method of measuring the scale of production fragmentation and the related trade in value-added. They decomposed exports and imports, which made it possible to estimate the country's net value added, i.e., its trade balance. The country's A gross exports (GE) consist of two components. The first is the domestic direct, and indirect value added (DVA) that country A exports to other countries. The second element is foreign value added (FVA), consisting of previously imported components, parts, and raw materials used in production processes.

Estimating domestic and foreign value added is the basis for determining the country's specialisation within GVCs. In the chapter, it was made based on: (1) the share of domestic value added in Poland's gross exports in individual sectors, (2) forward linkages – the share of exports of intermediate goods to the first importer and its further re-exports to third countries in gross exports, and (3) backward participation – share of foreign value added in gross exports (vertical specialisation).

The study uses the most recent version of the WTO and OECD database (OECD, 2021). The 2021 database covers 66 countries and 45 industries classified within a hierarchy based on ISIC Rev. 4. Data are available for 1995–2018.

Poland's Participation in GVCs – Evidence and Assessment

The turn of the 1980s and 1990s marked the beginning of profound structural changes in the Polish economy. Opening to the world initiated changes consisting in the growing importance of international economic cooperation. The increasing interdependence was observed in the area of trade, investment, and production. This was characteristic for all the countries of the former Eastern Bloc, which entered the phase of political and economic transformation in the early 1990s. Developing their specialisations, Polish enterprises were increasingly involved in international production processes at the regional and global levels. This process is illustrated by the growing difference between gross exports, and domestic value added included in the country's gross exports (Fig. 1).

Fig. 1 shows that since 1995 both values have been growing steadily, with gross exports increasing to a greater extent. By 2018, gross exports increased from 31.3 to 293.3 USD billion (an increase of 838%), while the domestic value added (DVA) in gross exports increased from 26.2 to 202.3 USD billion (671%). On the one hand, this proves the rapid growth of Poland's trade, and on the other hand, the growing importance of the country's international production cooperation. The declining share of domestic value added in gross exports (69% in 2018 compared to 83.8% in 1995) meant an increasing share of foreign value added (FVA) in Polish exports. Thus, it proves the growing significance of GVC for the Polish economy and foreign trade. This is confirmed by the *GVC participation index*. The combined share of foreign value added and domestic value added in partners' gross exports, related to Poland's gross exports, increased from 32.1% to 53.7%, which meant an increase of 67.1%. It was the most significant increase in the group of Central and Eastern European countries. Only in the case of Bulgaria and Hungary did the increases exceed 60% (63% and 62%, respectively), and in the case of other countries, they were clearly lower (OECD, 2021). As suggested by Koopman et al. (2014, pp. 485–486) and (Aslam et al., 2017, pp. 17–18), to assess the importance of GVCs for a given country, the GVC participation index should be supplemented with the indicator of the country's position

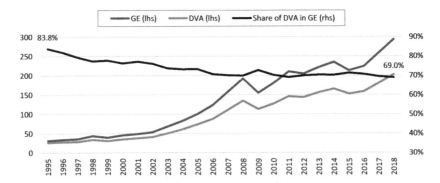

Fig. 1.   Value of Gross Exports (GE) and Domestic Value Added (DVA) to Gross Exports of Poland, and Share of DVA in GE in 1995–2018, USD Billion and %. *Source:* Authors' own elaboration based on publicly available data from OECD (2021).

in the GVC (*GVC position index*). When this indicator is calculated at the level of individual industries, it will determine whether a given country is in the initial or final stage of the production chain. Relevant calculations for Poland indicate that, on an overall level, Poland was positioned slightly at the initial phase of the production chains, which meant that foreign countries contributed more to Poland's exports than Poland to other countries' exports (the value of the position index ranged from −0.3 to −0.013).

The analysis of the geographical structure of Polish trade provides interesting evidence of changes in Poland's share in GVCs. Regardless of whether we analyse the structure using the gross exports method or using the share of domestic value added in gross exports, the share of regions is almost identical. Poland is most strongly connected with Europe, which, in 2018, accounted for about 80% of Polish exports. The following continents were North America (4.8%), East and Southeast Asia (4.1%) and South and Central America (0.6%). Other continents accounted for 10.6% of Polish exports (OECD, 2021). Since 1995, the geographical structure has not changed significantly – the differences in shares have not exceeded 1.5 p.p. The situation was different from the perspective of using the foreign added value in Poland's exports. Here, far-reaching changes can be observed in the analysed period. For virtually every region, the share of domestic value added in Poland's gross exports decreased from more than 80% (in the case of North America, it was even 85.2%) to less than 70% (the lowest value was recorded in South and Central America: 67%). This proves that Poland has become much more integrated into GVCs.

It is worth paying attention to the geographical structure of the origin of parts and components that Poland later exports as elements of its final products. The information in Fig. 2 indicates that Europe was the dominant region of Poland's supply of parts and components used as input to export production.

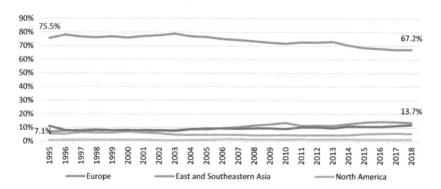

Fig. 2. Geographical Origin of FVA in Polish Gross Exports, 1995–2018, %. *Source:* Authors' own elaboration based on publicly available data from OECD (2021).

In 1995, the share of this continent was 75.5% of the total FVA, and since 2004, a downward trend has been observed. In 2018, the share was 67.2%, which meant a decrease of over eight percentage points. The continent that was increasing its importance as a supplier of FVA was East and Southeast Asia. Its share increased from 7.1% to 13.7%. However, this does not change the fact that the dominant region constituting the source of supply of intermediate goods for Polish exporters was Europe.

Table 1 shows the most important countries from which foreign added value originated. In the case of Europe, Germany played the most important role throughout the period, with a share in imports of intermediate goods used as inputs for Polish export production amounting to 22.9% in 1995 and 18.6% in 2018. The Russian Federation came in further positions (up from 6.5% to 10%), Italy (down from 8.7% to 4.9%), France (down from 5.3% to 4.7%) and the United Kingdom (down from 5.2% to 3.3%). In the case of East and Southeast Asia, the most significant change was the increase in China's share (from 0.7% to 7.7%, i.e. by as much as 7 p.p.). There was also a slight decrease in the case of Japan (from 2.7% to 1.9%) and a slight increase in the importance of South Korea (a rise from 1.1% to 1.7%).

The analysis of the product structure of Poland's exports in gross and value-added terms gives a picture of the structural changes that have taken place in the country's economy (see Table 2). Regardless of the measurement method, the *manufacturing sector* was the most significant group in commodity exports, whose share far exceeded 90%. Between 1995 and 2018, this share increased to 95.8% (in gross terms) and 94.7% (in value-added terms).

Table 1. Geographical Origin of FVA From Europe and East and Southeast Asia in Poland's Gross Exports, 1995 and 2018, %.

1995		2018	
Europe	*75.5%*	*Europe*	*67.2%*
Germany	22.9%	Germany	18.6%
Italy	8.7%	Russian Federation	10.0%
Russian Federation	6.5%	Italy	4.9%
France	5.3%	France	4.7%
United Kingdom	5.2%	United Kingdom	3.3%
East and Southeastern Asia	*7.1%*	*East and Southeastern Asia*	*13.7%*
Japan	2.7%	China	7.7%
Korea	1.1%	Japan	1.9%
Taiwan	1.0%	Korea	1.7%
China	0.7%	Taiwan	0.5%
Indonesia	0.5%	Singapore	0.5%

Source: Authors' own elaboration based on publicly available data from (OECD, 2021).

Table 2. Sectoral Breakdown of Poland's Exports Based on Gross Exports and Domestic Value Added, % and p.p.

	Gross Exports (GE)		Domestic Value Added (DVA)		GE-DVA	
	1995	2018	1995	2018	1995	2018
Agriculture, hunting, forestry and fishing	2.1%	2.0%	2.4%	2.5%	0.24	0.47
Mining and quarrying	3.8%	2.1%	4.2%	2.8%	0.41	0.65
Manufacturing	94.1%	95.8%	93.4%	94.7%	−0.65	−1.12
Food products, beverages and tobacco	7.3%	12.4%	8.1%	14.8%	0.87	2.41
Textiles, wearing apparel, leather and related products	11.3%	3.0%	11.7%	3.1%	0.43	0.13
Wood and paper products and printing	7.6%	5.1%	8.0%	5.9%	0.43	0.78
Chemicals and non-metallic mineral products	14.6%	20.1%	14.2%	19.2%	−0.40	−0.89
Basic metals and fabricated metal products	13.1%	11.4%	13.3%	11.3%	0.12	−0.14
Computer, electronic and electrical equipment	9.3%	11.5%	8.8%	9.7%	−0.49	−1.76
Machinery and equipment n.e.c	5.3%	5.8%	5.3%	5.9%	0.03	0.03
Transport equipment	17.5%	19.1%	15.6%	16.4%	−1.88	−2.70
Manufacturing nec; repair and installation of machinery and equipment	8.1%	7.4%	8.3%	8.5%	0.25	1.02

Source: Authors' own elaboration based on publicly available data from OECD (2021).

Initially (1995), the most important commodity groups were *Transport equipment* (17.5% and 15.6% in gross and value added terms, respectively), *Chemicals and non-metallic mineral products* (14.6%; 14.2%) and *Basic metals and fabricated metal products* (13.1%; 13.3%). By 2018, the situation changed, and the most important groups were *Chemicals and non-metallic mineral products* (20.2%; 19.2%), *Transport equipment* (19.1%; 16.4%) and *Food products, beverages and tobacco* (12.4%; 14.8%). The *Computer, electronic and electrical equipment* group also increased its share (11.5%; 9.7%). These changes testify to the modernisation of Polish production and exports, consisting in the increasing importance of more advanced groups of goods in exports and the decline in the importance of traditional groups (e.g. *Textiles, wearing apparel, leather and related products*).

Based on Table 2, it is also possible to indicate some changes in the involvement of Polish producers in GVCs. In the case of several product groups, the share of DVA in gross exports decreased significantly, which meant an increase in the involvement of Polish exporters in GVCs – parts and components previously imported from abroad constituted an increasing part of the Polish export value. This concerned mainly such groups as *Transport equipment* (the difference between the share in gross terms and in terms of added value −2.7 p.p.), *Computer, electronic and electrical equipment* −1.76 p.p.) and *Chemicals and non-metallic mineral products* (−0.89 p.p.). At the same time, there was an increase in the share of domestic value added in the production of such groups as *Food products, beverages and tobacco* (+2.41 p.p.) or *Manufacturing nec; repair and installation of machinery and equipment* (+1.02 p.p.). For these groups, involvement in GVCs has declined.

Main Influencing Factors

The analysis of Poland's participation in GVCs confirms the country's increasing involvement in international production processes. It is therefore worth considering the reasons for this process. In the literature on the subject, the most critical factors shaping participation in GVCs are, among others, factors of production availability, market size, geographical factors, national production capacity, level of economic development, industrial structure, trade policy, foreign direct investment, quality of institutions, connectivity, or macroeconomic factors (see, among others, Antràs, 2020; Cieślik et al., 2019; Fernandes et al., 2022). Also, participation in GVCs can be viewed from the point of view of competitiveness of the country in which such chains are developed. Both approaches will be used in this chapter.

Factors that strongly influenced Poland's participation in the GVCs include technology transfer resulting from the inflow of foreign direct investments, the transformation of the economic structure, improving institutional conditions and geographical factors.

At the beginning of the 1990s, Poland had a low economic and technological development level, with clear capital needs. The initiated political and socio-economic transformation enabled the inflow of foreign capital in the form of FDI. It was an important factor in the modernisation of the economy because foreign investments undertaken by foreign corporations led not only to an increase in the availability of capital but also to the improvement of labour productivity and production processes, increasing their overall efficiency and the level of technological development. The result of the modernisation of the economy was the improvement of the economic structure, which determines the production specialisation and, thus, the possibility of participating in GVCs. Since the beginning of the 1990s, Poland has been among the countries most often chosen as a location for FDIs by foreign corporations. According to UNCTAD data (2023), the value of investments increased from USD 88 million in 1990 to USD 24.8 billion in 2021, and the average annual inflow of investments in

1990–2021 amounted to USD 9.34 billion. It was one of the highest levels among the countries of Central and Eastern Europe. FDI per capita increased from just 2 USD (1990) to 657 USD (2021). Foreign capital flowing into Poland largely supplemented the internal investment fund. For 1990–2021, the annual average foreign capital accounted for 13.55% of gross fixed capital investments, but there were years when this share exceeded 20% (2000, 2004, 2006–2007, 2021). It can be said with certainty that the inflow of FDI, combined with technology, contributed to the modernisation of the economy and changes in its structure, which encouraged people to engage in international production networks.

Over time, the structure of the Polish economy was approaching the structures of more developed countries. In the case of Poland, the regularity was confirmed that the more modern the structure, the greater the possibility of joining inter-national production networks. At the beginning of the transformation, after years of functioning in the socialist economy, the structure of the Polish economy was significantly outdated. There was a relatively high share of the agricultural sector, and the share of industry and services was relatively low. Nevertheless, positive changes took place over time. In 1995, the share of agriculture in creating added value was 6.3% (percentage of employment in agriculture as much as 22.9%), while industry was 38% (33.2%), and services 55.7% (44%) (The World Bank, 2023; UNCTAD, 2023). By 2020, favourable changes took place: the share of agriculture fell to 2.8% in creating added value (9.1% in employment); the per-centage of the industry fell to 31.4% (32.1%), while the share of services increased to 65.7% (58.7%). The developing process of economic transformation, the growing servitization of the Polish economy, and the strengthening of the role and structural transformation of industry determined the increasing possibilities of joining international value chains.

In addition, the supporting role of institutional factors should be emphasised. Regulatory stability resulting from membership in the World Trade Organization (1995), the European Union (2004) and other organisations created favourable conditions for joining international production chains. The global production chains in which Poland participates have mostly a European range, so the importance of accession to the European Union should be underlined. From the beginning of the 1990s, Poland was oriented towards integration with the Euro-pean Union. Poland's Association Agreement with the EU clearly indicated the direction of change. Finally, Poland became a member of the European Com-munity in 2004, when it was officially admitted to the EU structures together with the other nine countries. Unifying the framework under which enterprises oper-ated on the single European market created a favourable climate for developing production chains. Foreign corporations from developed EU countries were even more willing to invest in increasingly stable and predictable economies. Poland was just such a market, confirmed by the FDI inflow data. Regional, European production chains were being created, in which Polish companies began to specialise in the assembly of final products and the production of parts and components, then mainly exported to other European countries. According to The World Bank data (2020, pp. 24–25), in 2018, in an average European country, about 65% of the foreign value added included in the country's gross exports came from another European country.

This specific regionalisation of production chains also illustrates the favourable impact of geographical factors. The proximity of suppliers and recipients reduces the time and cost of transport. This is of great importance in today's conditions of constant movement of goods (parts, components or final goods). As a medium-sized economy neighbouring the strongest European economy – Germany, Poland undertook production cooperation with European partners. On the other hand, relatively low production costs offered by geographically close countries of Central and Eastern Europe, including Poland, encouraged enterprises from developed countries of Western Europe to create European production networks. In addition to the production costs themselves, more factors improved the Polish economy's competitiveness and attractiveness under the GVCs.

Attributes of Poland as a participant of GVCs are addressed by international competitiveness and business rankings, supportive, certainly not sufficient, in respect of location decisions of foreign investors. Although there is no single, widely accepted definition of international competitiveness, it can be considered a nation's capacity to preserve conditions that promote greater value creation for its businesses and greater prosperity for its citizens (Garelli, 2005). It can also be associated with a set of institutions, laws, policies and other elements that affect a nation's output level (Schwab, 2009). In Poland's participation in GVCs, competitiveness can be understood as the economy's capacity to derive the most considerable economic gains from involvement in the international division of labour, augmented by factors related to the nation's potential.

Regular publications prepared by international organisations, forums, consultancy and research institutes, i.e. World Competitiveness Ranking (WCR; International Institute for Management Development), Global Competitiveness Index (GCI; World Economic Forum), Ease of Doing Business Ranking (EDBR; World Bank Group), Global Innovation Index (GII; World Intellectual Property Organization), are particularly appreciated. Irrespective of ranking, the number of countries considered, and the criteria applied, the position of Poland has been similar in recent years in most of them, clustering around 30–40th place. In the previous years, however, Poland was ranked relatively worse in the GII, EDBR, and GCI (in the case of the latter, since 2007) compared to WCR (see Fig. 3). On the other hand, we cannot neglect that IMD's ranking includes 63 countries in recent years, whereas EDBR analyzes 190 countries, GCI – 141, and GII – 132.

The oldest and continuously issued is the first mentioned above (WCR), assessing the competitiveness of countries using 163 hard and 92 survey data, categorised into four main criteria: economic performance, government efficiency, business efficiency and infrastructure, each divided into five sub-criteria.

According to Executive Opinion Survey by IMD, numerous indicators of the attractiveness of Poland impact participation in GVCs, with particular regard to a skilled workforce, effective labour relations, open and positive attitudes, the dynamism of the economy, high educational level, cost competitiveness, business-friendly environment, access to financing, and reliable infrastructure.

Fig. 3.   Position of Poland in International Competitiveness
Rankings, 1997–2022. *Source:* Authors' own elaboration based on publicly
available data from IMD (2023), WB (2023), WEF (2023), and WIPO
(2023).

When considering hard data, Poland is mainly appreciated for economic performance and infrastructure. On the other hand, however, IMD's recent reports
emphasised several challenges faced by Poland that may be crucial in respect of
participation in GVCs. These include skills development through reskilling and
upskilling programs, enhancement of public–private partnerships to narrow skill
gaps and deficits, development of digital technologies, green and digital infrastructure, technologies, and industry to stimulate innovation and productivity
growth, the establishment of user-friendly, predictable business legislation, reform
of immigration policy and the healthcare system.

GCI ranks 141 countries basing on 12 pillars of competitiveness: institutions,
infrastructure, ICT adoption, macroeconomic stability, health, skills, product
market, labour market, financial system, market size, business dynamism and
innovation capability, divided in total into 103 sub-criteria. Alike in the case of
WCR, both hard and survey data are used.

The GCI of Poland has been relatively stable through the years. In the latter
period, the position of Poland was almost analogical to the one achieved in IMD's
ranking (WCR). Among the key attributes of Poland, WEF's report points to
macroeconomic stability, market size, infrastructure, skills and innovation
capacity. On the other hand, relatively worst scores were recorded in the case of
the financial system, business dynamism, institutions and labour market. Pretty
challenging appeared to be such aspects as internal labour mobility, diversity of
the workforce, time to start a business, the efficiency of the legal framework in
challenging regulations and the government ensuring stability policy.

EDBR studies the business environment of 190 countries, using quantitative
indicators grouped in 12 areas: starting a business, dealing with construction
permits, getting electricity, registering property, getting credit, protecting minority
investors, paying taxes, trading across borders, enforcing contracts, resolving
insolvency, employing workers and contracting with the government.

Poland has gradually improved its performance through the years. Among the best regulatory performance, Poland was appreciated in area trading across borders, in respect of time required to comply with export documentation and get electricity. On the other hand, unfavourable changes were identified regarding transferring property in Poland.

GII ranks 132 countries in respect of their innovation capacities, relying on two sub-indices: the innovation input index (consisting of five pillars: institutions, human capital, and research, infrastructure, market sophistication and business sophistication) and the innovation output index (composed of two pillars: knowledge and technology outputs, creative outputs). In total, 80 indicators grouped in sub-indices and pillars are included in calculating a country's final score.

Poland's ranking performance has improved over time. According to GII 2022, Poland is assessed slightly better in innovation output than input. Among indicators positioning Poland as attractive from the perspective of providing an added value to GVCs, there are domestic industry diversification, PISA scales in reading, math, and science, e-participation, creative goods export as % of total trade, domestic market scale, pupil-teacher ratio, applied tariff rate (weighted average) and labour productivity.

In summary, there are some commonalities in respect of the evaluation of Poland as a participant of GVCs, including strengths like geographic location, macroeconomic performance, market size, cost savings, human capital, tariff rates, infrastructure and innovation potential. On the other hand, among the most critical weaknesses identified in most rankings were the efficiency of the government, public administration and procedures, stability, and clarity of legal frameworks and adoption of green technologies.

Conclusions

Participation in GVCs is considered as an inherent attribute of an open, competitive national economy. Poland, due to economic, institutional and political transformation since the 1990s, has been involved in the international division of labour, becoming an attractive recipient of technology-related FDI, mostly from the EU. Accession to the EU has consolidated Poland's position as an important node for production networks created by companies from Western Europe, mainly Germany.

Statistical analysis of product structure of Poland's exports in gross and value-added terms proved structural changes and modernisation of the Polish economy through the years. In particular, there was a decrease in share of DVA in Poland's gross exports in high-end product groups such as transport, electric and electronic equipment and chemicals, translating into increased integration with GVCs.

It is true that international competitiveness rankings indicate a number of advantages of Poland as a GVC participant, including geographical location, macroeconomic stability, market size, human capital and technical infrastructure;

however, there are several challenges related to legal and administrative environment, green transformation and labour mobility. Strengthening Poland's international competitive position requires, on the one hand, effective use of the country's potential, and, on the other hand, efforts to eliminate aforementioned barriers. Only then will the benefits from Poland's participation in GVCs continue to grow.

Note

1. Taxes and subsidies excluded for simplicity.

References

Ambos, B., Brandl, K., Perri, A., Scalera, V. G. and Van Assche, A. (2021), "The Nature of Innovation in Global Value Chains", *Journal of World Business*, Vol. 56 No. 4, 101221, https://doi.org/10.1016/j.jwb.2021.101221

Ancarani, A., Di Mauro, C. and Mascali, F. (2019), "Backshoring Strategy and the Adoption of Industry 4.0: Evidence from Europe", *Journal of World Business*, Vol. 54 No. 4, pp. 360–371, https://doi.org/10.1016/j.jwb.2019.04.003

Antràs, P. (2020), "Conceptual Aspects of Global Value Chains", *The World Bank Economic Review*, Vol. 34 No. 3, pp. 551–574.

Aslam, A., Novta, N. and Rodrigues-Bastos, F. (2017), *Calculating Trade in Value Added*, Vol. 17, No. WP/17/178, IMF Working Papers, Washington, DC, https://doi.org/10.5089/9781484311493.001

Buckley, P. J. and Tian, X. (2017), "Transnationality and Financial Performance in the Era of the Global Factory", *Management International Review*, Vol. 57 No. 4, pp. 501–528, available at https://www.jstor.org/stable/44985701

Cattaneo, O., Gereffi, G. and Staritz, C. (2010), "Global Value Chains in a Postcrisis World: Resilience, Consolidation, and Shifting End Markets". in: *Global Value Chains in a Postcrisis World: A Development Perspective*, eds. Cattaneo, O., Gereffi, G. and Staritz, C., World Bank, Washington, DC, pp. 3–20.

Cieślik, A., Michałek, J. J. and Szczygielski, K. (2019), "What Matters for Firms' Participation in Global Value Chains in Central and East European Countries?" *Equilibrium. Quarterly Journal of Economic and Economic Policy*, Vol. 14 No. 3, pp. 481–502.

Coe, N. M. and Yeung, H. W. C. (2015), *Global Production Networks: Theorizing Economic Development in an Interconnected World*, Oxford University Press, Oxford.

Fernandes, A. M., Kee, H. L. and Winkler, D. (2022), "Determinants of Global Value Chain Participation: Cross-Country Evidence", *The World Bank Economic Review*, Vol. 36 No. 2, pp. 329–360.

Garelli, S. (2005), *Competitiveness of Nations: The Fundamentals, IMD World Competitiveness Yearbook 2005*, International Institute for Management Development, Lausanne.

IMD (2023), IMD World Competitiveness Online, available at https://worldcompetitiveness.imd.org/customsearchresults/consolidatedresult (accessed 4 January 2023).

Kano, L., Tsang, E. W. K. and Yeung, H. W. (2020), "Global Value Chains: A Review of the Multi-Disciplinary Literature", *Journal of International Business Studies*, Vol. 51, pp. 577–622, https://doi.org/10.1057/s41267-020-00304-2

Koopman, R., Wang, Z. and Wei, S.-J. (2014), "Tracing Value-Added and Double Counting in Gross Exports", *The American Economic Review*, Vol. 104 No. 2, pp. 459–494.

OECD (2021), "Trade in Value Added (TiVA) 2021 ed", available at https://stats.oecd.org/ (accessed 26 November 2022).

Schwab, K. (2009), *The Global Competitiveness Report 2009–2010*, available at http://www.weforum.org/pdf/GCR09/GCR20092010fullreport.pdf (accessed 2 January 2023).

Shih, W. (2020), "Is it Time to Rethink Globalized Supply Chains?" *MIT Sloan Management Review*, March 19, available at https://sloanreview.mit.edu/article/is-it-time-to-rethink-globalizedsupply-chains/

The World Bank (2020), *Trading for Development in the Age of Global Value Chains*, Washington, DC, https://doi.org/10.1596/978-1-4648-1457-0

The World Bank (2023), "World Development Indicators | DataBank", available at https://databank.worldbank.org/source/world-development-indicators (accessed 15 January 2023).

UNCTAD (2023), "UNCTADstat Database", available at https://unctadstat.unctad.org/wds/TableViewer/tableView.aspx (accessed 15 January 2023).

WB (2023), *Doing Business Archive*, available at https://archive.doingbusiness.org/en/reports/global-reports/doing-business-reports (accessed 5 January 2023).

WEF (2023), *Global Innovation Reports*, available at https://www.weforum.org/reports (accessed 5 January 2023).

WIPO (2023), *Global Innovation Index*, available at https://www.wipo.int/edocs/pubdocs/en/economics/gii (accessed 6 January 2023).

Zhan, J. X. (2021), "GVC Transformation and a New Investment Landscape in the 2020s: Driving Forces, Directions, and a Forward-Looking Research and Policy Agenda", *Journal of International Business Policy*, Vol. 4, pp. 206–220.

Chapter 16

Board Diversity Policy: The New Challenges of Corporate Governance in Poland

Anna Wawryszuk-Misztal and Tomasz Sosnowski

Abstract

Research Background: Poland generally has a homogeneous society, conservative towards changes and diversity. The corporate culture in Polish companies reflects this mindset, leading to a lack of inclusion on the corporate board. Additionally, many companies may not fully understand the benefits of an inclusive workplace and legal requirements for gender diversity.

The Purpose of the Chapter: The main objective of the study is to provide a better understanding of the attitude of Polish companies towards diversity policies and reveal differences in actual and expected levels of gender diversity in corporate boards. Thus, we examine compliance with the gender diversity guidelines in the corporate governance code.

Methodology: Using a sample of 367 Polish companies listed on the Warsaw Stock Exchange, we study the composition of the management and supervisory boards to check if they meet the expected gender diversity criteria. We also look at companies' explanations for non-compliance with the main principles regarding diversity policy.

Findings: We find that the current composition of corporate boards of stock companies in Poland is male-dominated. Women represent only 12.72% and 17.12% of the management board and supervisory board members, respectively, and 68.94% (42.23%) of companies have no women on their management (supervisory) board. Moreover, only a small percentage of companies comply with the principles related to gender diversity. Qualifications, experience and education are pointed out as the most important criteria for decision-making on board appointments, with only

Modeling Economic Growth in Contemporary Poland, 249–265
Copyright © 2024 Anna Wawryszuk-Misztal and Tomasz Sosnowski
Published under exclusive licence by Emerald Publishing Limited
doi:10.1108/978-1-83753-654-220231021

2% of companies applying gender as an additional criterion. The study suggests that larger companies are more likely to implement diversity policies.

Keywords: Board diversity policy; gender quotas; corporate governance codes; management board composition; supervisory board composition; Warsaw Stock Exchange

Introduction

Equality between women and men is one of the fundamental rights of the European Union (EU). Thus, the European Commission addresses many actions to increase the gender balance in economic decision-making positions. The gender balance on corporate boards is part of the board diversity policy that not only refers to women's representation but also includes other dimensions of diversity among people, such as age, education and professional experience, among others.

Poland has developed voluntary initiatives, such as corporate governance codes, to promote board diversity. The 'comply or explain' mechanism, which is part of corporate governance codes, allows owners to decide if the company will follow a specific rule. If not, it must provide an explanation for its non-compliance with the rule and, in particular, describe the practices in relation to the issue included in the rule. This explanation is part of the statement on the company's compliance with corporate governance principles.

While Poland still uses voluntary tools to increase board diversity, other EU countries (e.g. France, Germany, Italy and Belgium) implemented gender quota laws for corporate boards of public companies to increase board diversity. There are also EU members that have not implemented any tools to achieve gender balance (e.g. the Czech Republic, Slovakia and Hungary). Although many initiatives have been taken to promote gender diversity in leadership positions in EU countries, the data revealed by the European Institute for Gender Equality shows that women's presence in such positions is still insufficient, especially in countries that have not implemented gender quotas.

With the ongoing institutional and social changes in Europe in mind, our research aims to ascertain the attitude of Polish companies listed on the Warsaw Stock Exchange (WSE) towards diversity policy under new rules included in corporate governance codes. In particular, we want to verify whether Polish stock companies implement a diversity policy or if only a specific type of company implements it. We also expect to reveal the difference between the actual and expected levels of gender diversity.

To achieve this aim, we analysed the explanations provided by companies included in their statement on compliance with corporate governance principles. Such a statement must be published after new corporate governance codes entered into force in July 2021. We focused on the reasons for non-compliance with two main principles that refer to diversity policy. Thus, our results might be important in the context of the legislative changes that must be introduced by the end of 2024, i.e. the transposition of Directive 2022 on gender equality to Polish law.

Although our study includes Polish companies, we hope our findings will be important not only in the Polish context. As the study shows the role of voluntary regulations in ensuring gender equality in decision-making bodies, it reveals how effective such regulations are. It also uncovers the obstacles and fears that prevent Polish companies from implementing a board diversity policy and appointing women to board positions. Those obstacles are not specific to Poland but might also occur in other countries that have not introduced gender quotas yet, especially in other countries from Central and Eastern Europe that share similar values, social and cultural backgrounds and economic conditions. Overcoming such obstacles and explaining the advantages of diversity should be the aim of policymakers responsible for issuing new gender quota laws.

Literature Review

The role of a board diversity policy was emphasised in Directive 2014/95/EU of the European Parliament and of the Council of 22 October 2014 regarding the disclosure of non-financial and diversity information by certain large undertakings and groups. It states that large companies must reveal information on their diversity policy concerning the administrative, management and supervisory bodies. According to the rule of 'comply and explain', companies are not required to implement a diversity policy of the board; however, the decision about non-implementation should be explained and included in the corporate governance statement (Directive 2014/95/EU, p. 3). In Poland, which has a two-tier corporate governance system, regulations concerning information revealed by public companies have been adjusted to the above Directive.

For the first time, the issue of a diversity policy was included in the corporate governance code for companies listed on the Warsaw Stock Exchange (WSE) that entered into force on 1 January 2016 (The Best Practice for GPW Listed Companies, 2016). This self-regulation included the principle of revealing information on the board diversity policy. It also contained a recommendation that the management board and supervisory board should be diverse in terms of gender, education, age and professional experience.

On 1 July 2021, the next corporate governance code (The Best Practice for GPW Listed Companies, 2021) entered into force. It also includes two rules regarding board diversity policy, but they are more restrictive than those in the previous document. The first principle (no. 2.1) requires companies listed on the WSE to have a diversity policy applicable to the management board and the supervisory board. Furthermore, it states that diversity goals and criteria (i.e. gender, education, expertise, age and professional experience), target dates and monitoring systems should be defined by a diversity policy. The principle specifies the measurable aim for gender diversity, which should be at least 30% for the minority group in each government body. The second principle (no. 2.2) states that bodies that elect members of the management board or supervisory board should take decisions that lead to the appropriate diversity of boards, in particular, at least 30% must be a minority group.

Directive (EU) 2022/2381 of the European Parliament and of the Council of 23 November 2022 on improving the gender balance among directors of listed companies and related measures was then adopted. It requires EU countries to introduce a gender quota law before 28 December 2024. Namely, large public enterprises should develop a diversity policy that allows them to achieve the required level of gender diversity − 40% of non-executive positions or 33% of all director positions should be held by underrepresented sex by 30 June 2026. If a company has not yet reached the required level of diversity, selection and appointment procedures should be adopted. They must impose fair and transparent procedures based on clear and neutral criteria. However, if there are two or more equally qualified candidates, gender criteria should be enabled and a candidate of a less represented sex should be prioritised.

Policymakers and researchers who analyse the role of gender-balanced boards refer to ethical and economic arguments for gender diversity. Ethical arguments refer to social equality and justice, and thus are not 'a means to an end, but [...] a desirable end in itself' (Brammer et al., 2007, p. 395). Economic arguments for gender diversity suggest that gender balance provides financial benefits to the company. These economic arguments arise from both theoretical conceptions and empirical research (Hoobler et al., 2018). Academics analysing the role of board gender diversity usually refer to agency theory and resource dependence theory, social capital theory and signalling theory (Kagzi and Guha, 2018), and they provide arguments for gender board diversity. For example, since female directors are more likely to reveal voluntary financial information (Gyapong and Afrifa, 2019) or increase the quality of financial or non-financial reporting (De Masi et al., 2021; Pucheta-Martínez et al., 2016), they contribute to decreasing information asymmetry and agency conflicts. According to resource dependence theory, female directors provide the company with unique skills, abilities and knowledge, thus providing critical resources (Hillman et al., 2000).

There is no doubt that board gender diversity brings many advantages. Still, the question remains: What kind of tools should be applied to increase board diversity, i.e. voluntary or obligatory ones? Since Norway was the first country to introduce gender quotas in 2003, researchers have analysed the results of the gender quota adoption by Norwegian public companies (Ahern and Dittmar, 2012; Wang and Kelan, 2013). Gender quota laws introduced by other European countries (e.g. France, Italy and Spain) attract the attention of practitioners, policymakers and researchers.

For example, since the introduction of mandatory gender quota for listed companies leads to investor reactions, some researchers use the event study method to explore the impact of new regulations on investors' decisions (Greene et al., 2020; Groening, 2019). For example, research on Californian companies shows, on average, negative impact of new law on the firm value. Still, the stock market reaction is less negative for companies with a smaller gap between the required and actual level of gender diversity (Greene et al., 2020). Groening

(2019) document that gender diversity in Italian companies might benefit investors, but only under certain conditions.

The recent literature presents sets of solid reasons for obligatory board gender quotas, such as correcting moral, social and ethical injustices related to gender inequality, accelerating the progress of achieving gender equality, breaking the glass ceiling and overcoming the issue of inside directorships, where a small group of male directors hold positions in multiple organisations (Hamplová et al., 2022, p. 746). These arguments might be used in the discussion on introducing gender quotas since possible problems and obstacles might occur when a country imposes mandatory quotas. Generally, quotas are seen as a simplistic solution to a very complex problem, and there are a number of reasons against them, for example, they encourage tokenism, there is a limited pool of experienced female directors (so-called golden skirts), discrimination against well-qualified men and increasing the perception of women as being given an unfair advantage, which can undermine their credibility and legitimacy ('decorative additions') (Hamplová et al., 2022, p. 746). Because the decision on obligatory board gender quota law in large EU public companies has been taken, the question is not if the country has to introduce the gender quota but how to encourage companies to change their attitude towards gender balance.

In contrast to the obligatory gender quota law, the corporate governance codes for listed companies exemplify a voluntary initiative to increase gender balance in leadership positions. The self-regulation mechanism increases the quality of the corporate governance system. However, the effectiveness of such a mechanism depends on the company's inclination to adopt the principles included in this document (see Krenn, 2015). According to institutional theory, the decision to comply with the principles included in the best practice code is perceived as the company's response to environmental expectations (Aguilera and Cuervo-Cazurra, 2004; DeCleyn, 2008). It also helps the company to gain acceptance in the financial market (Zattoni and Cuomo, 2008, p. 4).

The extant literature explores the level of compliance with codes of best practice (see De Cleyn, 2008) and points to determinants of this compliance (Tagesson and Collin, 2016; Wawryszuk-Misztal, 2021a). Tagesson and Collin (2016) revealed that companies with more concentrated ownership, smaller boards or that hired long-tenured directors were less likely to comply with the Swedish Code of Corporate Governance in 2010. Wawryszuk-Misztal's (2021a) investigation of Polish companies focuses on the two principles in The Best Practice for GPW Listed Companies 2016, i.e. those that regard the board diversity policy. It documents that if the company is larger, has a larger board size and a woman acts as president of the supervisory board, it is more inclined to develop a diversity policy.

The board's diversity policy is the issue that is included in corporate governance codes as recommendations. Therefore, some researchers explore if these recommendations lead to more diversified boards. Wawryszuk-Misztal's (2021b) research on Polish companies provides evidence that voluntary initiatives that promote the implementation of board diversity through corporate governance codes are not an effective tool. She measured management and supervisory board diversity in terms of gender, age, education and experience two times: at the end of December 2015 and then three years later in 2018, after the adoption of corporate governance codes. She concluded that the level of diversity had not changed significantly after three years. This result is in line with previous research by Mensi-Klarbach et al. (2019) for Austrian companies. They document that the corporate governance code has been ineffective unless the two forces have occurred. The first was the introduction of targets for women's representation in decision-making bodies, and the second was the threat of a gender quota being introduced if they had not achieved the expected level of diversity. These two coercive means effectively increased female representation in leadership positions.

Methodology

The empirical part of our analysis of the corporate governance environment aims to determine the attitude of public companies in Poland towards implementing diversity policies in practice and including women in corporate boards as an under-represented gender. Therefore, we employ a research sample of 367 Polish companies listed on the WSE at the end of 2021. Out of a total of 430 companies listed on the Polish stock exchange at the time – the leading stock market in Central and Eastern Europe – we excluded foreign companies, companies with bankruptcy proceedings undertaken and those that had not published a statement on compliance with Best Practice 2021.

Firstly, we investigated how many Polish companies meet the gender diversity criteria in The Best Practice 2021 for both management and supervisory boards, i.e. the percentage of under-represented gender accounts for 30%, bearing in mind that Directive 2022 will have to be implemented into Polish national law. Thus the gender quota will be adopted for large public companies. We also analysed how many companies from our research sample fulfill the two alternative criteria of gender diversity introduced by Directive 2022. This investigation provides evidence of the distance between the actual and expected level of diversity in the decision-making bodies of companies listed on the WSE.

We then analysed the companies' statements on compliance with Best Practice 2021 that were published after this regulation entered into force on 1 July 2021. We focused on the companies' explanations for their non-compliance with two principles regarding diversity policy, i.e. principle 2.1, according to which diversity policy must be developed, and, principle 2.2., which imposed the inclusion of expected diversity and the participation of minority groups in the boardrooms.

After analysing the company's explanations for non-compliance with the principles, it was possible to answer the following questions:

a. What criteria are applied by companies and their bodies when new members are selected for management and supervisory positions?
b. What obstacles prevent companies from adopting a diversity policy and allowing women to be appointed to leadership positions?

Answering these questions allows us to reveal the attitude of companies towards a diversity policy and their inclination to introduce it under a voluntary regime.

In the last stage of our study, we will ascertain if companies that introduced a diversity policy are somehow different from those that have not done so. Therefore, we examine certain characteristics of companies related to their size, profitability, leverage and market valuation and compare companies that have adopted a diversity policy with those that have not.

Statements from individual companies about their attitudes towards diversity policies are hand-collected from the stock investors relation and current reports section on the companies' websites. The management and supervisory board members' information and relevant financial data are gathered from the same source. Meanwhile, market valuation data are obtained from the WSE's website. All data are publicly available.

Findings

There is a consensus in the societies of developed countries that any form of discrimination based on gender or ethnicity is not socially acceptable. Thus, there is no rational basis for a different approach when forming company management or supervisory teams. However, when the current composition of corporate boards of public companies in Poland is analysed, it turns out that this is a male-dominated universe. Fig. 1 shows the most common compositions of the management and supervisory boards of companies listed on the WSE.

In the overwhelming majority of listed companies in Poland, only men are on the management board. The most common boards comprise two, one or three men. A woman (one in a three-member board) as a board member appears only in fifth place in the ranking of the most common types of board composition. It is slightly more common to find women as members of supervisory boards, although in 25% of listed companies (the most common composition model), the supervisory board consists of only five men. In only 15% of listed companies can one woman and four men be found on the supervisory board. Extremely symbolic for the Polish stock market is that among the most common models of corporate boards, there are no women at the head of them, neither on the management board nor the supervisory board. Men chair these boards.

In general, analysing the gender of all members of all management and supervisory boards in the research sample, the representation of women is very low and accounts for 12.72% and 17.12% for the management board and the supervisory board, respectively. Thus, most companies did not meet the gender diversity criteria in July 2021. Table 1 provides more detailed information on the current status and target criteria for gender diversity in corporate boards on the WSE.

Regarding the presence of women in decision-making bodies, companies without any women on the management board (68.94%) or supervisory board (42.23%) prevail. Furthermore, 28.61% of the companies have both management

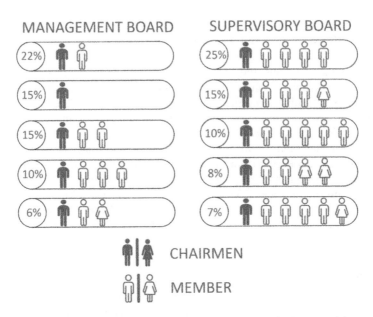

Fig. 1.   Top 5 Most Popular Corporate Boards Composition
According to Gender in Polish Stock Companies in 2021. *Source:* Authors'
own elaboration.

and supervisory boards composed only of men. Only 19.89% of companies fulfill the board diversity criteria included in Best Practice 2021 for the management board, and 21.53% of companies do for the supervisory board. Although the gender diversity requirements introduced by Directive 2022 apply to large public companies, it is interesting that only 16.62% of companies in the research sample (i.e. a sample that includes small, medium and large companies) have supervisory boards on which at least 40% members belong to an under-represented gender. The alternative aim for board diversity specified by Directive 2022 is achieved by 16.08% of companies only. Hence, these data show how far Polish companies are from the expected level of gender diversity.

Our research into the propensity of listed companies to accept the gender diversity guidelines in the corporate governance code Best Practice 2021 shows that only 6.3% and 8.2% of companies comply with principles 2.1 (see Fig. 2) and 2.2., respectively. Thus, we aim to determine why so many companies have not introduced a diversity policy, why they have homogenous boards in terms of gender or why they do not aim to reach the appropriate level of diversity. Therefore, next, we investigated the sample of 345 companies that do not comply with the 2.1. principle.

The detailed explanations for non-compliance with principles 2.1 and 2.2 provided by companies allows us to identify two subsamples. Generally speaking,

Table 1. Composition of the Management and Supervisory Board in Terms of the Expected Gender Diversity Criteria on the WSE in July 2021.

Specification	Management Board	Supervisory Board
Companies without any woman on the board	68.94%	42.23%
Companies without any woman on the management and supervisory board together	28.61%	
Companies with at least one woman on the board, but less than 30% are women	10.35%	35.42%
Companies with at least 30% of women on the board	20.71%	22.34%
Companies that meet the best practice 2021 criteria for 30% presence of a gender minority on the board	19.89%	21.80%
Companies that meet the best practice 2021 criteria for the management and supervisory board together	4.36%	
Companies that meet the Directive 2022 criteria for at least 40% presence of a minority on the supervisory board	16.62%	
Companies that meet the Directive 2022 criteria for at least 33% minority presence in the management and supervisory board	16.08%	

Source: Authors' own elaboration.

a lack of outright acceptance of principle 2.1 does not imply a lack of favour for the solutions promoted by the diversity policy. The first group includes 42 companies that have introduced a diversity policy for their management and supervisory bodies (or they are developing such a policy), but the level of gender diversity is lower than 30%, and thus they do not comply with the 2.1 principle. The second group includes 303 companies that still need to introduce a diversity policy. Among this group, only 49 companies are considering or declare that they will develop and adopt such a policy in the future; 25 companies are not going to adopt a diversity policy at all.

Table 2 shows comprehensive explanations and comments on the tendency to implement gender diversity policies, providing a range of information on the selection criteria for management and board members and the obstacles that stop the companies from adopting a diversity policy and appointing women to leadership positions.

Table 2 shows that the most important criteria when deciding on a new appointment to the board are the qualifications, experience and education of the

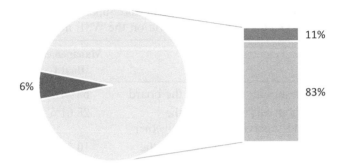

■ Comply with the 2.1. principle
■ Introduce or develope diversity policy, but the diversity rate of gender is below 30%
▨ No diversity policy

Fig. 2.   Polish Listed Companies' Attitude Towards the Diversity
Policy Recommendations of Best Practice 2021. *Source:* Authors' own
elaboration.

candidates, as well as company needs. This explanation was provided by 76% of companies that do not comply with principle 2.1. This result is in line with previous research on Polish companies, which documents that these criteria are the most important when new candidates are selected (Wawryszuk-Misztal, 2021a).

Unfortunately, 34% of companies stated that gender and age are not considered when a new person is appointed to leadership positions. Only 2% of companies apply gender as an additional criterion, and 7% aim to increase gender diversity on board. These results are not optimistic in the context of expected regulatory changes. Although 26% of companies appreciate board diversity and strive to increase the level, they do not specify specific aspects of diversity. Regarding the reasons for not complying with principle 2.1, 30% of the companies stated that their ability to affect the composition of the board is limited since final decisions regarding the appointment of the manager and supervisor position are taken by the supervisory board and at a shareholder's meeting, respectively. Therefore, the company can only indirectly influence these decisions. There are also companies (29%) that apply the general principle of equality and non-discrimination, which is a sufficient approach according to some of them. Nineteen percent of firms state that the composition of the corporate governance bodies is diversified in all or some aspects of diversity. Therefore, it is likely that the formal adoption of a diversity policy is not necessarily to increase diversity.

Looking at attitudes towards accepting solutions that promote diversity policies, we examine whether certain characteristics of these companies differentiate their approaches. Table 3 offers insight into attributes that relate to these companies' financial standing and market valuation (regardless of whether they comply with the 2.1 rule).

Table 2. The Explanations for Non-compliance With Principle 2.1. Given by
Companies in July 2021.

Specification	Companies That Do Not Comply With Principle 2.1.		
	All (*N* = 345)	A Diversity Policy Exists, But There Is an Inadequate Level of Gender Diversity	No Diversity Policy
Panel A. Criteria applied in the board member selection procedure			
Qualifications, experience, education, company needs.	76%	6%	70%
Gender and age are not applied for the selection procedure.	34%	2%	32%
Gender is only an additional criterion.	2%	0%	1%
Striving for board diversity.	26%	6%	20%
Striving for board gender diversity.	7%	2%	4%
Panel B. The obstacles that stop companies from adopting a diversity policy and appointing women to leadership positions			
The policy of equal opportunities and non-discrimination is applied in the company.	29%	3%	26%
Decisions regarding appointment to the position of management and supervisory member are taken by the supervisory board and shareholder's meeting, respectively. Therefore, the company's role in creating the structure of these bodies is limited.	30%	3%	27%
The composition of corporate governance bodies is diversified in all or some aspects of diversity.	19%	2%	17%

Table 2. *(Continued)*

Specification	Companies That Do Not Comply With Principle 2.1.		
	All (N = 345)	A Diversity Policy Exists, But There Is an Inadequate Level of Gender Diversity	No Diversity Policy
The type of industry (i.e., there are no female candidates with specific qualifications).	3%	0%	3%
One person on the management board or a few members.	3%	0%	3%
Family company – family members and the founders take leadership positions.	3%	0%	3%
The composition of the corporate boards is stable.	1%	0%	1%
The small size of the company.	1%	0%	1%

Source: Authors' own elaboration.

In the Polish stock market, larger companies have implemented the diversity policy more often. Statistically significant differences are found in characteristics such as asset size, sales (median only), market capitalisation and book value. This observation is consistent with institutional theory and resource dependence theory. Institutional theory suggests that a company must achieve both economic success and obtain legitimacy. Complying with corporate governance principles regarding board diversity policy legitimises its existence and gives the firm access to other resources such as advice, counsel and communication channels (Hillman et al., 2000). Since larger and more visible companies are more dependent on external resources (Hillman et al., 2007), they are more likely to respond to societal pressure and thus develop a board diversity policy and increase female representation on boards. It was confirmed by Hillman et al. (2007) for US companies and Wawryszuk-Misztal (2021a) for Polish companies. Furthermore, our results may also suggest that the market better values these companies. The average value of the P/E ratio for companies that have implemented a diversity policy is higher than the other companies, with a statistical significance of 0.1. In turn, looking at the profitability ratios, we found no statistically significant differences between the compared groups of companies.

Table 3. Financial and Market Characteristics of Companies (at the End of 2021) According to Diversity Policy Adoption.

Panel A. Descriptive Statistics

Specifi-cation	Companies Adopting the Diversity Policy				Companies With No Diversity Policy			
	Mean	Median	Std. Dev.	N	Mean	Median	Std. Dev.	N
Assets	30614.59	721.23	79147.53	57	4371.96	235.30	26685.41	298
Sales	2330.79	441.14	3747.25	57	2397.15	205.34	10156.67	291
ROS	-0.1841	0.0635	1.6029	56	-4.2023	0.0570	69.4460	291
ROE	0.1116	0.1020	0.2517	54	0.0903	0.1012	0.3594	279
ROA	0.0192	0.0429	0.2565	57	0.4817	0.0455	8.0291	297
DR	0.6652	0.5323	0.7507	46	0.6966	0.4826	1.9799	296
MV	4807.74	410.00	10864.19	57	1360.45	126.18	4826.28	308
BV	3504.81	327.18	8049.84	57	1201.13	118.20	5133.37	308
P/E	40.44	10.40	148.71	45	19.19	9.35	41.40	222
P/BV	3.05	1.28	7.99	56	3.12	1.08	9.47	290

Panel B. Statistical Tests of Equality

	t-Test	p Value	Wilcoxon Rank-Sum Test	p Value
Assets	4.55***	0.0000	3.88***	0.0001
Sales	-0.05	0.9612	3.27***	0.0011
ROS	0.43	0.6657	0.44	0.6568
ROE	0.42	0.6775	0.20	0.8391
ROA	-0.43	0.6643	0.77	0.4396

Table 3. (*Continued*)

Panel B. Statistical Tests of Equality

	t-Test	p Value	Wilcoxon Rank-Sum Test	p Value
DR	−0.11	0.9155	1.75*	0.0805
MV	3.88***	0.0001	4.03***	0.0001
BV	2.81***	0.0052	3.47***	0.0005
P/E	1.82*	0.0699	1.51	0.1317
P/BV	−0.05	0.9610	1.37	0.1713

Source: Authors' own elaboration.

Note: Assets – total assets as reported (in million PLN). Sales – total revenue as reported (in million PLN). ROS – net income to sales ratio. ROE – net income to equity ratio. ROA – net income to total assets ratio. DR – debt ratio. MV – capitalisation (in million PLN). BV – book value at the end of 2021 (in million PLN). P/E – price-to-earnings ratio. P/BV – price-to-book value ratio. ***, **, and * denote significance levels of 1%, 5%, and 10%, respectively.

Summary

Attitudes towards board diversity in Poland are gradually changing. Poland has traditionally been a conservative and homogeneous society, and this is reflected in its corporate culture, where there has been a lack of diversity on corporate boards. However, in recent years, there has been an increasing awareness of the importance of diversity and inclusion in the workplace, and many companies in Poland are beginning to implement diversity policies for their boards. In 2021, the Polish stock exchange introduced a new law enhancing diversity that is seen as a significant step towards achieving gender parity on corporate boards in Poland. Despite these efforts, there is still a long way to go to achieve true diversity and inclusion on corporate boards in Poland. Many companies still lack diversity policies, and there is a shortage of women and people of minority backgrounds in leadership positions. There is still much work to be done to achieve true diversity and inclusion in Polish companies.

Polish companies encounter numerous obstacles in implementing board diversity policies, such as cultural and social barriers, a lack of awareness and motivation to implement diversity policies, a limited pool of qualified candidates (especially in certain industries), resistance from existing board members, as well as a lack of clear guidelines and support from the government or other organisations to implement diversity policies. However, with the right attitude, resources and commitment, Polish companies can overcome these challenges and achieve greater diversity and inclusion on their boards. Companies can seek guidance and support from external organisations, such as industry associations or government agencies that promote diversity and inclusion. Furthermore, it is important to invest in education and awareness programmes to promote understanding of the benefits of diversity and the legal requirements in this regard.

References

Aguilera, R. V. and Cuervo-Cazurra, A. (2004), "Codes of Good Governance Worldwide: What Is the Trigger?", *Organization Studies*, Vol. 25 No. 3, pp. 415–443, https://doi.org/10.1177/0170840604040669

Ahern, K. and Dittmar, A. (2012), "The Changing of the Boards: The Impact on Firm Valuation of Mandated Female Board Representation", *Quarterly Journal of Economics*, Vol. 127 No. 1, pp. 137–197, https://doi.org/10.1093/qje/qjr049

Best Practice of GPW Listed Companies (2016), *"Warsaw Stock Exchange"*, available at https://www.gpw.pl/pub/GPW/o-nas/DPSN2016_EN.pdf (accessed 10 March 2023).

Best Practice of GPW Listed Companies (2021), *"Warsaw Stock Exchange"*, available at https://www.gpw.pl/pub/GPW/files/DPSN2021_EN.pdf (accessed 10 March 2023).

Brammer, S., Millington, A. and Pavelin, S. (2007), "Gender and Ethnic Diversity Among UK Corporate Boards", *Corporate Governance: An International Review*, Vol. 15 No. 2, pp. 393–403, https://doi.org/10.1111/j.1467-8683.2007.00569.x

De Cleyn, S. H. (2008), "Compliance of Companies With Corporate Governance Codes: Case Study on Listed Belgian SMEs", *Journal of Law and Governance*, Vol. 3 No. 1, pp. 1–16, https://doi.org/10.15209/jbsge.v3i1.127

De Masi, S., Słomka-Gołębiowska, A., Becagli, C. and Paci, A. (2021), "Toward Sustainable Corporate Behavior: The Effect of the Critical Mass of Female Directors on Environmental, Social, and Governance Disclosure", *Business Strategy and the Environment*, Vol. 30, pp. 1865–1878, https://doi.org/10.1002/bse.2721

Directive (EU) 2022/2381 of the European Parliament and of the Council of 23 November 2022 on Improving the Gender Balance Among Directors of Listed Companies and Related Measures. Text with EEA Relevance. (Official Journal of the EU L 315/44).

Directive 2014/95/EU of the European Parliament and of the Council of 22 October 2014 Amending Directive 2013/34/EU as Regards Disclosure of Nonfinancial and Diversity Information by Certain Large Undertakings and Groups. Text with EEA Relevance. (Official Journal of the EU L330/1).

Greene, D., Intintoli, V. J. and Kahle, K. M. (2020), "Do Board Gender Quotas Affect Firm Value? Evidence from California Senate Bill No. 826", *Journal of Corporate Finance*, Elsevier, Vol. 60 No. October 2019, p. 101526, https://doi.org/10.1016/j.jcorpfin.2019.101526

Groening, C. (2019), "When Do Investors Value Board Gender Diversity?", *Corporate Governance*, Vol. 19 No. 1, pp. 60–79. https://doi.org/10.1108/CG-01-2018-0012

Gyapong, E. and Afrifa, G. A. (2019), "The Simultaneous Disclosure of Shareholder and Stakeholder Corporate Governance Practices and Their Antecedents", *International Journal of Finance & Economics*, Vol. 24 No. 1, pp. 260–287, https://doi.org/10.1002/ijfe.1661

Hamplová, E., Janeček, V. and Lefley, F. (2022), "Board Gender Diversity and Women in Leadership Positions – Are Quotas the Solution?", *Corporate Communications: An International Journal*, Vol. 27 No. 4, pp. 742–759, https://doi.org/10.1108/CCIJ-02-2022-0022

Hillman, A. J., Cannella, A. A. and Paetzold, R. L. (2000), "The Resource Dependence Role of Corporate Directors: Strategic Adaptation of Board Composition in Response to Environmental Change", *Journal of Management Studies*, Vol. 37 No. 2, pp. 235–256, https://doi.org/10.1111/1467-6486.00179

Hillman, A. J., Shropshire, C. and Cannella, A. A. (2007), "Organizational Predictors of Women on Corporate Boards", *Academy of Management Journal*, Vol. 50 No. 4, pp. 941–952.

Hoobler, J. M., Masterson, C. R., Nkomo, S. M. and Michel, E. J. (2018), "The Business Case for Women Leaders: Meta-Analysis, Research Critique, and Path Forward", *Journal of Management*, Vol. 44 No. 6, pp. 2473–2499, https://doi.org/10.1177/0149206316628643

Isidro, H. and Sobral, M. (2015), "The Effects of Women on Corporate Boards on Firm Value, Financial Performance, and Ethical and Social Compliance", *Journal of Business Ethics*, Vol. 132 No. 1, pp. 1–19, https://doi.org/10.1007/s10551-014-2302-9

Kagzi, M. and Guha, M. (2018), "Does Board Demographic Diversity Influence Firm Performance? Evidence from Indian-knowledge Intensive Firms", *Benchmarking:*

An International Journal, Vol. 25 No. 3, pp. 1028–1058, https://doi.org/10.1108/BIJ-07-2017-0203

Klettner, A. (2016), "Corporate Governance Codes and Gender Diversity: Management-Based Regulation in Action", *UNSW Law Journal*, Vol. 39 No. 2, pp. 715–739.

Krenn, M. (2015), "Understanding Decoupling in Response to Corporate Governance Reform Pressures: The Case of Codes of Good Corporate Governance", *Journal of Financial Regulation and Compliance*, Vol. 23 No. 4, pp. 369–382, https://doi.org/10.1108/JFRC-04-2014-0019

Mensi-Klarbach, H., Leixnering, S. and Schiffinger, M. (2019), "The Carrot or the Stick: Self-Regulation for Gender-Diverse Boards via Codes of Good Governance", *Journal of Business Ethics*, No. November, https://doi.org/10.1007/s10551-019-04336-z

Pucheta-Martínez, M. C., Bel-Oms, I. and Olcina-Sempere, G. (2016), "Corporate Governance, Female Directors and Quality of Financial Information", *Business Ethics*, Vol. 25 No. 4, pp. 363–385, https://doi.org/10.1111/beer.12123

Tagesson, T. and Collin, S. O. Y. (2016), "Corporate Governance Influencing Compliance with the Swedish Code of Corporate Governance", *International Journal of Disclosure and Governance*, Vol. 13 No. 3, pp. 262–277, https://doi.org/10.1057/jdg.2015.15

Wang, M. and Kelan, E. (2013), "The Gender Quota and Female Leadership: Effects of the Norwegian Gender Quota on Board Chairs and CEOs", *Journal of Business Ethics*, Vol. 117 No. 3, pp. 449–466, https://doi.org/10.1007/s10551-012-1546-5

Wawryszuk-Misztal, A. (2021a), "Determinants of Board Diversity Policy Implementation by Companies Listed on the Warsaw Stock Exchange. Equilibrium", *Quarterly Journal of Economics and Economic Policy*, Vol. 16 No. 3, pp. 617–637, https://doi.org/10.24136/eq.2021.022

Wawryszuk-Misztal, A. (2021b), *Finansowe czynniki i konsekwencje różnicowania składu osobowego zarządów i rad nadzorczych polskich spółek giełdowych* (eng. *Financial Factors and Consequences of Diversifying the Composition of Management and Supervisory Boards of Polish Public Companies*), Wydawnictwo UMCS, Lublin.

Zattoni, A. and Cuomo, F. (2008), "Why Adopt Codes of Good Governance? A Comparison of Institutional and Efficiency Perspectives", *Corporate Governance: An International Review*, Vol. 16 No. 1, pp. 1–15, https://doi.org/10.1111/j.1467-8683.2008.00661.x

Chapter 17

Corporate Resilience and Financial Flexibility in Times of Crisis – Case of Poland

Elżbieta Bukalska and Michał Bernard Pietrzak

Abstract

Research Background: Poland was coined a 'green island' during the Global Financial Crisis (GFC) of 2007–2009 with a stable growth in Gross Domestic Product (GDP), while other countries experienced a dramatic drop in the GDP growth. We assumed that this is due to the stronger resilience of Polish economy and Polish companies.

Purpose of this Chapter: The aim of the research is to identify the companies' stability (resilience) in the crisis situations (especially the GFC and COVID-19 crisis). We also wonder whether corporate resilience is accompanied by the financial flexibility.

Methodology: We use GDP growth rate and Profitability as the measures of the resilience. Additionally, we include in our research financial flexibility measured by debt and cash ratio as factors affecting corporate resilience. Our research covers the period 2000–2021. Our data refer to three European countries: France and Germany as the leading European countries and Poland as the leader of changes in Central and Eastern Europe.

Findings: We found that Polish economy – against German and French – have higher GDP growth and profitability ratio over the 2000–2021 period. These ratios also show lower volatility around the trend. We proved that higher corporate resilience is accompanied by higher financial flexibility of Polish companies.

Keywords: Corporate resilience; financial flexibility; GDP growth rate; profitability; cash ratio; debt ratio

Modeling Economic Growth in Contemporary Poland, 267–279
Copyright © 2024 Elżbieta Bukalska and Michał Bernard Pietrzak
Published under exclusive licence by Emerald Publishing Limited
doi:10.1108/978-1-83753-654-220231024

Introduction

Recently, there has been a rise in the number, degree and range of challenges that threaten organisations. The challenges and turbulences might be of political, economic, social and environmental nature, which affect the operations of an enterprise. Some of these turbulences include natural crises (floods, earthquakes, fire incidents, diseases or pandemics such as COVID-19), and some include human-induced crises (wars, financial crises). Despite the nature of instability, increasing turbulences should make the companies be prepared to survive and adapt to new conditions.

In response to the increasing trend in disruptive external shocks, there have been a number of calls for organisational research on crisis management or even anti-crisis management. The crisis is a process of weakening or degeneration that can culminate in a disruption event to the actor's (i.e. individual, organisation and/or community) normal functioning. The crisis affects the main economic categories of business activity – sales revenue, costs, profits, investment and employment. That is why companies should be prepared for such a disruptive impact of the crisis.

Crisis management should explain how individuals and organisations prepare, anticipate and respond to adversity. Williams et al. (2017) think that crisis management should explain how organisations effectively prepare for, respond to and overcome their various forms and degrees to preserve performance, recover or prevent decline and even failure. Coombs and Hollady (2012) present an approach describing crisis management as a three-stage process – the pre-crisis (prevention and preparation), the crisis (response) and the post-crisis (learning and revision). Thus, crisis management is an activity to restore equilibrium at all stages of crisis impact.

Much of the empirical research has focused on a linear progression of response after the crisis appears but crisis management should include not only how to respond to adversity but also how to mitigate it before it arises – organisational resilience. Crisis management is the ability to return organisations and systems to normal functioning after a disruption while resilience is the ability to maintain reliable functioning despite adversity (John-eke and Bayo, 2021). We believe that the first phase is crucial for company survival and give a good ground for a company to bounce back from an external shock. The purpose of prevention is to establish a procedure and content of activities, including the securing of resources, to diminish the impact of a crisis (Mikušová and Horváthová, 2019).

In corporate finance, the equivalent meaning of corporate resilience has financial flexibility. Financial flexibility appears to be an important determinant of investment and performance of 1,068 East Asian firms over the period 1994–2006. In particular, firms that are financially flexible prior to the crisis (i) have a greater ability to take investment opportunities, (ii) rely much less on the availability of internal funds to invest, and (iii) perform better than less flexible firms during the crisis. The analysis covering the post-crisis period does reveal more benefits for flexible than for inflexible firms (Arslan-Ayaydin et al., 2014).

Ramelli and Wagner (2020) find that companies with lower financial flexibility experience a larger stock price drop. For example, Gittell et al. (2006) investigated the resilience of the airline industry after the September 11th terrorist attack in the United States and found that airlines with strong financial reserves adjusted to the strains imposed by adversity and performed better than their less well-off counterparts. Fahlenbrach et al. (2021) discuss and provide evidence that financial flexibility is particularly valuable given that the COVID-19 shock has led to a sudden and, in many cases, complete stop in firms' revenues.

The aim of this chapter is to identify the resilience of the Polish economy and Polish companies and compare it to the resilience of companies from France and Germany. We also identify financial flexibility as the main factor affecting corporate resilience with two financial flexibility elements: cash holdings and financial leverage. We wonder whether higher resilience is accompanied by higher cash holding and lower financial leverage.

Literature Review on Corporate Resilience

The concept of corporate resilience has evolved over time. In psychology, resilience is the ability of adults in otherwise normal circumstances who are exposed to an isolated and potentially highly disruptive event, such as the death of a close relation or a violent or life-threatening situation, to maintain relatively stable, healthy levels of psychological and physical functioning (Bonanno, 2004). Ong et al. (2006) define psychological resilience as a 'relatively stable personality trait characterised by the ability to overcome, steer through, and bounce back' from daily adversity and challenge.

The term resilience has been used freely across a wide range of academic disciplines and in many different contexts. There is little consensus regarding what resilience is, what it means for organisations, and, more importantly, how organisations might achieve greater resilience in the face of increasing threats. Lengnick-Hall et al. (2011) think that corporate resilience is an enterprise's ability to effectively absorb, and develop situation-specific responses to a crisis. Resilience is the feature of organisations that provides the ability to react to and ability to recover from disturbances with minimal effects on stability and functioning (Linnenluecke, 2017). This is the organisation's ability (embodied in the existence of resources, ideologies, routines and structures) to absorb a discrete environmental jolt and restore prior order (Williams et al., 2017). This definition shows the ability to survive and sustain its activities. That is why resilience is quite often mixed with sustainability or sustainable management (Ortiz-de-Mandojana and Bansal, 2016).

Resilience involves using generic resources (e.g. knowledge or financial resources) to avoid a catastrophe or to mitigate its evolution (Williams et al., 2017). In a business context, resilience addresses the 'capacity for an enterprise to survive, adapt, and grow in the face of turbulent change' (Dahles and Susilowati, 2015). Company practices should make the company more adaptive, more flexible and more shock resistant, in a word, more resilient (Palmi et al., 2018). Resilience is the ability to 'absorb' strain or change with a minimum of disruption (Somers, 2009).

The basic essence of resilience means that it is a trait, capacity or ability to sustain the first shock and recover. Resilience is inclusive of pre-adversity capabilities, in-crisis organising, adjusting and post-crisis responding. Resilience should be built in the pre-crisis process, thus it is sometimes called preparedness. Preparing includes managing the company in order to face risks and reduce vulnerability (e.g. in sales revenue, profits, investment and employment). In economics, this notion is associated with the ability to self-restore the system through compensating mechanisms towards the pre-shock equilibrium state (Duval and Vogel, 2008; Martin, 2012). A second definition of resilience, known as ecological resilience, focuses on the ability of the system to absorb a shock without changing its structure, identity and function (Gunderson and Pritchard, 2002; Walker et al., 2004).

Resilience is the ability to stay relatively stable when encountering problems and when coping with shocks (Alessi et al., 2020). Resilience is the capacity of a system to absorb disturbance and reorganise while undergoing change so as to still retain essentially the same function, structure, identity and feedback (Walker et al., 2004). Erol et al. (2010) define enterprise resilience as the ability to decrease vulnerability, the ability to change and adapt and the ability to recover quickly from disruption. Using this definition, they identify metrics that evaluate, more specifically: (1) an enterprise's capability to decrease its level of vulnerability to expected and unexpected events, (2) its ability to change itself and adapt to changing environment; (3) its ability to recover in the least possible time in case of a disruptive event. Based on the discussed enterprise resilience metrics, they use several examples and evaluate a set of illustrative responses to common disruptions.

There are a number of individual, organisational and community variables that have been demonstrated to impact the level of disaster 'preparedness' (Somers, 2009). Thanks to these variables, Lengnick-Hall and Beck (2003) believe that 'organisational resilience can be developed, measured and managed'. Annarelli et al. (2020) measured resilience using seven indicators – adaptability, agility, reliability, flexibility, effectiveness, recovery level and recovery time. Flexibility is one of the indicators of resilience and is commonly used in corporate finance.

Literature Review on Financial Flexibility of Corporations

Financial flexibility is a financial dimension of resilience. The definition of financial flexibility reflects those related to corporate resilience but within the financial area. The term financial flexibility represents 'the ability of a firm to respond effectively to unanticipated shocks to its cash flows or its investment opportunities' (Bancel and Mittoo, 2011). More specifically, financial flexibility is the ability of an enterprise to acquire or adjust resources, seize opportunities to invest in due time (Gamba and Triantis, 2008) and provide resilience to face any future unexpected events. Financial flexibility refers to the inherent comprehensive strength of enterprises to reduce financial risks and make effective use of financial resources in the face of dynamic financial environmental changes. It assists in reconfiguring enterprise resources to adjust and increase financial resources (Arslan-Ayaydin et al., 2014). Financially flexible enterprises have greater access to capital markets and are able to raise capital at lower costs in order to fund new growth opportunities, even during a crisis (Islam et al., 2020).

Financial flexibility provides enterprises with different options to cope with future unpredictable investment and financing demands. Financial flexibility is considered the optimal allocation of financial resources to make the company able to sustain performance and investments during a crisis. With financial flexibility, companies are able to sustain the investment rate and survive the decline in sales revenues and profits. Having financial flexibility makes the company more stable and less vulnerable to external shocks. Following seminal work by Bernanke and Gertler (1989), previous studies have shown that the impact of economic shocks is amplified for firms with lower financial flexibility or weaker balance sheets (e.g. Giroud and Mueller, 2017; Kahle and Stulz, 2013).

Some studies have supported the argument that financial flexibility has a positive effect on enterprise performance during non-pandemic periods (Kuo et al., 2006; Rapp et al., 2014) and during the pandemic period (Fahlenbrach et al., 2021). Teng et al. (2021) reveal that financial flexibility has a significant positive effect on the overall enterprise performance of the Taiwan Stock Exchange's listed manufacturing companies during the COVID-19 crisis.

Prior research has emphasised the importance of appropriately stockpiling resources (e.g. slack) in anticipation of the need to withstand adversity (Williams et al., 2017). A way for firms to increase financial flexibility is through greater retention of cash flow and diminishing financial leverage (see, e.g. DeAngelo et al., 2018). Corporations would have been more resilient had they received higher cash holding and lower debt ratios. That is why in existing studies, financial flexibility has been measured with two main indicators which include: cash holdings and financial leverage (Arslan-Ayaydin et al., 2014). Firms are considered to be more financially flexible if they hold more cash and have less debt (Fahlenbrach et al., 2021).

Methodology

The aim of our research is to identify the stability of the whole economy and corporations, corporate resilience and financial flexibility – factors affecting corporate resilience (debt ratio and cash holdings).

We use several variables: GDP growth rate and Profitability (calculated as the relation of net profit to total assets, return on assets (ROA)). These ratios reflect the economy and corporations' response to external shocks and thus they measure resilience. Additionally, we include in our research debt ratio (total liabilities to total assets) and cash ratio (cash and cash equivalents to total assets). These ratios reflect financial flexibility and thus factors affecting corporate resilience.

The parameters of the trend model were estimated for all variables, which made it possible to identify development trends during the period under study. Due to the nature of the trend, a linear trend specification was adopted. Depending on the period and the variable, the occurrence of all types of the trend was established: downward, upward and horizontal.

Our data comes from publicly available sources. Our research covers the period 2000–2021.

Our data refer to three European countries: France and Germany as the leading European countries and Poland as the leader of changes in Central and Eastern Europe.

Findings

Table 1 and Figs. 1–4 present the data with the trend in changes in GDP growth, profitability, cash ratio and debt ratio in Poland over the 2000–2021 period. The variables allow an analysis to be carried out to assess the performance of companies, including – in particular – aspects of corporate resilience and financial flexibility. In addition, the analysis was spread to Germany and France, allowing the situation in the three selected countries to be compared simultaneously. Germany and France were selected as the largest and dominant member countries of the European Union, to which Poland also belongs.

As for GDP growth, Poland got quite a stable growth, approximately 3% annually over the whole period (except 2020 – the pandemic year). But in Germany and France, the GDP growth rate is lower (than in Poland) – approximately 1.8–1.9% annually with two strong breakdown points – during the financial crisis of 2007–2009 and the pandemic year of 2020. The breakdown in 2020 was much deeper in Germany and France than in Poland.

Additionally, volatility around the trend is much lower in Poland (41.59%) than in Germany (78.95%) and France (77.23%). The results show that situation in Poland is better (Poland has a higher GDP growth rate) and more stable (a lower volatility).

The results prove the higher resilience of Poland to external shocks.

All countries included in the research (Poland, France and Germany) show decreasing profitability.

Although Poland got a downward profitability trend, the profitability of Polish companies is much higher (approximately 6%) than in France and Germany (approximately 3%). While German and French companies experienced quite a deep drop in profitability during the financial crisis of 2007–2009, Polish companies show only a slight decrease. However, there is no profitability drop in the 2020 pandemic year – probably due to state aid.

Additionally, volatility around the profitability trend is much lower in Poland (8.09%) than in Germany (10.79%) and France (9.61%). The results show that situation in Poland is better (Poland has a higher profitability) and more stable (lower volatility).

Table 1. The Trends in Changes in GDP Growth, Profitability, Cash Ratio, and Debt Ratio in Poland, Germany, and France Over the 2000–2021 Period.

GDP Growth — Cash Ratio

Poland

Characteristics	2000–2021		2020	Characteristics	2005–2020
Type of trend	Horizontal (mean = 3,928)		Breakdown	Type of trend	Upward
Trend parameter	0		−6.649	Trend parameter	0.098
Volatility around the trend	41.59%			Volatility around the trend	4.98%

Germany

Characteristics	2000–2008	2009	2010–2021	2020	Characteristics	2000–2020
Type of trend	Horizontal (mean = 1,782)	Breakdown	Horizontal (mean = 1,782)	Breakdown	Type of trend	Upward
Trend parameter	0	−7.448	0	−5.762	Trend parameter	0.069
Volatility around the trend	78.95%				Volatility around the trend	9.39%

France

Characteristics	2000–2008	2009	2010–2020	2020	Characteristics	2000–2020
Type of trend	Horizontal (mean = 1,926)	Breakdown	Horizontal (mean = 1,926)	Breakdown	Type of trend	Upward
Trend parameter	0	−4.785	0	−10.034	Trend parameter	0.112
Volatility around the trend	77.23%				Volatility around the trend	9.77%

Profitability — Debt Ratio

Poland

Characteristics	2005–2020	Characteristics	2005–2020
Type of trend	Downward	Type of trend	Upward
Trend parameter	−0.12	Trend parameter	0.281
Volatility around the trend	8.09%	Volatility around the trend	1.54%

Germany

Characteristics	2000–2008	2009	2010–2020	Characteristics	2000–2020
Type of trend	Horizontal (mean = 3.114)	Breakdown	Downward	Type of trend	Downward
Trend parameter	0	−0.644	−0.177	Trend parameter	−0.347
Volatility around the trend	10.79%			Volatility around the trend	1.17%

France

Characteristics	2000–2008	2009	2010–2020	Characteristics	2000–2020
Type of trend	Horizontal (mean = 4.332)	Breakdown	Downward	Type of trend	Downward
Trend parameter	0	−1.213	−0.08	Trend parameter	−0.363
Volatility around the trend	9.61%			Volatility around the trend	9.77%

Source: Authors' own calculations based on publicly available data from Eurostat.

The results prove again the higher resilience of Polish companies to external shocks.

The cash ratio for Poland is higher (approximately 5–6%) than for Germany and France (approximately 4.5%). Poland got a strong upward trend of cash ratio increase – higher than in Germany but lower than in France.

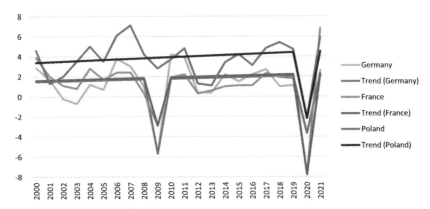

Fig. 1.   GDP Growth With the Trend for Poland, Germany, and France Over the 2000–2021 Period. *Source:* Authors' own elaborations based on publicly available data from Eurostat.

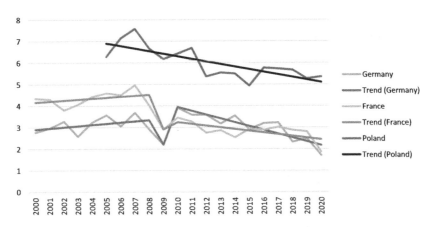

Fig. 2.   Profitability With the Trend for Poland, Germany, and France Over the 2000–2021 Period. *Source:* Authors' own elaborations based on publicly available data from Eurostat.

The trend for Poland is quite stable (with volatility around the trend of 4.98%), while in France and Germany, the cash ratio is floating to a bigger extent (with volatility around the trend of 9.39% and 9.77, respectively).

The results prove that higher corporate resilience is accompanied by a higher cash ratio.

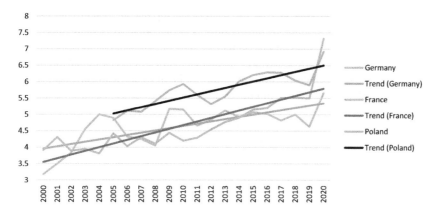

Fig. 3.   Cash Ratio With the Trend for Poland, Germany, and France
Over the 2000–2021 Period. *Source:* Authors' own elaborations based on
publicly available data from Eurostat.

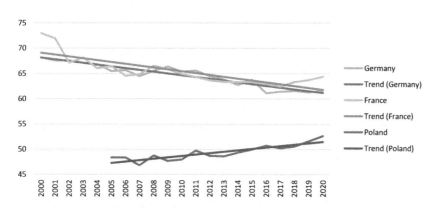

Fig. 4.   Debt Ratio With the Trend for Poland, Germany, and France
Over the 2000–2021 Period. *Source:* Authors' own elaborations based on
publicly available data from Eurostat.

The debt ratio for Poland is much lower (47%) than for Germany and France
(60%). Poland got an upward trend of debt ratio increase – while Germany and
France got a downward trend. The trend for Poland is quite stable (with volatility
around the trend of 1.54%), while in France, the debt ratio is floating to a bigger
extent (with volatility around the trend of 9.77).

The results prove that higher corporate resilience is accompanied by a lower
debt ratio.

Our results prove that the Polish economy and Polish companies achieved higher GDP growth and higher profitability. This is achieved with lower volatility and lower decrease in times of financial crisis of 2007–2009 and the pandemic year of 2020. Lower volatility and lower changes in times of crisis mean that Polish companies are less vulnerable and thus more resilient to external shocks. They are able to absorb strain and maintain reliable functioning despite adversity. Our results confirm that higher resilience is accompanied by a higher cash ratio and lower debt ratio. This is in line with previous findings on factors affecting corporate resilience and financial flexibility.

Summary

The aim of the research was to identify the resilience of the Polish economy and Polish companies and compare it to the resilience of companies from France and Germany. We also identify financial flexibility as the main factor affecting corporate resilience with two financial flexibility elements: cash holdings and financial leverage.

We found that Polish economy – against German and French – have higher GDP growth ratio over the 2000–2021 period. Additionally, profitability of Polish companies is higher. This higher GDP growth ratio and profitability is achieved with lower volatility around the trend and smaller decreases in crisis time (both the Global Financial Crisis of 2007–2009 and COVID-19 crisis).

We proved that higher corporate resilience is accompanied by higher financial flexibility of Polish companies. This higher financial flexibility is depicted by higher cash holdings ratio and lower debt ratio. Higher financial flexibility of Polish companies is present over the whole analysed period of 2000–2021. We believe that having higher financial flexibility prior to the crisis was of help to cope with sudden hit of external shocks.

However, the idea of financial flexibility is in the opposition to the free cash flow theory (Jensen, 1986). Free cash flow theory argues that managers have the incentive to be financially flexible through the internal fund to increase the assets under their control which leads to performance. Financial economists have argued that financial flexibility might be used to hurt shareholders (Jensen, 1986), and investor activists have campaigned to force firms to decrease cash holdings and increase leverage, and the west European companies have made the reduction of financial flexibility intrinsic to its business model. But, the results of this research should remind us that financial flexibility is also a key risk management tool. However, this tool does not come for free. Future research should help us understand better how to value the downside of financial flexibility to help shareholders and managers trade off the benefits and costs of financial flexibility more effectively (Fahlenbrach et al., 2021).

References

Alessi, L., Benczur, P., Campolongo, F., Cariboni, J., Manca, A. R., Menyhert, B. and Pagano, A. (2020), "The Resilience of EU Member States to the Financial and Economic Crisis", *Social Indicators Research*, Vol. 148 No. 2, pp. 569–598.

Annarelli, A., Nonino, F. and Palombi, G. (2020), "Understanding the Management of Cyber Resilient Systems", *Computers & Industrial Engineering*, Vol. 149, 106829.

DeAngelo, H., Gonçalves, A. S. and Stulz, R. M. (2018), "Corporate Deleveraging and Financial Flexibility", *The Review of Financial Studies*, Vol. 31 No. 8, pp. 3122–3174, https://doi.org/10.1093/rfs/hhx147

Arslan-Ayaydin, Ö., Florackis, C. and Ozkan, A. (2014), "Financial Flexibility, Corporate Investment and Performance: Evidence from Financial Crises", *Review of Quantitative Finance and Accounting*, Vol. 42 No. 2, pp. 211–250.

Bonanno, G. A. (2004), "Loss, Trauma, and Human Resilience: Have We Underestimated the Human Capacity to Thrive after Extremely Aversive Events?", *American Psychologist*, Vol. 59 No. 1, pp. 20–28, https://doi.org/10.1037/0003-066X.59.1.20

Bernanke, B. and Gertler, M. (1989), "Agency Costs, Net Worth, and Business Fluctuations", *The American Economic Review*, Vol. 79, pp. 14–31.

Bancel, F. and Mittoo, U. R. (2011), "Financial Flexibility and the Impact of the Global Financial Crisis: Evidence from France", *International Journal of Managerial Finance*, Vol. 7 No. 2, pp. 179-216, https://doi.org/10.1108/174391311 11122157

Coombs, T. and Hollady, S. J. (2012), *The Handbook of Crisis Communication*, Wiley, New York.

Dahles, H. and Susilowati, T. P. (2015), "Business Resilience in Times of Growth and Crisis", *Annals of Tourism Research*, Vol. 51, pp. 34–50.

Duval, R. and Vogel, L. (2008), „Economic Resilience to Shocks: The Role of Structural Policies", *OECD Journal: Economic Studies*, Vol. 1, pp. 1–38.

Erol, O., Sauser, B. J. and Mansouri, M. (2010), "A Framework for Investigation into Extended Enterprise Resilience", *Enterprise Information Systems*, Vol. 4 No. 2, pp. 111–136.

Fahlenbrach, R., Rageth, K. and Stulz, R. M. (2021), "How Valuable Is Financial Flexibility when Revenue Stops? Evidence from the COVID-19 Crisis", *The Review of Financial Studies*, Vol. 34 No. 11, pp. 5474–5521.

Gamba, A. and Triantis, A. (2008), "The Value of Financial Flexibility", *The Journal of Finance*, Vol. 63 No. 5, pp. 2263–2296.

Gittell, J. H., Cameron, K., Lim, S. and Rivas, V. (2006), "Relationships, Layoffs, and Organizational Resilience: Airline Industry Responses to September 11", *The Journal of Applied Behavioral Science*, Vol. 42 No. 3, pp. 300–329.

Gunderson, L. H. and Pritchard, L. (2002), *Resilience and the Behavior of Large Scale Systems*, Island Press, Washington.

Giroud, X. and Mueller, H. M. (2017), "Firm Leverage, Consumer Demand, and Employment Losses during the Great Recession", *The Quarterly Journal of Economics*, Vol. 132 No. 1, pp. 271–316.

Islam, M. R., Hossain, M. A., Uddin, M. S. and Bahta, D. T. (2020), "Does Financial Flexibility Foster Investment Efficiency? Evidence from an Emerging Market", *Asian Business Review*, Vol. 10 No. 2, pp. 121–136.

Jensen, M. C. (1986), "Agency Costs of Free Cash Flow, Corporate Finance, and Takeovers", *The American Economic Review*, Vol. 76 No. 2, pp. 323–329.

John-eke, E. C. and Bayo, P. L. (2021), "Crisis Management and Corporate Resilience in Hotel Presidential: The Theoretical Perspective", *International Journal of Economics and Business Management*, Vol. 7 No. 3, pp. 21–34.

Kahle, K. M. and Stulz, R. M. (2013), "Access to Capital, Investment, and the Financial Crisis", *Journal of Financial Economics*, Vol. 110 No. 2, pp. 280–299, https://doi.org/10.1016/j.jfineco.2013.02.014

Kuo, H. C., Li, Y., Wang, L. H. and Ding, C. Y. (2006), "Flexibility and Performance of MNEs: Evidence from Taiwan", *International Journal of Business*, Vol. 11 No. 4, pp. 417–432.

Lengnick-Hall, C. A., and Beck, T. E. (2003), Beyond Bouncing Back: The Concept of Organizational Resilience. *National Academy of Management meetings*, Seattle, WA.

Lengnick-Hall, C. A., Beck, T. E. and Lengnick-Hall, M. L. (2011), "Developing a Capacity for Organizational Resilience through Strategic Human Resource Management", *Human Resource Management Review*, Vol. 21 No. 3, pp. 243–255.

Linnenluecke, M. K. (2017), "Resilience in Business and Management Research: A Review of Influential Publications and a Research Agenda", *International Journal of Management Reviews*, Vol. 19 No. 1, pp. 4–30.

Mikušová, M. and Horváthová, P. (2019), "Prepared for a Crisis? Basic Elements of Crisis Management in an Organization", *Economic research-Ekonomska istraživanja*, Vol. 32 No. 1, pp. 1844–1868.

Martin, R. (2012), "Regional Economic Resilience, Hysteresis and Recessionary Shocks", *Journal of Economic Geography*, Vol. 12 No. 1, pp. 1–32.

Ong, A. D., Bergeman, C. S., Bisconti, T. L. and Wallace, K. A. (2006), "Psychological Resilience, Positive Emotions, and Successful Adaptation to Stress in Later Life", *Journal of Personality and Social Psychology*, Vol. 91 No. 4, pp. 730–749, https://doi.org/10.1037/0022-3514.91.4.730

Ortiz-de-Mandojana, N. and Bansal, P. (2016), "The Long-term Benefits of Organizational Resilience Through Sustainable Business Practices", *Strategic Management Journal*, Vol. 37 No. 8, pp. 1615–1631.

Palmi, P., Morrone, D., Miglietta, P. P. and Fusco, G. (2018), "How Did Organizational Resilience Work before and after the Financial Crisis? An Empirical Study", *International Journal of Business and Management*, Vol. 13 No. 10, pp. 54–62.

Rapp, M. S., Schmid, T. and Urban, D. (2014), "The Value of Financial Flexibility and Corporate Financial Policy", *Journal of Corporate Finance*, Vol. 29, pp. 288–302.

Ramelli, S. and Wagner, A. (2020), What the Stock Market Tells Us About the Consequences of COVID-19, in: *Mitigating the COVID Economic Crisis: Act Fast and Do Whatever It Takes*, eds. Baldwin R. and Weder di Mauro B., CEPR Press Centre for Economic Policy Research, London, pp. 63–70.

Somers, S. (2009), "Measuring Resilience Potential: An Adaptive Strategy for Organizational Crisis Planning", *Journal of Contingencies and Crisis Management*, Vol. 17 No. 1, pp. 12–23.

Teng, X., Chang, B.-G. and Wu, K.-S. (2021), "The Role of Financial Flexibility on Enterprise Sustainable Development During the COVID-19 Crisis—A Consideration of Tangible Assets", *Sustainability*, Vol. 13, 1245, https://doi.org/10.3390/su13031245

Williams, T. A., Gruber, D. A., Sutcliffe, K. M., Shepherd, D. A. and Zhao, E. Y. (2017), "Organizational Response to Adversity: Fusing Crisis Management and Resilience Research Streams", *The Academy of Management Annals*, Vol. 11 No. 2, pp. 733–769.

Walker, B., Holling, C. S. Carpenter, S. R. and Kinzig, A. (2004), "Resilience, Adaptability and Transformability in Social-Ecological Systems", *Ecology and Society*, Vol. 9 No. 2, 5, http://doi.org/10.5751/ES-00650-090205

Chapter 18

The Entrepreneurial Ecosystem in Poland: A Panacea for Growth?

Marek Angowski and Mariusz Sagan

Abstract

Research Background: The entrepreneurship ecosystem is one of the most important elements determining the conditions for the development of modern enterprises. The structure and tools of the system are the subjects of research and analysis by practitioners and researchers dealing with the issues of entrepreneurship. The main objective of these studies is to search for the optimal use of the potential and opportunities of the enterprise sector in relation to current socio-economic problems.

Purpose of the Chapter: The purpose of the chapter is to present and discuss the possibilities of the impact of the entrepreneurship ecosystem on the development of enterprises in Poland.

Methodology: The analysis includes directions, support instruments and an assessment of the effectiveness of activities related to supporting entrepreneurship in Poland. To prepare the chapter, a review and analysis of literature, analysis of programs and documents as well as an analysis of statistical data describing the development of entrepreneurship in Poland were used.

Findings: Entrepreneurial ecosystems are an essential factor determining the development of entrepreneurship in Poland. There are visible problems related to the implementation of an effective entrepreneurial ecosystem. The experience and adaptation processes of institutions and organisations related to its functioning make the system and its elements work correctly.

Keywords: Entrepreneurship; enterprise; business ecosystems in Poland; institutions; startups; support for enterprises

Modeling Economic Growth in Contemporary Poland, 281–294
Copyright © 2024 Marek Angowski and Mariusz Sagan
Published under exclusive licence by Emerald Publishing Limited
doi:10.1108/978-1-83753-654-220231026

Introduction

Entrepreneurship plays a huge role in many spheres of human activity. It is most often associated with business activity, but entrepreneurship is also essential and visible in areas related to social, technological, ecological and educational development. This is the reason why it is so important to create appropriate conditions for sustainable and effective stimulation and development of entrepreneurship. One of the support tools is the creation and management of an entrepreneurial ecosystem.

Entrepreneurship is defined as the ability and way of thinking, creating, developing and managing business ventures in order to achieve profit and sustainable development. It includes an analysis of market opportunities, the development of a new product, service or solution to meet identified needs (Belitski et al., 2021). Entrepreneurship can take many forms, such as setting up and running a business, developing innovative projects within enterprises or organisations or undertaking various non-business activities. It requires a range of skills, including planning, decision-making, resource management and soft skills such as creativity, assertiveness and collaboration skills (Apostolopoulos et al., 2018).

Entrepreneurship is often associated with the creation and operation of enterprises. Enterprises play a very important role in the development of the economy. They are responsible for creating jobs, generating revenue and driving innovation, which in turn contributes to economic growth (Tavassoli et al., 2021).

One of the primary roles of enterprises is to create jobs. Enterprises employ people and provide them with salaries and benefits, which in turn helps to boost consumer spending and stimulate economic activity. Additionally, the growth of enterprises leads to the creation of new jobs, which helps to reduce unemployment and improve overall living standards (Jarosz-Angowska and Angowski, 2014). Enterprises also generate revenue, both for themselves and for the economy as a whole. They contribute to the tax base, which in turn helps to fund public services and infrastructure. Moreover, enterprises drive economic growth by investing in new technologies, products and services, which can open up new markets and create new business opportunities (Abdesselam et al., 2018). Innovation is another key role of enterprises in economic development. Enterprises are often at the forefront of technological advances, and they invest heavily in research and development to stay competitive. As a result, enterprises can create new products and services that help to drive economic growth and improve the quality of life for people (Kijek and Angowski, 2014).

The main barriers to enterprise development in the present economy are diverse and multifaceted. Some of the most significant barriers include (Ateljević and Budak, 2018; Aarstad et al., 2022; Angowski et al., 2015; Ateljević and Budak, 2018; Bichler et al., 2022):

- Access to finance: Many enterprises face difficulties in obtaining funding to start or grow their businesses. This can be due to a lack of collateral or a high level of risk associated with their business models, which makes it difficult for them to secure loans or investment.

- Regulatory barriers: Enterprises often face significant regulatory barriers, such as bureaucratic red tape, complex licencing requirements, and excessive taxation. These barriers can make it difficult for enterprises to comply with regulations and may also limit their ability to innovate and grow.
- Lack of skilled labour: The availability of skilled labour is critical for the development of enterprises. However, in some cases, there may be a shortage of skilled workers in certain industries or regions. This can limit the growth of enterprises and make it difficult for them to remain competitive.
- Market access: Access to markets is crucial for enterprises to grow and succeed. However, in some cases, enterprises may face barriers to accessing domestic or international markets, such as trade barriers, tariffs, or restrictive regulations.
- Infrastructure: Inadequate infrastructure, such as poor transportation networks, unreliable power supply or limited access to broadband internet, can also be a significant barrier to enterprise development. This can limit the ability of enterprises to operate efficiently and reach new markets.

To overcome these barriers, policymakers need to focus on creating an enabling environment that supports entrepreneurship, reduces regulatory barriers and provides access to finance and skilled labour. Additionally, investments in infrastructure and efforts to expand market access can help to support the growth and development of enterprises in the present economy.

Literature Review

One way to help business grow is to create an entrepreneurial ecosystem. An entrepreneurial ecosystem is a network of individuals, institutions and organisations that support and encourage entrepreneurship in a particular region or industry (Malecki, 2018). It is a dynamic and complex system that includes various elements, such as policies, funding and infrastructure. The ecosystem includes a variety of stakeholders, including entrepreneurs, investors, mentors, educators, government agencies and support organisations (Penco et al., 2021). An effective entrepreneurial ecosystem provides a supportive environment that enables entrepreneurs to start and grow successful businesses. The ecosystem includes several elements that work together to support entrepreneurship, which can be divide into the following groups (Audretsch et al., 2019; Content et al., 2020; Cumming et al., 2019; Fredin and Lidén, 2020; Penco et al., 2021; Stamand van de Ven, 2021; Wurth et al., 2022):

- Entrepreneurial culture: A supportive and entrepreneurial culture is essential to the success of an entrepreneurial ecosystem. This culture is characterised by a willingness to take risks, a focus on innovation and a strong sense of community.

- Human capital: Access to talent is critical to the success of an entrepreneurial ecosystem. This includes a pool of skilled and motivated entrepreneurs, as well as a supportive network of mentors, advisors and investors who can provide guidance and support.
- Funding: Access to funding is critical to the success of startups. An entrepreneurial ecosystem should have a range of funding options available, including angel investors, venture capitalists, crowdfunding platforms and government grants.
- Infrastructure: Access to supportive infrastructure, such as co-working spaces, incubators, accelerators and other support organisations, is essential to the success of an entrepreneurial ecosystem.
- Government support: Government policies and support programs can play an important role in creating a favourable environment for entrepreneurship. This includes tax incentives, regulatory support and access to government grants and loans.
- Industry collaboration: Collaboration between industry and academia can help to drive innovation and support entrepreneurship. This can include partnerships between startups and established companies, as well as collaborations between universities and industry.
- International connectivity: Access to international markets and global networks can help startups to grow and scale their businesses. This includes access to global funding sources, international mentorship and networking opportunities and access to international markets.

In recent years, Poland has been making strides to develop a more effective and supportive entrepreneurial ecosystem. The country has made significant progress in creating a more friendly and favourable environment for entrepreneurs, contributing to the realisation of many business ideas in various industries. In Poland, there are several models of institutional support that have been developed to support entrepreneurship. These models include (Kubera, 2016; Walendowski, 2021):

- Public institutions: The Polish government has implemented several policies and programs to support entrepreneurship, including tax incentives, grants and loans and support for research and development.
- Incubators and accelerators: There are several incubators and accelerators in Poland that provide support to startups, including mentoring, networking opportunities and access to funding.
- Venture capital firms: There are several venture capital firms in Poland that provide funding to startups.
- Academic institutions: Several academic institutions in Poland have established entrepreneurship programs to support the development of startups. These programs provide access to mentors, funding and networking opportunities.
- Business support organisations: Private sector organisations, such as chambers of commerce and industry associations, provide support to entrepreneurs by offering networking opportunities, access to funding and other resources.

The entrepreneurial ecosystem in Poland is still developing; there are many positive signs of progress. The country has a highly educated workforce, access to funding, growing support organisations, supportive government policies and a growing community of entrepreneurs. These elements create a favourable environment for entrepreneurship and suggest that the ecosystem will continue to grow and develop in the years to come. While Poland has made significant progress in developing its entrepreneurial ecosystem, there are still several barriers that need to be addressed to create a more supportive environment for entrepreneurship. Some of these barriers include (Fazlagić et al., 2021; Kubera, 2016; Murzyn, 2021; Zajkowski and Domańska, 2019):

- Limited access to funding: While there is a growing number of venture capital firms and angel investors in Poland, access to funding remains a significant barrier for many entrepreneurs. Many start-ups struggle to secure funding, which can limit their ability to grow and scale their businesses.
- Lack of experienced mentors: While there are a growing number of support organisations in Poland, such as incubators and accelerators, there is a shortage of experienced mentors who can provide guidance and support to entrepreneurs. This can limit the growth and success of startups.
- Limited access to international markets: While Poland has a large domestic market, many start-ups struggle to access international markets, which can limit their growth potential.
- Limited collaboration between universities and industry: While Poland has several leading universities that produce skilled graduates, there is often a lack of collaboration between these institutions and the industry. This can limit the ability of startups to access the talent and resources they need to grow and succeed.
- Bureaucratic barriers: While the Polish government has implemented policies to support entrepreneurship, there are still bureaucratic barriers that can make it difficult for entrepreneurs to start and operate their businesses. This can include complicated regulations, high taxes and lengthy administrative processes.

The regional system of supporting entrepreneurship in Poland is based primarily on the use of regions as local government units for the transmission of financial resources from the national and EU levels to entrepreneurs located in a given region. This is done in a grant model (transfer of EU funds to local entrepreneurs, mainly from the SME sector) and through repayable financing (regions provide financing to independent repayable financial institutions or directly create or manage such institutions).

The structure of business financing in the regions in Poland is most often derived from the guidelines and strategies of the European Union, contextualised by the development situation of the region and the smart specialisations implemented there. In 2007–2013, during the first full EU budget perspective, the priority was to support basic investments of enterprises, regardless of the sector, and to strengthen the competence of employees. In the next perspective (2014–2020), funding was mainly provided for innovative projects, research and development and investments to improve the energy efficiency of enterprises (Kawałko and Sagan, 2015).

Regional support for the SME sector in Polish regions also includes promotional and informational activities. Polish regions have implemented a number of activities to support, for example, the internationalisation processes of their entrepreneurs, by financing participation in hundreds of foreign missions, participation in international trade fairs, study visits, etc.

Another element of supporting regional entrepreneurship is preparing and providing companies with business infrastructure. Local government provinces and their dedicated companies (institutions) have carried out a number of activities in building infrastructure for fairs and exhibitions, congresses, meetings, incubators, technology parks, etc.

All the activities discussed above improved to a significant extent in 2010–2021 to strengthen the potential of SMEs, mainly through investment and training support. On the other hand, they contributed to a small extent to increase the internationalisation of Polish SMEs and to a limited extent to improve their innovation potential. As noted earlier, national support systems had a significant impact.

The importance of local government support for the development of local entrepreneurship, innovation and competitiveness of urban economic ecosystems is highlighted in the literature as conclusive. The concept of coordinating local entrepreneurial ecosystems in a model of cooperation of key stakeholders is slowly ceasing to be just an academic theory, becoming a developmental paradigm in many cities. Also in Polish cities, local authorities are pursuing policies to support local business, mainly through available tax tools. Very few Polish cities implement sophisticated support tools, coordinating the cooperation of key stakeholders, such as business and universities (Brooks et al., 2019), in order to implement joint projects between urban actors, share resources and build a climate for creating and implementing innovations.

The toolkit of entrepreneurial support in Polish cities and other local communities is mainly traditional in nature. It includes the following tools: (1) financial (real estate tax exemptions for companies investing in SEZs or for the creation of new jobs), (2) investment (preparation of investment areas, mainly for large companies, construction of business infrastructure such as technology parks, innovation laboratories, etc. subsidising micro-businesses with funds from labour offices), (3) competence (training for entrepreneurs), (4) relational (participation in the co-creation of clusters) and (5) educational (entrepreneurship support programs for young people).

Local business support systems in Poland are more a complement to the national support system than individual models in cities, operating largely independently. The development of local business support models depends very much on either national or EU funding, while cities themselves allocate a limited portion of their budgets and human resources to support entrepreneurship.

Dynamics of Change in the Polish Entrepreneurial Ecosystem

The analysis of changes in the basic indicators characterising the Polish entrepreneurial ecosystem was carried out for the years 2010–2021, in order to capture the phenomenon over a longer period of time and to indicate to what extent the systemic solutions adopted in Poland actually support the development of entrepreneurship. The second argument for this choice of time series for the study was Poland's accession to the EU in 2004. Most of the EU solutions for supporting the SME sector had been adopted in Poland by 2008, while tangible financial support for the entrepreneurship sector has been taking place since 2010.

In 2020, the share of the SME sector in GDP creation in Poland by primary business area was as follows: services 44.5%, commerce 26.1%, industry 17.4% and construction sector 12.0% (Raport o stanie, 2022).The SME sector has been responsible for about 50% of gross value added in Poland for many years, and this ratio has been stable. Entrepreneurship boomed in Poland between 2010 and 2021, while the number of all companies increased by almost 25% to 4.84 million (see Table 1). At the same time, the growth in the number of companies in the SME sector was virtually identical and mainly involved micro and small companies. This was the result of strong state support especially for new businesses operating in traditional sectors and markets, although also for e-commerce

Table 1. Number of Enterprises in Poland (2010–2021).

Enterprise Size/ Year	2010	2015	2020	2021	Change 2021/ 2010
All companies	3,909,802	4,184,409	4,663,378	4,836,214	23.69%
Mikro (0–9)	3,713,677	4,003,599	4,497,099	4,670,749	25.77%
Small (10–49)	161,550	147,124	134,600	133,936	−17.09%
Medium (50–249)	29,731	29,243	27,381	27,263	−8.30%
SME sector (0–249)	3,904,958	4,179,966	4,659,080	4,831,948	23.74%
All companies	3,909,802	4,184,409	4,663,378	4,836,214	23.69%
Mikro (0–9)	3,713,677	4,003,599	4,497,099	4,670,749	25.77%
Small (10–49)	161,550	147,124	134,600	133,936	−17.09%
Medium (50–249)	29,731	29,243	27,381	27,263	−8.30%
SME sector (0–249)	3,904,958	4,179,966	4,659,080	4,831,948	23.74%

Source: Authors' own elaboration based on publicly available data from Raport o stanie sektora małych i średnich przedsiębiorstw w Polsce 2022, Polska Agencja Rozwoju Przedsiębiorczości, Warszawa 2022.

companies. On the other hand, there was a decline in the number of small (10–49) and medium-sized (50–249) companies, so the fragmentation of the SME sector was increasing.

The growth in the number of companies was also accompanied by a significant increase in their revenues to GDP. The share of gross value added of all companies as a share of GDP increased by 1.7% in 2010–2019, while the SME sector increased by more than 5%, mainly due to the very rapid growth of revenues to GDP in the group of small companies (10–49 people) – in this case by as much as 20% (Raport o stanie, 2022). The importance of the SME sector in Poland's GDP was also growing thanks to the increasing innovativeness of companies in this sector, while the fastest progress was made in the group of service companies (see Table 2). This was related to the SME sector's increasing R&D spending, both in absolute terms and as a proportion of GDP. This share rose to 1.21% in 2018 from 0.72% in 2010 (see Table 3).

The hallmark of Polish entrepreneurship over the years has been a focus on traditional sectors and a relatively low level of SME innovation. Polish companies excelled as entities producing relatively high-quality traditional products and services at low costs. State support for the start-up environment started late, relative to other European countries, as de facto only in 2012–2014. The effects of the activities of state institutions and private investors can be seen relatively recently, as only from 2019/2020, while the dynamics of the development of this environment are significant (see Table 4).

The industry specialisation of Polish start-ups is also changing rapidly. While in 2016 most of them operated in the areas of big data, IoT or BA in 2019 start-ups dealing with artificial intelligence dominated. This shows the great flexibility of this environment, which, despite still being characterised by low market maturity, is actively seeking its international specialisation. This is very important in the context of Poland building its domains of competence, basing its economic development on innovation and high-tech, and consequently breaking the middle-income trap. The vast majority of Polish start-ups are active in IT, BA,

Table 2. Share of Innovative Enterprises in the Industrial and Service Sector (in % of SME).

Years	2010–2012	2011–2013	2012–2014	2013–2015	2014–2016	2015–2017	2016–2018
Enterprises from the service sector	12.4%	11.4%	11.4%	9.8%	13.6%	10.4%	19.6%
Enterprises from the industrial sector	16.5%	17.1%	17.5%	17.6%	18.7%	18.5%	24.0%

Source: Authors' own elaboration based on publicly available data from Raport o stanie sektora małych i średnich przedsiębiorstw w Polsce 2022, Polska Agencja Rozwoju Przedsiębiorczości, Warszawa 2022.

Table 3. Investments in Innovative Activities in SME Enterprises and Expenditures on R&D in Relation to GDP (in %).

Years	2010	2011	2012	2013	2014	2015	2016	2017	2018
Investments in innovative activities in SME enterprises in relation to GDP (in %)	2.39%	2.03%	2.25%	1.99%	2.19%	2.43%	2.10%	2.07%	1.72%
Expenditures of SME on R&D in relation to GDP (in %)	0.72%	0.75%	0.88%	0.87%	0.94%	1.00%	0.97%	1.03%	1.21%

Source: Authors' own elaboration based on publicly available data from Raport o stanie sektora małych i średnich przedsiębiorstw w Polsce 2022, Polska Agencja Rozwoju Przedsiębiorczości, Warszawa 2022.

IoT and e-commerce, prospective areas of international business in the coming years (see Table 5).

The Polish start-up environment, thanks to its interesting technological offerings, is attracting increasing interest from international and domestic investors (see Table 6). In the last few years, there has been a leap in value when it comes to the committed capital of VC funds in the Polish market (see Table 6), mainly locating their ventures in the areas of e-platforms.

Problems and Challenges for the Future

The Polish entrepreneurship ecosystem has been an interesting example of evolution over the past several years, both when we analyse its structural changes and the models of institutional support for entrepreneurship by Polish authorities at

Table 4. Estimated Number of Startups in Poland.

Years	2015	2016	2017	2018	2019	2020	2020/2015 Dynamics
The number of start-ups	2,432	2,677	2,790	n/a	4,700	4,700	93%

Source: Authors' own elaboration based on publicly available data fromRaport – Polskie Startupy 2015–2020, Fundacja Startup Poland, Warszawa 2016–2021.

Table 5. The Most Popular Industries Among Polish Startups.

2016 (The 10 Most Popular)		2019 (The 10 Most Popular)	
Big data	15.0%	AI/Machine learning	22.0%
Internet of things (IoT)	14.0%	Business intelligence	14.0%
Business intelligence	13.0%	Fintech	11.0%
Fintech	11.0%	Big data	11.0%
Marketing technology	10.0%	CRM/ERP	11.0%
CRM/ERP	10.0%	Internet of things (IoT)	11.0%
Education	9.0%	Marketing technology	10.0%
Tools for programmers and developers	9.0%	Industry 4.0	10.0%
Machine learning	9.0%	Edutech	9.0%
Social services	9.0%	Electronics/robotics	8.0%

Source: Authors' own elaboration based on publicly available data fromRaport – Polskie Startupy 2015–2020, Fundacja Startup Poland, Warszawa 2016–2021.

different taxonomic levels. The legal and institutional solutions of entrepreneurship support in Poland are a kind of hybrid of tools programmed and implemented in member countries by the EU and individual national and local solutions. They form an emerging ecosystem of entrepreneurship in Poland, which is still at an early stage of development compared to the formed economies of highly developed countries.

Despite the relatively fast pace of development of the SME sector and the start-up environment, the development of entrepreneurship in Poland takes place

Table 6. The Value of VC Funds' Investments in Polish Startups and Structure of Capital Origin in VC Transactions.

Years	2019	2020	2021	2022
The value of VC investments (mln PLN)	1,266	2,127	3,624	3,616
International funds that have invested in Polish companies	28%	21%	50%	26%
Co-investment of Polish and international funds in a company in Poland	14%	27%	21%	38%
Polish funds that have invested in Polish companies	58%	52%	29%	35%

Source: Authors' own elaboration based on publicly available data fromTransakcje na polskim rynku VC w 2022 roku, PARP, Warszawa 2022.

more in the traditional-imitative model than in the innovation-high-tech model. There are many reasons for this state of affairs, including historical and geopolitical conditions and contexts which are not considered in this chapter. A key problem and at the same time a challenge of the Polish entrepreneurial ecosystem is the low innovativeness of enterprises and the difficulties in stimulating it. This problem is widely discussed in the literature. The most important related problems include too low a level of investment in research and development (both by the government and businesses), too low public financial support for the most promising Polish innovative enterprises and a lack of tools at the national level to support the retention of breakthrough technologies in the country (Radło and Sagan, 2021). Another extremely important barrier to the Polish entrepreneurial ecosystem achieving higher maturity is the varying quality of institutional support. Despite Poland's extensive support system for the enterprise sector, it is uneven. Support for the entrepreneurial ecosystem at the level of cities and local governments is rated best, while it is rated worst on the part of national institutions, including in particular the quality of Polish economic diplomacy, constantly changing legislation and the Polish government's belated responses to external shocks.

Another significance in the development of Poland's entrepreneurial ecosystem is its relatively low degree of internationalisation. We signal this problem as important for further business development in Poland, although the purpose of this chapter is not to analyse it. Despite Poland's very good export performance as a country, this success is primarily attributable to the export sales performance of branches of multinational corporations in locating particular elements of their global value chains in Poland. The export performance of the Polish SME sector is much weaker. Also, Polish VC funds are virtually absent with investments in foreign start-ups and other innovative ventures. For example, Polish funds' investments in foreign companies in 2021 and 2022 did not exceed €100 million annually, which is negligible (Transakcje, 2022).

Summary

Poland's entrepreneurial ecosystem continues to be a panacea for the country's economic growth and stabilises Poland's labour market, making it one of the best employment rates among EU countries. A big plus of Polish entrepreneurship is its mass character and high development dynamics, as well as the structural diversity of the Polish economy, which is not based on a single specialisation. Added to this are a relatively large market and a multifaceted system of state support for businesses. However, it seems that such a model for the development of Polish entrepreneurship will slowly run out of steam: without the establishment of true innovation, and true and competitive city entrepreneurial ecosystems (Brooks et al., 2019), the seeds of domains of competence, and large national champions, Polish entrepreneurship will face a development drift.

The experiences of the development of Polish entrepreneurship indicate the necessity of continuous and possibly quick adaptation to the dynamically changing market environment. The Polish entrepreneurship ecosystem should not only help in overcoming market barriers but also actively use the potential and specialisation of the region. That is why it is so important to constantly monitor the changes taking place in the market and the related needs of the enterprise sector.

References

Aarstad, J., Jakobsen, S.E. and Foss, L. (2022), "Business Incubator Management and Entrepreneur Collaboration With R&D Milieus: Does the Regional Context Matter?", *The International Journal of Entrepreneurship and Innovation*, Vol. 23 No 1, pp. 28–38.

Abdesselam, R., Bonnet, J., Renou-Maissant, P. and Aubry, M. (2018), "Entrepreneurship, Economic Development, and Institutional Environment: Evidence from OECD Countries", *Journal of International Entrepreneurship*, Vol. 16 No. 4, pp. 504–546.

Angowski, M., Jarosz-Angowska, A. and Lipowski, M. (2015), "Comparison of Computerisation and Innovation Activity of the Companies in Rural and Urban Areas", Raupelienė A, eds. *Proceedings of the 7th International Scientific Conference Rural Development 2015*, Aleksandras Stulginskis University, https://doi.org/10.15544/rd.2015.097

Apostolopoulos, N., Al-Dajani, H., Holt, D., Jones, P. and Newbery, R. (2018), *Entrepreneurship and the Sustainable Development Goals*, Emerald Publishing Limited, Bingley.

Ateljević, J. and Budak, J. (2018), *Entrepreneurship in Post-Communist Countries New Drivers Towards a Market Economy*, eds. J. Ateljević and J. Budak. 1st ed, 2018. Jovo. Ateljević and Jelena. Budak, Springer International Publishing, Cham.

Audretsch, D. B., Cunningham, J. A., Kuratko, D. F., Lehmann, E. E. and Menter, M. (2019), "Entrepreneurial Ecosystems: Economic, Technological, and Societal Impacts", *The Journal of Technology Transfer*, Vol. 44 No. 2, pp. 313–325.

Belitski, M., Grigore, A. M. and Bratu, A. (2021), "Political Entrepreneurship: Entrepreneurship Ecosystem Perspective", *The International Entrepreneurship and Management Journal*, Vol. 17 No. 4, pp. 1973–2004.

Bichler, B. F., Kallmuenzer, A., Peters, M., Petry, T. and Clauss, T. (2022), "Regional Entrepreneurial Ecosystems: How Family Firm Embeddedness Triggers Ecosystem Development", *Review of Managerial Science*, Vol. 16 No. 1, pp. 15–44.

Brooks, Ch., Vorley, T. and Gherhes, C. (2019), "Entrepreneurial Ecosystems in Poland: Panacea, Paper Tiger or Pandora's Box?", *Journal of Entrepreneurship and Public Policy*, Vol. 8 No. 3, pp. 319–338, https://doi.org/10.1108/JEPP-04-2019-0036

Content, J., Bosma, N., Jordaan, J. and Sander, M. (2020), "Entrepreneurial Ecosystems, Entrepreneurial Activity and Economic Growth: New Evidence from European Regions", *Regional Studies*, Vol. 54 No. 8, pp. 1007–1019.

Cumming, D., Werth, J. C. and Zhang, Y. (2019), "Governance in Entrepreneurial Ecosystems: Venture Capitalists vs. Technology Parks", *Small Business Economics*, Vol. 52 No. 2, pp. 455–484.

Fazlagić, J., Szulczewska-Remi, A. and Windham Loopesko, W. (2021), "City Policies to Promote Entrepreneurship: A Cross-Country Comparison of Poland and Germany", *Journal of Entrepreneurship, Management and Innovation*, [Online] Vol. 17 No. 2, pp. 159–185.

Fredin, S. and Lidén, A. (2020), "Entrepreneurial Ecosystems: towards a Systemic Approach to Entrepreneurship?", *GeografiskTidsskrift-Danish Journal of Geography*, Vol. 120 No. 2, 87–97. https://doi.org/10.1080/00167223.2020.1769491

Jarosz-Angowska, A. and Angowski, M. (2014), "Innovation Practices of Enterprises Located in Rural Areas of LubelskieVoivodeship", *Annals of the Polish Association of Agricultural and Agribusiness Economists*, Vol. 16 No. 5, pp. 73–78.

Kawałko, B. and Sagan, M. (2015), "LubelskieVoivodeship Development Strategy for the Years 2014–2020: Context of Metropolitan Lublin", in: *Peripheral Metropolitan Areas in the European Union*, eds. Z. Pastuszak, M. Sagan and K. Żuk, ToKnowPress, Bangkok-Celje-Lublin.

Kijek, T. and Angowski, M. (2014), "Enabling Knowledge Creation: Does Employees' Training Stimulate R&D Activities?", in *European Conference on Knowledge Management. 2014 Kidmore End*, Academic Conferences International Limited. p. 556.

Kubera, P. (2016), Evaluating the Impact of Regulation and Regulatory Policy – Towards Better Entrepreneurial Ecosystem. The Case of Poland, *ProblemyZarządzania*, Vol. 15, No. 1 (65), 237–253.

Malecki, E. J. (2018), Entrepreneurship and Entrepreneurial Ecosystems, *Geography Compass*, Vol. 12 No. 3, 4–21.

Murzyn, D. (2021), Social Entrepreneurship and Selected Elements of the Entrepreneurship Ecosystem, *PrzedsiębiorczośćEdukacja*, Vol. 17 No. 1, p. 165.

Penco, L., Ivaldi, E. and Ciacci, A. (2021), "Entrepreneurial Ecosystem and Well-Being in European Smart Cities: a Comparative Perspective", *The TQM Journal*, Vol. 33, No. 7, pp. 318–350.

Radło, M-J. and Sagan, M. (2021), "Opportunities and Challenges for Moving Up the Value Chains Before and After the Pandemic. The Case of Central and Eastern European Countries", in: *Report of SGH Warsaw School of Economics and the Economic Forum 2021* eds. Chłon-Domińczak, A., Sobiecki, R., Strojny, M. and Majewski, B. SGH Publishing House, Warsaw, pp. 341–374.

Raport – Polskie Startupy 2015–2020, Fundacja Startup Poland, Warszawa 2016–2021 (2021), available at https://startuppoland.org/report/polskie-startupy-2022/ (accessed: 1 March 2023).

Raport O Stanie Sektora Małych I Średnich Przedsiębiorstw W Polsce 2022, (2022), Polska Agencja Rozwoju Przedsiębiorczości, Warszawa.

Stam, E. and van de Ven, A. (2021), "Entrepreneurial Ecosystem Elements", *Small Business Economics*, Vol. 56 No. 2, 809–832.

Tavassoli, S., Obschonka, M. and Audretsch, D. B. (2021), "Entrepreneurship in Cities", *Research Policy*, Vol. 50 No. 7, 104255.

Transakcje na polskim rynku VC w 2022 roku, PARP, Warszawa (2022), available at: https://pfrventures.pl/aktualnosci/transakcje-na-polskim-rynku-vc-w-2021.html (accessed: 1 March 2023).

Walendowski, J. (2021), *Fostering Collaboration through Mapping, Analysing and Interlinking of European Entrepreneurial Regions: Phase II : Regional Ecosystem In-Depth Mapping for the Region of Pomorskie*, Publications Office, Luxembourg.

Wurth, B., Stam, E. and Spigel, B. (2022), "Toward an Entrepreneurial Ecosystem Research Program", *Entrepreneurship: Theory and Practice*, Vol. 46 No. 3, pp. 729–778.

Zajkowski, R. and Domańska, A. (2019), "Differences in Perception of Regional Pro-entrepreneurial Policy: Does Obtaining Support Change a Prospect?" *Oeconomia Copernicana*, Vol. 10 No. 2, pp. 359–384.

Printed and bound by CPI Group (UK) Ltd, Croydon, CR0 4YY

08/02/2024

08234031-0003